Nudism in a Cold Climate

THE VISUAL CULTURE OF NATURISTS IN MID-20TH-CENTURY BRITAIN

atelier éditions

Table of Contents

Nudism in a Cold Climate

Getting the Picture

There's an old joke about pornographic magazines: *I only read them for the articles!* It regularly popped into my mind while researching 50 years of nudist publications packed full of photographs of naked people. In my case the defence was true: nudist articles have complex and interesting things to say about the movement's principles and its public identity. Nudist authors were earnest in the face of ridicule. They are worth taking seriously for what they reveal about bodily ideals and realities in a period of rapid social and cultural change in 20th-century Britain.

Nude and nudist images also matter. I spent a long time looking at them too. The naked body and its visual depictions have always attracted attention and generated heated debate. What and who should be seen and shown, by whom and where, form the basis of the social and moral codes that shape behaviour and belief across place and time. Similarly, the visual portrayal of nudism has always been important to the communication of its moral message. How should nudism look to a public audience? What kind of bodies best represent nudism's ideals? What were the merits and perils of looking and being looked at? What makes a nudist nude different from others? As attitudes and practices in nude photography changed fundamentally in mid-20th-century Britain, these were key questions that shaped the fledgling nudist movement.

From the early 1920s to the early 1970s, debates about undressed bodies took a distinctive form while social nudism, later known as naturism, was first establishing itself in Britain. Nudist books and magazines were initially philosophically dense and filled with moral arguments about the value of nudism for personal freedom and social transformation. Latterly, they operated as vehicles for the photographic depiction of nude bodies, attracting an audience both inside and outside the movement.[1] Through their now yellowing pages we meet surprising personalities: political philosophers promising radical utopias; feminist campaigners stripping away convention; naked clergymen and sexual permissives gathering together in the woods; nude models who seized the visual means of production; queer participants pushing at the door of the closet; communist spies, royal portraitists, and proto-pornographers who made their photographic names and fortunes. The public display of nude bodies in mid-century Britain was highly contentious, tangled up in moral panics and court cases that addressed big issues about bodies and selves, sex and gender, race and class, freedom and censorship.

Nudism in a Cold Climate makes play with the title of Nancy Mitford's 1949 novel *Love in a Cold Climate*, which in turn builds on a phrase from George Orwell's 1936 novel *Keep the Aspidistra Flying*. Orwell's central character aspires to be a poet and lover but he is frustrated by having no money and nowhere to go in a country condemned to poor weather. Mid-century Britain was a cold climate for nudists in both temperature and social attitudes. As an American visitor put it in 1936: "In Great Britain nudism is nothing short of heroism."[2] Early efforts could be received with amusement and scepticism but they also met with serious hostility and prosecution. Going naked and circulating naked images were subject to punitive laws in a place and time that expected bodies to be covered for respectability and where the open discussion of intimate matters was largely "not done".

Early nudists were caught between utopian desires for a radical new unclothed world and the cultivation of public acceptability within the buttoned-up boundaries of British decency and reserve. From the start there were clashes between dreamers and realists, and a moderate line was argued to be a particularly British resolution in a movement originally established on the continent. What was nationally distinctive about nudism was a concern to British nudists, who measured themselves against their European neighbours and their American rivals, and developed complex superior–inferior relations with the rest of the world. British nudism was mostly English, as clubs clustered in the more populous, sunnier south, although geographical terms were used interchangeably.[3] While prudery was seen by nudists to be endemic to England, the nations of Scotland, Wales, and Northern Ireland were perceived as even less liberated.[4]

"Nakedness" and "nudity", "nudism" and "naturism" are also terms that can be used synonymously, but for mid-century practitioners they had distinctive meanings that were not always agreed upon. To be naked is to be without clothes, but British nudism was not always wholly undressed. Nudity's shared human aspect—that we are all born naked regardless of class, gender, ability, or ethnicity—underpinned nudism's ideal of social and cultural levelling.[5] Despite this, to borrow another Orwell phrase, in the nudist movement some bodies were more equal than others.

If nudity is as old as humanity, nudism as a movement—with manifestos and membership cards, physical premises and belief systems—has much more recent origins. In Britain, nudism emerged in the early 1920s as an organized practice under a range of different names. By 1931, nudism had entered the *Oxford English Dictionary*. How nudism related to *naturism*—beliefs rooted in modern ideas about exercise, diet, and exposure to the sun—was a debate begun in the 1920s but only resolved in the 1960s, when British naturists formally adopted it as a title to distinguish their practices from nudism's increasingly sexualized associations. What was "natural" in naturism, however, could be highly ideological.

The difference between nudism and the nude was also a site of conflict. The nude as an idealized artistic genre is not the same as photographs of nudists. Practitioners used photographic illustrations to recruit members and attract readers through their publications, but nude photography in mid-century Britain could also be seen on gallery walls and in camera manuals, in books of anthropology, sexology and pornography, in cheap pin-up magazines and expensive art albums. How naturist nudes could be distinguished legally, morally and stylistically was a source of much discussion in the courts and in an increasingly crowded marketplace for the consumption of nude bodies, and particularly for those of young, slim, able-bodied white women. Youth, beauty, physical health, and skin colour were all subjects for value-laden debate in nudist visual culture.

Women were nudism's principal photographic subject, but they played a more minor role in the male-dominated movement. They participated in and sometimes led nudist clubs, wrote about nudist philosophy, and photographed nude bodies, but they were also regularly objectified, anonymized, and allegorized. Women could be sceptical about the sexual motives of nudist men and of male photographers. They were concerned about the effect of nudism on their reputations, and they were self-conscious about their appearance in a movement founded on bodily beauty rather than inclusivity.

Mid-century nudist publications were largely edited and authored by men and addressed to men. Men, however, were much less regularly depicted as subject matter. Too many men were attracted to nudist clubs, according to organizers, and numbers were policed to moderate voyeurs. Anxieties about homosexuality can be read into these debates. Same-sex desire was mostly unmentionable in mid-century Britain, but heterosexual desire was also barely discussed. To achieve public respectability, early practitioners denied any link between nudism and sex, focusing instead on its psychological and physical benefits. As the movement distanced itself from its intellectual and health origins and as sexualized nude bodies achieved greater cultural acceptance in the 1960s, some practitioners began to champion naturism's sensuality, leading to institutional splits

between "permissives" and "prudes". These controversies reached a peak at the start of the 1970s,
at the same time as the photographic depiction
of women's naked bodies in everyday print media
became normalized.

EXPOSING MYSELF
Some may assert that only a card-carrying club
member could properly appraise the movement's history, and I am not a naturist. An insider perspective
would offer interesting insights, but I have different
motivations. The first is my interest in the history of
photography in Britain, especially photographic
images outside the narrow canon of art. My earlier
investigations into the practices of popular photography, for example, used magazines such as *Amateur
Photographer* from the 1920s and 1930s to explore
how subject and style was shaped. I later returned
to the periodical to investigate amateur photography
in Britain in the 1980s.[6] The dramatic gulf that lay
between the dry, high-minded guidance of the interwar period, where nude photography was virtually
non-existent, and the titillating content of the same
magazines in the 1980s—which included glamour as
a genre alongside portraiture and landscape, and
where young female models, topless or barely clad in
wet T-shirts, were prominent content including on
most covers—led me to wonder what moral and aesthetic shifts had occurred to change photographic
practice so profoundly. Equally, in reading nudist
publications I was struck not only by the significance
of photography to the movement's visual identity but

also to the discussions of photography's meaning more broadly. Nudism is a profoundly visual culture, and the camera is one of its principal tools. As *Sun Bathing Review* wrote in 1951, "Nudism and photography seem to go hand in hand, whether we all like it or not."[7]

Another of my interests is historic attitudes to the British countryside, specifically the woodcraft camping and hiking groups established in the 1920s, whose utopian understanding of the moral and spiritual potential of outdoor health and exercise is directly related to early British nudism in ideas and personnel.[8] Some of my fascination with these early 20th-century countercultures comes from my personal participation in their later iterations: for example, in the naked festivities of the hippies, pagans, witches, and weirdos with whom I joyfully hung out in the early 1990s. As a member of a women's art collective in my twenties, I posed nude for photographs among the stone circles of Dartmoor, full of mystical belief about the purity and power of naked bodies in wild places, happy to be depicted as a subject on my own terms. In the same years I earned income by life modelling, including sitting for photographic portraits at nine months pregnant. Through these experiences I understand first-hand what it means to be the voluntary recipient of the artistic (and usually male) gaze as a model; these experiences have influenced my perspectives as a feminist art historian.

There is merit in being both a nude sympathizer of sorts and an inhabitant of the enemy position as a "textile" (the contemporary term for a non-naturist). I can read mid-century nudist publications as they were intended: many address the sceptic and the novice to persuade the reader that the movement is legitimate. As a woman, analysing images intended for a heterosexual male viewer also gives additional perspective on what is and what is not shown. "Living in a female body is different from looking at it," as art historian Lisa Tickner has put it. "Even the Venus of Urbino menstruated, as women know and men forget."[9] Finally, being middle-aged with a figure that is far outside mid-century nudist ideals and standing on the brink of a menopausal phase of cultural invisibility offers me a good vantage point from which to appraise afresh images of bodies in public culture. The only middle-aged female viewer evoked in mid-century nudist publications is Mrs Grundy, the figurative prude who disrupts the pleasures of others. Those who created her seemed unable to imagine that she had any of her own.[10]

Nudist publications in mid-century Britain marginalized many kinds of bodies in the belief that youth and beauty were moral virtues and that physiques could be divided into "good" and "bad", natural and unnatural. Nudism was the alchemy that would transform the flawed into the fit; fresh air, exercise, and sunshine would produce new best selves. It would return the seeker to the paradise that had been lost and to an original state of splendour. It was a practice simultaneously full of transcendental possibility and one that reinforced restrictive norms.

THINKING VISUALLY

Mid-20th-century British nudes continue to circulate in print and online in the 21st century, mostly decontextualized and often trivialized. They may have been transformed over time into objects of comedy and nostalgia, but they still operate as objects of desire. What is now seen as their innocence, quaintness, and charm serve them well in the vintage erotica market, where they provide a pornographic niche as masturbatory material. Nude photographs command high prices as collectors' items, and nude photographers are retrospectively reframed as masters of the form. Equally, pin-ups and the glamour photography of the mid-century have been revived and reinterpreted by a new |generation of feminists who see the promise of sexual subjectivity in their alternatives to mainstream contemporary representations of beauty and sexuality.[11]

Photographs are always ambiguous. They are open to a wide range of readings and counter-readings depending on how they are seen, by whom, and when. Nude and nudist photographs are no different. They may have been produced for artistic, health, educational, or sexual purposes, but their categorical certainty was always unstable, and the same models, photographers, and photographs crossed the boundaries between these domains. The fluid status of nudes as beautiful and repulsive, normative and liberatory, spiritually uplifting and sexually arousing caused consternation and controversy in the contexts in which they originally circulated. In selecting and presenting images in this book, I acknowledge their original purposes, their alternative adaptations, and their continuing potential to be read in multiple ways. The irony is not lost on me that in reproducing nude photographs this book adds to the discourse even as it scrutinizes it. I have chosen illustrations to include nudist and nudist-adjacent imagery across the candid and the romanticized, the elegant and the crude, the professional and the amateur, the earnest and the comic, the common and the unusual. I have aimed to include a cross-section of bodies (within early nudism's narrow range) but exercised caution when showing images of children, as consent could not have been given. The visual culture of naturists in mid-20th-century Britain was riddled with complications, and to assess it even-handedly means to celebrate its pleasures as well as its shortcomings. I have spent many years looking at its striking imagery and reading its strident philosophy; I hope this book communicates my frustration as well as my fascination.

1

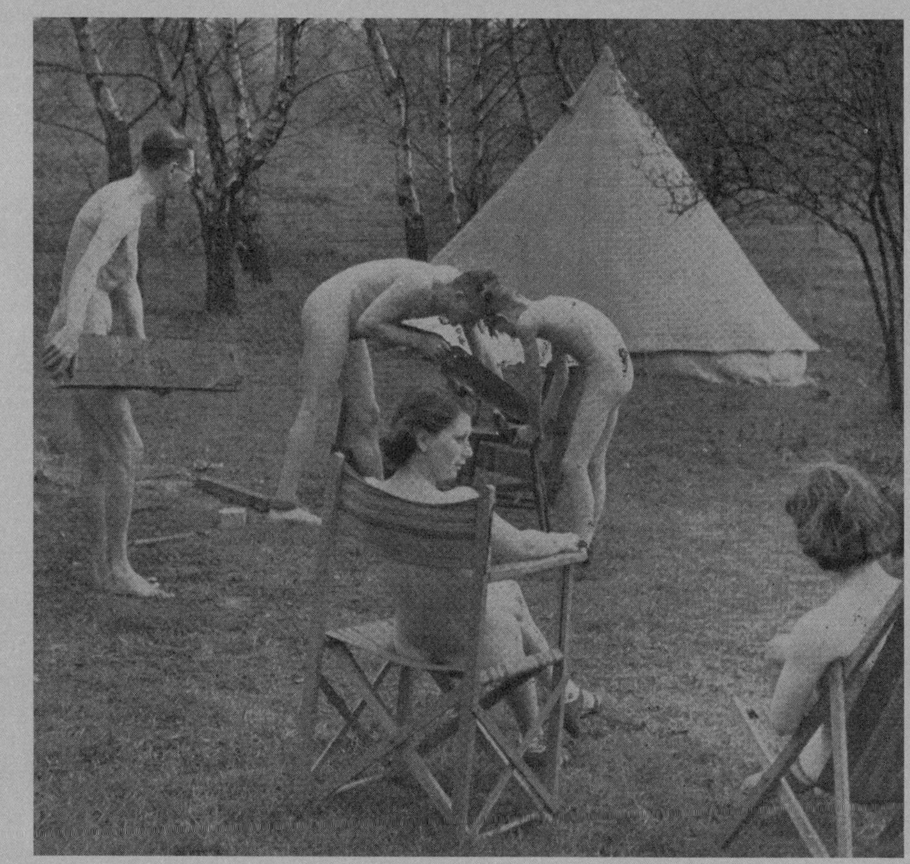

Establishing an Ideal

A nudist camp
somewhere in England:
A ring of mature trees
and freshly planted
rhododendrons; a hand-
built wooden hut and
a clutch of lightweight
canvas tents. Deckchairs
and woven blankets sit
on rough grass alongside
an axe and wheelbarrow.
A folding table is laden
with tea in floral cups
and saucers, plates
of sliced brown bread,
and a hardback book of
poetry. Leather sandals
are cast aside.

18

Previous spread - To establish the British nudist movement, groups of enthusiasts purchased plots of land in the 1920s and 1930s as simple camp sites. Slowly and steadily, these developed these into formal clubs.

The scene was set for the social nudism movement in Britain in the 1920s. Its hardy pioneers were modernist artists and authors, sex reformers and spiritual seekers, experimental educationalists, physicians, and psychologists. With passionate beliefs in the transformational power of sun on skin for radiant health and freedom from repression, they enthusiastically embraced new ways of living, eating, and dressing—as well as undressing. They shared their developing ideas in the pages of political and physical culture magazines, drank to them over non-alcoholic beverages and nutmeat salad in London's first vegetarian restaurants, and pooled their resources to purchase rough plots of what they called "virgin jungle" for "sun and air bathing" in London's suburbs.[1] The seeds they planted and the spadework they undertook led to Britain's first organized nudist societies and clubs.[2]

Interwar nudism began as a small-scale endeavour in Britain but, for those who subscribed to its cause, it offered radical physical, mental, and even spiritual liberation from a debilitating social and cultural affliction broadly defined as "civilization".[3] As much a mental condition as a time and place, civilization, according to its complainants, was embodied in the artificial conveniences of tinned food, mechanized culture, and monotonous labour. It was polluted by stale urban air and smog but also a regimented rigmarole of rules and manners, by sophistication that took the place of authentic experience, and by superficial pleasures that disrupted the instinctive enjoyment of simple things. Together, these aspects of modern British life, their opponents argued, had produced a weak and weedy nation with poor bodily health and a collective neurosis rooted in sexual anxiety. In a period of self-scrutiny after the physical and cultural devastation of the First World War, radical social reformers sought new beginnings. As a country dominated by Conservative political leadership and widespread financial hardship, Britain saw the proliferation of single-issue societies and campaigns in the 1920s, each promising new dawns. For those who sought salvation in natural health and the sun, metaphors of illumination were models to live by. The fundamentals of what was natural and true, they argued, had become confused and corrupted. Pure and bright radical solutions were sought to counteract physical and cultural "diseases of darkness".[4]

Artificiality and convention were nowhere more entrenched than in the heavy, uncomfortable, and complex garments that were required by British men of good standing to convey class, authority, and respectability in working life, in formal leisure locations from restaurants to the theatre, and even in outdoor sports. They blocked the body from the sun and stood between humanity and its liberation. Women were beginning to achieve greater freedom in dress, but to attain radiant health, so the argument went, formal clothes needed to be cast aside en masse. Several parallel events took place to start the ball rolling. In 1921, a series of articles in the *New Statesman* by "Lens", a pseudonym of eminent physician Dr Caleb Williams Saleeby, who was devoted to the use of light and air as healing tools, espoused the natural benefits of exposing naked bodies to the elements. Under the heading "Modern Sun Worship", he detailed the profound effects that sunlight had on conditions such as rickets and tuberculosis in the experimental Swiss clinic of Dr Auguste Rollier at Leysin, and the positive results in parallel British heliotherapy experiments by Sir Henry Gauvain.[5] Among supportive correspondents was one Harold Booth, who shared his transformational experiences in pre-war German nudist camps. The ensuing conversations demonstrated that there was a small but critical mass of enthusiasm for therapeutic sun bathing in Britain. By 1923 Saleeby extended his thoughts in a crusading book, *Sunlight and Health*, which aimed to illuminate the "malurbanised millions" of "blackened, bleached and blighted" British citizens.[6]

A similar exchange flourished in the pages of *Health and Efficiency*. Established at the start of the 20th century, and by the 1920s calling itself "The National Magazine of Health, Physical Culture, Sociology, Hygiene, Natural Healing, Reformed Diet", the illustrated periodical had long covered social and self-improvement matters from bodybuilding to birth control, aiming to improve the podgy and stodgy national body, coaxing it out of its armchairs and away from its stewed steak and kidney puddings.[7] In 1921, it published a letter calling for nude bathing facilities in public swimming baths. This led to an editorial, followed by eager responses, including by one Harry "Dion" Byngham, who went by "Elan Vital". A young writer committed to outdoor living, natural health, and ecstatic pagan spirituality, Byngham had been in touch with Booth, and proposed to establish a national society for "Nude Life Culture" in the summer of 1922.[8] From there, a dozen or so devotees calling themselves the English Gymnosophist Society met to discuss these ideas and to put them into practice. In 1924 they established a site, The Camp, in the private garden of a member's house in Wickford, Essex.

Discussion about nudism as a new social movement in Britain developed in the pages of *Health and Efficiency* magazine in the 1920s, amid articles and illustrations on national fitness topics.

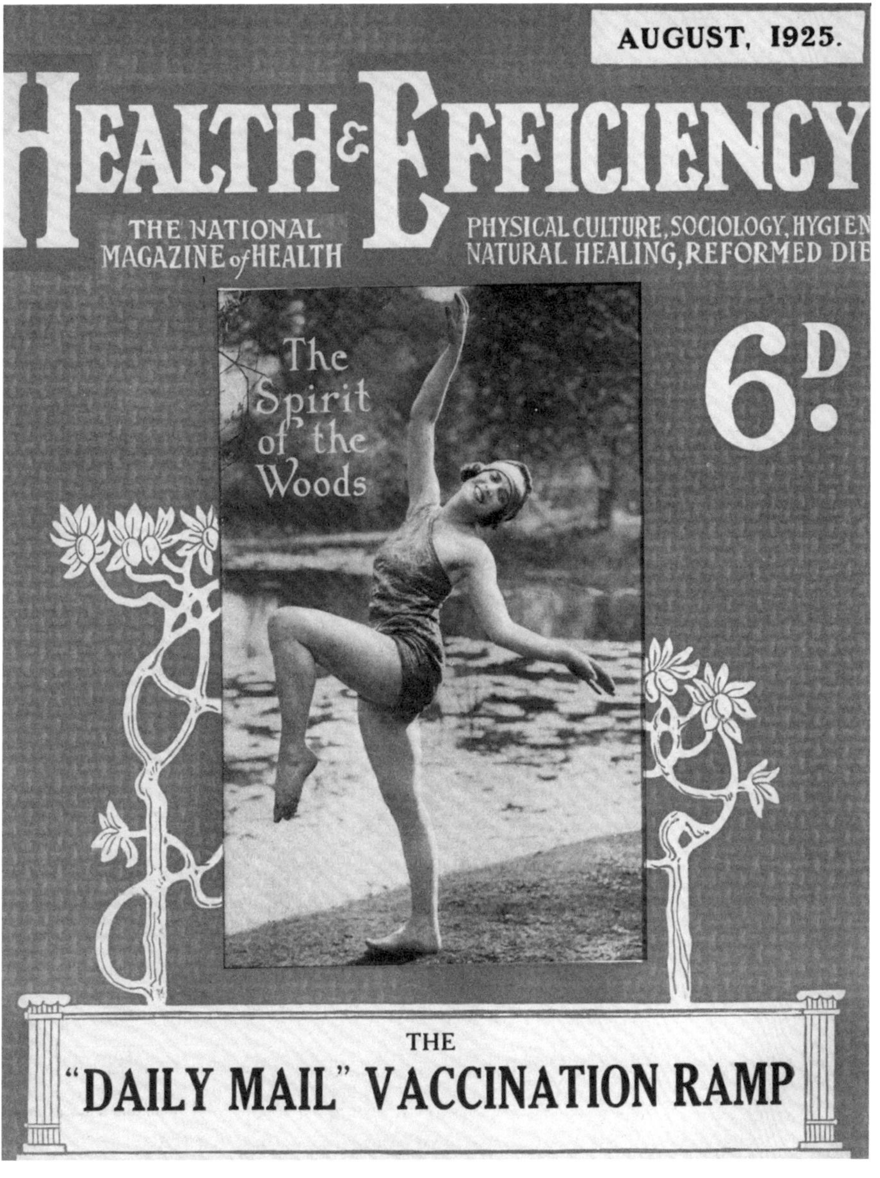

The plain name gave nothing away about its core purpose, but it was from these modest beginnings that the first nudist club in England was born.

The term "gymnosophy" neatly combined the Greek words for nakedness and wisdom. Its classical title gave its activities legitimacy and, crucially, concealed the naked aspect that could cause scandal in a buttoned-up society. While early nudists sought to break the automatic link made in the popular imagination between the naked body and sex, and while they repeatedly noted the purity of their motives, secrecy was paramount, hence the widespread use of pseudonyms for those who attended clubs and published on the subject. "Moonella", "Zex", "Flang", "Thwang", and friends were an elite, well-educated, mixed-gender group who collectively disrobed at The Camp for the purpose of "self-realization", but Zex acknowledged in his invitation to members that "the rocks upon which this experiment may be wrecked are numerous".[9] Gymnosophists' pseudonyms show that secrecy was required to protect members' identities, but their fanciful alter egos also demonstrate the romantic nature of their cause. In 1927 the group purchased four acres of "picturesque wilderness" near Bricket Wood, Hertfordshire, 20 miles outside London. What would later become Four Acres and finally Five Acres nudist club was established "for the purpose of inaugurating a playground and camp settlement wherein a group of congenial persons, united in a desire to detach themselves from the trivialities and less valuable artificialities of conventional existence, may find opportunity for vigorous, healthy exercise and stimulating thinking—for vitalising recreation and refreshing social intercourse".[10] Little more than a patch of land for a clutch of tents for members to use during sunny weekends and holidays, the first nudist camp was a rough-and-ready affair boasting few amenities but a wealth of utopian possibilities.

By 1927, gymnosophy was a modest society with a permanent site, a members' newsletter, and public activities including lectures by Booth on "clothing and its conflict with health and morality".[11] Gymnosophy's target member was the radical visionary. The society advertised among groups that attracted vegetarians and healthy eaters, campers and hikers, simple-lifers and handicrafters, yoga practitioners and enthusiasts of new religions. Their advertisements sat alongside promotions for food-reform restaurants offering meat substitutes washed down with fruit juice, vitalizing nature cures using water, air, mud, and magnetism, and bookshops selling tomes on self-improvement and sex education. These communities might boast wealth and university educations among their membership, but they were more commonly populated by aspiring intellectuals who were white-collar workers with nine-to-five office jobs living in suburban locations. They wanted to change the world but needed to do so cheaply and on their spare weekends.

Word spread among sympathizers, who developed new branches from these roots, each with distinctive characteristics. N. F. Barford, for example, along with his wife Leila, recognized that a moderate approach to the cause was needed in order to appeal to "the English man and woman in the street", most especially to women, for whom public mixed nudity was anathema to conventional expectations about respectability.[12] Barford's carefully named Sun Bathing Society expressly appealed to married couples and families and, notably, did not require full bodily exposure. Instead, at its Sun Lodge in Upper Norwood, Surrey, established in 1929, men wore "slips"—loose briefs—and "women, slips and brassieres, and children little or nothing".[13] "Sun bathing" came close to nudism in its claims for open-air health and natural freedom, and it was, at times, a polite synonym for full nakedness, but Barford's model offered a more modest entry point.

The need for caution was clear. While social experiments were flowering in the 1920s, the dominant norms were conservative and closed, and churchgoing remained strong. Nudism threatened establishment certainties and fed its fears of social collapse. Nesta H. Webster's 1926 book *The Socialist Network*, for example, provided a paranoid account of an international, interlocking, and well-financed system of left-wing groups whose "disintegrating doctrines" were designed to incite world revolution. The book included a fold-out diagram that mapped the most formal of political organizations in Russia and across Europe onto the most modest of cultural organizations in Britain, from youth clubs to sports groups, including gymnosophists. Webster drew links between them and the more established German nudist cultures, which she collectively dismissed as sexually promiscuous, economically communist, and anti-Christian, binding them together as part of her conspiracy theory into a terrifying international force that would devastate all that right-minded people held dear.[14] In another instance of public condemnation, when nudists of

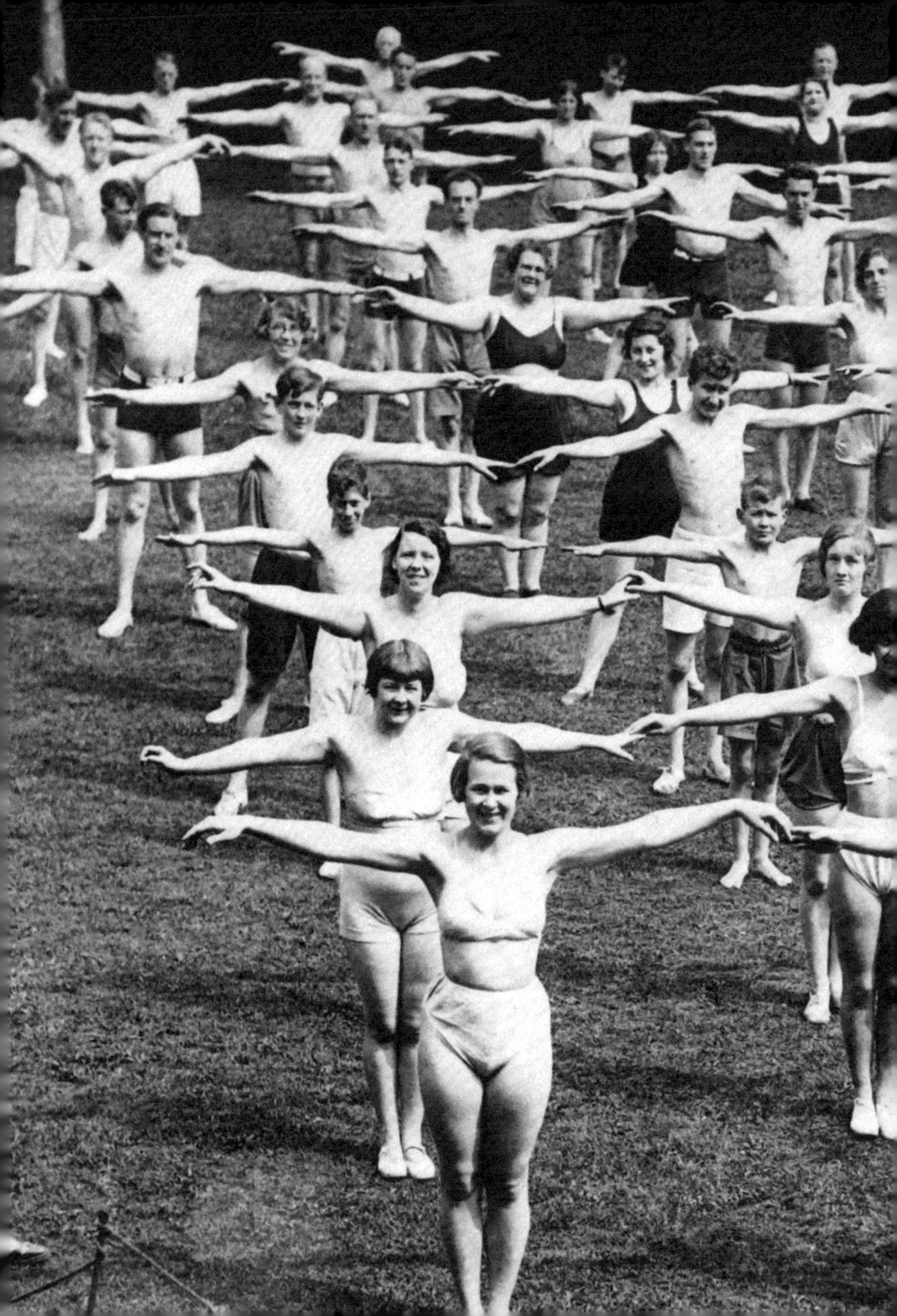

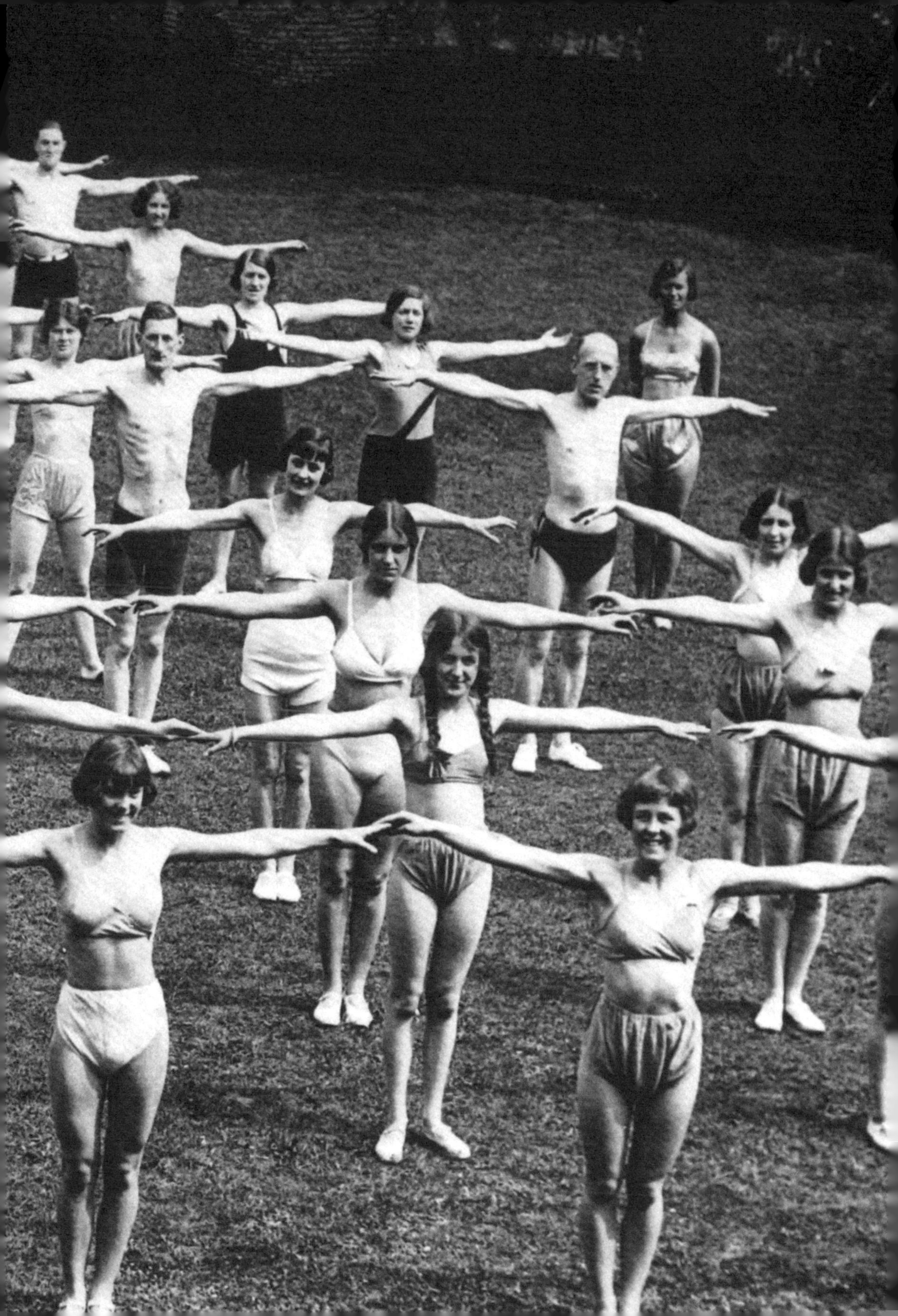

the Sun Ray Club and New Health Society in Hendon, north London, assembled in 1929 on private land at the Welsh Harp reservoir, they were attacked by passers-by in violent clashes described by the *Daily Express* as a "Sun Bathing War". At this time bathers were expected to cover torsos fully; men's chests could not even be exposed without controversy. Members were accused of being "sexual maniacs". Hecklers shouted at them: "Even cannibals wear loincloths." Bathers were arrested for indecency and threatened with imprisonment.[15]

OUR FRIENDS IN GERMANY

British nudists looked to their more established German counterparts for inspiration and leadership. Booth and Barford had both visited nudist camps in Germany, and their activities were supported by German literature translated into English in the 1920s. These evangelical works espoused full-body exposure to light and air as part of a transcendental philosophy of health and fitness and provided the intellectual basis for British endeavours. They included Hans Surén's bestselling *Man and Sunlight*, which carried an endorsement by prominent British physician, sexologist, and eugenicist Havelock Ellis.[16] Surén was a former army physical training officer but his book was more than an exercise manual. It provided a detailed anti-civilization tract alongside a daring photographic view of nude German bodies in nature, from massed ranks of sun-bronzed men tossing medicine balls high into the sky to coordinated groups of slim, young women dancing gymnastically in pastoral settings. Surén's own body, taut, muscular, and tanned, clad only in a tiny black posing pouch to conceal his genitals for legality, also featured centrally as a demonstration of both methods and results.

German organized nudism, known as *freikörperkultur* (free body culture) or *nacktkultur*, had its roots in the late 19th century, when it was aligned with wider life-reform practices including vegetarian diet, simple living, and experimental, anti-urban approaches to natural health. The German nudist movement was much larger than in Britain, and more wide-ranging, reaching across class factions and the political spectrum. By the 1920s Germany boasted over 200 formal nudist clubs as well as dozens of illustrated periodicals for supporters.[17] When London gymnosophists Charles and Dorothy Macaskie bought 12 acres of undeveloped land in Hertfordshire,

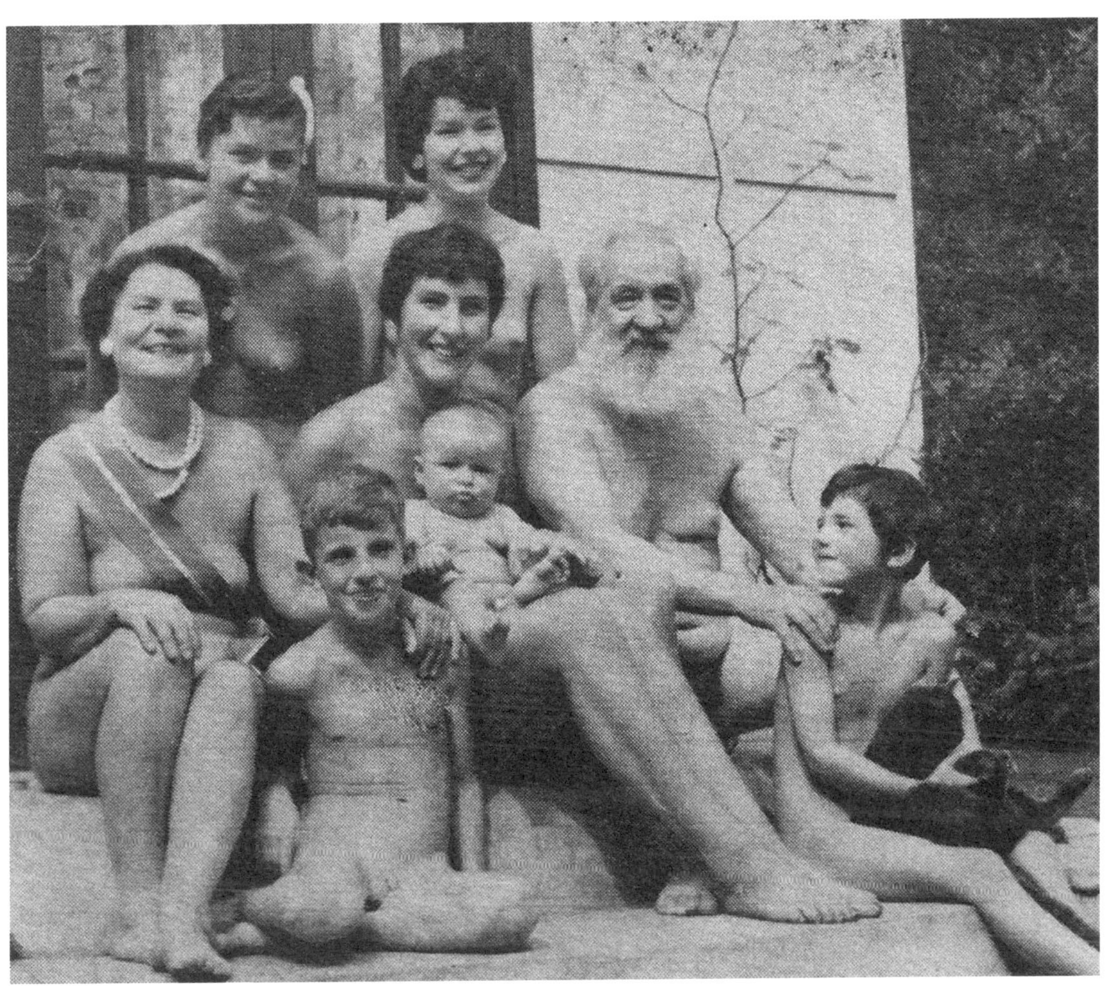

Above - The Macaskie family, headed by Charles (with beard) and Dorothy (with sash), pictured c. 1960, were the symbolic parents of British nudism as the founders of Spielplatz nudist camp in 1930.

Previous spread - Sun bathing societies in the 1920s and 1930s gathered members for collective outdoor exercise to achieve the health benefits of sun and air. Complete nudity was not always required.

adjacent to The Camp where they were early members, they named the business they launched in 1930 Spielplatz (Playground) in honour of the German movement whose *freikörperkultur* practices were advertised by name, alongside net sports and swimming, as "Everything for the Discriminating Nudist". With its large site, visitor accommodations, permanent living spaces, and increasingly well-appointed facilities, Spielplatz would become the cradle of nudism in Britain in the 20th century.[18] Its owners and principal residents, the John the Baptist-like bearded Scotsman Charles and the diminutive, pearl-wearing Dorothy, were both former life models at London's Slade School of Fine Art. With their growing naturist family of children and grandchildren, they became British nudism's poster figures and symbolic parents.[19]

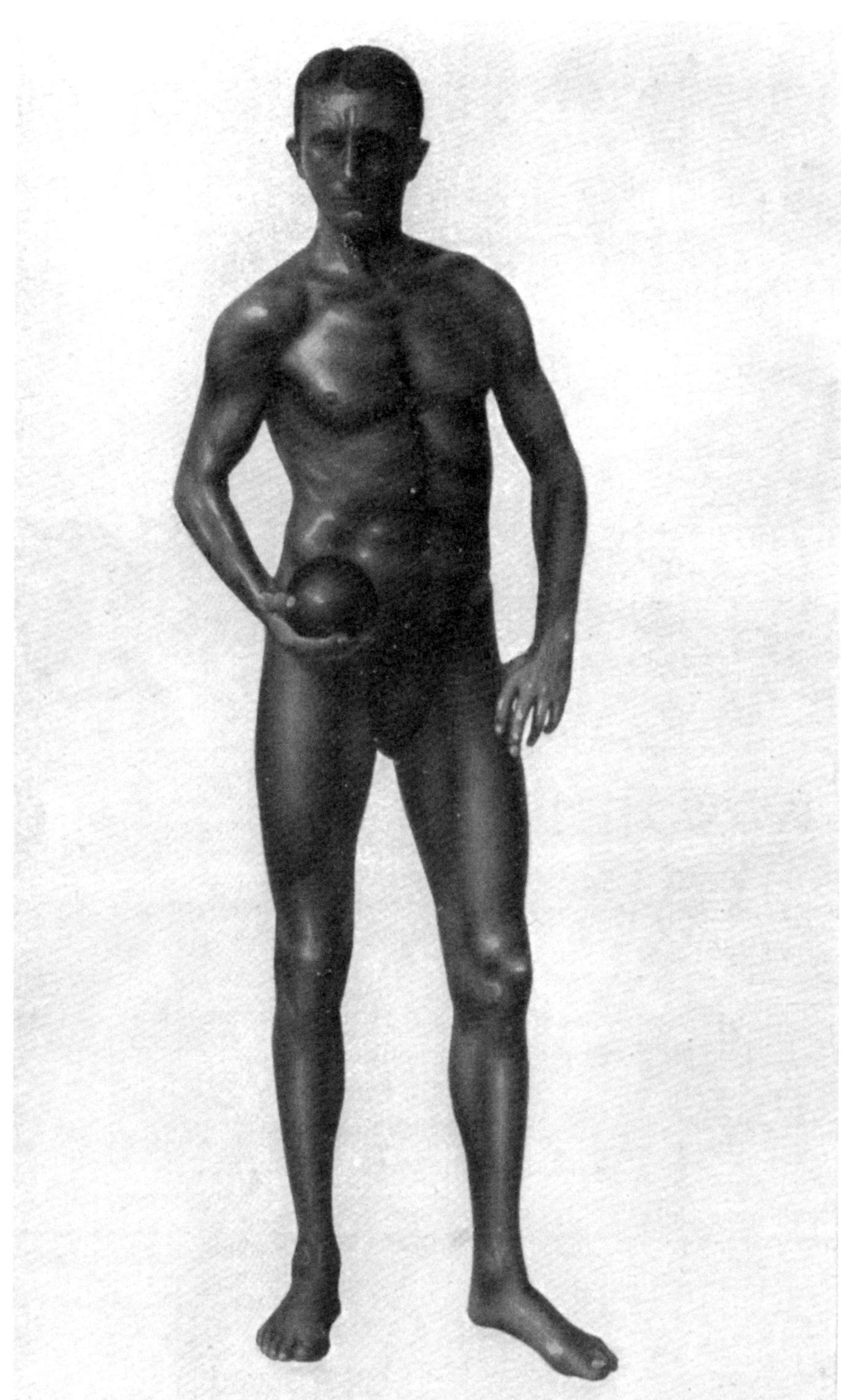

Early British nudism was influenced by continental practices. Hans Surén's evangelical manual, *Man and Sunlight*, translated into English in 1927, provided philosophical and practical guidance for naked health alongside demonstration photographs of the tanned German author.

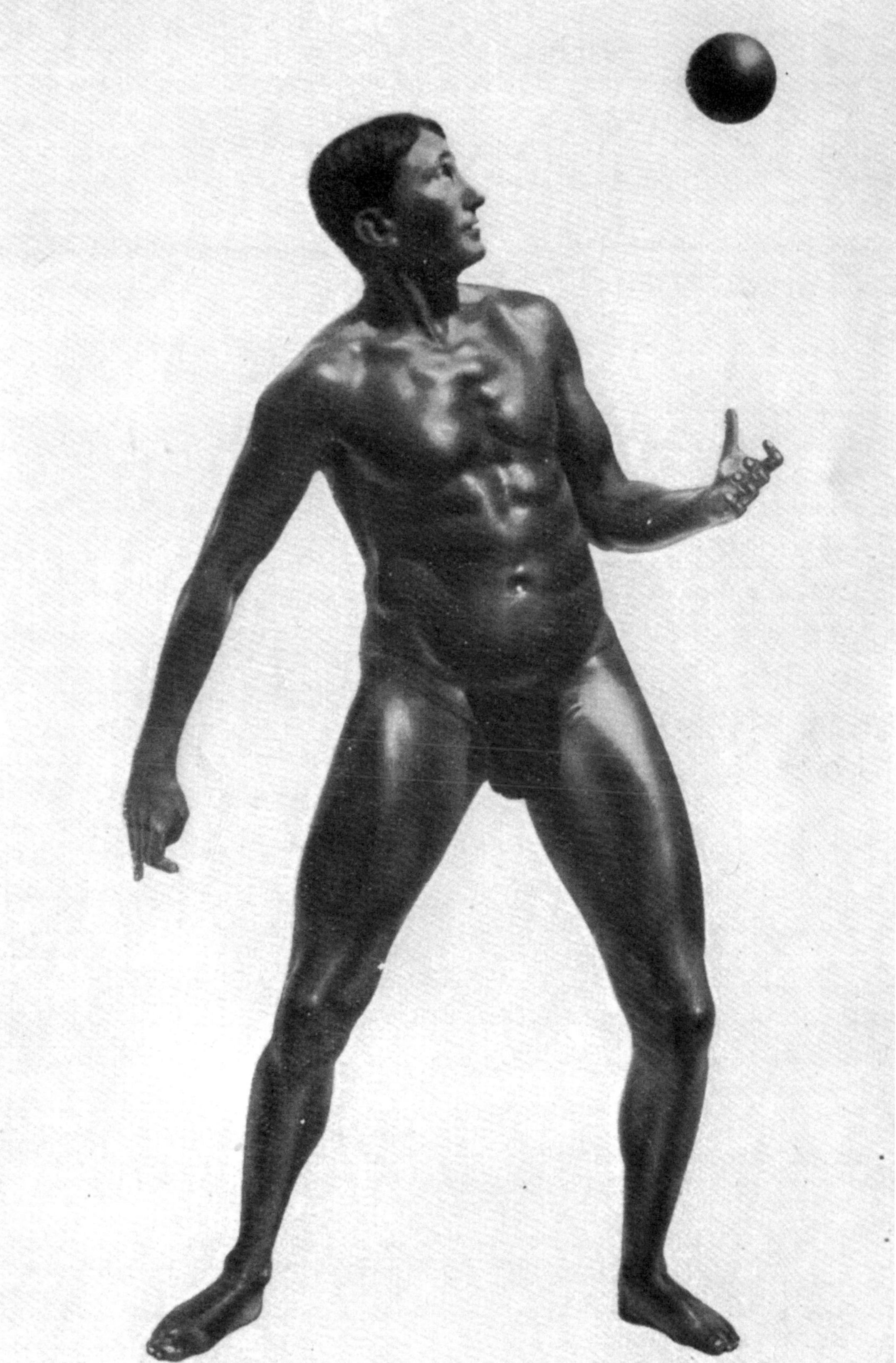

As the most promoted and documented of nudist clubs, the establishment of Spielplatz offers a useful inside view of daily life in British camps and their early development from rough ground to leisure site. In 1929 the Macaskies pitched their canvas bell tent and cooked baked beans and jacket potatoes over a campfire as they mowed, dug, and scythed the site into submission, always in the nude, with the assistance of nudist friends. Together they laid the tarmac paths for cars and caravans, and constructed wooden chalets to accommodate visitors alongside a nude restaurant with table service catering for both vegetarian and what they called "ordinary" diets. An 80-foot windmill provided electricity, and a pump raised water from an underground stream.

Spielplatz paying guests—always pre-approved via application forms—could opt for modest one-off daily rates of a few shillings or purchase monthly or annual passes to attend more regularly for weekends or holidays.[20] They arrived dressed but were greeted at the front desk by naked female receptionists who directed them to gender-segregated changing spaces; public undressing was considered sexually alluring and therefore taboo. Once disrobed, members could socialize nude in deckchairs while soaking up the sun, or build muscle at the outdoor gymnasium with parallel bars, swings, and ropes. Nude folk dancing took place in circles while nude group exercise classes took place in neatly spaced rows. The self-built 60-foot swimming pool was a particular Spielplatz attraction, with competitive water polo. For visiting families there was a children's corner with see-saws and a sandpit. Dorothy roamed Spielplatz with an usherette's tray of chocolates for sale. Waitresses, dressed only in armbands that showed their staff status, served tea al fresco. On rainy days, a "sun lodge" with Vita Glass windows and an artificial sun lamp stood in for the real thing.[21] A radio kept utopians in touch with the outside world; nudist reading matter filled the shelves.

THE NUDIST'S LIBRARY
The first generation of English language books dedicated to nudism were split along practical and utopian lines. John Langdon-Davies's 1929 *The Future of Nakedness* made play with nudism's comic potential in a country where class status was performed in part through propriety in dress.[22] In a context where "half London would be

terrified if it had to walk along Regent Street in the *wrong* clothes, let alone in no clothes at all", he proposed, tongue firmly in cheek, that it would be "a short time only before a person who wears more than a loin cloth in Regent Street will be stigmatised as indecent and degenerate". Langdon-Davies's assertion that "nakedness to-day is a crime in all civilised countries and a sin in all Christian congregations" provided a pertinent basis for why an urgent reappraisal was needed. He proposed that reasonable solutions would bring about the change. "We shall get rid of our clothes inevitably," he prophesied, "because of the contradictions and conflicts inherent in their nature. But though this is inevitable we must not sit idly waiting for the working out of immutable laws; the inevitable needs our assistance to bring it about." Success, however, should follow a softly-softly approach. "It will be safest not to be doctrinaire about this taking off of our clothes, to attack it in a spirit of compromise; we may even have to strike some sort of bargain with the tailors; and had best not shout too loud about nakedness in our time."[23]

The gauntlet gently thrown by Langdon-Davies was taken up by a series of American authors including married couple Frances and Mason Merrill in their 1931 work *Among the Nudists*. The Merrills travelled across Europe to survey continental nudism as participant-observers, and a similar path was trod by fellow American Jan Gay, whose resulting book, *On Going Naked*, published in 1932, included charming life drawings of realistic body types by her female life partner, Zhenya. As was the pattern for many devotees, they detailed their inspirational experiences at Paul Zimmerman's 100-acre nudist holiday camp, Freilichtpark, established in 1903 in Klingberg, Germany. Britain received less than a page of coverage by the Merrills. They acknowledged nudism's tentative existence in a few societies and as an educational method at the progressive Priory Gate School in Norfolk. "Even England," they observed, "the European stronghold of Puritanism, is being invaded."[25]

Nudism in Modern Life: The New Gymnosophy was another work of theory by an American that achieved popularity in Britain and endorsement by Havelock Ellis.[26] As a widely published British author on matters of sexual and social reform, Ellis's status added authority to the book although the sexologist, aged 70 at the time of publication, noted that he had no intention of joining any nudist societies.[27] For Maurice Parmelee, an early sociologist, criminologist, and New York resident, gymnosophy was more than an absence of clothes. It was "a philosophy both of nature and of cultural evolution"; a world-changing world view that "stands for simplicity, temperance and continence in every phase of life. It is useful in the rearing of the young, in the relations between the sexes, and in promoting a democratic and humane organization of society. Consequently," he continued, "the implications of gymnosophy extend far beyond the practice of nudity alone, for it connotes a thoroughgoing change in the outlook upon and mode of life."[28] Parmelee's appraisal was informed by his wide travels and his direct experiences in Germany, France, and England; it was produced with input from Booth. As such, it provides useful perspectives on the social and political alignments and demographics of the nudist movement in Britain in its beginnings.

Most gymnosophists, Parmelee observed, were middle class and urban but he counted as many as 50 different occupations among members, from manual labourers to professionals, and a range of political positions and beliefs, from communists to monarchists, Catholics to occultists. "Some are influenced by principles of freedom from convention and other restrictions. Others wish to simplify life and return to nature as far as possible. They sometimes call themselves 'naturists', and are very likely to be vegetarians as well." A "considerable percentage", he noted, promote health cures, abstain from smoking and drinking and are thus labelled "cranks" by "the Philistine world". Parmelee conceded that aspects of gymnosophy's body culture could be adopted by chauvinists and militarists "as a means for developing a physically strong and healthy race which will exalt the nation, crush its enemies in combat, and demonstrate its superiority to other races". His observation made oblique reference to nude culture's ideological adaptability in a time of rising political extremism in Europe, especially in relation to the eugenic ideas that provided some of nudism's intellectual undertow. Nonetheless, he concluded that "naturistic, libertarian, democratic and humanitarian ideals and principles are characteristic of the most genuine gymnosophists".[29]

Parmelee also had distinctive claims to make about nudism's value for women.[30] As a panacea to many social ills, his ideal gymnosophic world was classless, casteless, and egalitarian. He claimed gymnosophy to be "a powerful aid to feminism, because it abolishes the artificial and unnecessary sex barrier and distinction of dress. The gymnosophic movement is indeed the logical continuation and consummation of the woman's movement, for it at last brings woman into the man's world and man into the woman's world, so that they can see each other as they really are." Women had more to gain, he argued, from gymnosophy as it "gratifies their desire to see male nudity"—a rare stance at the time—while men, apparently, already had other means, including "houses of prostitution".

Looking at the bodies of others, Parmelee noted, was a central part of gymnosophy's appeal, but he cautioned that attention to aesthetics could warp its potential. He observed a "cult of beauty" in some gymnosophic groups, where "ill-formed, deformed and mutilated persons are excluded". While his own aesthetic preferences were couched in concerns about health, they betrayed moral values. These were visible in his disgusted descriptions of "adipose rumps" and of fat stomachs, particularly among women. "This unwieldy mass of flesh, sometimes containing folds and creases, and shaking jellylike with the motion of the body," he cringed, "is one of the most unpleasant sights in gymnosophic circles." He proposed nudism as "the most effective measure for eliminating this monstrous distortion by spreading an ideal of human beauty and shaming those who fall so far short of it".[31] Parmelee's summary of nudism's class positions, utopian ambitions, and gendered aesthetics established core aspects of the movement that would endure for decades. The conflict between nudism's egalitarian principles and its exclusionary practices would also form a longstanding contradiction in its visual culture, both in how nudists should look as individuals but also in how nudism should be depicted as a whole.

HOME-GROWN NUDISM
The year 1933 was a key one for the fledgling nudist movement in Britain. It saw the publication of a home-grown account by a member of "one of the earliest English societies". The slim book, *Nudism in England*, was authored by Reverend Clarence Norwood, an Anglican vicar who had visited German nudist camps and Swiss light-treatment clinics. He had considered concealing his identity behind a pseudonym, a common practice among early nudists, but his faith convinced him of the importance of transparency: "nudist truth is very important [...] it is His truth", he wrote. Christianity and nudism were compatible to Norwood; the old idea of the mortification of the body was

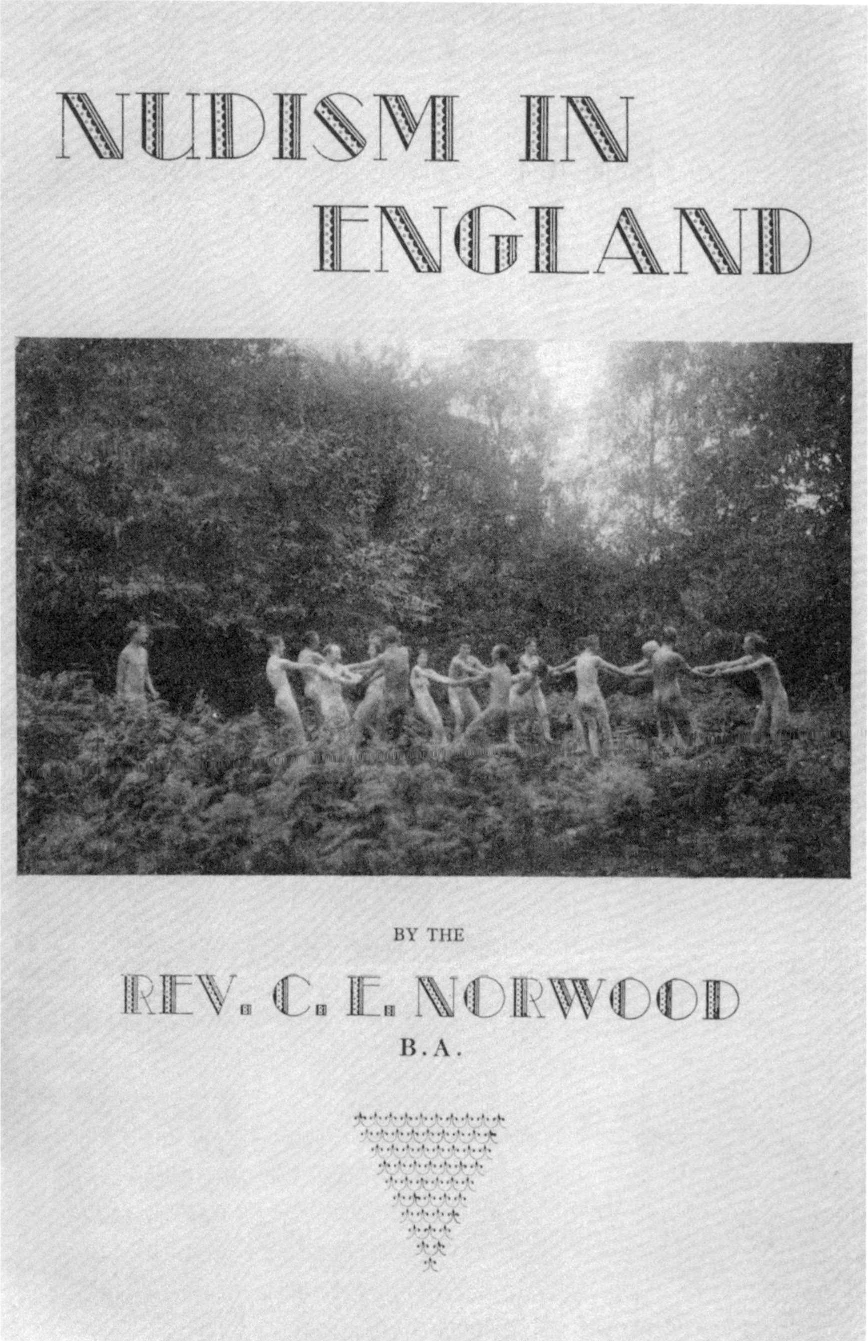

Nudism in England, published by the Anglican vicar Clarence Norwood in 1933, provided an early account of the national scene and an appraisal of nudism's health and spiritual benefits.

outmoded. Using the language of his profession, he argued that the bathing costume was a "satanic invention" as it promoted titillation through part-concealment. Norwood believed that the naked body and sexual desire should be decoupled, and the nudist camp provided the ideal place to achieve this psychological deprogramming. His book's short list of English clubs and associations, mostly in the south-east, offered a direct route.[32]

In the same year, another religious-themed study was published with a very different tenor. *In a Nudist Camp! (Somewhere in England)* was a cheap pamphlet with a shouted title page, authored "by an Eye-Witness" and circulated by the Scottish Protestant League. It was claimed to be "An Exposure of Nudism, the New Menace to Christianity"; the anonymous researcher was reporting back from their visit to an unnamed site.[33] Mostly the author complained about the food—heavy brown bread and small portions—for there was little that was salacious to be found. The site provided "every privacy"; communal games without clothes were "jovial and innocent-like". He ended with: "There was no sex in that Camp." While he admitted, "I saw nothing objectionable," he added, rather hopefully, "had we stayed longer perhaps we would have seen more". Despite this unsensational experience, the author concluded that nudism was anti-Christian, with leading practitioners characterized as material- ists and free thinkers. "Your average Nudist", he complained, "spends his Sundays as he spends his Saturdays, going about naked among naked women." At the close of the pamphlet, instead of a list of nudist clubs to join, membership details were provided for Scottish Protestant organizations, along with advertisements for further "stirring" texts in the series, including "Convent Life Unveiled".[34]

The year 1933 was also a key one for British nudist periodicals. Although *Health and Efficiency* had shown occasional naked bodies as part of its coverage of physical culture matters in the 1920s, it first included full-length and illustrated articles on nudism as a theory and practice in 1931 and 1932. By 1933 its contents were wholly nudist, and it became a leading and enduring voice for the movement. The first born-nudist magazine in Britain was *Gymnos,* which described itself as "For Nudists who Think".[35] Available by subscription from early 1933, the professionally printed monthly comprised only a few stapled-together illustrated pages, but it was internationally connected and intellectually minded, with ecstatic poetry and

scholarly articles by British and European progressive educationalists, experimental psychologists, and social reformers.[36] From its first
pages, *Gymnos* argued that nudism could fulfil spiritual emptiness:
"The vague sense of something lacking, of complete happiness never
quite achieved. Our experience leads us to suggest that nudity will
supply the need." Aware that nudism was not yet fully respectable,
they added, emphatically: "WE DO NOT PRACTICE NUDITY FOR
NUDITY'S SAKE." Nudism must be practised "under proper conditions
and under the guidance of men and women whose character is
beyond reproach".[37] Only then would its profound healing powers
of body and mind be unlocked.

Aligned with the wider European nudist movement, *Gymnos*
included anxious reports on the changing political circumstances in
Germany from its first issue. Official government decrees had been
issued in 1932 by Dr Bracht banning nude bathing; by early 1933 all
nacktkultur organizations were supervised by police under the direction of Hermann Göring. Restrictions included the termination of
nudists' contracts with public swimming baths and the banning of
municipal financial support for nudist societies.[38] By summer 1933,
Gymnos reported that "suppressionists say that Free-Physical-Culture
is anti-German and a cultural aberration" *Freikörperkultur*, "like every
other organisation, must pledge its full support to the Nazi movement" and convert to military training. *Gymnos* concluded that the
German nudist movement, "as we knew it, is dead".[39] The British
movement had been described by *Gymnos* in its first issue as being
"still in its infancy".[40] No sooner had it taken its first tentative steps
than it needed to stand alone.[41]

Sun Bathing Review, a quarterly, quickly followed *Gymnos*.
Founded by Barford and operating as a commercial enterprise, the magazine's promotion of partially dressed "sun bathing" rather than full
nudism enabled it to be sold on British newsstands and to reach a wider
audience. "We have nothing against complete nudity," the editors
noted, but neither did they advocate it as a scientific necessity.[42] The
magazine's centrist approach resulted in a circulation of 50,000 after
just two issues.[43] Its contents were substantial and high-minded, with
contributors of noted professional calibre including the leading physicians of light and air Saleeby and Rollier. Major public intellectuals,
including writer George Bernard Shaw and biologist Julian Huxley, were
supporters alongside prominent humanists, pacifists, socialists, and

feminists including Naomi Mitchison, Vera Brittain, and Winifred Holtby.

The magazine's intellectual community reflected the signatories of a 1932 letter to *The Times* asserting the physical and mental health value of what they euphemistically called "air bathing" and criticizing its current status as a furtive activity denied public respectability. The distinguished authors complained that its practitioners "have found it necessary to secrete themselves in the woods round London in order to avoid the attention of the public, the Press, their friends, and their neighbours. This need for secrecy is an iniquitous state of affairs!"[44] The letter argued for greater public acceptance for nudism (although not by name), yet the signatories did not go so far as to identify themselves as practitioners. Nonetheless, nudism's elite authorization by upper-class or otherwise privileged figures, who prided themselves on challenging conventional boundaries while also being socially and financially insulated from the reputational risks that experimental and bohemian lifestyles could bring, helped pave the way for nudism's wider acceptance across a broader demographic. Emboldened by support for this letter, *Sun Bathing Review* was born of the belief that "once the people of Britain were able to overcome their timidity, they will flock to enjoy the activities offered under the banner of naturism".[45]

WHAT SHOULD NUDISTS WEAR?

Among early sun bathing enthusiasts, the question of whether exposure of the whole body to the sun was necessary was a key sticking point.[46] All agreed on the positive therapeutic value of sunshine. To what extent additional benefits could be enhanced by *total nudity*, however, was a cause for dispute between moderates and completists. Some of the discussions related to physical health, including the therapeutic value of the sun's rays and vitamin D, were a core aspect of early nudism's healthy status, but other debates concerned social norms and attitudes. A range of voices promoted full disrobing, from psychologists who vouched for its capacity to "dispel fear", to physicians who advocated "the whole light on the whole skin".[47] Reverend Norwood claimed, for vaguely asserted "medical" reasons: "It is important that the sexual organs are exposed."[48] A core claim of nudism was that it released the naked body from its dominant association with sex, so swimming costumes and "slips" were strongly condemned by some as they drew attention to specific areas of the body.

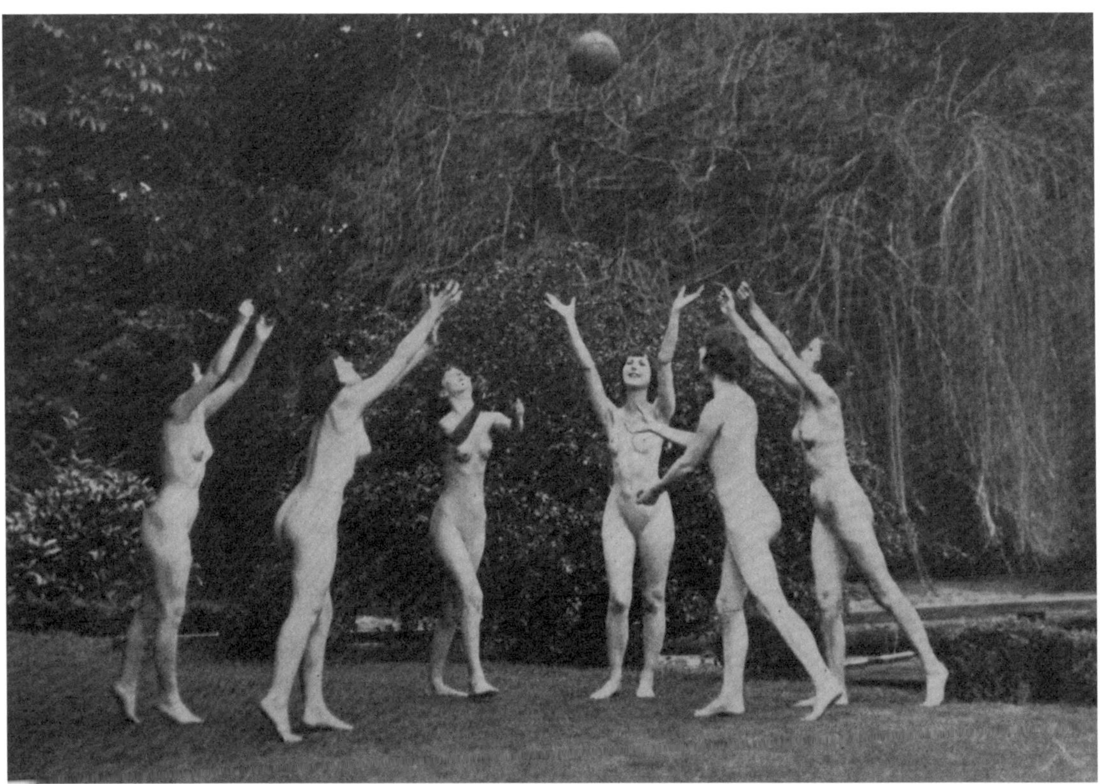

Exalted postures were common visual motifs in early nudist and sun bathing photographs. Stretching bodies, especially of young women, communicated poise and *joie de vivre*.

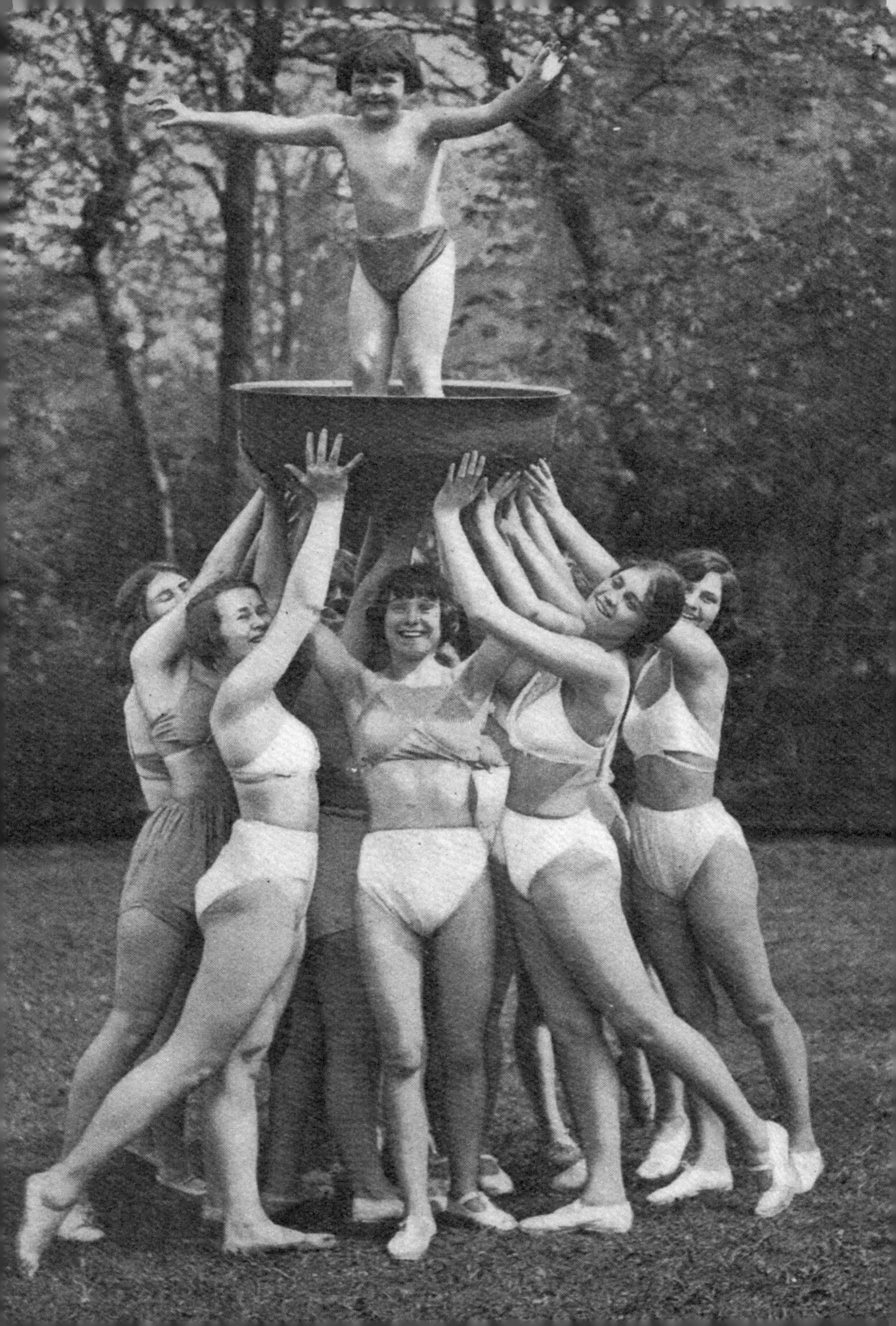

GYMNOS

The Official Organ of the Gymnic Association of Great Britain

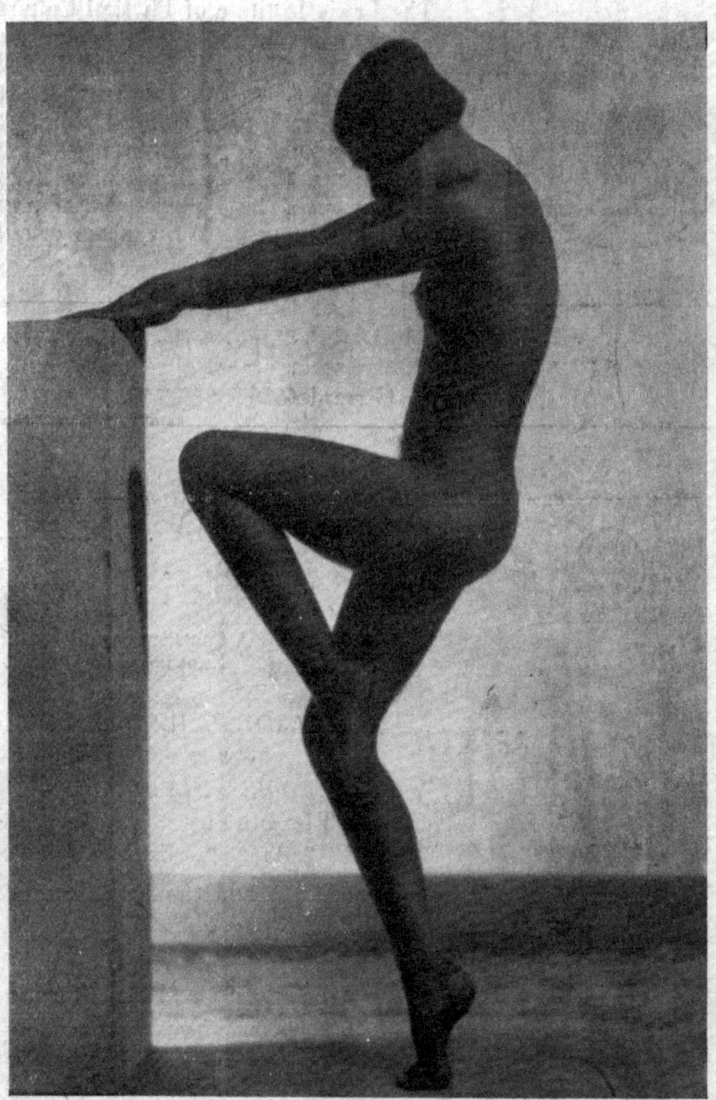

1/-

MAY, 1933

Establishing an Ideal

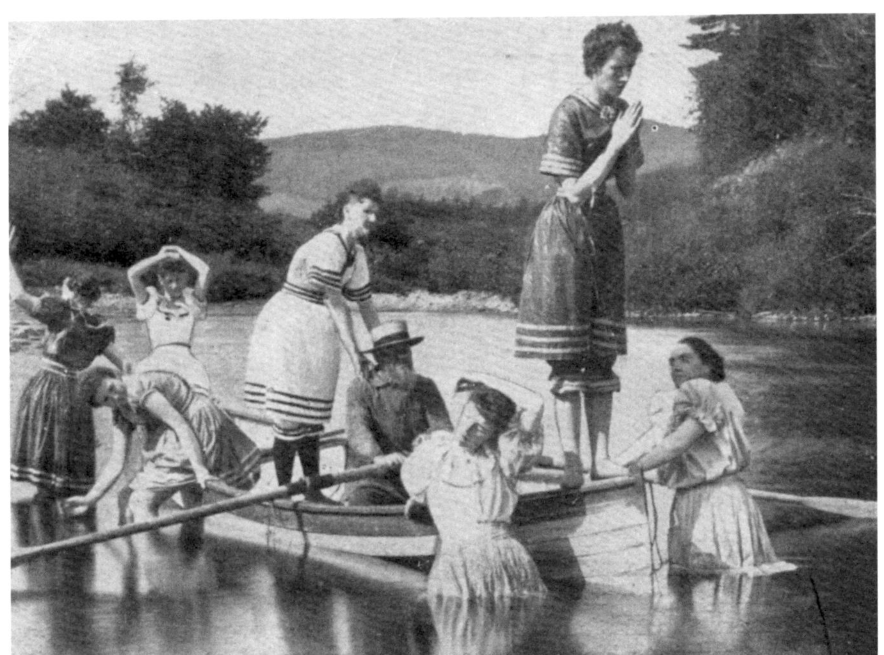

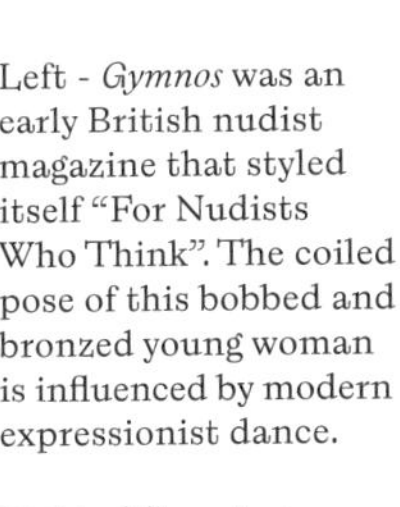

Left - *Gymnos* was an early British nudist magazine that styled itself "For Nudists Who Think". The coiled pose of this bobbed and bronzed young woman is influenced by modern expressionist dance.

Right - These two photographs, entitled "1880" and "1933", were included as a contrasting pair in *Gymnos* to show the stuffy swimsuit styles of the past and the new freedoms of nude bathing.

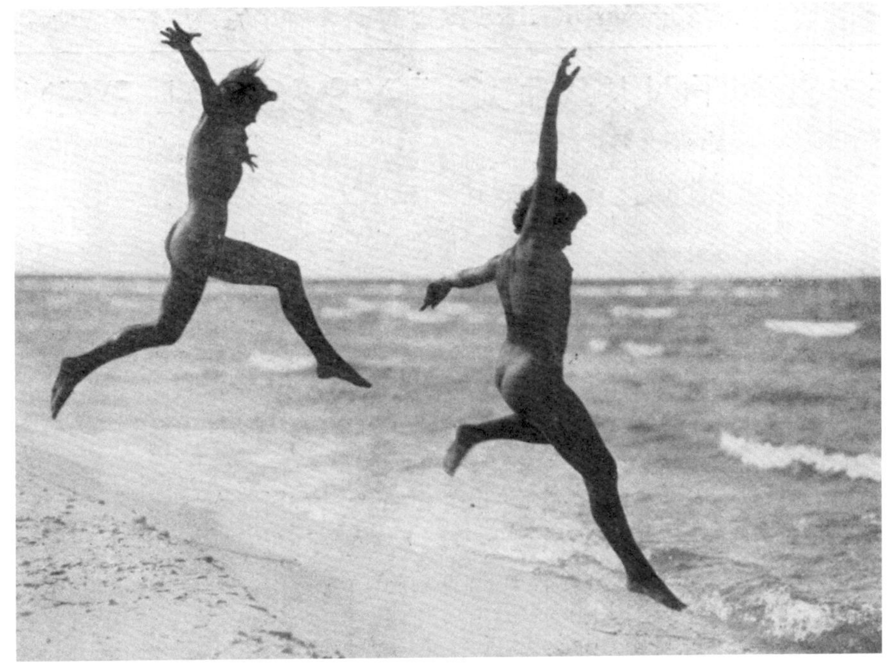

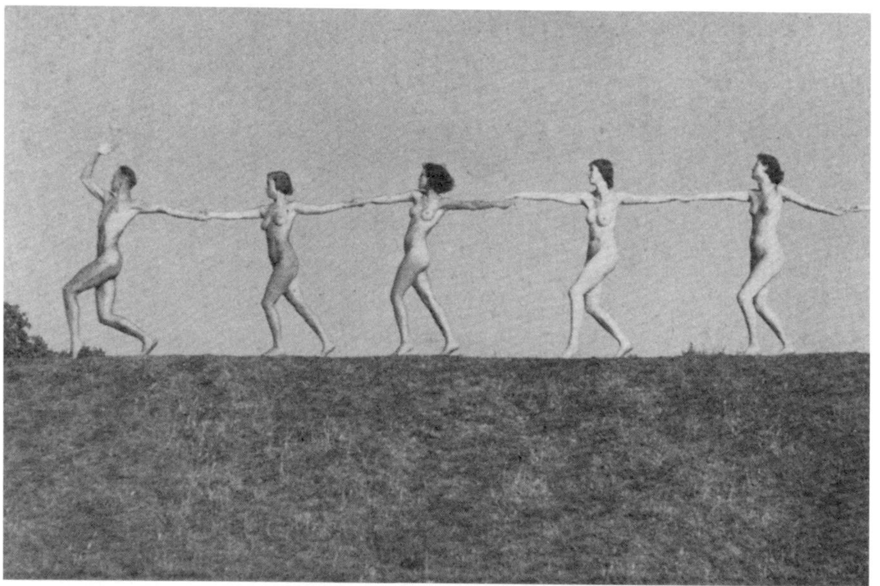

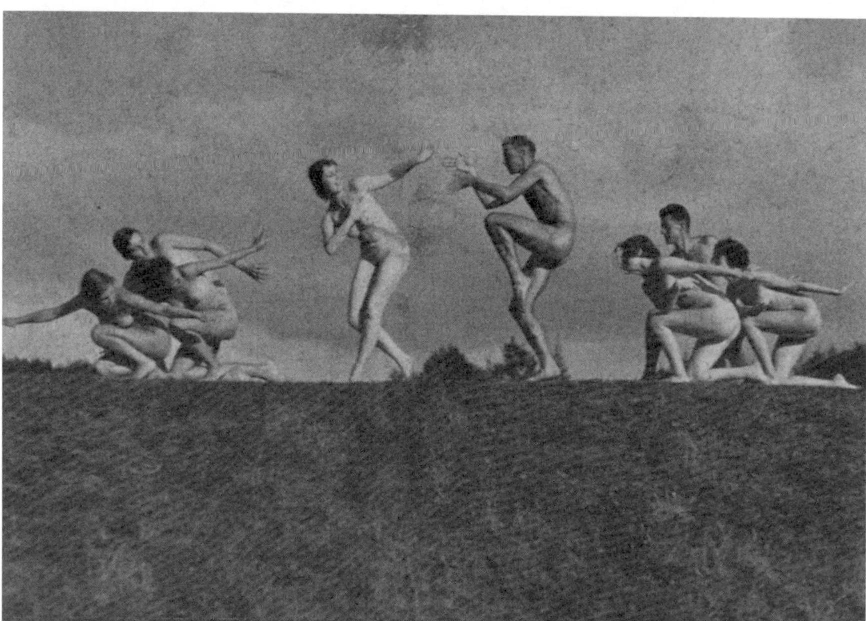

Via Greek-style friezes, angular leaps and expressionist gestures, attendees of the 1933 Sun Bathing Society Summer School perform athletic nudism for the camera of Yvonne Gregory.

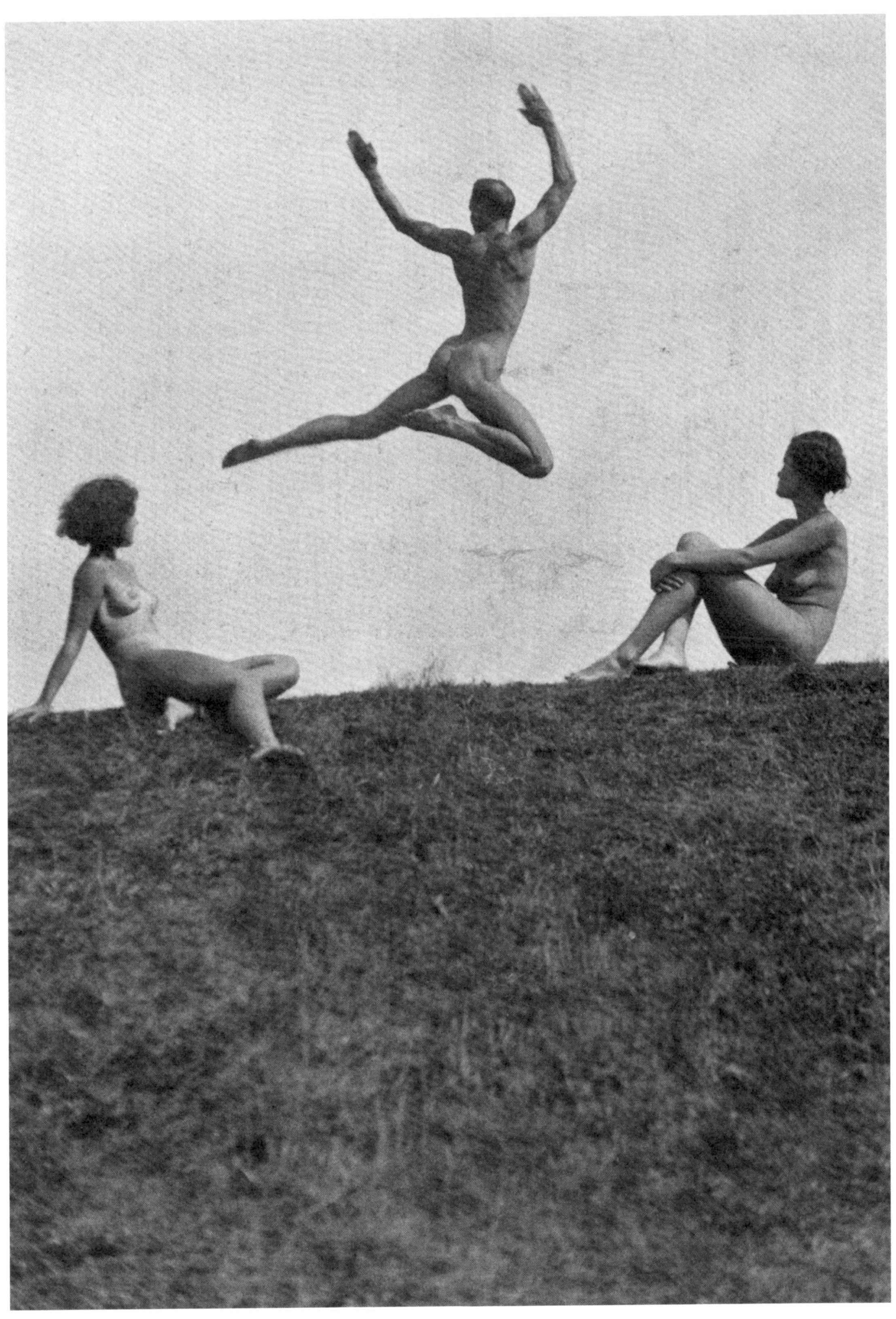

43

A *Gymnos* article debating "partial nudity" argued that "false ideas of modesty should not be engendered by covering the sexual organs or the breasts".[49] A *Health and Efficiency* article argued for total nudity as essential: "The idea is completely defeated if you have a thread of clothing on you. It is a thing which you cannot possibly appreciate unless you are completely naked. [...] You don't get anywhere near as much physical and mental benefit without complete nudity. A sense of absolute freedom is a *sine qua non*."[50]

For those who followed this line of argument, nudism was a total practice that need not be confined merely to the leisure spaces of nudist clubs on sunny weekends and summer holidays. There, the norm was to arrive clothed, privately disrobe, and then collectively sun bathe and swim, play net sports and team games, enjoy picnics and maintain the site, all in the nude, before dressing to return to conventional society. But this was too modest a practice for some. Those in favour of "universal nudism" looked forward to a fully nude world when people would "permanently discard clothes" at all times.[51] Others saw these visionary ideals as a bridge too far. Norwood observed, "Clothing has an important place to fill and no one but a crank would propose its total abolition."[52] *New Health* magazine articulated a middle position between clashing camps: "Somewhere between superabundance of dress and complete nakedness lies the happy mean, a mean which will permit of dress or undress as circumstances change."[53] This flexible approach allowed nudists to cover themselves as situations suited and explains the clothing worn in nudist photographs.

What nudists should wear might seem obvious—nothing!—but given that total nudity was too strong a medicine for many and was not possible year-round in Britain's climate, dress was a central discussion point for nudists, ironic as it may seem. Whether clothes were positioned as the enemy, a necessity, or an enhancement, nudists talked about them constantly. Prominent playwright and pacifist Laurence Housman, a sun bathing supporter if not a full nudist himself, suggested an outfit for when minimal decency was required. He drew inspiration from what he vaguely described as "pictures of natives", comprising a loose short apron hanging over a belt to cover the genitals. As he put it in *Sun Bathing Review*, "What they wear is decorative and easy; it is something to be seen and admired; it has not that wretched appearance of exposed underwear which characterises most of your present sun-bathing costumes." To Housman, "The bunched loin cloths your devotees are at present wearing are to my mind both silly and ugly, and in the case of some of your males a little bit 'exhibitionistic' in tendency." When breasts must be concealed, he suggested "the fashions of ancient and eastern civilisations", making cups "decorative and beautiful" with "rich, strange colour and pattern". Finally, he recommended "a loose Indian wrap" to add "real social beauty combined with the freedom you so much desire—and need".[54]

For other nudists, bodily decoration was vetoed. One contributor, Clifford Coudray, who had extensive experience of German nudist camps, described a female nudist there who "got hauled over the coals", as he put it, "for wearing a gold and ruby pendant, as we are supposed to cultivate bodily beauty, but unadorned. Women were not made by God to stick jewels on their necks or bosoms."[55] Parmelee's accounts of womenswear in English camps differ, and some practices seemed to sustain the feminine glamour that certain nudists hoped to destroy. He observed that women "often wear bands or garlands of flowers around their heads, usually retain such jewelry as they are in the habit of wearing, such as rings, bracelets, earrings, and necklaces, and sometimes don slippers with brightly coloured ribbons. More rarely they drape a transparent veil about the shoulders."[56] No similar practices of decoration were recorded among nudist men.

Much was written in nudist publications on dress as a form of deception and trickery, and the removal of clothes was promoted to draw attention to men and women's potential as suitable breeding partners. Eugenics is a racist, classist, and ableist pseudoscience, but many nudists in the 1920s and 1930s, including those who considered themselves to be politically progressive, incorporated eugenic theory into their bodily and social improvement project.[57] Better knowledge about exercise, diet, and physical health was promoted as a positive drive to enhance the health of the nation but discriminatory ideas about fitness (including for reproduction or "breeding") were also rooted in ideas about biological imperatives and pecking orders or, put more simply, right and wrong bodies. Sun bathing supporter W. Hope-Jones of the Eugenics Society despaired of the current "debased" state of modern sexual attraction, particularly "its painted and powdered women angling for masculine favour with the bait of expensive clothes and cosmetics". Setting up a contrast between what he considered artificial and natural, he lamented, "We may well hope that our descendants will be privileged to live in a freer and saner world, where they may meet each other as God made them and not as their tailors have disguised them."[58]

To those nudists who supported full body exposure, nudism was utopian and escapist while dress was its inverse: dystopian and enslaved. Clothing as a concept carried the weight of a variety of moral charges using a range of metaphors. Garments were "dirty cloth jails", a "tyranny", and "the iron chains which civilisation and custom have riveted on suffering humanity."[59] Disease, danger, and deathliness were common characterizations; for example, it was noted that illness "is largely an inevitable result of the enslavement of the body within the dark walls of its own clothing". An excess of dress was claimed to be fatal. Those who clung to their "astrakhan collars and have no use for the Sun and Air and freedom of the body" offered "one consolation" to nudists: it was believed "they will die off quicker than those who follow the sun".[60] In uncompromising language, some nudists declared: "Clothes are dead."[61] In particular, the fashionable garments of the period's immediate forebears, from tight corsets to complex bathing costumes, were slighted as "ludicrous, insanitary, uncomfortable, imbecile".[62]

Modern clothing fared little better, being described as "crude, unimaginative and unattractive".[63] The problem particularly concerned clothes worn by men: "They fray their necks with the rings of collars and bore into them with protruding studs, they encase their bodies irrespective of the state of the weather in thick black or grey cloth and wear on their heads little black boxes which they call bowlers or taller ones called silk hats."[64] The argument that menswear was not progressing at the same speed as womenswear featured prominently in early nudist literature and overlapped with contemporaneous British campaigns for men's dress reform. Many dress reformers were nudists and vice versa. Proposed solutions ranged from moderate revisions to existing garments to make them more lightweight, "rational", and washable, to a complete eradication of offending items and the introduction of colourful, comfortable, and flamboyant alternatives, from velvet knickerbockers and pussycat bow blouses to men's skirts.[65]

Artist Eric Gill, for example, well known for his dress diatribes and for wearing nothing but a smock and sandals in public, proclaimed: "I should like to see collars, ties and trousers abolished."[66] Parmelee argued, "All the implements of torture with which mankind voluntarily adorns itself [...] as if in straitjackets in prisons and asylums, should be discarded." These "abominations" included boots and shoes: "In no other way has mankind deliberately caused itself more misery than by the use of these monstrous agencies of deformation."[67] The release was expected to produce a utopian state of being. Nudists looked forward to "liberation from these heavy draperies that shut out from our mind the fresh draught of independent thought, and that screen our souls and bodies from the divine light which Heaven pours out day by day to save us from our padded dinginess".[68]

Emancipation from all that clothing represented included escape from industrialization. The artist Gill, as part of his wider arguments about the loss of craftsmanship in contemporary culture, argued that mass production was producing uniformity. By casting off factory-made dress, he claimed nudism would return individuality.[69] This yearning for individual distinction, however, contrasted sharply with other claims that nudism as a means of dissolving hierarchies and creating universal equivalence. For those who supported a more exclusive view, nudism offered a chance to regain authority when securities of social status were being challenged. George Ryley Scott, a regular contributor to nudist magazines, identified the problem: "the increased prosperity and higher standard of living among the working classes, the remarkable rise in democracy, the emancipation of women, the enormous spread of popular education". These factors created "a herd" from which cultural elites found it difficult to stand apart.[70]

The three central purposes of dress were widely agreed by nudist authors to be adornment, modesty, and protection.[71] The first two could be debunked but the last remained a challenge for bare feet on rough ground and regular bad weather. Several authors claimed that nudism created resilient bodies: "Vagaries of climate, cold winds, even snow need be no obstacle to a fit hardened, unabashed and sensible people."[72] Parmelee stated that nudity at work was "entirely feasible": "in most occupations no protection is necessary" and nudity could improve efficiency. Manual work especially should be undertaken naked.[73] Others keenly emphasized that sun bathing did not merely mean "lying about" but the pursuit of pigmentation through effort and exercise. Net sports, group activities, swimming, and the physical labour involved in the creation of the nudist camp, from felling trees to digging latrines, should be conducted naked. As one author put it, "Notice how supple and harmonious are the movements involved in the wielding of the axe or mattock!"[74] Beyond selected club tasks and games, however, vigorous naked exercise was discouraged. As was noted in an article on mountaineering, "Anyone who intended real climbing [...] would, of course, wear full clothing and breeches, unless he wished to lose his life in the cause of naturism."[75] The health aspect of nudism was rarely discussed in terms of safety or hygiene, where clothes might offer a further pragmatic function as a buffer for bodily fluids. Its transcendental promise was mostly above such daily details. In promoting nudism as a theory and an ideal, practical aspects of daily needs were often passed over. That nudists might sometimes be cold or uncomfortable, and that they might need coverage and protection from stony ground and splintery picnic benches, went mostly unacknowledged.

NO PICTURES!

Given the arguments about dressed versus undressed bodies, and that modest, warming, or reformist clothes were needed in certain situations, it is perhaps not so surprising that nudist magazines advertised garments for sale, from men's breathable Aertex sports shirts to skimpy beach briefs to be worn where authorities permitted or demanded. Photographs of women in fashionable bathing costumes and swimming caps appeared on magazine covers alongside advertisements on its back pages for so-called "natural" corsetry. These images often undermined the claims of the articles they bookended, while debates about how nudist culture should be depicted visually was a dominant focus from its very earliest publications.

Langdon-Davies's 1929 book had been wholly unillustrated, and Norwood's *Nudism in England* featured a sole photograph of a mixed-gender folk dance scene in woodland on its cover, sufficiently distanced for identities to go undetected. (The copy I ordered from the British Library had been defaced by a previous reader with an outraged annotation about its content: "No Pictures!".) Gay, the Merrills, and Parmelee had all included professional photographs of energetic and youthful participants taken at continental camps. Some of these European illustrations, including images from Surén's book, were reproduced in the pages of early British nudist magazines.[76]

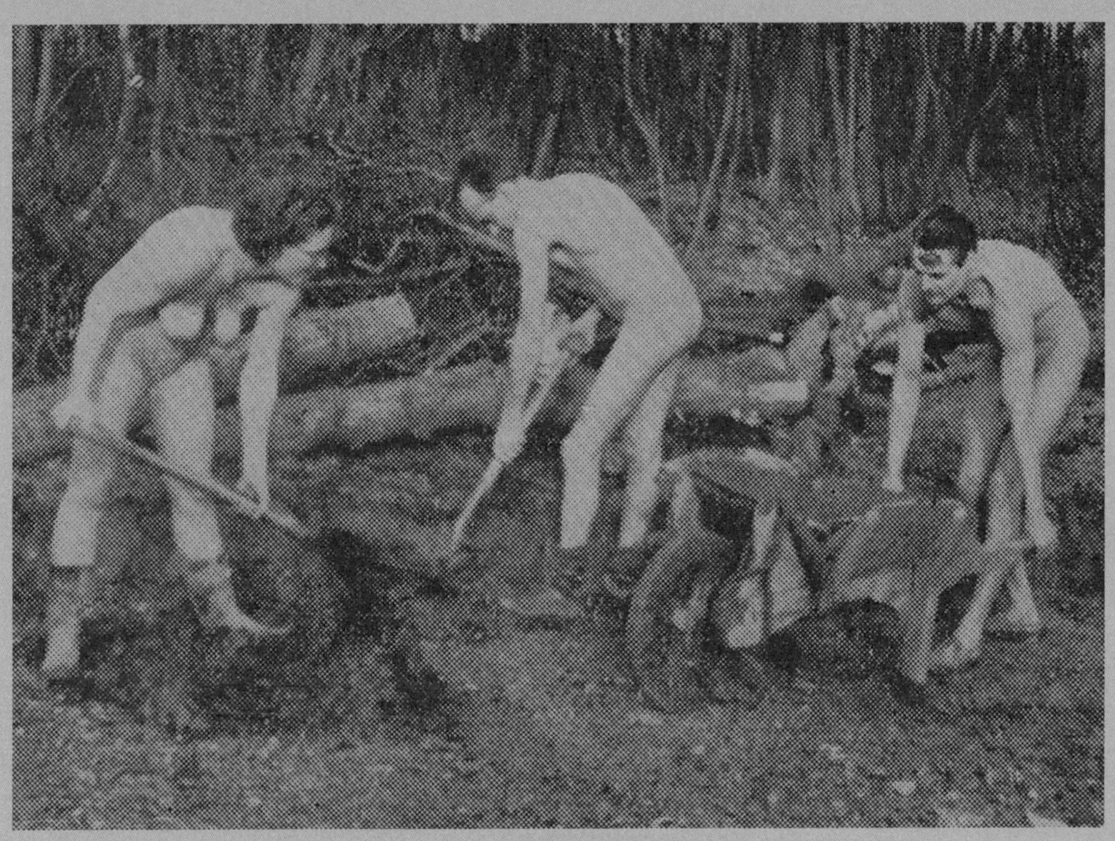

The hard work of
nudism's pioneers,
turning basic grounds
into leisure clubs, was
frequently depicted
in nudist magazines.
Nude members scythed,
raked, and dug rough
sites into submission.

Many of nudism's British founders were also dress reformers. The Men's Dress Reform Party advertised flamboyant garments, including highly patterned golf wear, in pre-war nudist magazines.

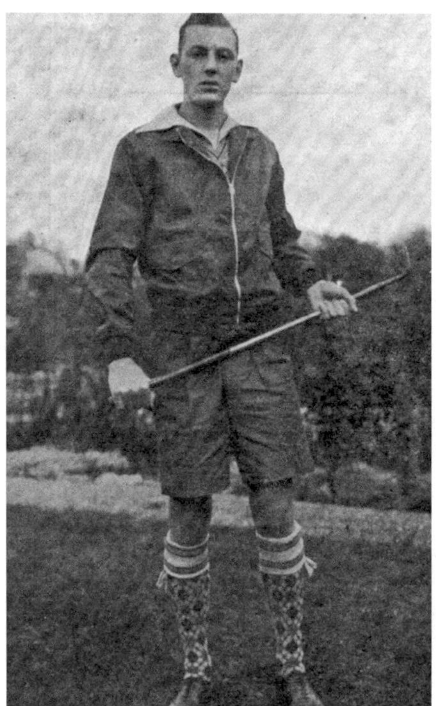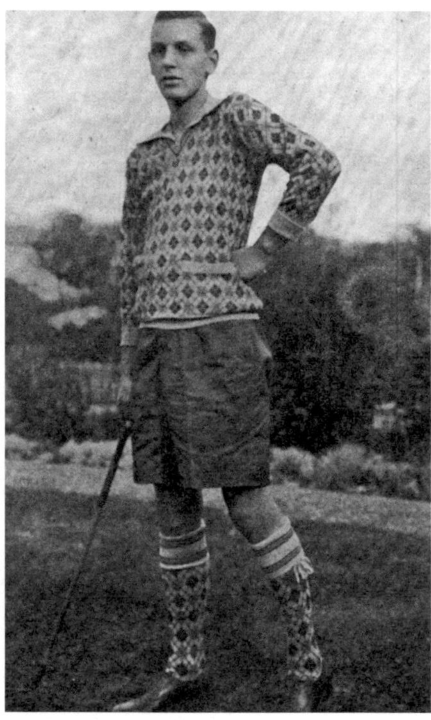

Gymnos included photographs of partially dressed and wholly naked men, women, and children on its covers and inside pages. These were mostly presented without credit but showed a mixture of European youthful bodies engaged in exercise alongside candid family scenes of British club activity.

While full, natural, and truthful nakedness was *Gymnos*'s stated philosophy, photographs in British publications concealed adult genitals by strategic posing or by retouching prints so penises, vulvas, and pubic hair were smoothed away or clouded out. Letters-page correspondents repeatedly drew indignant attention to the fact that the magazine's illustrations contradicted its published morals, but it was noted with regret that British laws dictated what could be shown. "The camera," the *Gymnos* editor asserted, "when used in conjunction with live models, unfortunately lends itself to abuse, as witness the filthy photographs, desecrating sexual life, which all too frequently find their way into this country from places abroad." He continued, "Penal legislation is aimed mainly at the potential evil-doer, with the result that the legitimate photographic artist is denied the privilege of reproducing natural specimens of his art."[77] This moral position underscored *Gymnos*'s aims, as stated in its "Planks of Nudism", which claimed "pure motives", "chastity", and "true propriety".[78] *Desecration*, *filth*, *abuse*, and *evil* in this statement were euphemisms for sexual desire, its visual depiction, and, by extension, the use of such images for sexual arousal (blamed, conveniently, on foreign imports). British nudists disputed the definition and value of "obscenity" as a category—several were also prominent anti-censorship campaigners—but British law in the 1930s was still beholden to the 1868 interpretation of the term; that is, any material, textual or visual, with the potential to "deprave and corrupt".[79] In order to build public acceptability and to stay in print, British nudist magazines needed to be seen to uphold unimpeachable moral standards through word and image.

As a result of these rules and requirements a certain sameness of visual style developed across British nudist publications before the Second World War. Legality and propriety dictated nudist visual aesthetics to a certain degree, but other influences came into play. *Health and Efficiency*, the most commercial of the 1930s nudist magazines, was abundantly illustrated including with advertisements for health foods (Hovis bread, Shredded Wheat breakfast cereal, and Marmite spread), compensatory treatments (for height, weight, and baldness), and nudist clubs, literature, and products, such as artificial light treatments. The bodies shown in its pages paid a debt to the magazine's long tradition of physique and posing competitions, with shots of oiled and muscular men in heroic poses, indoor and out. By the 1930s the title's application of fig leaves to men's genitals had given way to discreet G-string "jock slips" or posing pouches, which were also offered for sale in the back pages. Monthly competitions attracted contributions from amateur photographers (who went uncredited), and these featured alongside regular art supplements of professional photographs by well-known names, including society portraitists Dorothy Wilding and Bertram Park, which were presented in larger format on higher-quality paper, sometimes in soft colour. While photographs of men were included in the mix, *Health and Efficiency*'s covers exclusively featured women from 1933 onwards. These photos were mostly of nude, though occasionally lightly clad, women, often in pastoral settings, singly or in choreographed groups, but always of a particular kind: white, slim, able-bodied, athletic, and young. Photographs of nudist camps were a core part of the magazine's

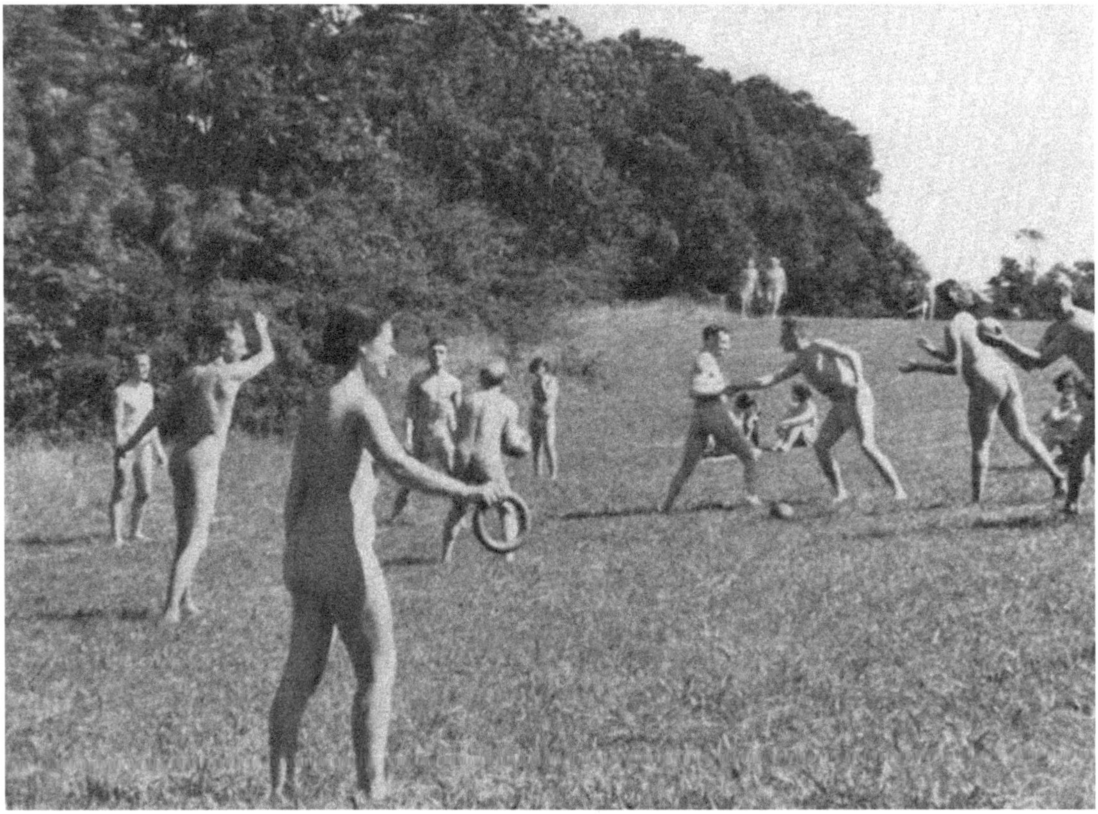

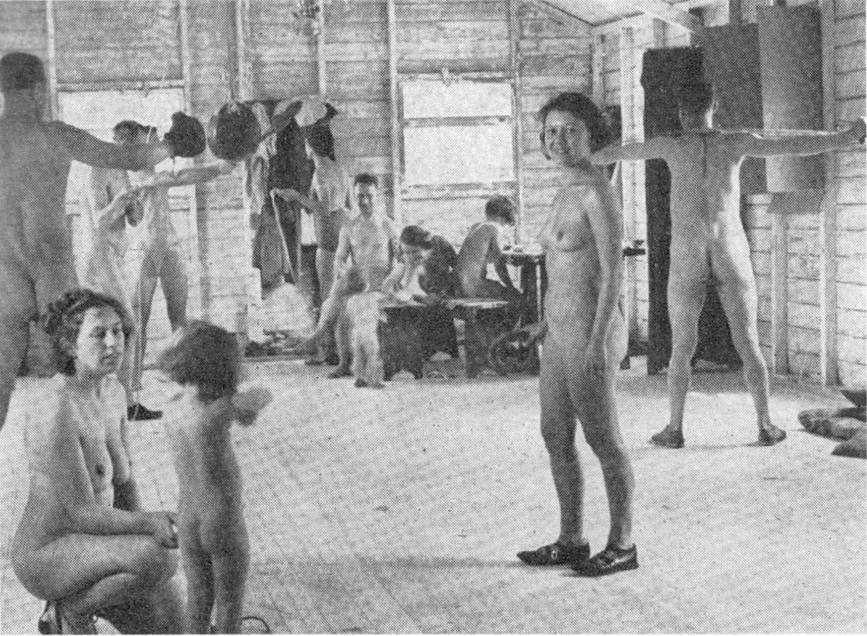

Gymnastics, weight training and team sports were all regular nudist camp activities. As a health movement, British nudism was underpinned at the outset by ideas of bodily improvement.

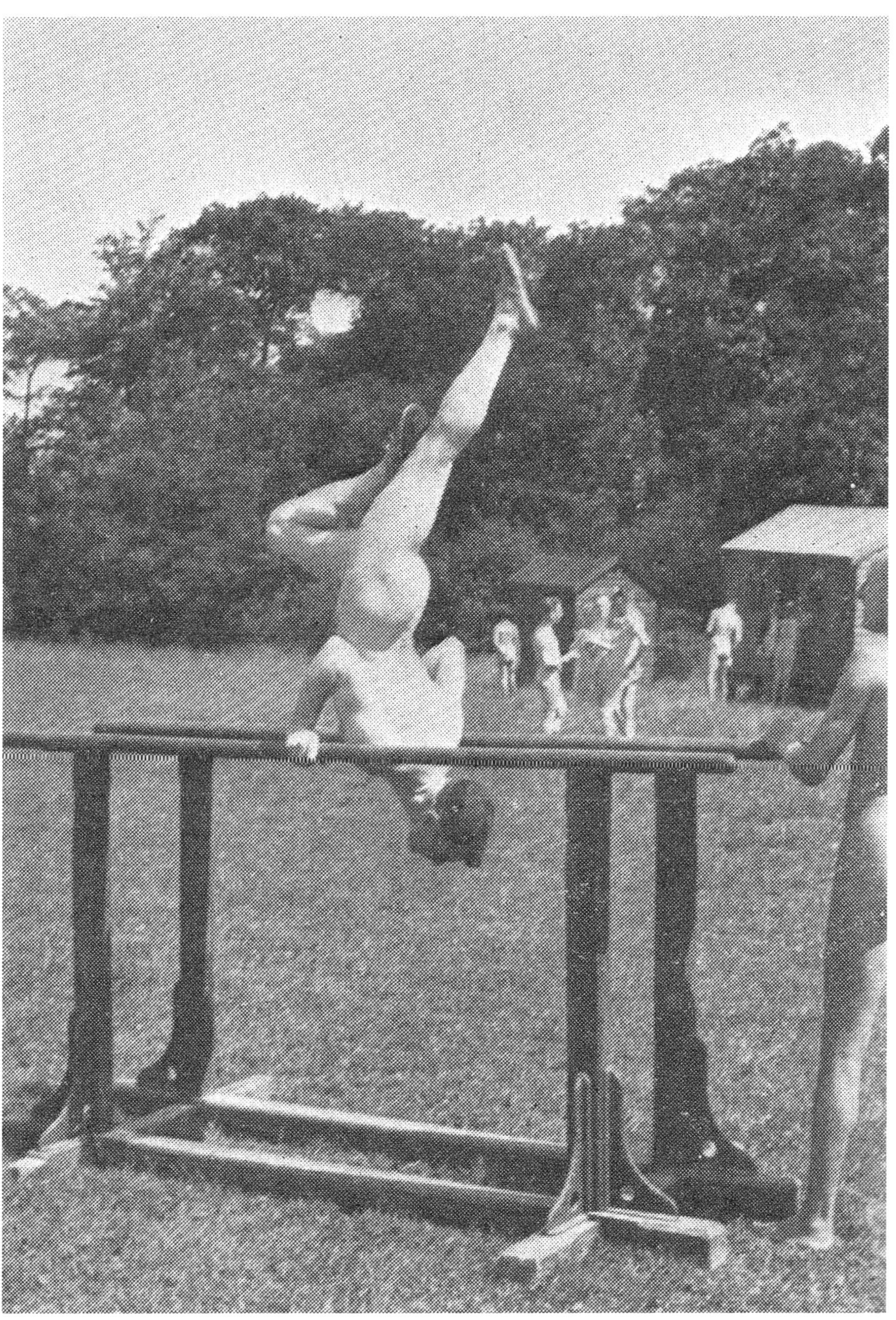

visual repertoire, covering all ages in more informal arrangements, but its most dominant imagery was the youthful female body in stylized poses that variously spoke to classical painting, Grecian statuary, and gymnastic postures.

The first eight issues of *Sun Bathing Review* featured a woodcut by prominent artist and nudist Robert Gibbings on its coloured card covers.[80] His bold monochrome treatment of a nude nuclear family, arranged among waterside foliage, was sufficiently modern in its styling and shading to suggest a new aesthetic vision, while being sufficiently timeless in its antiquarian format to convey the ancient rural wisdom that the magazine wished to evoke. Its depiction of nude men, women, and children together also diffused suspicion of nudism's sexual motivations and reflected the family ethos of the magazine, where modern methods in childcare and schooling were regularly profiled. The words "Copiously Illustrated", pronounced under the journal's title, highlighted the central importance of its illustrations as a selling point. Like *Gymnos*, its photographs were split between posed depictions and candid camp scenes, but *Sun Bathing Review*'s aesthetic ambitions were greater, with Bertram Park appointed as an honorary art editor in 1935 when the magazine moved to exclusively photographic monochrome covers. As a result, the magazine claimed, "the artistic quality of the illustrations—another important point for the good name of the movement—is assured". Photography was seen to strike an especially "modern note [...] in keeping with the times".[81]

A contemporaneous book, *Photography of the Figure* by artist Charles Simpson, observed that new aspects of nude photography were emerging in the 1930s; instead of imitating painting, as had once been the case, modern practice, Simpson stated, "ranged from photographs of nudist camps and others taken from the point of view of physical culture to the more advanced phases of nude photography in which the photographers make use of many devices to get away from representational realism".[82] All aspects of this range appeared in the nudist press in the 1930s, on covers, in features, and in advertisements. Key practitioners emerged with recognizable aesthetics and, in some cases, theories about subject and style. Nude photographs and photographs of nudists were, importantly, not the same thing.

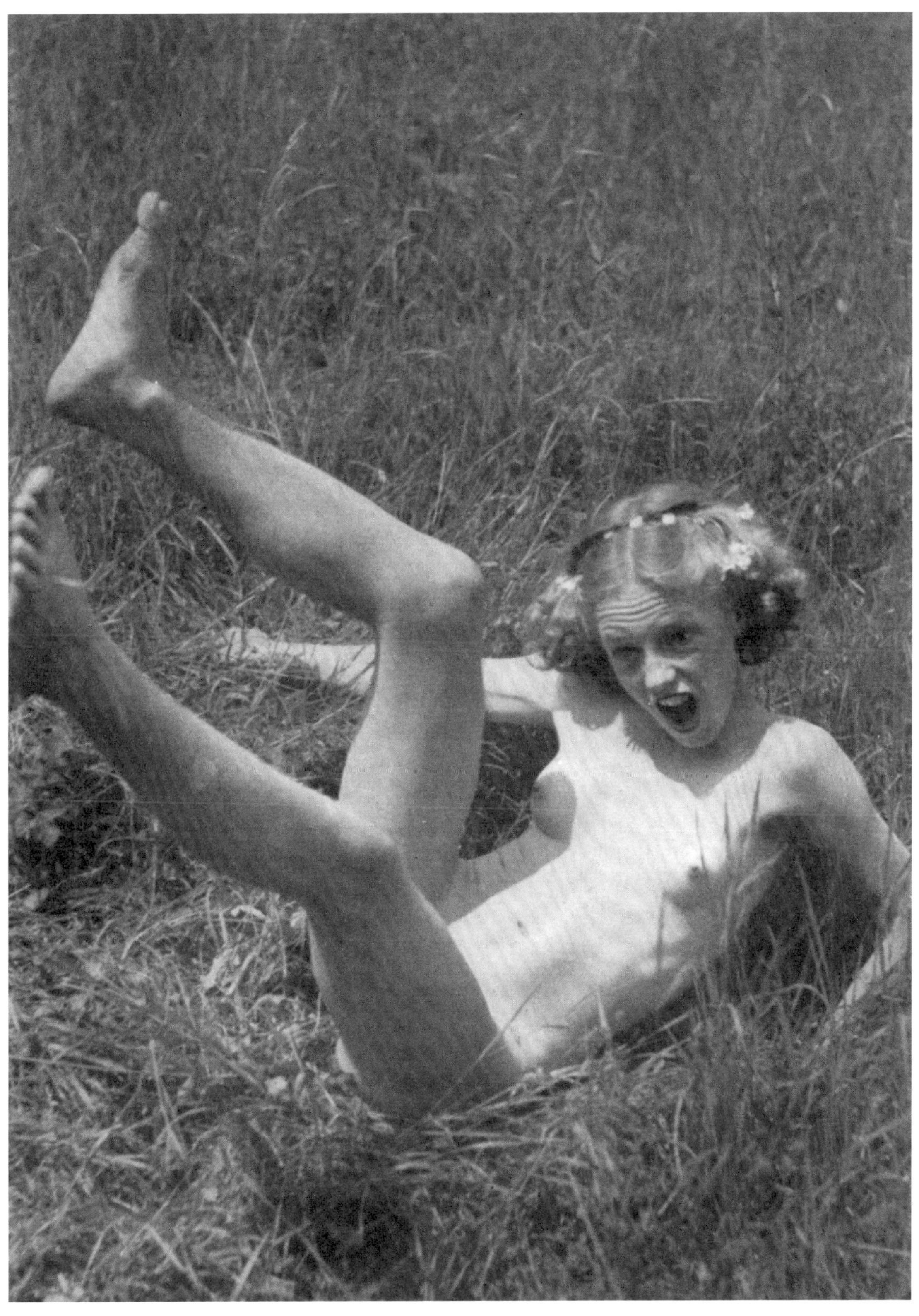

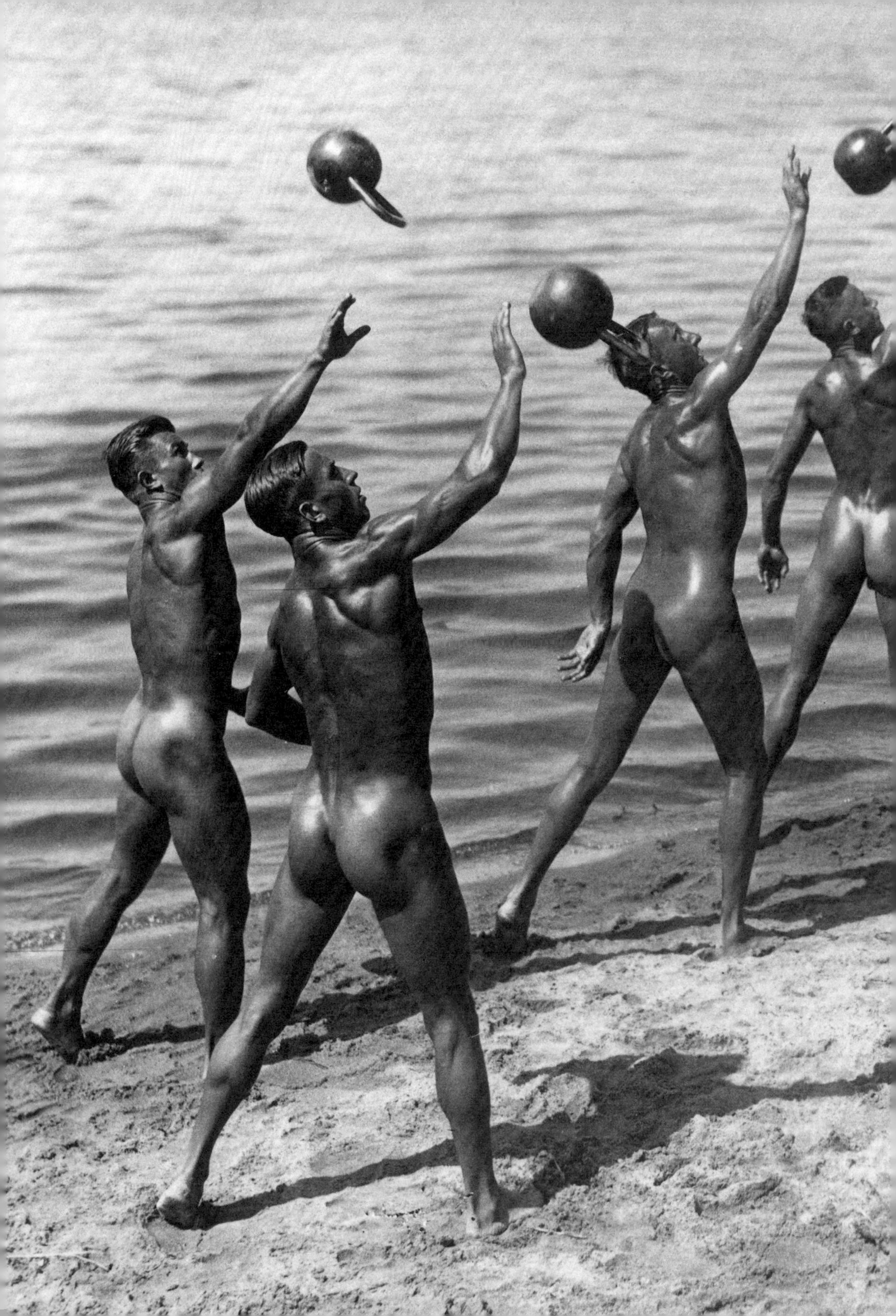

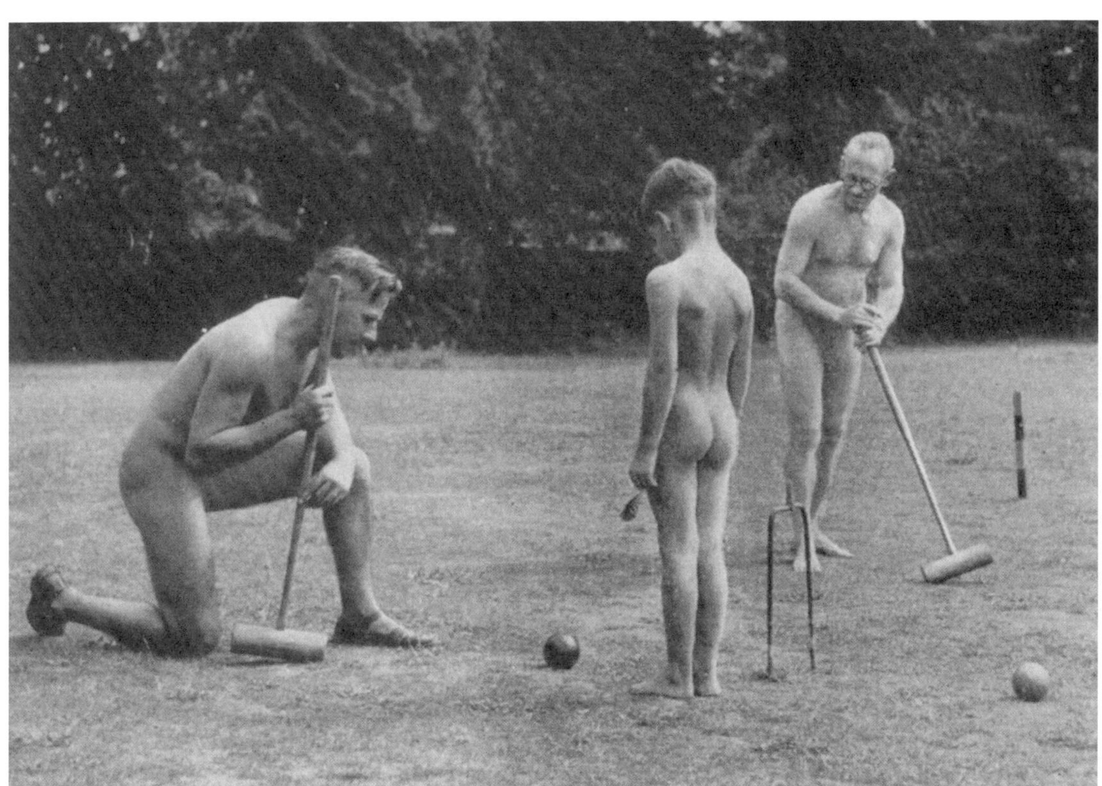

Photographs of nude activity illustrated in early nudist periodicals ranged from highly choreographed European exercise regimes to more sedate British lawn games, including croquet.

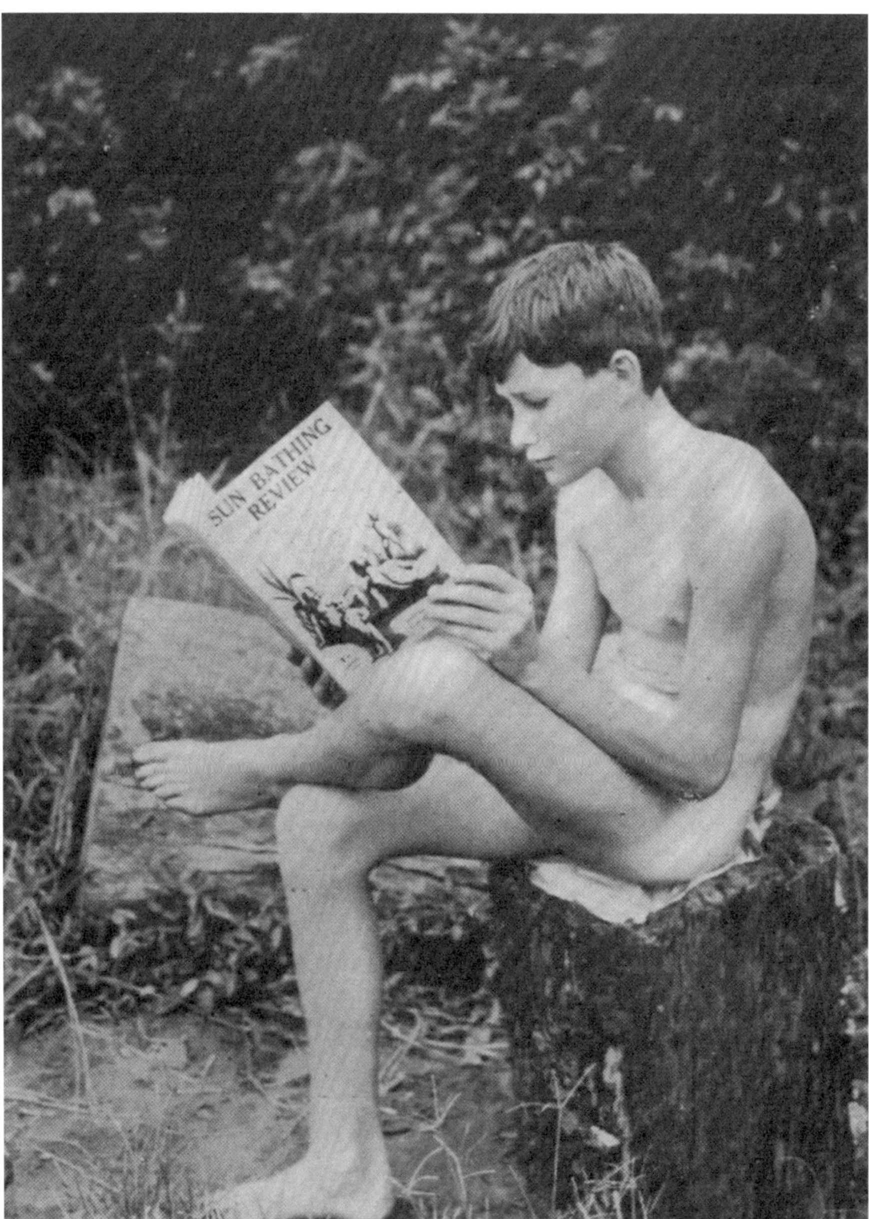

Sun Bathing Review, founded in 1933, saw nudism as an intellectual as well as a recreational pursuit. Early woodcut covers were provided by artist and nudist Robert Gibbings.

MODEL SUN BATHERS

Park, for example, with his wife and collaborator Yvonne Gregory, was a regular photographic contributor to the nudist press. Together, they jointly authored six books of photographic nudes between 1926 and 1939. They also ran a major portrait studio in central London with Marcus Adams, another regular nudist magazine photographer. Their studio clients included kings, politicians, and prominent figures in society and the arts, and they were founding figures in leading photographic salons.[83] Park's royal photographs circulated the world, appearing on British postage stamps and banknotes, and he achieved pre-war royal honours of Member and Order of the British Empire (MBE and OBE). These establishment credentials did not prove to be incompatible with nude photography, and the development of the movement gave Park and Gregory new photographic focus and justification.

As was common in early British nude publications, their first books claimed to provide instruction for painters and sculptors studying the figure. The photographs, mostly female studio nudes, were given abstract nouns as titles, as was the painterly tradition. Their accompanying annotations explicitly drew attention to the photographs' anthropological, anatomical, and artistic value. By the time they produced *Sun Bathers* in 1935, the outdoor photographs continued with titles such as "Awakening" or "Naiad", but the text spoke more directly to the nudist cause. The book's introduction, written by Alan Warwick, a regular contributor to nudist magazines, described it as a "new movement born of an unstable world".[84]

Park and Gregory claimed that their sun bathers could be seen "revelling in the full enjoyment of the freedom and health which the casting off of clothes promotes".[85] Poses, however, tended to be static and sculptural; lively revels were not much pictured. Some even come close to what Simpson noted as modern photography's tendency to position models as rigidly as the ornamental figurines on car bonnets.[86] For all the talk of freedom and honesty in the book's introduction, the models' genitals and pubic hair were retouched for legality, leading to some fundamental contradictions in claims. Another Park photograph from the period, given the grand title "Nudity knows no Falsehood", for example, features a groin cleared of any indication of the male model's genitals, and provides a telling case of the relative meanings of naturalism and truth in early British nudist depictions.[87] Although all *Sun Bathers* photographs were monochrome, Park and Gregory stated that recent years had brought a "rich sun bronze" to the formerly "washed out and colourless model". They argued, of their exclusively white sun bathing subjects, "the warm tints of the air-tanned body have infinitely more life and luminosity than the almost dead complexion of a skin that has never really been touched by the light of day".[88] The racial undertones of these early observations underscored nudism's dominant whiteness, which would come to a crisis in later decades, as will be shown.

All *Sun Bathers* photographs were "open-air", variously taken in rural and coastal settings, by the slightly grotty pools of early nudist clubs, or sometimes in the married photographers' back garden. Despite the variety of settings, they offer a repetitive view, in part because Park and Gregory preferred one type of model. Park advised on the subject for aspiring photographers in *Sun Bathing Review*. He supported nudism's key philosophy that the regular sight of the unclothed body is important for the betterment of the "moral and physical welfare of Society", but for photographic purposes he argued that only certain bodies should be depicted. Nudists, he noted, wore admirably less camera-conscious than most, which was crucial because awkwardness of attitude was one of the biggest obstacles to successful nude photography. He believed, however, that professional models rather than everyday nudists should be used, as "good proportions are required, meaning, for women, being 5 foot 7 (1.70 meters)". By contrast, "the majority of what might be called the average middle class girl are [*sic*] out of proportion from the head to the hips". For the avoidance of doubt, the article provided a chart that sliced a woman's body into equidistant dividing lines to show which distribution of parts was "perfect".[89] Park and Gregory's sun bathers, all unnamed, were women that fit this ideal.

Although Park and Gregory each preferred different camera technologies and sometimes published individually in magazines under their own names, in their jointly authored books they shared credit and their images cannot be told apart, even as they experimented with a range of nude styles, including more straightforward depictions in naturist clubs, mythological allegories of fauns and nymphs, and modernist cropping, dramatic angles, and chiaroscuro lighting in their studio work. Anyone looking for a distinctive female perspective through Gregory's lens will struggle to find it.

Autobiography was suppressed beneath commercial appeal during a time when new markets were growing for books of so-called nude camera studies, as well as illustrations for nudist publications, where many of their photographs were repurposed again and again.[90] Gregory had been a former model for Park, but by the 1930s they were in their forties and fifties respectively. As middle-aged photographers, clothed behind the viewfinder, they focused their gaze on nude youth.

THE NATURIST NUDE

John Everard, a former newspaper photographer, and Walter Bird, a society portraitist, followed Park and Gregory's lead by producing lavish book series of female nudes, with image content also sold as illustrations to periodicals from *Sun Bathing Review* to the magazine *Men Only*.[91] Bird's *Beauty's Daughters*, for example, was populated by young, slim women in sometimes convulsive, contorted theatrical performances of complex inner emotional states, including torment, abandonment, and ecstasy. Limbs lamented and implored, hands yearned and reached, bodies voluptuously resisted and yielded in stylized poses that created dynamic, angular shapes. Sometimes dramatically lit with oppressive shadows and low-key chiaroscuro effects, and with props including skulls or primitivist statues, they signalled the externalization of intense, metaphysical dramas born of powerful unconscious forces. Other poses, showing physical recoil or shielded eyes, neatly concealed the model's identity but also symbolized something deep, mysterious, and unknowable.

Such photographs established a modern argot for the nude that extended the softly romantic pictorialist tropes, such as the hesitant young woman at the water's edge in the style of the early 20th-century oil painting *September Morn* by Paul Chabas, the classical modest "pudica" Venus, or the languorous reclining odalisque. But in order to be suitable for the nudist press, photographic nudes needed, ideally, to combine modern attitudes with outdoor environments. What might be called a "naturist nude"—reflecting the emerging preferred term for British nudists—relied on setting for its meaning.[92] Photographs were ideally taken in natural light and rural spaces. Much of naturism's moral power related to the stripping away of artifice and release from complex neuroses, therefore the drama of the

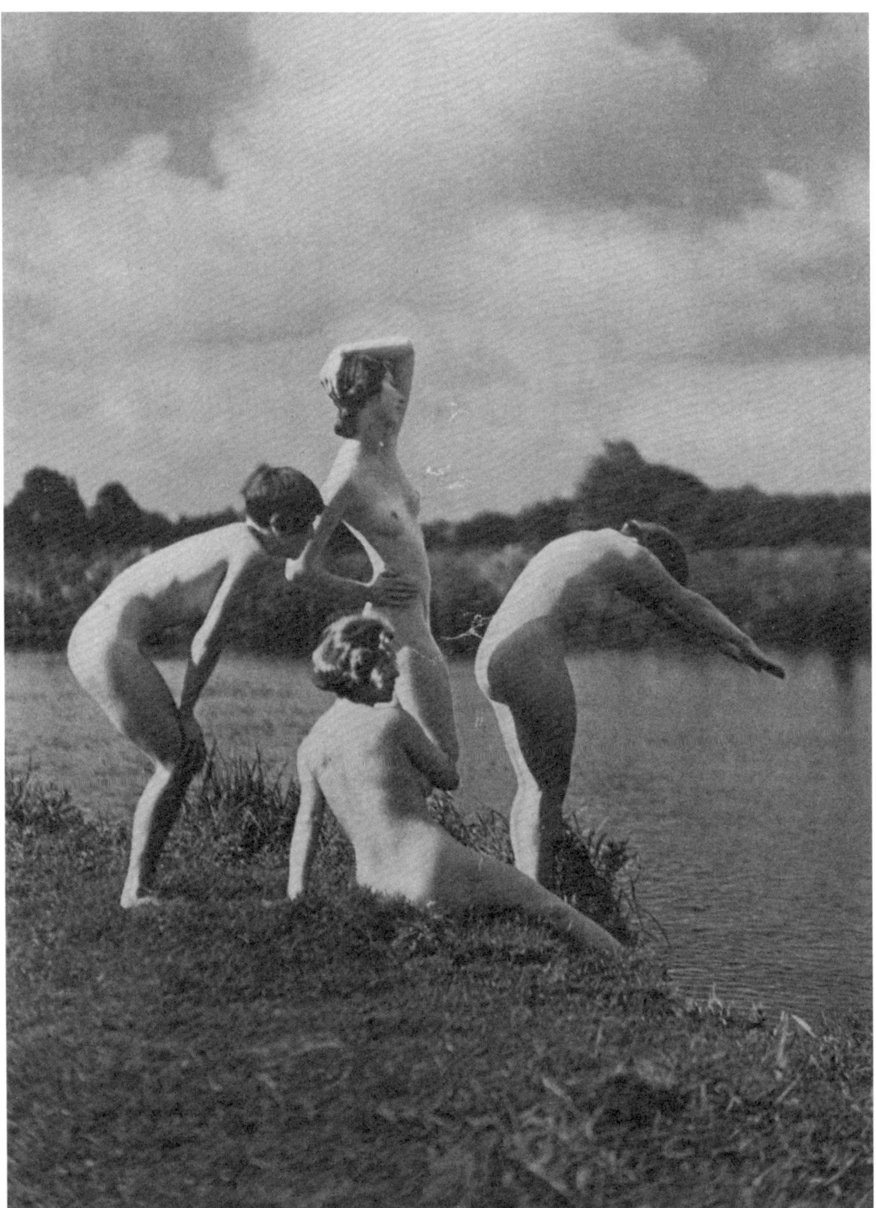

Nudist photography emerged as a distinctive genre in Britain in the 1930s, with poses and compositions drawing on painterly styles and sculptural ideals.

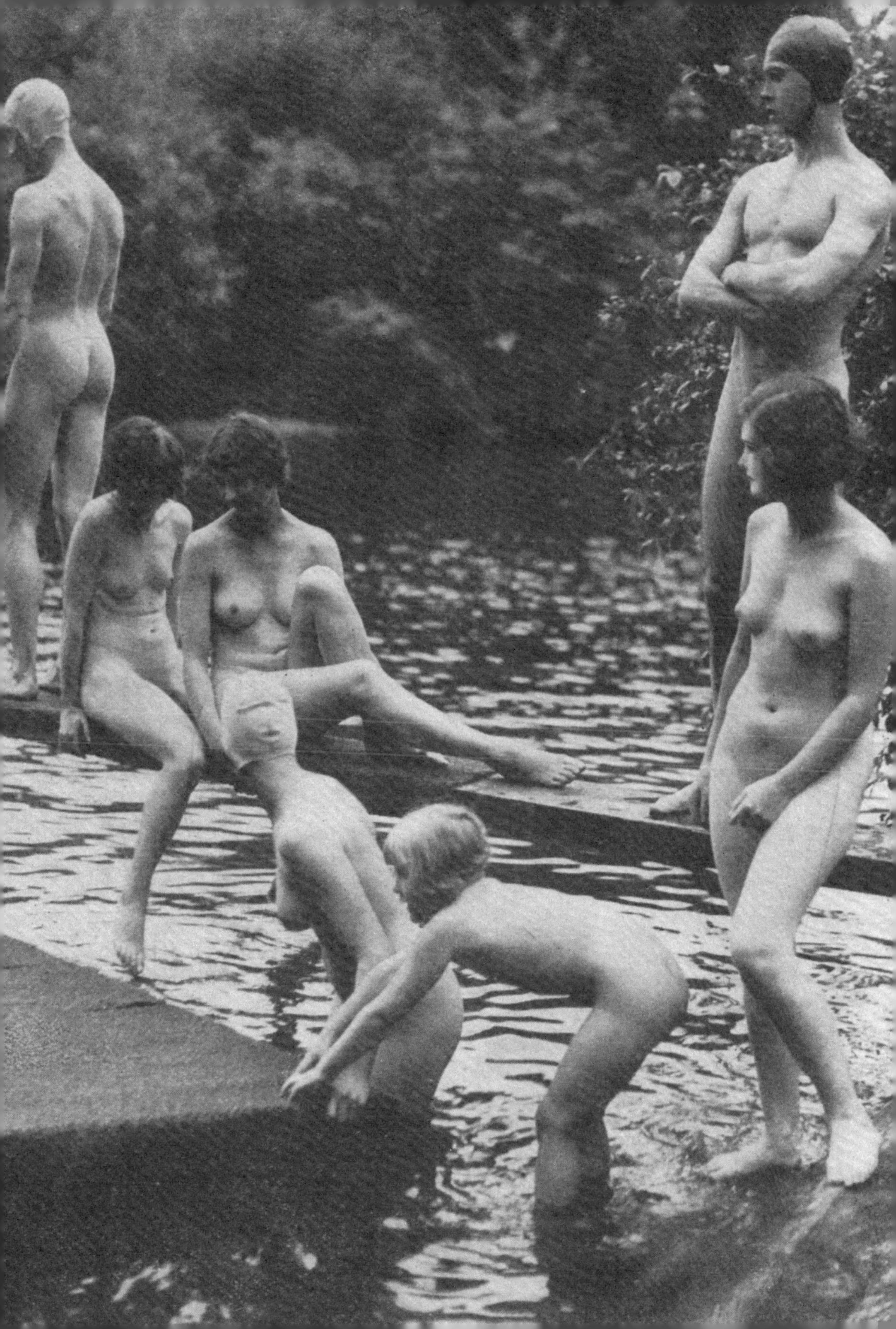

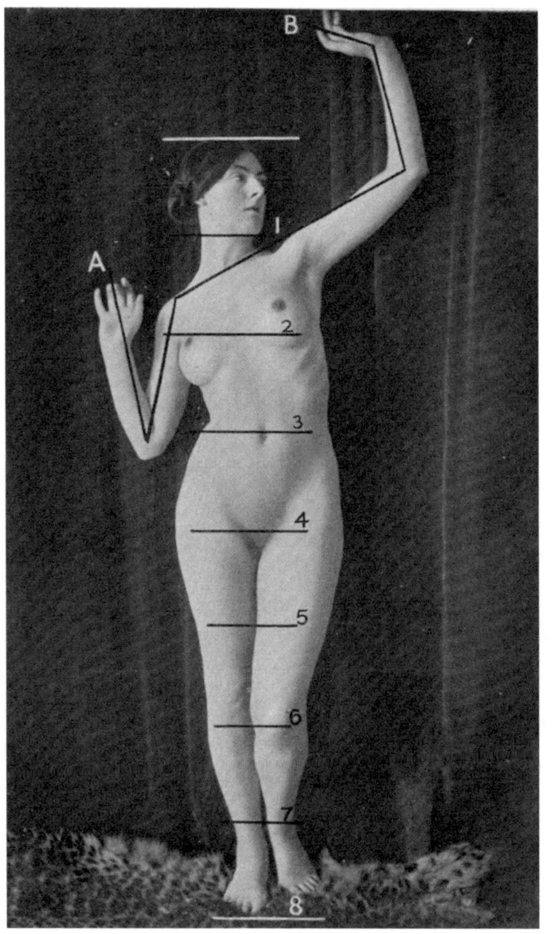

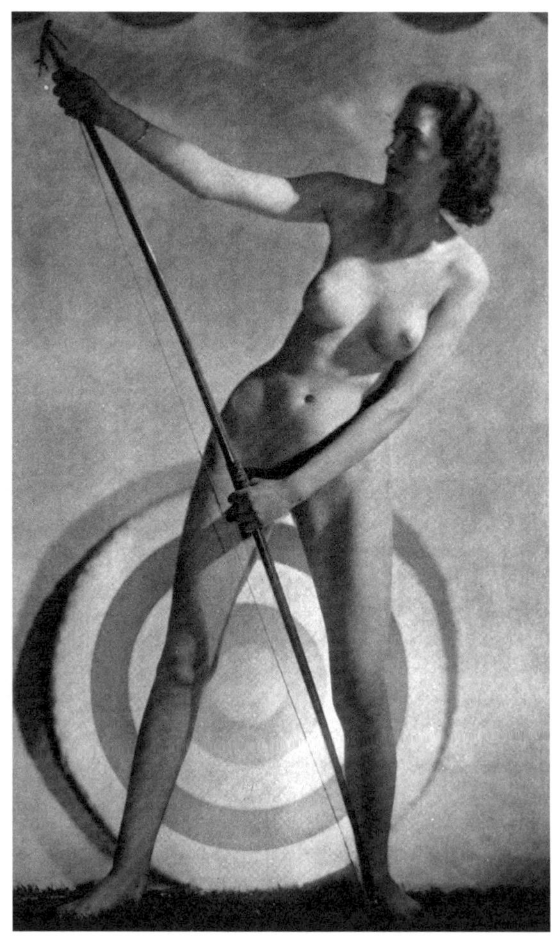

Nude photography
by husband-and-wife
photographers Bertram
Park and Yvonne
Gregory emphasized
ideal proportions,
classical traditions,
and new visions
informed by graphic
modernism.

artificially lit studio nude and the emotional performance of shadowy inner turmoil thus did not suit. Naturism, its practitioners argued, was more than an artistic mode of depiction. It combined simplification of life with vigorous healthy activity. Its pursuit of liberation meant that leaping and stretching poses and attitudes of exaltation could best communicate *joie de vivre* and fitness in outdoor settings in active and dynamic ways. Naturism simultaneously drew inspiration from ancient Greece alongside new scientific thinking, depicting future-focused mentalities alongside timeless values, even as present-day fashions were visible in models' rollered hairstyles and pencilled-in brows. As models in naturist photographs typically inhabited pastoral scenes without industry or mechanization, they communicated this temporal complexity symbolically through poses and props.

Balls were a popular inclusion, providing action and purpose, whether medicine balls in exercise (for men) or inflatables on the seashore (for women). Muscular heroics and taut bodies were perceived to be masculine, showing mastery and triumph. Rhythmic gymnastics' flowing movements suggested the elegance that women were meant to embody, including in all-female groups, which also demonstrated the geometry and harmony of collective exercise. Balletic moves with full-body extensions appeared in women's nude poses but more modern attitudes drew on the expressionist gestures of barefoot dance, featuring coiled and curved bodies with asymmetric angles of hand and wrist. In many photographic images, however, movement was merely suggested. Although shutter speeds were capable in the period, photography in early naturist magazines was rarely used to capture bodies truly in motion. Nude dancing was dangerously close to the titillating stage performances that naturists so strongly opposed.

The power of the British rural idyll was such that photographs in outdoor settings could achieve a moral superiority that studio nudes could not. What constituted a naturist nude photograph, however, could be flimsy. One taken in a club of practising naturists engaged in camp activities had the highest legitimacy, but professional models posed formally in seaside and woodland locations also passed. Nude subjects leaning on wooden gates or posed in fields of wheat might seem to indicate agriculture rather than wilderness or paradise; Park and Gregory posed models in their garden with ornamental ponds and rockeries visible and where models perched buttocks on bird baths: all these could be accommodated. When a nude appeared in naturist print, its location and title were often its main tethers to value and meaning. Variations on "Eve" were used to mythologize and anonymize models through associations with Eden. "Venus" was suitably classical but also signalled eroticism, which needed to be approached with caution in a movement that severed nakedness from sex. Maids and nymphs were popular as mythical evocations of abstracted womanhood; matrons and crones were not. Fit men might be framed as Apollos; older men with spectacles, bald patches, and paunches were harder to allegorize and were barely shown. Titles that conveyed nature, youth, energy, and radiance were most suited to sun and health audiences.

The appearance of model bodies in pre-war nudist publications was a concern to some readers. Many complained in the animated forum of letters' pages that images of women dominated magazines, and that photographs were too stylized. As one correspondent put it, "I am sure I am voicing the opinion of many of your readers when I say that there is perhaps too much of the female form divine about the *Sun Bathing Review*. All of the Art Supplements are devoted to it in languorous and enervating poses." One reader wrote in to criticize particular images for their aesthetic shortcomings: "'The Archer' is painfully posed, and has obviously never shot an arrow in his life before. In another photograph the lady appears to be suffering from delusions, while both girls are utterly and hopelessly bored."[93]

Another correspondent argued that there was something particularly British about female models' elite and haughty deportment, "as if their nostrils were assailed by a bad odour". What was wanted instead was more egalitarian: the "ordinary British Nudist crowd".[94] As a further letter put it, photographs should show "chopping wood for the campfire, putting up the tent, making the tea, or frying bacon and chips, and all the hundred and one other things that people do when camping".[95] Caught in the conflict between idealistic images and egalitarian principles, nudist magazines were supportive of these requests to a point. When a correspondent argued that photographs of nudists undertaking everyday tasks would be better than holiday imagery, the editor retorted that "pictures of happy girls on beaches" were "more encouraging than mothers scrubbing dirty kitchen floors".[96]

In an attempt to diversify visual content, *Sun Bathing Review* requested willing models from its readership, to include "children, girls and men", but the exclusion of mature women from this list and the note that photographs were welcome from those with "good figures" who were "accustomed to dancing" did not present a major deviation from the dominant aesthetic of fitness, grace, and youth.[97] Magazines encouraged amateur photographic submissions by readers, and gave stylistic and technical advice to produce desirable results. "Avoid all fixed 'posey' positions in your models," *Sun Bathing Review* told those wishing to submit snaps. "Muscular strain sometimes helps a male but it is quite out of place with a female nude. A naked man tugging at a fishing net may provide a grand subject, but substitute a woman and it looks ridiculous and even ugly."[98]

Nudist magazines carried regular advertisements for confidential photographic developing and printing services, inserted between product promotions for herbal tea, boundary fencing, and binoculars. "In order to retain the full tone value and contour of the human form, negatives require very careful development," one claimed.[99] It was more to the point that the production and circulation of photographs of naked bodies could fall foul of British laws on obscene libel. Alec Craig, nudist and vociferous anti-censorship campaigner, helpfully advised on legality. He reassured, "Snaps taken in a nudist camp cannot be considered 'obscene'. But it must be remembered that the circumstances of 'publication' affect the question of 'obscenity'. What may be perfectly innocuous in one set of circumstances may be 'obscene' in another. To take an extreme example," he noted, "nude photographs, quite unobjectionable in normal circumstances, might be held to be 'obscene' if circulated in a convent school."[100] Likewise, outside of the careful framing of the nudist magazine, a nude photograph carried a range of meanings that could prove hard to pin down in a court of law.

Some correspondents, aware of the gender imbalance in photographic representation, requested more images of men, but what kinds of men and what kinds of images remained contested. *Health and Efficiency* had long featured men in statuesque and sporting poses, hoisting spears and javelins, locked in wrestling holds, or other-wise demonstrating heroic aspects of classical masculinity, but highly developed bodies displaying exaggerated muscle were judged to be out of keeping with nudism's natural health principles.

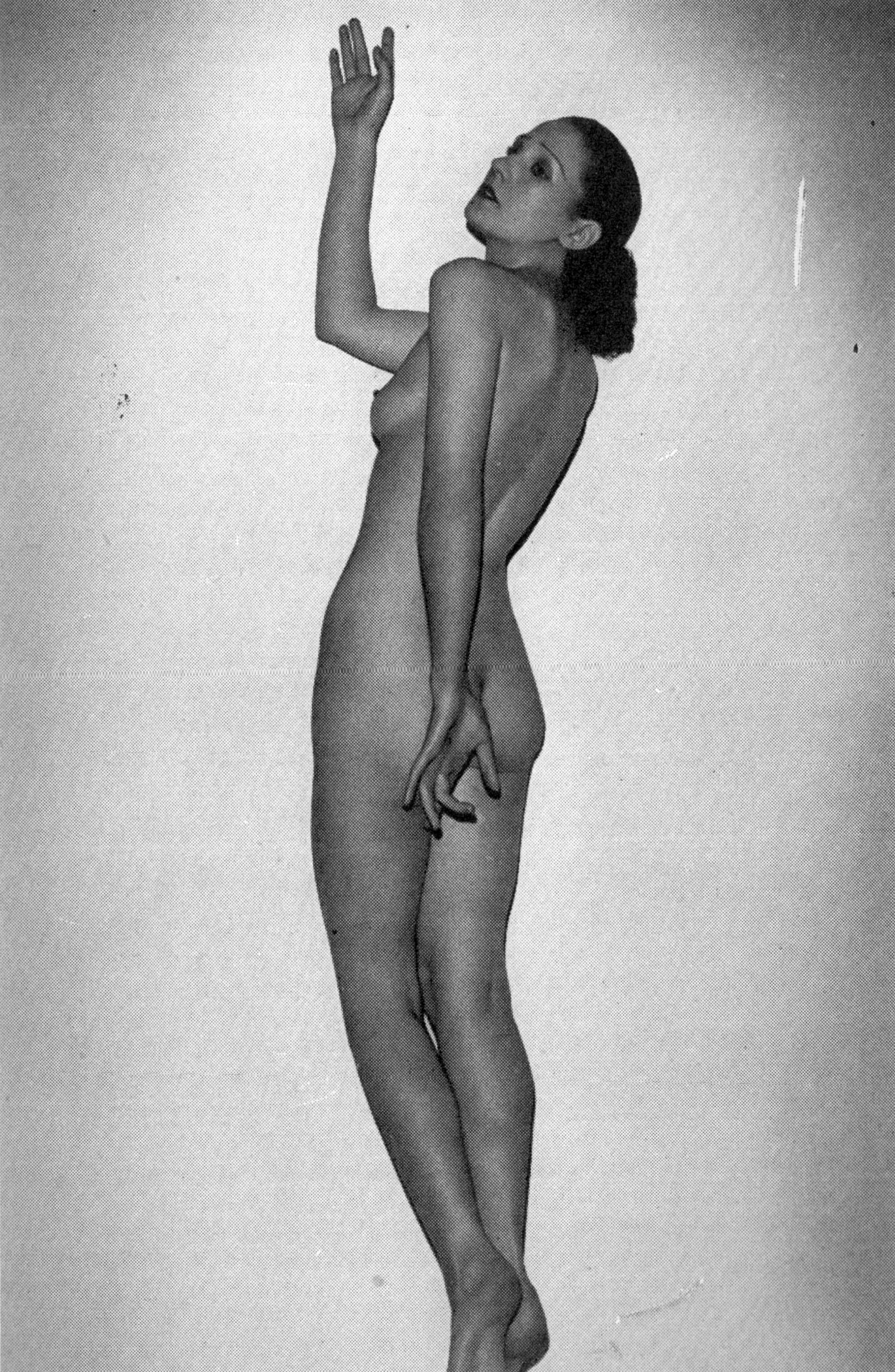

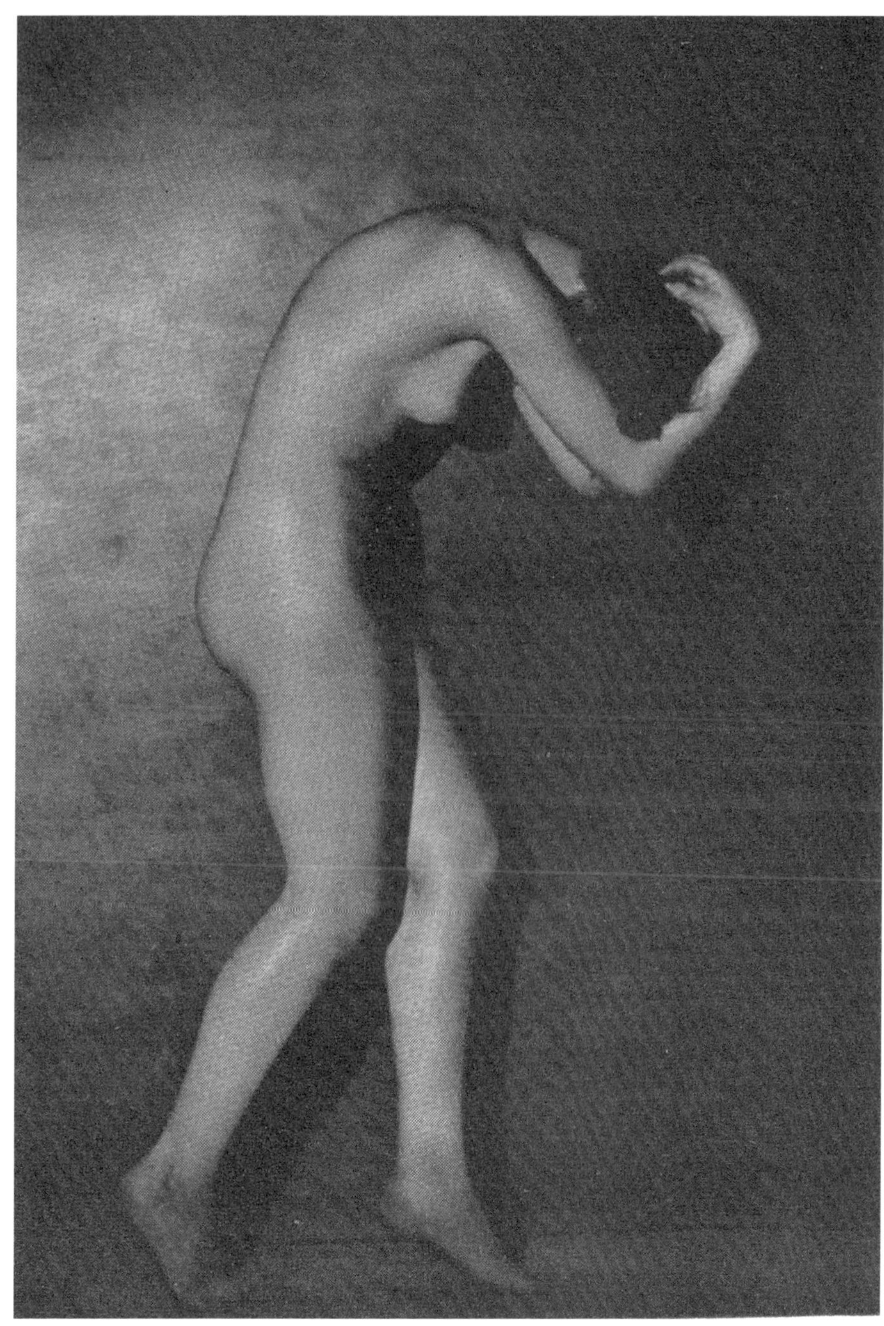

John Everard and Walter Bird were prolific producers of nude photographs from the 1930s in studio as well as outdoor settings. Their titles were often allegorical to secure their artistic meaning.

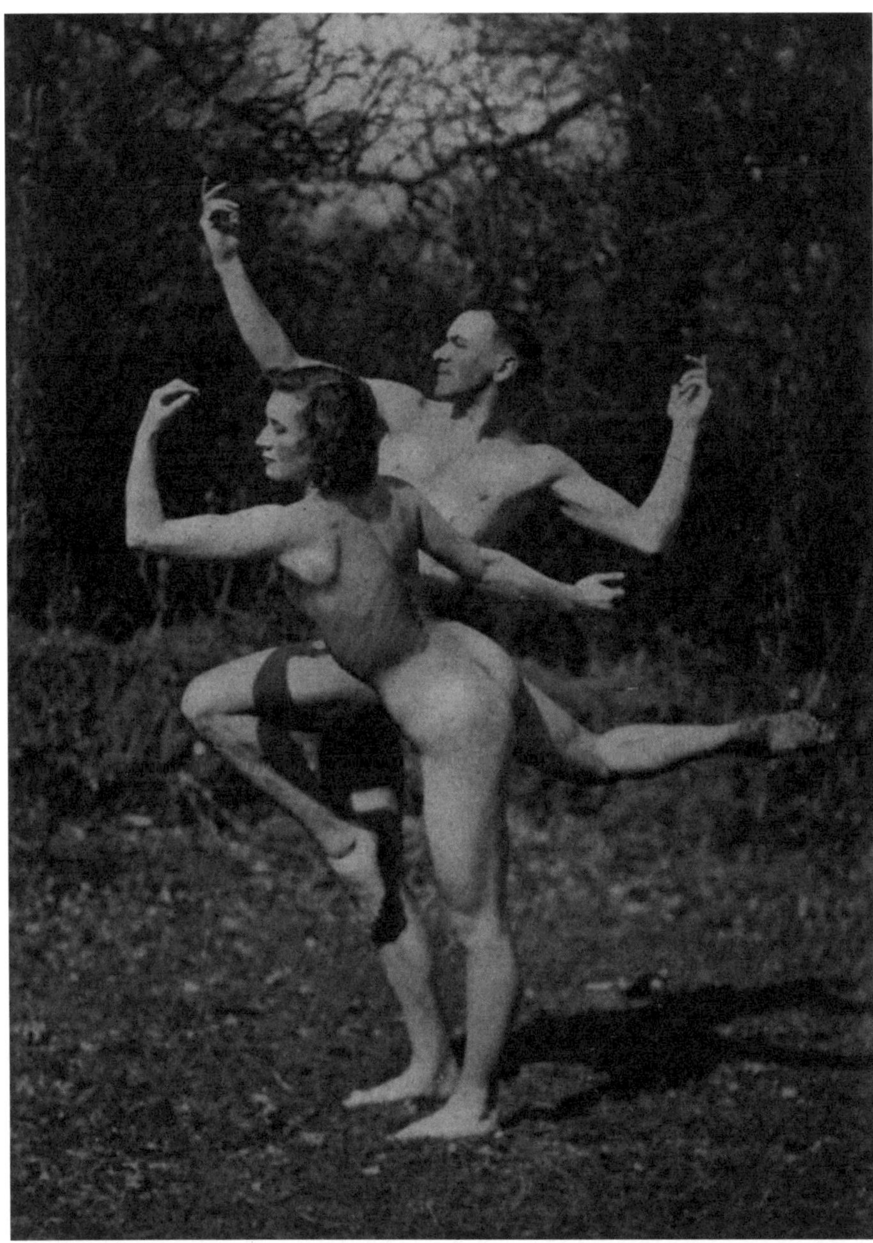

Static poses, suggestive of modern movement but held still for the camera shutter, were common arrangements for pre-war naturist nude photographs.

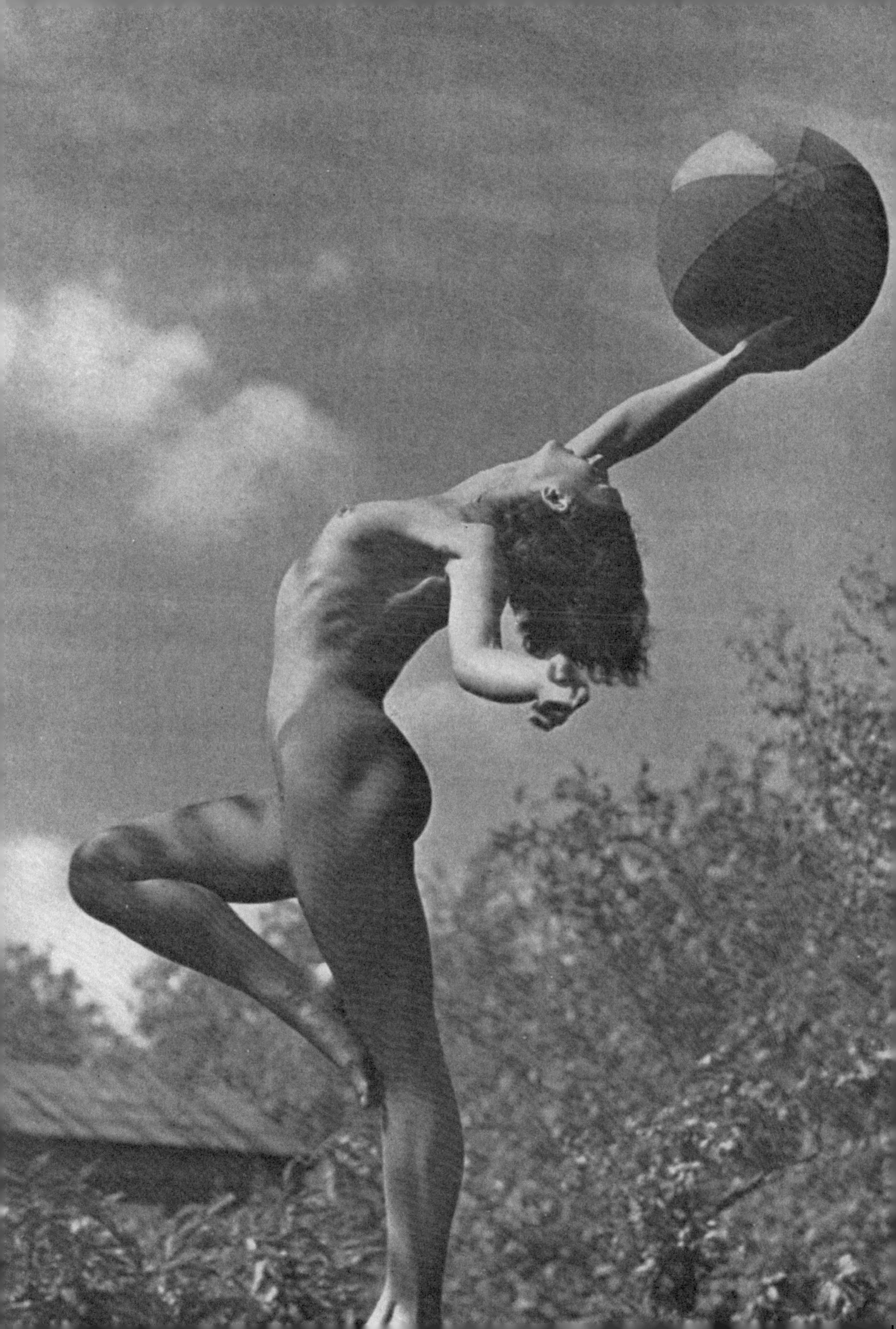

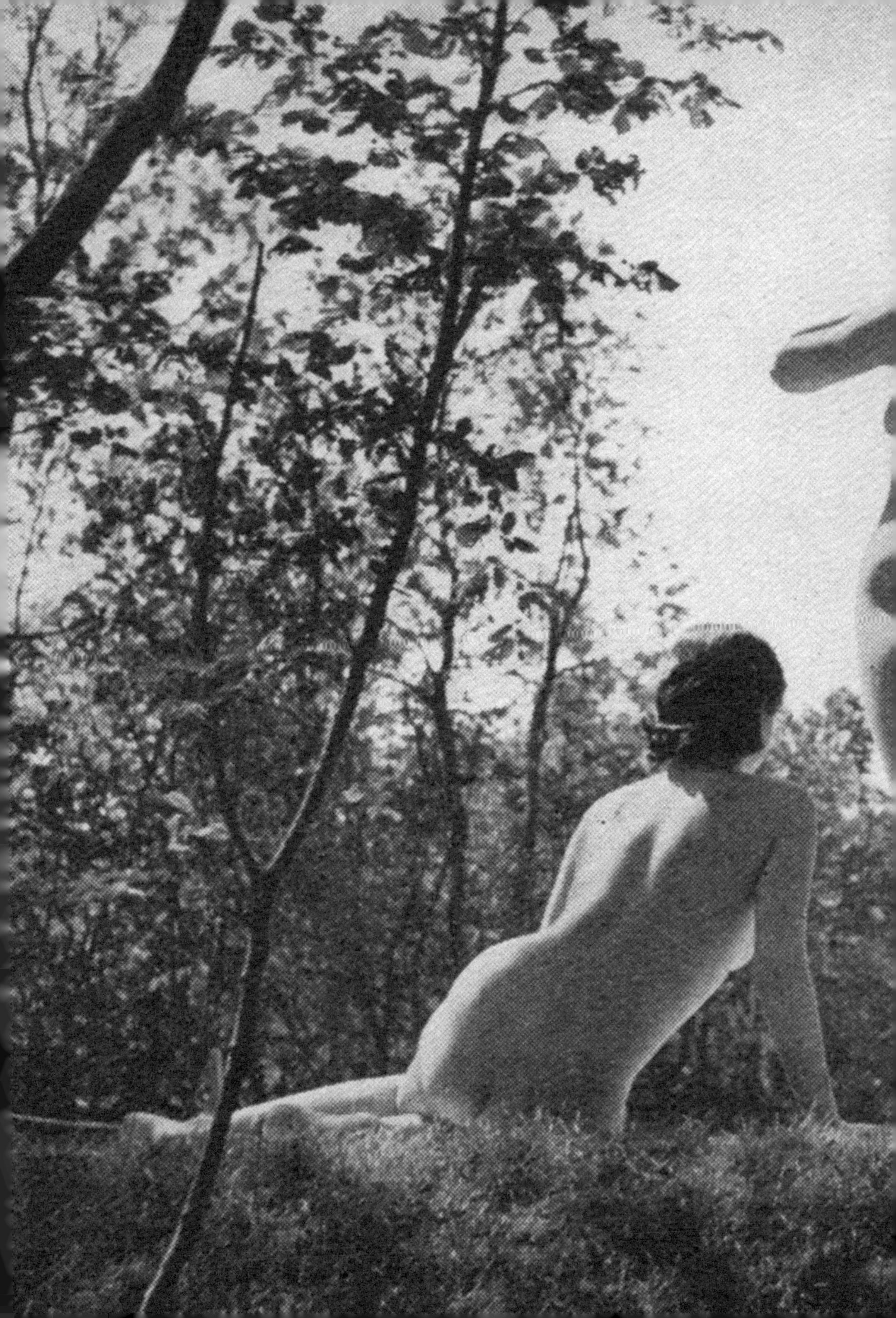

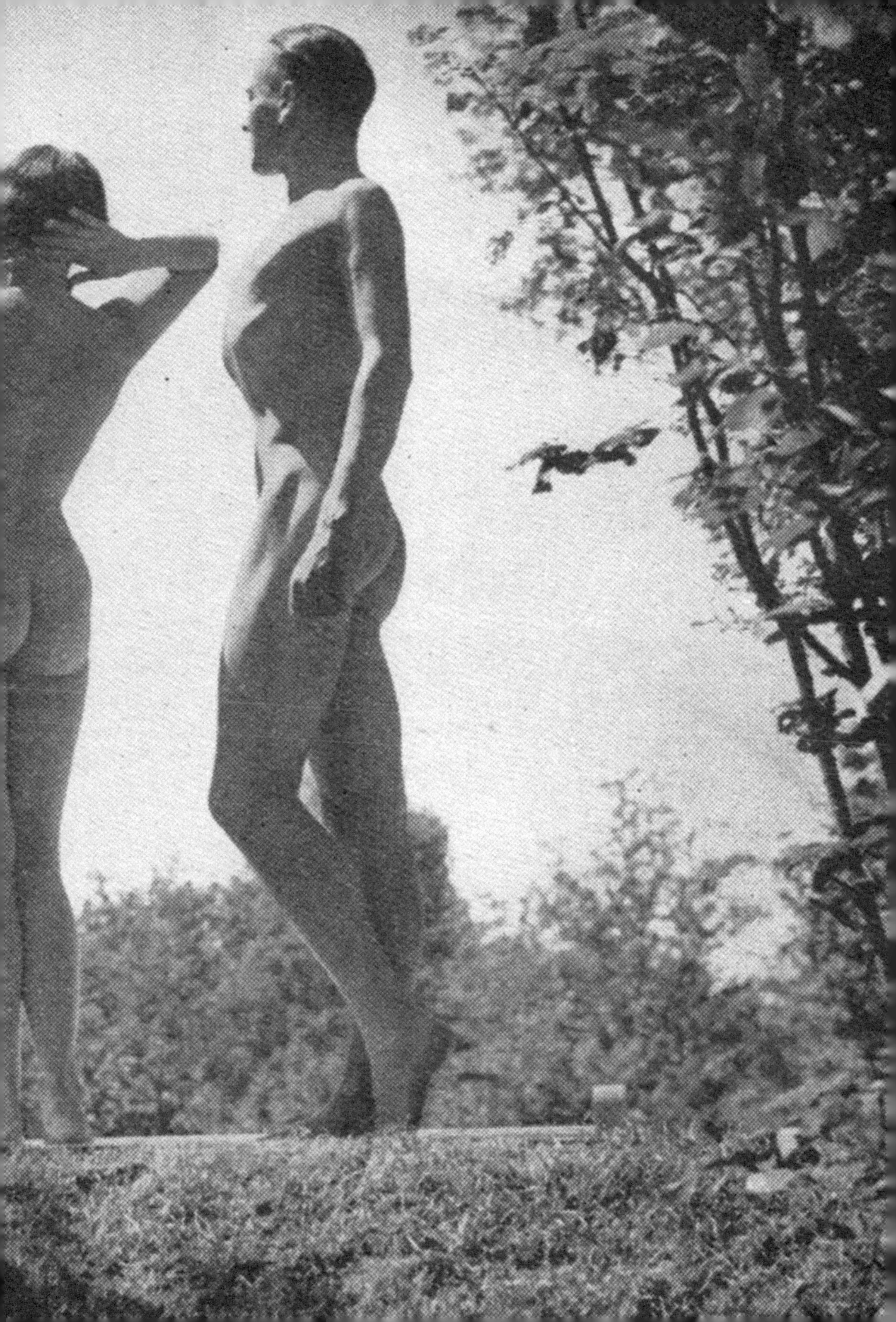

Magazines were conflicted as they simultaneously advertised muscle-building products but discouraged strained bodybuilding poses in competition photographs, repeatedly telling readers that what was wanted was "more natural relaxed pictures showing how you enjoy life in the outdoors".[101] The editor of *Sun Bathing Review* confessed that suitable photographs—amateur or otherwise—were hard to come by. The ideal was "neither muscle-bound, as so many photographed gentlemen appear to be, nor 'narcissus'", meaning effeminate.[102] The spectre of homosexuality lurked beneath nudism's anxieties about too much or too little masculinity and in the repeated emphasis on nudism as a family practice. As with nudism's racial biases, the certainties of the heterosexual nudist subject would become a critical point of fracture in subsequent decades—more on this to come.

Retouching was the single biggest talking point about nudist photographs. After sculptor Eric Gill had been permitted by the Home Secretary to display male genitals on his carved stone figures for the new BBC building on London's Regent Street in the mid-1930s, surely a nudist magazine could show the same in its photographs? As correspondents noted, "Honest photography would induce mental honesty, and help sweep away the rude idea of sex-secrecy." They continued: "Dishonest devices are more likely to create squeamishness, hypocrisy, and misunderstanding, and thus retard the progress we are trying to make towards freedom and sanity."[103] Nudists described retouched bodies as "mutilated" and "repulsive", yet they acknowledged that the other legal alternative, "a pictorial world where everyone turns his or her back to the spectator", risked monotony.[104] Editors argued that caution kept magazines on the stands and helped spread a moderate message, but correspondents felt retouching was publicly damaging. "Not long ago," one reported, "I heard a group of working men commenting upon the figure on the cover of a nudist magazine displayed in a shop window, and the conclusion they arrived at was that, as the photograph had been faked, the nudist movement was also a fake and a fiction from beginning to end."[105]

The fundamental question behind these disputes was what nudist photographs were, in fact, for. "Nudity is not practiced for art's sake," it was argued, "and artistic effects are therefore not of primary importance." Instead, "The primary object is the educational influence of the photographs [...] as they reveal something that has hitherto been withheld from the eyes of many people."[106] Nudist photographs, in this argument, helped the novice grow accustomed to the shock of the nude. Some argued that magazines should carry no images at all to avoid attracting the wrong type of reader, implying that there was a correct way of viewing the photographs: educationally but not erotically. Amid the debate over whether or not to use idealized models who were not nudists, there was also a recognition that attractive bodies boosted sales; for those who dared acknowledged the fact, it was admitted that not all readers were practitioners. Nonetheless, it was hoped they might become nudists by photographs' propagandist persuasion. As correspondent "Woodsman" argued, "We need pictures of people who have already reached a high standard in physique. Illustrations of perfection set an example."[107]

Gender played a key part in recruitment. From the outset men were much keener nudists than women, as evidenced in abundant club applications from single men, which were "very greatly in excess of those from families and women". To mitigate the issue, membership restrictions were imposed in some clubs: "Men should always be accompanied by a lady or children." The Sun Bathing Society insisted that "the only way to maintain the family atmosphere, keep the numbers even and spread our ideals is to adhere to our rule".[108] Other clubs offered cheaper prices for single female members and higher prices for single men.[109] The plain-spoken George Ryley Scott, a prolific author of books about sex as well as articles about nudism, also noted the gender imbalance but explained that men's greater interest should be seen in parallel with "the greater interest of man in Parisian 'peep shows' and 'art studies'". He concluded, "In nine cases out of ten, he goes to the nudist park as he goes to a brothel." For Scott, club rules would not solve the problem, as he observed men's "coincident reluctance to bring with them their own wives and sweethearts". He noted, "Her presence, in most instances, would seriously cramp his own style."[110]

ENLIGHTENED FAMILIES
Gender norms went largely unquestioned in this movement that claimed, at its most utopian, to be creating a new social order. Nonetheless, in some nudist magazines of the 1930s, women were

not simply photographed but also photographers and authors. *Sun Bathing Review* in particular featured many contributions from women, often but not exclusively on what were styled as women's matters, such as childbirth, child-rearing, and schooling, with articles by radical sex educationalists and feminists including Elizabeth Sloan Chesser, Janet Chance, and Kathleen Vaughan.[111] A notable contributor of both word and image in the 1930s was Edith Tudor-Hart. Better known now for her documentary photography of working-class life in London and Wales, and for her communist politics, Tudor-Hart, née Suschitzky, had fled Austria for London in 1933, aged 25, following the Nazi rise to power. She produced photographs for international advertising and press in the 1930s and, in the same decade, operated as a spy for the Soviet Union and enlisted key figures in the notorious Cambridge Five ring of spies.[112]

Tudor-Hart's dual training, in photography at the Bauhaus art school and in Montessori child-centred teaching methods, is visible in her decade of contributions to *Sun Bathing Review*. These include not only pared-back beach photographs of naked women that bear comparison to other prominent photographic modernists, such as the famous images of bathers and divers by George Hoyningen-Huene, but, more prominently, naturalistic images of young children paddling, climbing, and playing in few or no clothes at a time when the magazine produced regular features on juvenile health and featured children on covers and in their glossy art-supplement sections. Children were sometimes depicted in nudist magazines performing gymnastics or group dances but mostly were pictured at play. Tudor-Hart's photographs of children show a particular ease and warmth. In the mid-1930s she extended her specialism in this work, establishing a studio for child portraiture after the birth of her son; she also photographed children treated by her English doctor husband. While her idealized rural nudist photographs may seem to have little visual relation to her urban documentary and politically committed practice, it is notable that the photomontage cover of one of her campaigning works uses a very similar image of a naked infant included in *Sun Bathing Review*.[113] *New Homes for Old* was published in 1934 and juxtaposed photographs of slums with the modern housing that would replace them. An image of a naked child, rising from the roof, operates as a symbol of a healthy new future, in harmony with the optimistic messaging of the nudist magazine.[114]

Children figured prominently in both text and image in nudist publications in the 1930s, where they were argued to be *natural nudists* and models for adults for whom paradise had been lost.[115] Raising children to be open minded and free spirited was an essential part of righting the wrongs that underpinned prudish contemporary attitudes. Norman Haire, for example, the President of the World League of Sexual Reform, wrote, "If parents are desirous of bringing up their children with a sane outlook on sex, then surely the first step is to refrain from making any mystery of the appearance of the human body, both as regards children and adults."[116] Incorporating children into nudism was part of the long-term work that nudists hoped to seed across generations. As Scott put it, "The children of tomorrow will reap the harvest, and grow up better in every way, physically, mentally and morally, for having discarded all the clothes, to which we of this generation are accustomed, some of the time, and some of these clothes all of the time."[117] This could be accomplished by integrating children into camp activities and by "enlightened parents" showing children their naked bodies in everyday life in the home to avoid the "suspicious curiosity" that "warp" adult attitudes.[118] It could also be achieved by making nudist choices in formal education.

Educational establishments promoted in nudist magazines included Pinehurst School, Sussex, where children aged three to 12 "bathe nude every day of the year"; a school in Woodhall Park, Hertfordshire, where pupils are "free of clothes and all their traditional implications", and St Christopher's School in Letchworth, Hertfordshire—a national gathering point for early 20th-century experimental life-styles—where meals were vegetarian, girls learned Greek dancing and Dalcroze eurythmics, and same-sex naked swimming was offered.[119] Dora Russell, an authority on progressive pedagogy and the founding principal of Beacon Hill School, wrote of sun bathing's psychological benefits of "peace and contentment for "children who are inclined to be strung up and nervous". She described clothes as "indignities imposed by arbitrary adult rule."[120] The photographs that accompanied these articles were sometimes retouched for legality so children's genitals were concealed, but there was never any discussion of children's consent or their potential for exploitation. The only issue raised about their depiction was from a teacher at Rocklands School, Hastings, who said, "We have not taken any photographs for three years because of the tendency it would rouse towards exhibitionism, and we only want our children to be absolutely free and happy in the mind."[121] Magazine correspondents generally praised images of children for their spontaneity, although one complained about their abundance, stating that there were 36 in one issue of *Sun Bathing Review* alone, outnumbering adults by four to one and misrepresenting children's place in clubs. The editor confessed that the photographs served a strategic protective purpose: "The preponderance of child studies is due mainly to the fact that we are anxious to encourage the family aspect of sun bathing."[122]

Tudor-Hart's photographs provide a range of functions in *Sun Bathing Review*, including illustrating her sister-in-law's account of Fortis Green School, in north London, "based on a natural philosophy of equality of rights and opportunities" where "the children wear nothing but sunsuits all day long"[123] and her own writing on the advanced nature of sun bathing in Vienna prior to Nazi control.[124] Her photographs of groups at outdoor pools and on the banks of the Danube were arranged at dynamic angles and in photomontage, during a period when the magazine was experimenting with modernist layouts and covers. Interestingly, while the article introduction states that Tudor-Hart is "a Viennese", throughout her authored piece, she uses "we English" as a collective mode of address in a magazine that repeatedly emphasized nudism's national distinctions.[125]

WAKE UP ENGLAND!

How British nudism might differ nationally was a key discussion point in a movement finding its feet. Early publications saw Britain's class formality as the root cause of the problems that nudism would cure. An outspoken "Clergyman" argued in *Gymnos*, "To hell with our 'decency' and 'reserve'. It is sapping the life of our country." He made grand claims: "Our 'unhappy marriages', our adulterers, our prostitutes, our helpless cases of masturbation and sexual neurasthenia will vanish when, and ONLY when, the British nation throws aside its silly, ignorant 'modesty', and goes out to cultivate respect for the body founded on knowledge."[126] Whereas Britain's complex system of social hierarchies had once been used to assert national superiority over the rest of the world, many nudist articles noted that Britain was being left behind internationally. *Sun Bathing Review*'s opening issue was a call to action: "Britannia no longer rules the waves, nor the air,

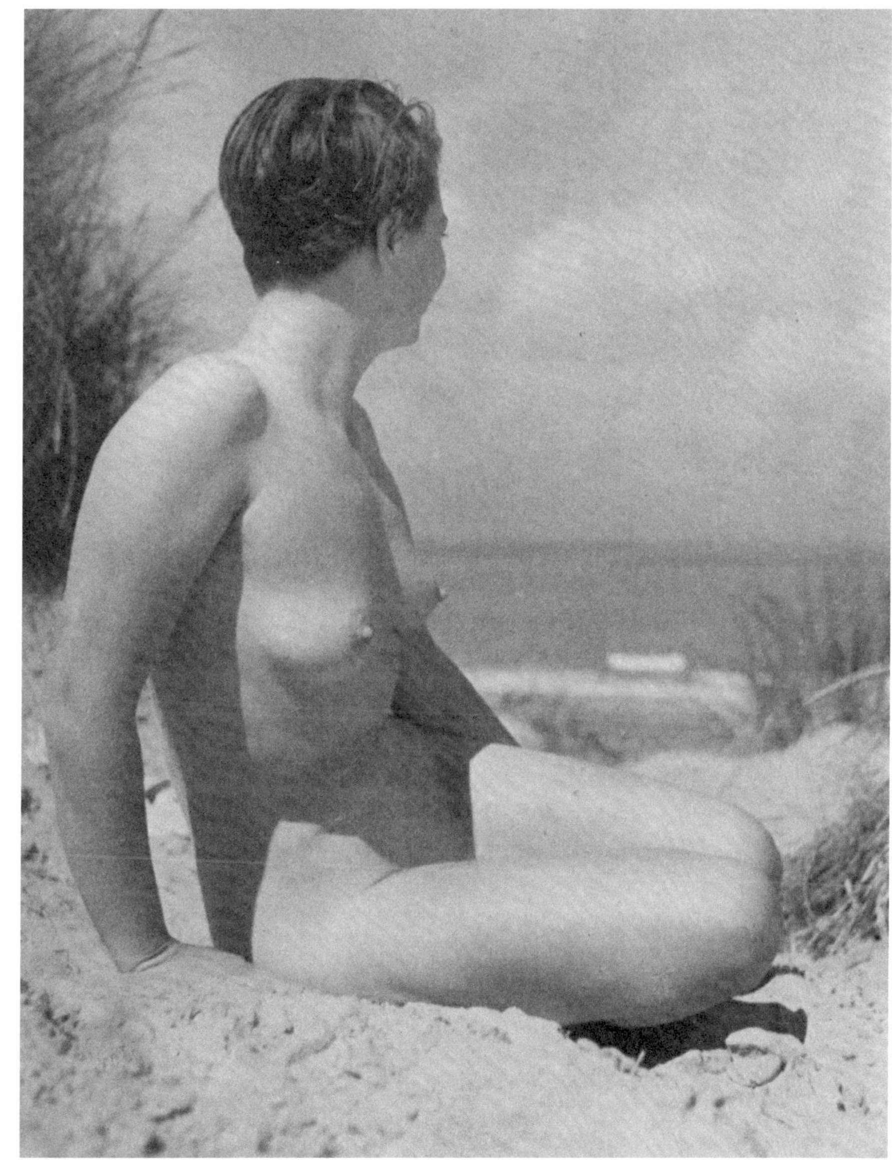

Edith Tudor-Hart's nudist photographs show young women and children at ease before the lens. While not as political in message as her other campaigning photographs, they communicate her interest and participation in radical, experimental lifestyles.

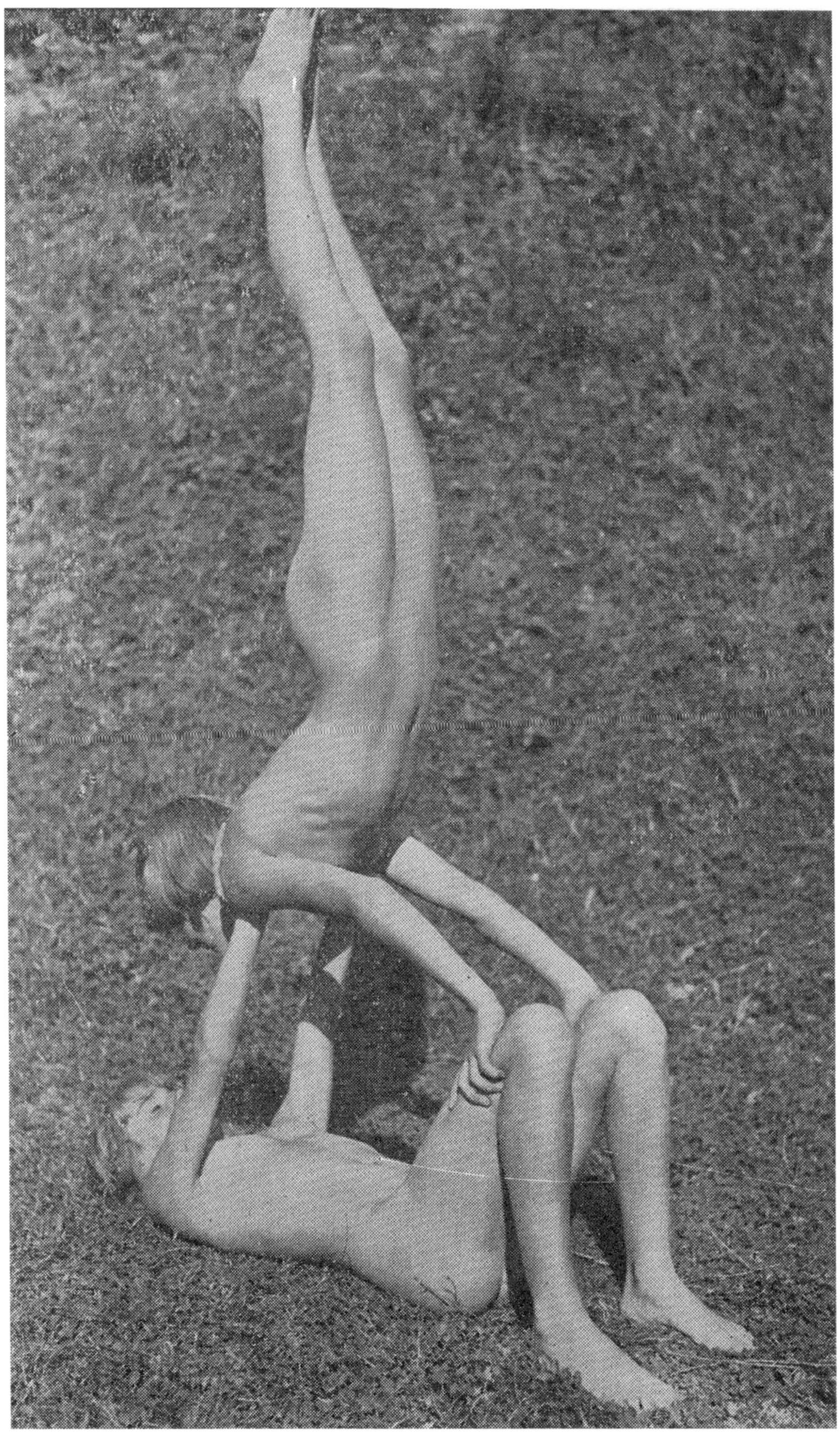

Children were regularly depicted in early nudist magazines, including as pupils of progressive schools. They also served as visual symbols of innocence and future potential.

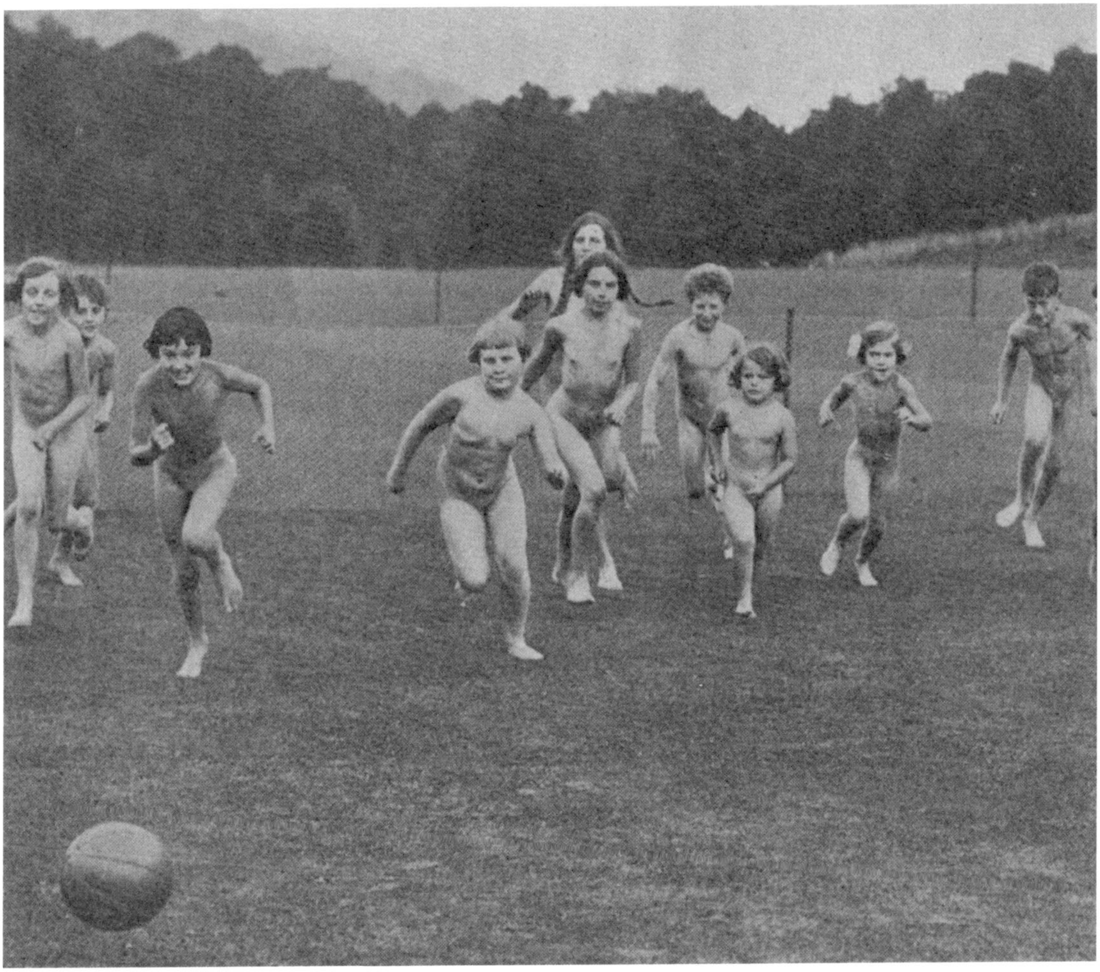

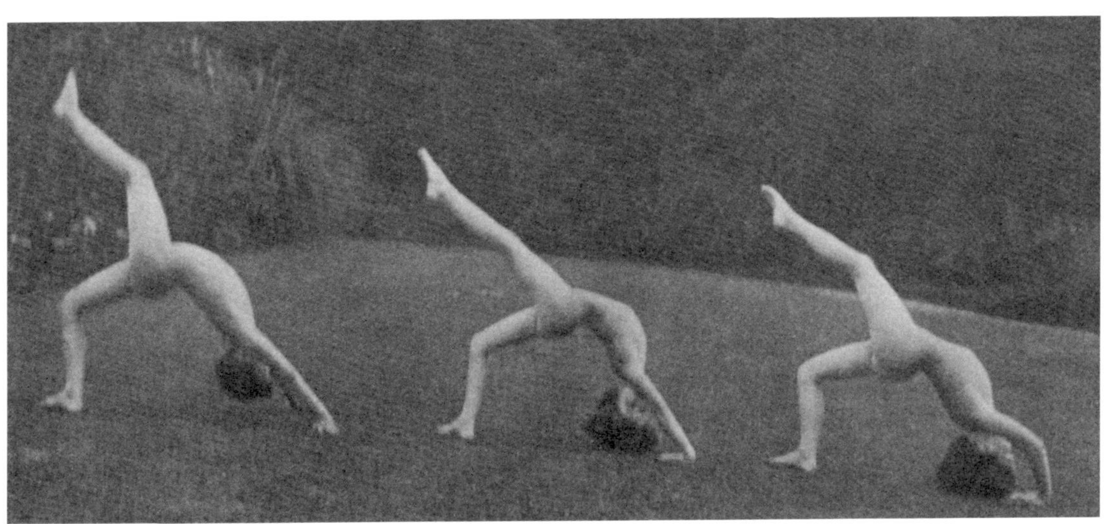

In their effortlessness, children were described in early sun bathing literature as the most natural of nudists. There was never any discussion of the potential of child photographs for exploitation.

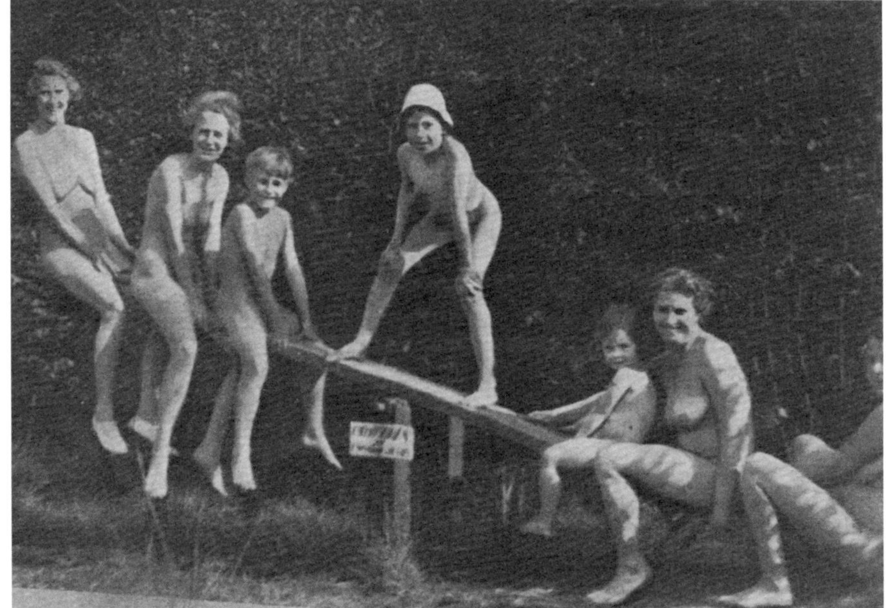

nor our land sports, and we are probably the biggest slaves to prudery and convention that ever existed!" A weary sense of rivalry, borne of wider circumstances of economic instability and a loss of imperial power, motivated the appeal: "Once again we are in the inevitable position of the cow's tail and watching all other European nations and even the USA going ahead with what we may call Sun or Air Bathing, Nudism or Nakedness."[127]

As British nudist culture took root in the mid-1930s, with home-grown clubs and publications, members and visitors reflected on its emerging national distinctiveness. Britain's small scale and its conservative cultural practices in comparison with continental Europe and America could be communicated as a source of pride as well as a problem. For some, moderation was the characteristic that set British nudism apart. Publications with titles such as *The Common Sense of Nudism* and *Sensible Sun-Bathing* reiterated that British nudism was reasonable, ordinary, or, in the argot of the period, "sane". As the movement matured, the utopian claims of its pioneers were frequently rejected as "cranky" or "faddish". Gymnosophy as a term came to seem pretentious.[128] Alignments with wider practices of life reform, including vegetarianism and abstention from alcohol and tobacco, were dismissed in an attempt to develop a more domestically

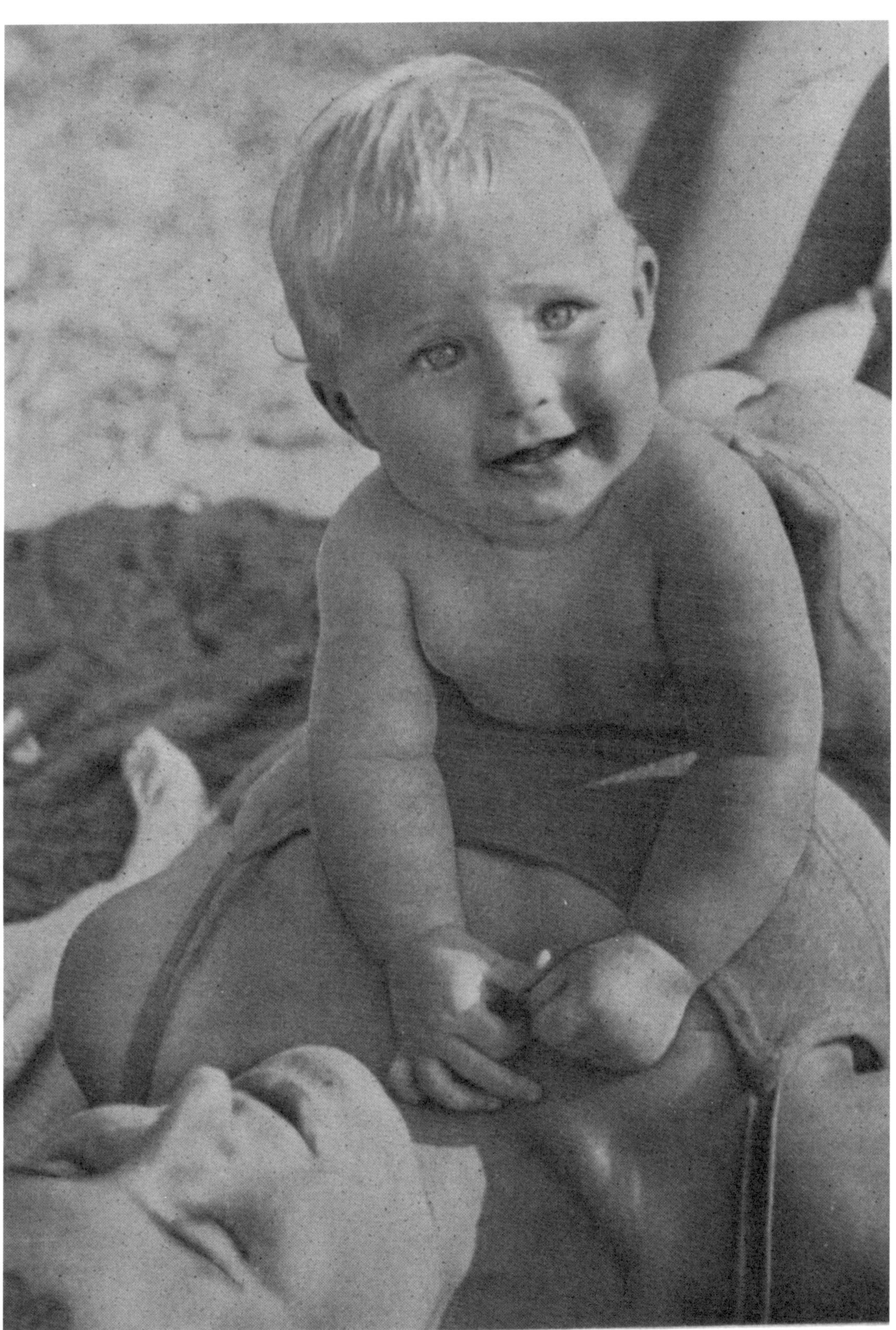

palatable variant that was more self-consciously ordinary. "Back to nature" aspects thought to be "cultish" were toned down, and car ownership, listening to gramophone records, and reading Dickens were all argued to be nudist-compatible.[129] I. O. Evans, the author of publications aimed at the "sensible" practitioner, even avoided the terms "nudist" and "nudism": "They suggest a philosophy and a cult, an earnest, humourless, proselytising spirit, and elaborate propagandist organisation; and they likewise suggest a foreign origin."[130] For those fundamentally opposed to the practice, such as a Sussex landowner neighbouring a proposed camp, nudism was an alien imposition to be "left to the Continentals and not imported into the sylvan glades of England".[131] Enthusiasts, however, saw its potential as "a logical development of that love of free activity in the open air, that healthy sportsmanship which distinguishes our island race".[132]

Perhaps the best comparative perspectives were given by international visitors. American nudist Julian Strange, for example, visited British clubs in 1936 and confirmed their conservative mentality: "The professional non-conformist, who embraces any and every unconventional movement, and who, in other countries, takes to nudism only because it is yet another way of shocking the staid, is conspicuous by his absence." He argued too that a benign British government created the right atmosphere for nudism as it "does not impose foolish laws, is not given to busybody activities, respects the individual's right of privacy, and molests no group which conducts itself in a manner inoffensive to the public". Strange noted particular national attitudes to food and drink among the British nudist: "He does not surrender the sacred tea-ceremony—nor his national habit of devouring food six, seven, or eight times a day, on the slightest pretext, or on none at all." Strange claimed to have witnessed "a formally attired butler" serving at a nudist club and he observed "nudists gathered in an indoor gymnasium gulping down three or four cups of tea apiece— to the accompaniment of miscellaneous Swiss rolls, cakes, sandwiches, and cream puffs" before exercise.[133]

Britain's chilly climate was a key matter when it came to undressing, and regular articles in the nudist press attested to the merit of "air bathing" in all weathers and the "tonic ting" of rain.[134] "Naked and unashamed, laughingly let us run, dance, swim and sing in all sorts of weather," proclaimed contributor Arnold Lane. "Cold winds, even snow need be no obstacle to a fit hardened, unabashed and sensible people."[135] Nonetheless, limits of climate led to innovations, and Strange observed that "the most interesting feature of the movement in Great Britain is indoor nudism".[136] When winter or weather necessitated, enthusiasts established covered social clubs in urban rented rooms where nudists could shelter. Offering artificial sunlight from the patented health gadgets whose scientific virtues were advertised in nudist magazines, indoor sites' benefits included hot soup, darts, table tennis, jazz bands, whist drives, knitting, a "Ladies Toilet Club and Beauty Institute", and a camera club.[137]

These arrangements were not without controversy. Authors noted their soft target for jokes about "the difficulty of resting a hot cup of tea on one's bare knee" but there were also greater reservations. Some suggested that gathering naked indoors, as a group, was sexually suspect.[138] Articles such as "Can Indoor Nudism Be Justified?" showed anxieties around the practice, which made fewer claims for health.[139] As Alec Craig put it, "Instead of the fresh open air the atmosphere is stuffy and, because of the necessity for avoiding draughts, often overheated. Space is cramped, and hygienic difficulties will occur to the fastidious." He concluded, "I am not alone in feeling that here is something different from the woodland sunbathing camp."[140] Colin Smithson, described as "a keen believer in sane naturism", declared, "It is uncomfortable and inconvenient—where does one keep handkerchiefs and the other accessories of civilised life? It is nudity for nudity's sake."[141] Sexologist Norman Haire raised legal concerns. "If a test case should come up, it might be easy enough to justify nudism in the sunlight and open air, but it might be more difficult to convince a British judge or a British jury of the innocent intention of those taking part in indoor nudism in a case where a number of naked people were found huddled around a fire in cold weather, by artificial light."[142] Despite the need to come in from the cold, indoor nudism remained limited as an interwar innovation. Nudism mostly remained a fair-weather practice for weekend warriors and alternative holidaymakers. The moral benefits of sun and countryside could not be claimed for naked gatherings in central London.

Many distinguishing characteristics of early British nudist clubs were tacitly related to class. As some nudists claimed that egalitarian ambitions were realized in the disposal of clothes, and as privacy was fiercely protected, club members were advised that questions about occupation were "tacitly taboo".[143] However, would-be nudists needed

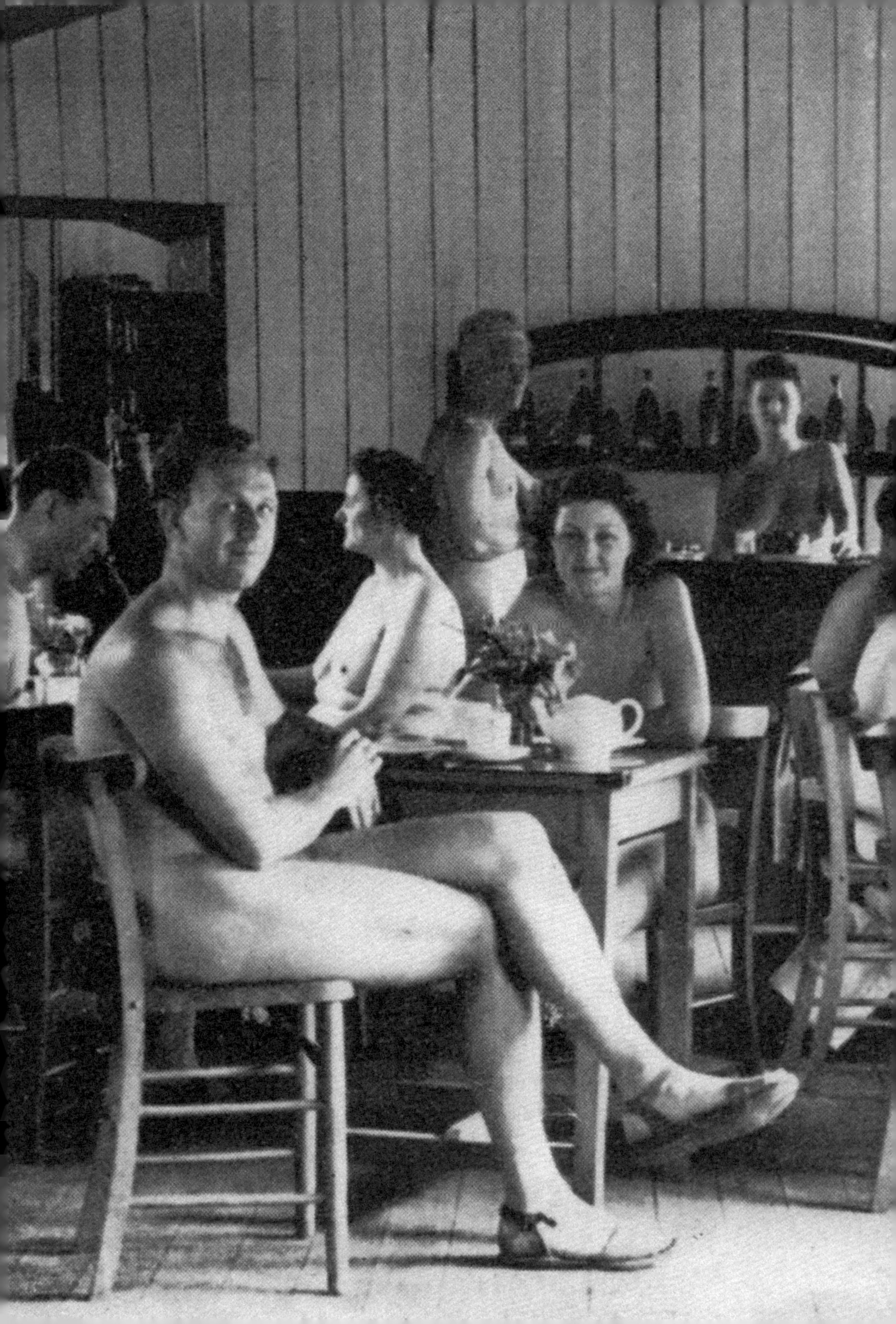

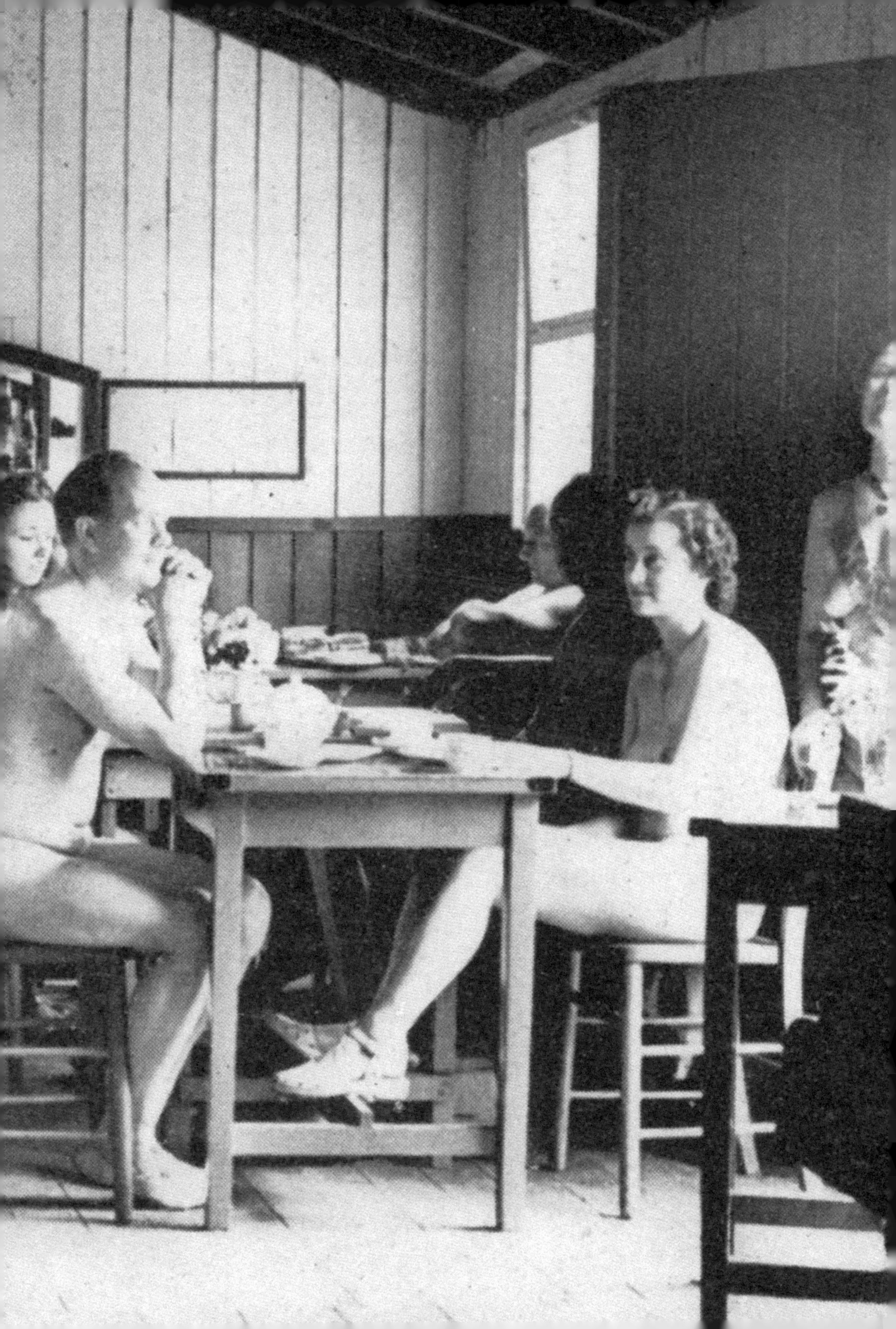

to pass stringent screening procedures before admission, including interviews, home visits, and extended questionnaires.[144] These were designed to maintain "standards" in moral conduct but they also evaluated social position. Nudism claimed to be "a great leveller" but Strange noted in Britain that "differences between classes are too great to permit a complete reconciliation". Nudists "of obvious culture" and the "rugged" met one another in clubs, he said, but not always harmoniously.[145] Prominent nudist commentators, including Evans, Craig, and C. E. M. Joad, all found class consciousness to be prominent in early British nudism, with clubs organized to appeal to different social groupings and with some high entry prices designed to keep out working-class "riff-raff".[146]

Class politics also related to political preferences. In the context of rising extremism at home and abroad, members in the 1930s variously claimed British nudism's position to be progressive and reactionary. Many asserted that all beliefs were welcome among the disrobed; nudist A. A. Burall said that both communists and fascists were members of his camp.[147] Craig, however, was certain that British nudism had an "ideological affinity" with the political left whether members liked it or not. To him, the "critical mind, free from the shackles of superstition, tradition, ignorance and convention" that nudists had applied to "the problem of clothing" could be equally applied to other problems of social and political life.[148] Novelist and nudist George C. Foster, the author of the articles "Nudism is not a Cult" and "Nudism and the Common Man", took the opposite stand. "The movement does not want the fanatics and the cranks. It needs Mr. Everyman and his wife. It needs people with jobs in the City and a proper pride in 'keeping up appearances'." He claimed to know nudists who went to camp after going to church or who popped in before visiting their Conservative club. To Foster, nudism "needs such people and their wives more than it needs cranky artists and authors, self-expressionists and parlour-bolsheviks".[149] He argued, "One of the most encouraging things about nudism in this country is that it is non-political. Politics have no more to do with nudism that they have with tennis or golf."[150] Despite their differences, the progressive and the conservative positioned the average nudist as male and middle class, and both agreed that nudism should cease to be secretive. For those who wanted a mass movement, openness was central. The nudist, Craig argued, "should be prepared to talk about nudism in railway carriages, in the office, and at his club".[151]

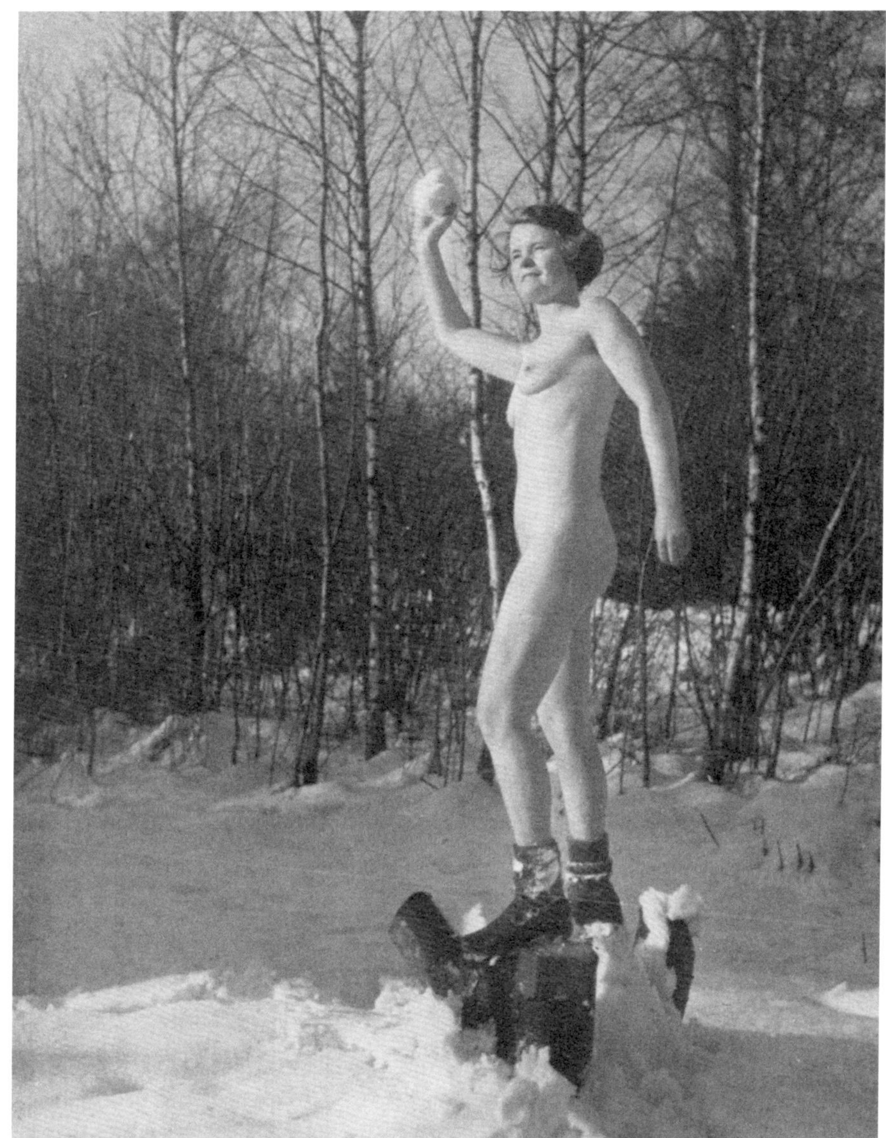

Previous spread
- Spielplatz, the most
well-appointed of early
nudist camps, provided
a sit-down restaurant
with nude waitress
service alongside
catering for vegetarian
diets.

Right - Early British
nudists espoused the
health value of
disrobing in all seasons
and all weathers
including rain, wind,
and snow.

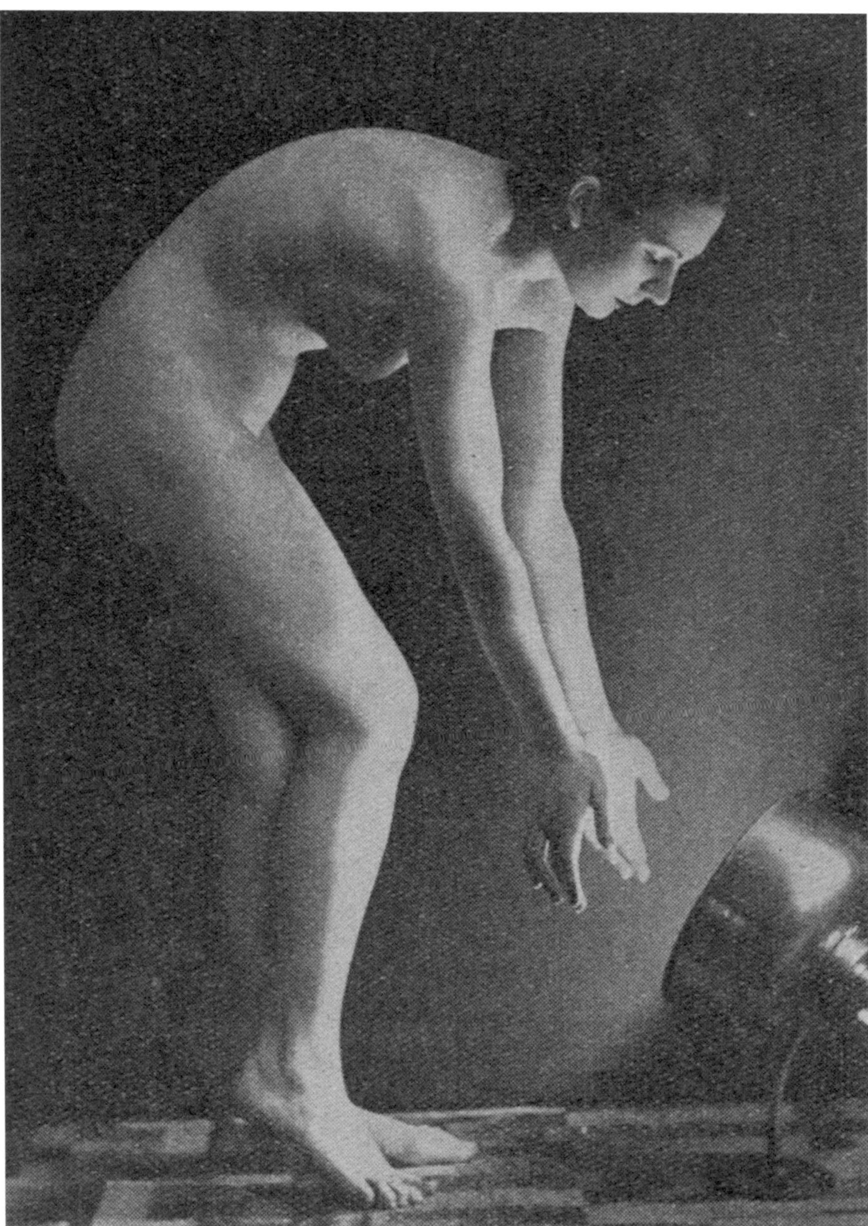

Due to Britain's poor weather, indoor nudist camps were a pre-war innovation. Practitioners found technological solutions —artificial light from sunlamps—for the problem of sunless days.

A GOLDEN AGE

British nudism in its first two decades developed from a private practice on a small scale, hesitant and imitative of its international counterparts, with a utopian and eccentric character, to a no-nonsense national nudism with its own distinctive discourse, appearance, and culture. By the later 1930s, as a result of incremental shifts in attitude and moderate appeals to the public, nudism could even claim some public respectability. When the conservative mass-circulation *John Bull* magazine first introduced nudism to its non-nudist readers in 1931, it assumed the movement to be full of undesirables, extremists, and degenerates, with camps one step away from "organised orgies". In 1936 when its reporter visited clubs around Greater London, he found clergymen, Harley Street medical specialists, schoolmasters, civil servants, and BBC officials.[152] In 1937, the *Daily Mirror*, a newspaper that then boasted daily sales of 4 million, made over 1,000 mentions of nudism and ran major articles that took the movement seriously, with first-hand accounts and a survey of readers' attitudes. While some respondents were outraged, many were accepting.[153] In the decade and a half since the first dozen gymnosophists established the first nudist club, British nudist numbers stood at 40,000 by 1938.[154] Claims that the movement was a "craze" seemed to have run their course. For the enthusiasts who braved the ill winds of negative opinion over many years, a golden age of British nudism seemed to be finally dawning.

As nudism boasted peak numbers and growing public acceptance, new publications showcasing the naked body followed thick and fast. *The Naturist* magazine, launched in late 1937, built on the success of *Health and Efficiency* and *Sun Bathing Review* but operated a new business model dedicated to the circulation of nude photographs by professional practitioners in book as well as periodical form.[155] Female photographic nudes in the 1930s could be found on the walls of photography exhibitions as well as in the pages of art, anatomy, and anthropology books, men's magazines, daily newspapers, photojournalist weeklies, and naturist monthlies. In some cases, with appropriately adjusted framing and context, the same images could appear in all these locations. This was the case with works by Horace Narbeth, professionally known as Roye, whose prolific and commercially adaptable oeuvre offers a telling example of how nude photographs could move in and out of the moral boundaries of naturism and be repurposed for a wider range of audiences and arguments.[156]

PERFECT SALESMANSHIP

Roye's autobiography, *Nude Ego*, paints a larger-than-life myth of a man who was, at various times, a dance instructor, colonial playboy, diamond smuggler, night club owner, and a studio assistant in the last days of silent cinema. He came to photography in the early 1930s; his friendship with the long-established photographer Walter Bird helped him build a career, and his first forays in Paris and London encompassed formal studio portraiture, street photography for art exhibitions, and advertising. Routledge had seen the sales that could come from books of female nudes, following their publication of Park and Gregory's *Sun Bathers*, and they commissioned Roye to produce a similar volume. 1938's *Perfect Womanhood* comprised 48 prints of unnamed models in outdoor settings, and launched Roye's reputation as a leading mid-century photographer of naked women.

One of the photographs in *Perfect Womanhood*, of a topless young woman holding a beach ball above her head was, Roye claimed, the first nude photograph to feature in a national newspaper.[157] Entitled "Sport", it won a 100 guinea prize in the *Daily Mirror* for its encapsulation of "the Spirit of Girlhood" in the same year that it appeared as an example of artistic achievement in the London Salon of Photography.[158] Along with many of Roye's other photographs, it also served as an illustration in the naturist press, which prescribed *Perfect Womanhood* for "The Naturists' Bookshelf".[159] *The British Journal of Photography*, the principal professional publication for all matters photographic, also gave the book an effusive review, stating that it was "filled with studies of excellent technique and in quite unimpeachable taste".[160] Roye's nudes were seen in these various settings as technically and aesthetically accomplished, youthful and healthy, newsworthy and morally pure. Roye was also particularly skilled at maximizing commercial mileage from his images. Photographs of attractive young women had long been used to promote consumer products, but his nudes proved especially saleable. By his own boasting, they sold British tractors in India, British suits in Argentina, and British machine tools in the USA.[161] For naturist purposes, Roye's nudes were not of naturists (he preferred showgirls as models); nor were they taken in naturist camps (*Perfect Womanhood* was born in a field outside Colchester, Essex, in view of the road).[162] They illustrated a movement in which they played no meaningful part.

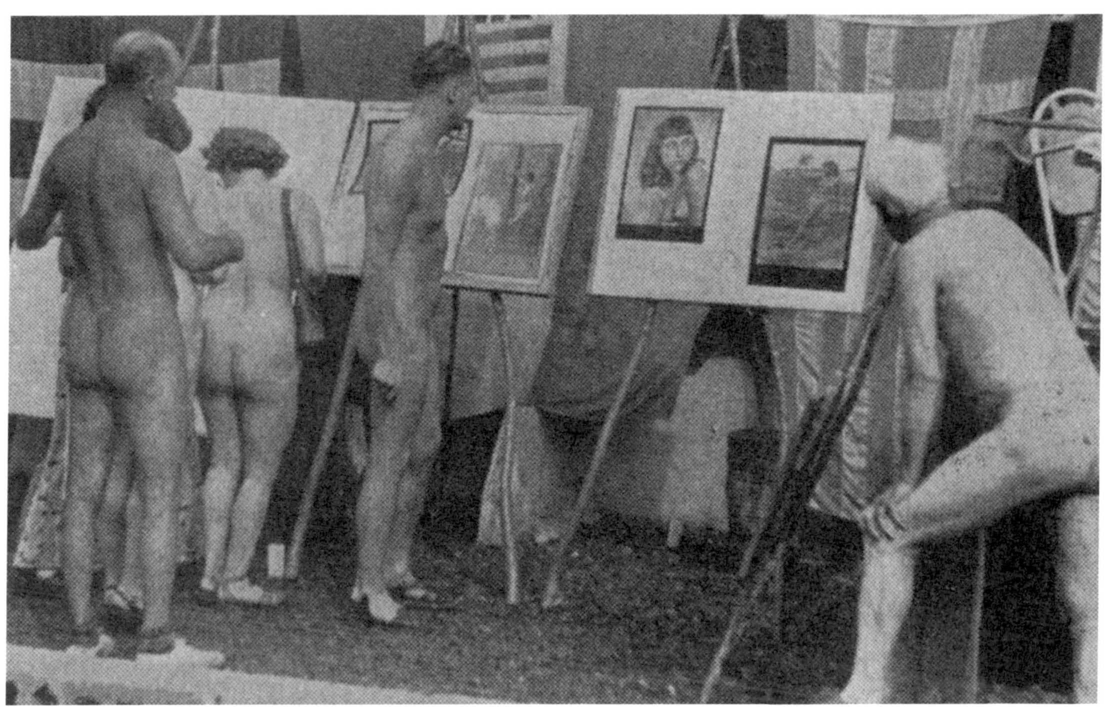

The nudist gallery:
an exhibition at
Spielplatz nudist camp
provided an egalitarian
opportunity for nude
spectators to view nude
photographs.

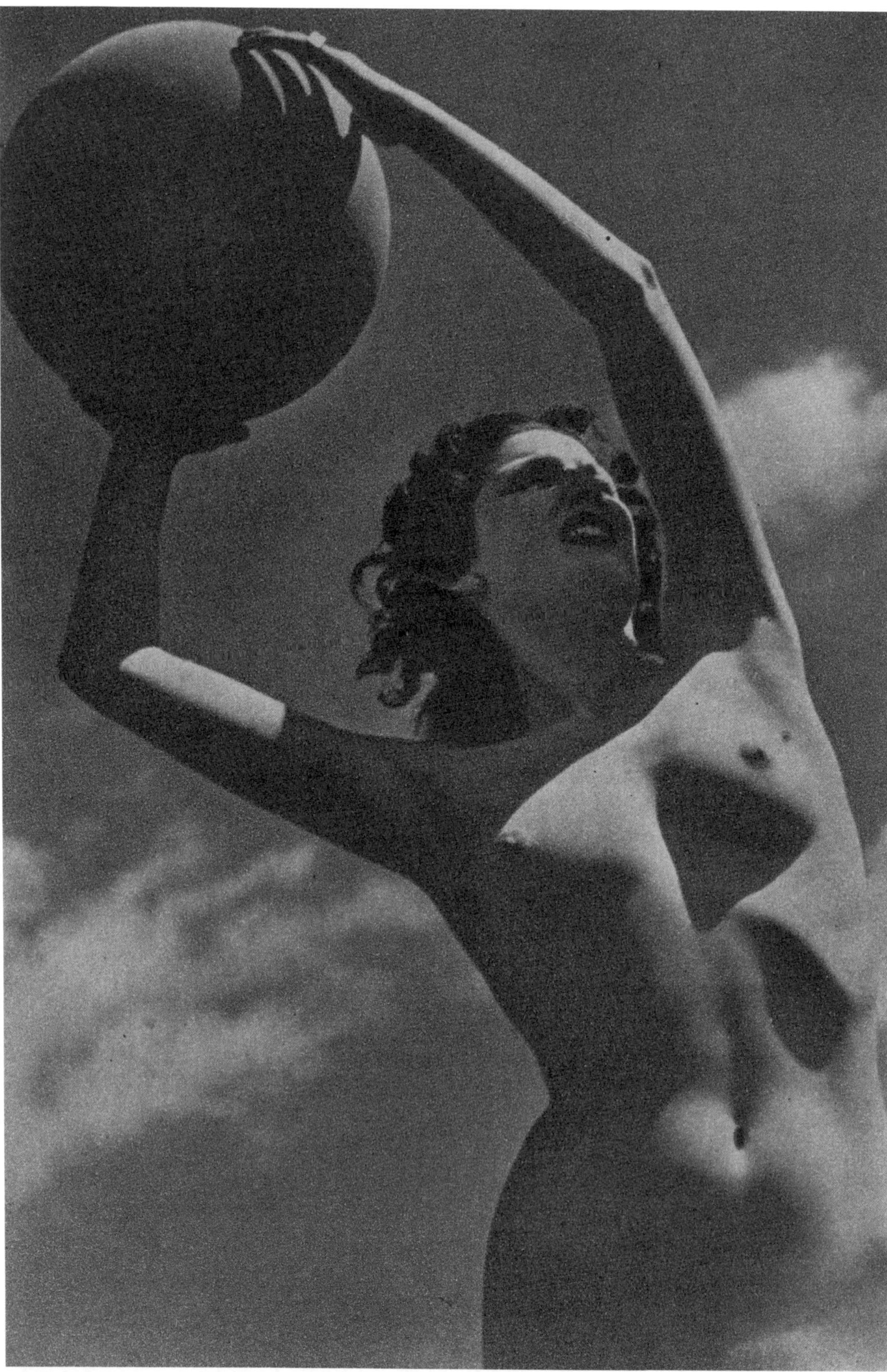

The Naturist sold itself, from the outset, as a magazine "for all interested in Physical Fitness, Hygiene, Diet, Sunbathing, and a Natural Healthy Life". It aimed "1) To provide a medium of expression for the many thousands of sunbathing, naturist and physical culture enthusiasts; 2) To make people appreciate the enormous benefits to the nation's health to be had from the proper use of the air and the sun's rays; 3) To spread the gospel of naturism and the cultivation of a perfect nation by natural means and resources."[163] In practice, it largely operated as a vehicle to publish nude photographs of professional white female models. They appeared on almost every page and accompanied almost all articles, no matter the subject matter (body odour, boils, piles, dandruff, carbuncles, catarrh, warts, varicose veins, ingrown toenails, and the role of cheese in the diet). Apparently without irony, youthful photographs even accompanied an article entitled "Age is no Bar to Nudism".[164] While the magazine covered health matters in its textual content, some articles were bogus, such as those that staged debate about the magazine's imagery as a means to show more of it: "We Can Do Without Pin-Ups", "In Defence of the Model", "What I Think of Those Naturist Photographs", and "Is it Wrong to Take Pleasure in Pictures Such as These?"

EXQUISITE POSES

Roye's photographs played a major role in *The Naturist* from its inception. They appeared regularly on its coloured covers and in multiples within. Readers received a free copy of *Perfect Womanhood* as a subscription incentive; six-packs of Roye's nude prints were also available to purchase through the periodical. "That an artist such as Roye is assisting us in providing beautiful photographs for this magazine indicates the merits of true Naturism," an editorial in 1938 gushed. "How truly right the human body is against natural backgrounds. Nature is above art, but here art interprets Nature."[165] Letters from practising naturists, however, expressed qualms about the photographs' naturist credentials. One complained that Roye's models do not "appeal humanly and directly" to the viewer but instead assume rather "exquisite" poses and facial expressions; they thus appeared "as beings from another sphere" rather than realistic representatives. Another griped that, in his club at Bricket Wood,

Hertfordshire, professional models had been shipped in for a photo shoot even though he reckoned there were "at least half a dozen genuine naturists with figures that were superior". When the models removed their "exotic beach wraps" and glamorous "cart wheel" hats, they were revealed to have "dead white skin".[166] As supposed representatives of a movement based on complete exposure to the sun, this reader perceived hypocrisy and inauthenticity.

Editors and authors who defended nude photography using models argued, "It is impossible to obtain a great many photographs of Naturists at the camps. Not every man or woman cares to be reproduced in a leading national publication—and for obvious reasons."[167] Nudists lobbied hard for their cause in the pages of the magazine but many wrote under pseudonyms; the risk to reputation in being recognized in a nudist photograph was even more fraught. As to the almost total dominance of women, it was claimed, "We publish fewer photographs of men rather than women because we have many more of the latter submitted to us."[168] While there may have been some truth in both areas, photographers and publishers recognized by the end of the 1930s that there was serious money to be made from images of naked women, and naturism provided the alibi for lucrative business. This commercial expansion was not dampened by the coming of the Second World War.

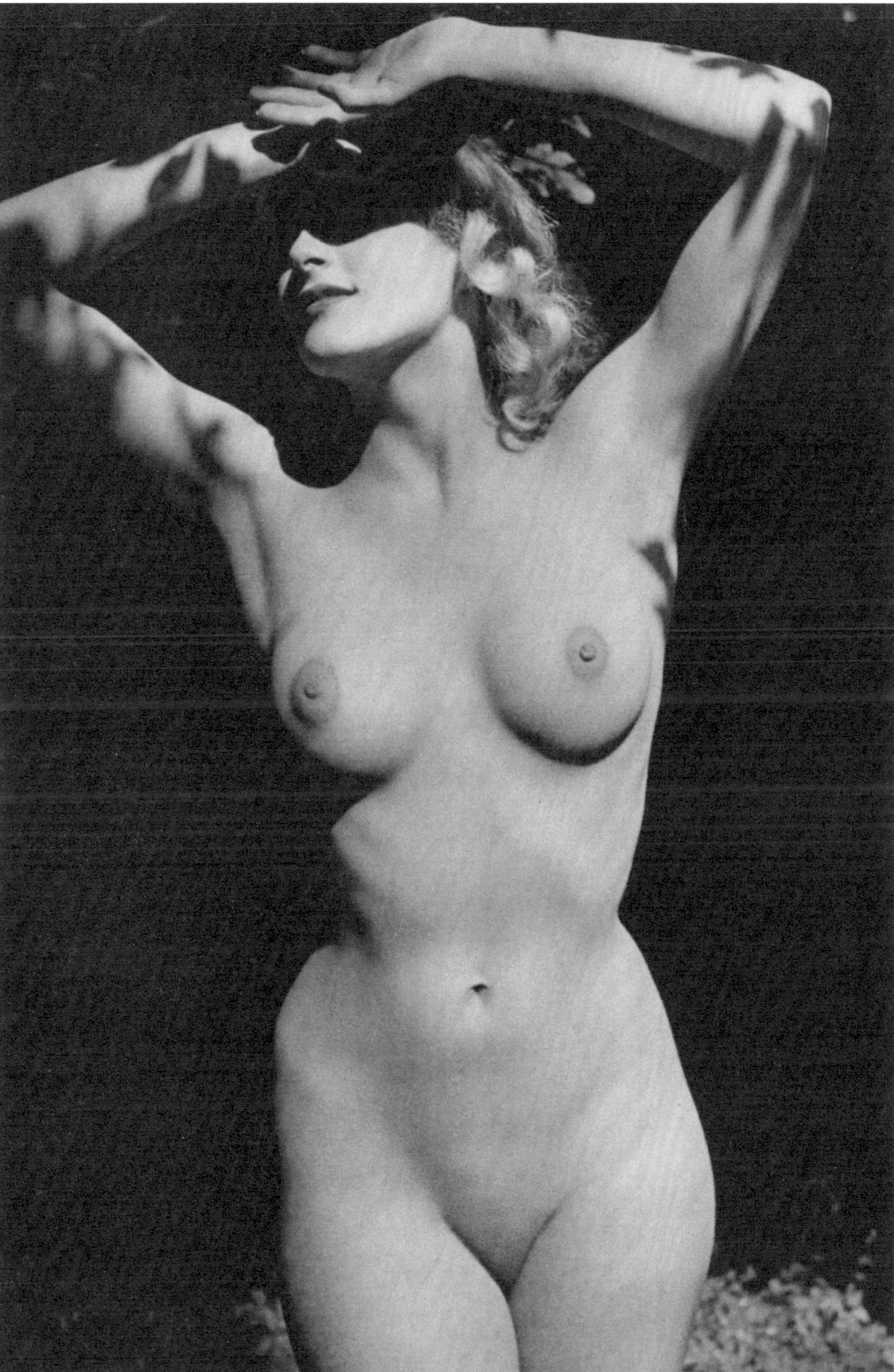

2

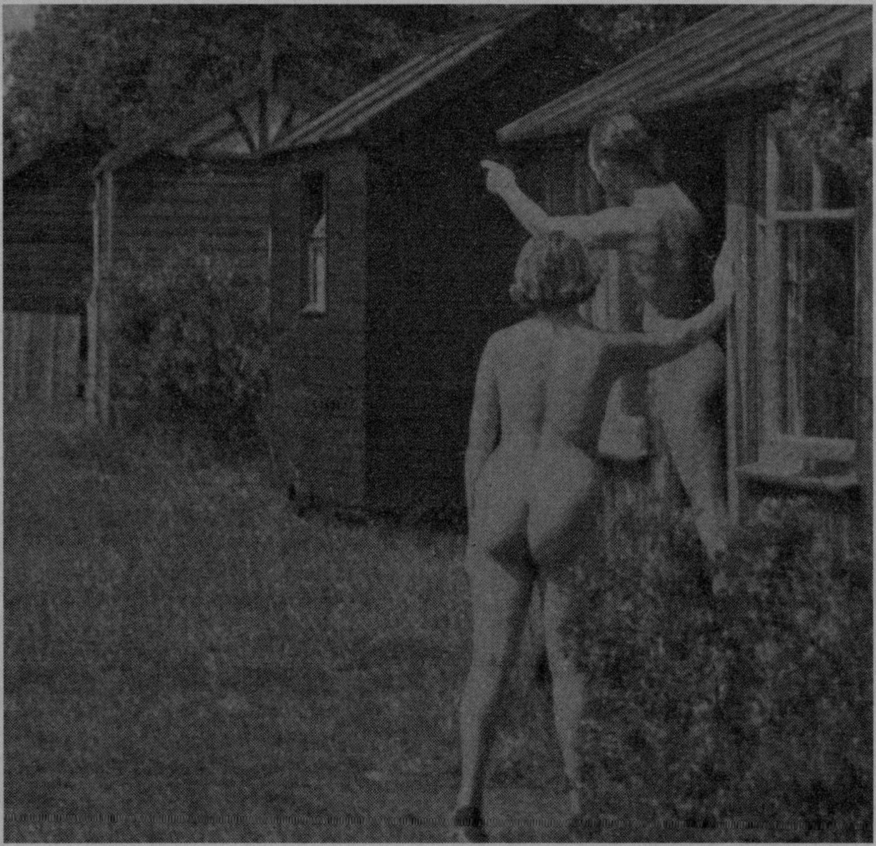

Building a Culture

A nudist camp somewhere in England: High wooden fencing encircles a row of matching prefab chalets. On the lawn, with volleyball net and cold-water swimming pool, there is a baize-topped card table with a radio, a packet of cigarettes, a meat pie, and a camera.

100

Previous spread – As British nudism consolidated post-war, its sites became better appointed with standardized chalet accommodation, running water, heating, and lighting.

As the Second World War began, British bookshops reported booming sales of *The Naturist*, *Health and Efficiency*, and *Sun Bathing Review*.[1] *The Naturist*, in particular, attracted thousands of readers each month with its visual style focused on professional nude models taken by professional photographers, and in 1941 began producing pocket-sized book-length guides, often with only slightly differing titles (*The Romance of Naturism*; *The Mystery of Naturism*; *The Beauty of Naturism*; *Sunshine and Naturism*) in a series that exceeded a dozen volumes, all sold through the magazine.[2] Each included a glossy "art supplement by leading camera artists" that often outnumbered in pages the text it was meant to support.[3] Singly or jointly, Roye, John Everard, and Walter Bird also produced at least a dozen books during the war, which was a thriving period for the sale of photographic nudes.[4]

In 1940 *The Naturist* asked, "What Can Naturists Do in Wartime?"[5] The answer was to persevere, just as they had been already doing in the face of poor weather and pre-war public ridicule. Naturists had long argued that their philosophy of life was essentially pacifist; many of its pioneers had been conscientious objectors in the First World War. So-called "war fervour" was seen to be life-denying; it capitalized on the contemporary malaise that joyful naturist life was designed to counter. "Every sexually repressed adolescent, every bored and exasperated office-worker, every film-struck, feather headed girl, sensation-starved, sensation-hungry, every unhappily married man and secretly disappointed woman", Dion Byngham argued, "are the precious pawns of the war-party. These are the subconsciously seething, fermenting precious material, as precious as any in the munition factories."[6]

As the Second World War hit, these pacifist claims were partly repeated but British naturists also recognized the battle against fascism could be interpreted as a broader campaign for liberation, including for bodies. One asked, in 1942, "What are we fighting for?" He provided the response by paraphrasing Kaiser Wilhelm II: for "every man's right to a place in the sun". With some poetic licence, the barrister author linked the famous German abdicator's call for power to British naturists' desire for radiant health.[7] Other authors also positioned the war effort in naturists' favour. William Welby, the author of several books of nudist philosophy, noted: "We are constantly being told that we are fighting for 'Democracy'." Naturism was its "very apotheosis".[8] The movement had always used the language of freedom and it served a new purpose in wartime. The knowledge that German nudist books and publications had been burned by the Nazis added further power to the oppositional charge.[9]

Naturist magazines called on British doggedness and stolidity to help see the movement through tough times.[10] Articles on "wartime nerves" noted the mental and physical drains of "long hours in the factory" and "queues for buses and trains".[11] Instead of days in the sun, "black-out regulations will mean long winter evenings by the fireside". They argued for the fresh value of their cause: "Now, more than ever before, the health of the nation should not be neglected".[12] Ever optimistic, even opportunistic, some naturists saw potential in the period. Fresh air and sunlight were "free, unrationed benefits". Casting off garments was "an antidote to the stresses and strains of war service".[13] With the coming of clothes rationing in 1941, some prominent critics of dress, notably J. C. Flugel, perceived "a great fillip to our movement" as "the public will be forced to wear less". He argued, "Liberation from our inherited prudery of mind is what we have been advocating for years, and now by a freak of Fate this is being brought about by War." He claimed, "Two of this war's most important legacies to mankind may well prove to be healthier minds and healthier bodies."[14]

Despite these aspirations, many camps closed between 1939 and 1945. Spielplatz, as an exception, by this time had expanded to form a permanent "nudist village" for 30 families, housing members displaced by the Blitz in its chalets and accommodating soldiers on lookout duties.[15] Welby observed in 1941 that some clubs had been bombed. "I know of more than one centre which has suffered from enemy action, yet is still carrying on in true British tradition," he stated. "I am sure their optimism will be justified and that when Peace comes, as come it must, the sane healthy atmosphere of the Nudist camps will be better understood and far more widely appreciated."[16] Wartime enthusiasts claimed that the movement "is still going strong in preparation for the day when its enjoyment will be unhampered by the shadow of the Swastika". They argued, "The thousands of men and women who have enjoyed wartime Naturism have not regarded it as a luxury, but as a necessity."[17]

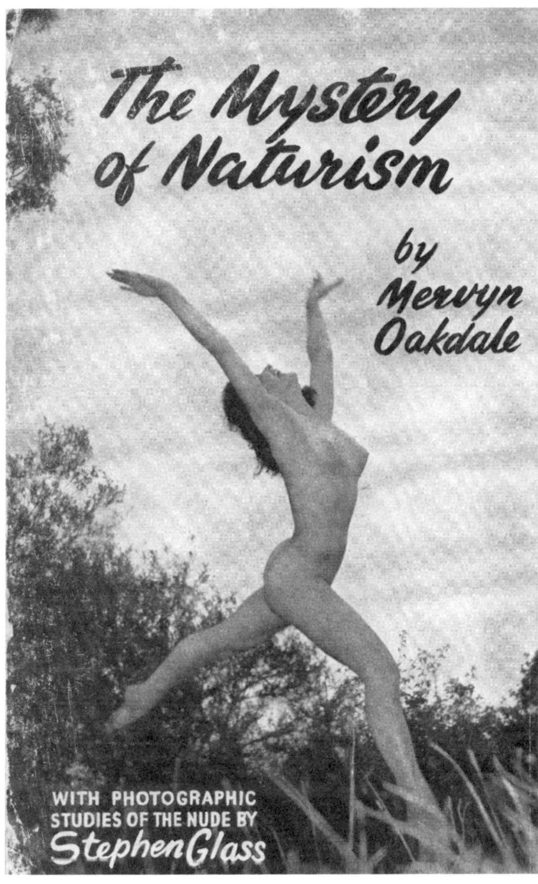

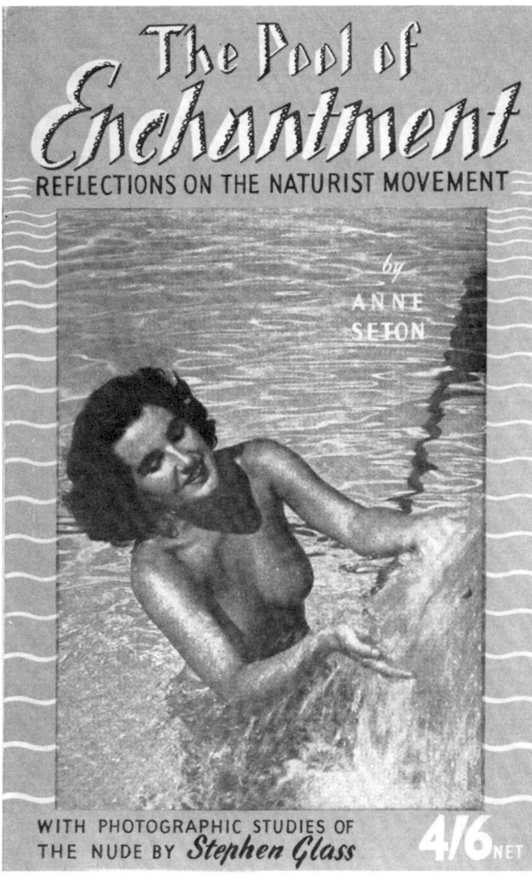

The Naturist produced over a dozen highly illustrated books in the 1940s and 1950s, capitalising on the growing commercial interest in nude bodies.

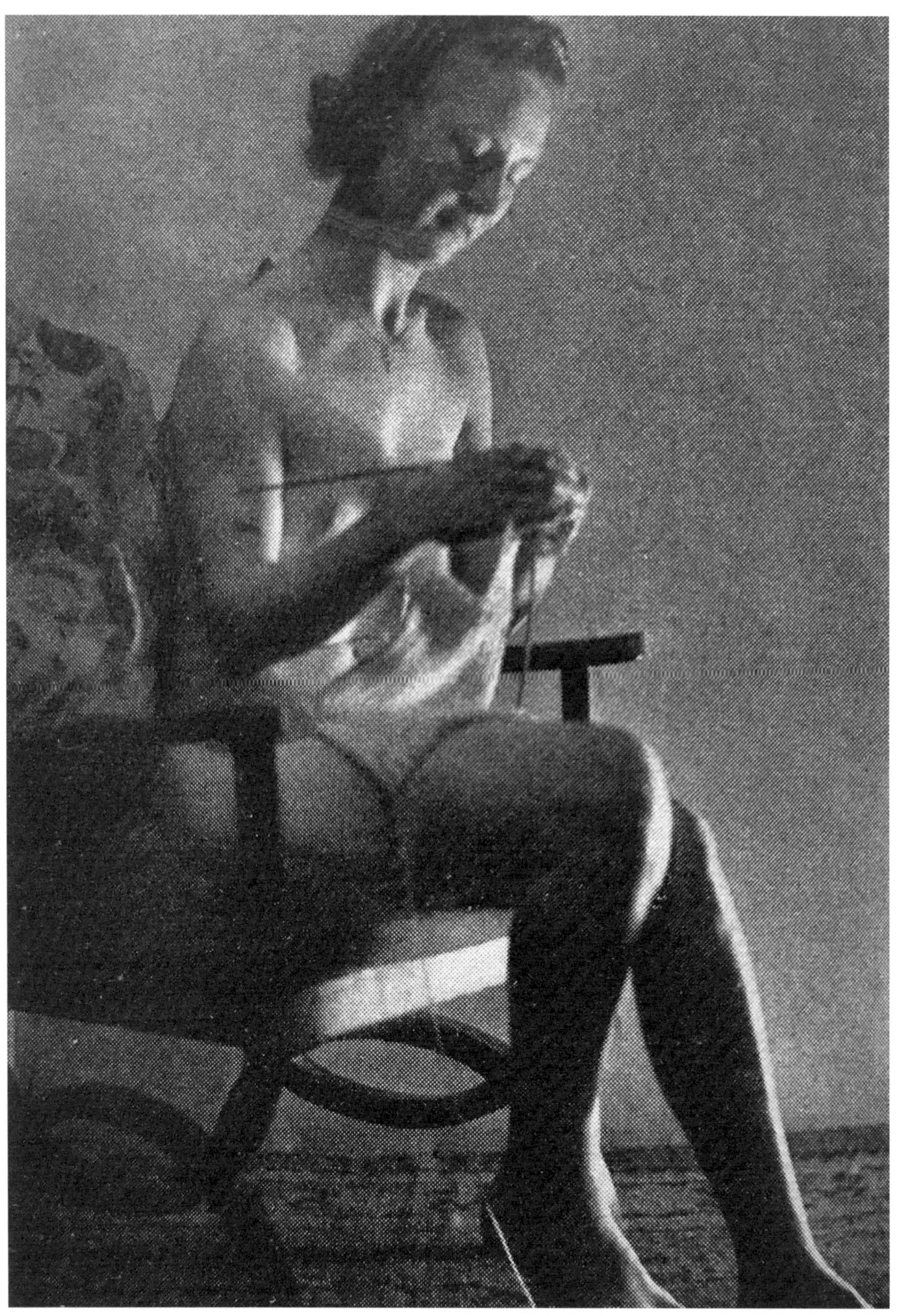

104

BODIES IN CONFLICT

The restorative effects of naturism in the context of war were provided in powerful personal testimonies. One woman wrote of how naturism brought a transformational sense of personal freedom after she lost her leg in an air raid.[18] Another account of "the healing touch of the sun and air" related to a former prisoner of war, whose emaciated body was marked by beatings from two years spent in Central Europe in "one of those horrible encampments erected for the political enemies of the Nazis". After his physical and mental recovery in a naturist club, he stated, "The sight of you people, spending your week-ends down here in the open air, without clothes or false shame, reminded me that there was still something inherently decent in mankind. I came from an atmosphere of jackboots and uniforms and found myself in company where clothes and the stupid, soul-destroying pomp of outward appearances did not matter."[19]

Notably, none of these accounts were illustrated with images of the authors. In the case of the latter, it appeared in a book, *British Naturism* by Michael Rutherford, accompanied by an "art supplement" by regular photographer Stephen Glass.[20] Rutherford reassured the reader that "the bronzed, athletic men and women shown in the photographs are all practising Naturists" and that they "were specially taken at British Naturist camps". He added, however, that "no person appearing in them is mentioned, specifically or by inference, in the text".[21] This manoeuvre was ostensibly to protect personal identities, but it reflected naturism's ongoing devotion to the body beautiful as propaganda. As one mid-century magazine correspondent put it, "although the weedy males and flat-chested matrons who, alas, form the largest percentage of small-club membership, may be charming enough people to their relatives and immediate friends, by no stretch of the imagination can they be regarded as photogenic enough to advertise the nudist movement at its best".[22] In the same years, parallel articles expressed concern about the lack of disabled or "imperfect" members in the clubs. One author noted, "many hundreds of men and women" fitted such a category and they might be "exactly those who need the benefits, and the comradeship, of naturism most". The movement's enduring emphasis on physical perfection, however, meant "men and women who are scarred or crippled [...] hesitate before applying for permission to join".[23]

Left - Nudism in wartime: a naturist, at an indoor club, knits clothes for the troops.

FORCES' SWEETHEARTS

The war also added rhetorical power to the presentation of idealized nude bodies in publications that were not strictly naturist but which were heavily promoted in naturist magazines and drew on similar imagery and similar justifications of freedom. *The English Maid*, for example, by Roye, published in 1939 as the first in a book series offering a pseudo-anthropological survey of young women's physical characteristics in four different countries, used the conflict to set the moral terrain. After accounting for England's release from Victorian prudery—a frequently recruited bogeyman—it was observed that the "Back to Nature" movement had a new national enemy. The book complained, "a mechanical civilisation is flooding the countryside with houses, petrol stations and factories. London and other cities sprawl over ever-larger areas of territory. The noise and smell of cars make roads intolerable. Aeroplanes roar overhead. It becomes harder and harder to find a quiet spot in which to retreat to enjoy in peace the beauties of Nature and the sensation of freedom." War was the great risk to men and women's "unrivalled opportunities to live as nature meant them to", the text warned. "Now they have to forsake the countryside and don the asbestos suit and the gas-mask, enclose themselves in tanks, aeroplanes and submarines, and ride forth with deadly weapons to destroy their fellows."[24] Predictably, the illustrations in *The English Maid* did not show men, tanks, or gas masks. The accompanying photographs showed only undressed and idealized bodies in unspoilt and unspecified rural locations.

Eves without Leaves was a joint book production that combined the photographs of Roye, John Everard, and Walter Bird for a wartime audience, reproducing Roye's "Sport" from *Perfect Womanhood*.[25] As a compilation of material that had previously appeared in the monthly magazine *Men Only*, the all-female nudes received a satirical introduction from Reginald Arkell, the magazine's editor.[26] Describing the leisure magazine *Men Only* as a "chaste" space into which "a certain number of nudes have been allowed to drift", he claimed that he would have preferred the publisher to have produced a book of "old village churches, thatched cottages and Brighton Pier by Moonlight". Arkell's sarcastic commentary skewers the high-minded moral and aesthetic justification that many texts provided for nude photographs, including the naturist press, while acknowledging its principal purpose as objects of heterosexual desire. His smirking tone carried through to his observations about the uses of the photographs, each of which could be ordered as prints: "They tell me that members of his Majesty's forces have a weakness for this sort of thing; they have grown so artistic that they even frame enlargements of these pictures and hang them in their ward rooms and what not." He joked: "Does this mean that war has a refining influence on those participating in it?" If so, the publisher "may be a public benefactor engaged upon work of national importance".[27]

Arkell's statement about the popularity of nude photography with the wartime armed forces was borne out by what was called an "experiment in taste" conducted in 1944 by British social research organisation Mass Observation, among members of a London Services Club. Mass Observation commonly investigated overlooked aspects of everyday life and popular culture using eccentric methods adapted from anthropology; this study was no exception. Published in the weekly illustrated *Picture Post* as "What is a Pin-Up Girl?", the survey asked soldiers, sailors, and airmen to evaluate 12 black-and-white reproductions of women from historic painting, graphic illustrations popular in both world wars, and photographs of cinema stars. All were displayed at the same size and without further information. The selection included a Roye nude from his book *The English Maid*, comprising a full-length view of a model part-concealed by her diagonal arrangement around a rock against a cloudy sky.

The results calculated which image the men "would most like to decorate their billets". Out of nude paintings by Renoir and Frederic Leighton, images of the scantily clad *Daily Mirror* cartoon character Jane, and Hollywood star Betty Grable, Roye's photograph was an "easy first", with 46 per cent giving it top ranking and 70 per cent of respondents placing it in their top three. Roye's was also "the only picture which no-one disliked". The outdoor nude was perceived as a breath of fresh air. It was described by reviewers as "full of life", "natural", "clean and decent". A 22-year-old army private stated that it should be titled "Worth Fighting For". Referencing a traditionally working-class part of London, the article concluded that it is "the Venus of Mile End, not the Venus of Milo, which men like to have around in the barrack room, gazing at them when they sink on their beds after an exhausting day".[28]

Nudism in a Cold Climate

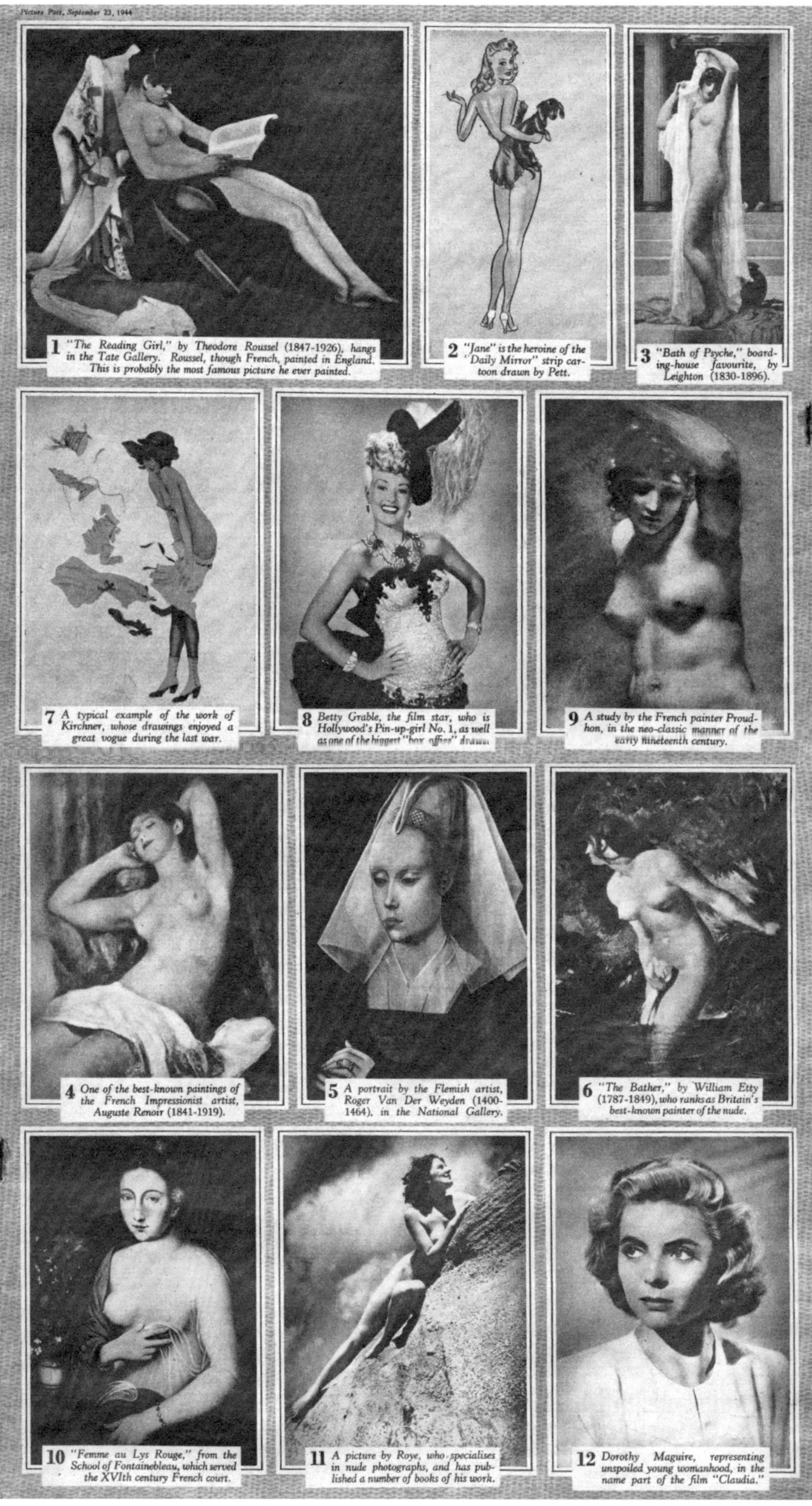

1 "The Reading Girl," by Theodore Roussel (1847-1926), hangs in the Tate Gallery. Roussel, though French, painted in England. This is probably the most famous picture he ever painted.

2 "Jane" is the heroine of the "Daily Mirror" strip cartoon drawn by Pett.

3 "Bath of Psyche," boarding-house favourite, by Leighton (1830-1896).

7 A typical example of the work of Kirchner, whose drawings enjoyed a great vogue during the last war.

8 Betty Grable, the film star, who is Hollywood's Pin-up-girl No. 1, as well as one of the biggest "box office" draws.

9 A study by the French painter Proudhon, in the neo-classic manner of the early nineteenth century.

4 One of the best-known paintings of the French Impressionist artist, Auguste Renoir (1841-1919).

5 A portrait by the Flemish artist, Roger Van Der Weyden (1400-1464), in the National Gallery.

6 "The Bather," by William Etty (1787-1849), who ranks as Britain's best-known painter of the nude.

10 "Femme au Lys Rouge," from the School of Fontainebleau, which served the XVIth century French court.

11 A picture by Roye, who specialises in nude photographs, and has published a number of books of his work.

12 Dorothy Maguire, representing unspoiled young womanhood, in the name part of the film "Claudia."

Worth Fighting For? Mass Observation, a social research organization, asked servicemen in the Second World War to rate pin-ups as an experiment in taste. Roye's naturist nude was the clear winner.

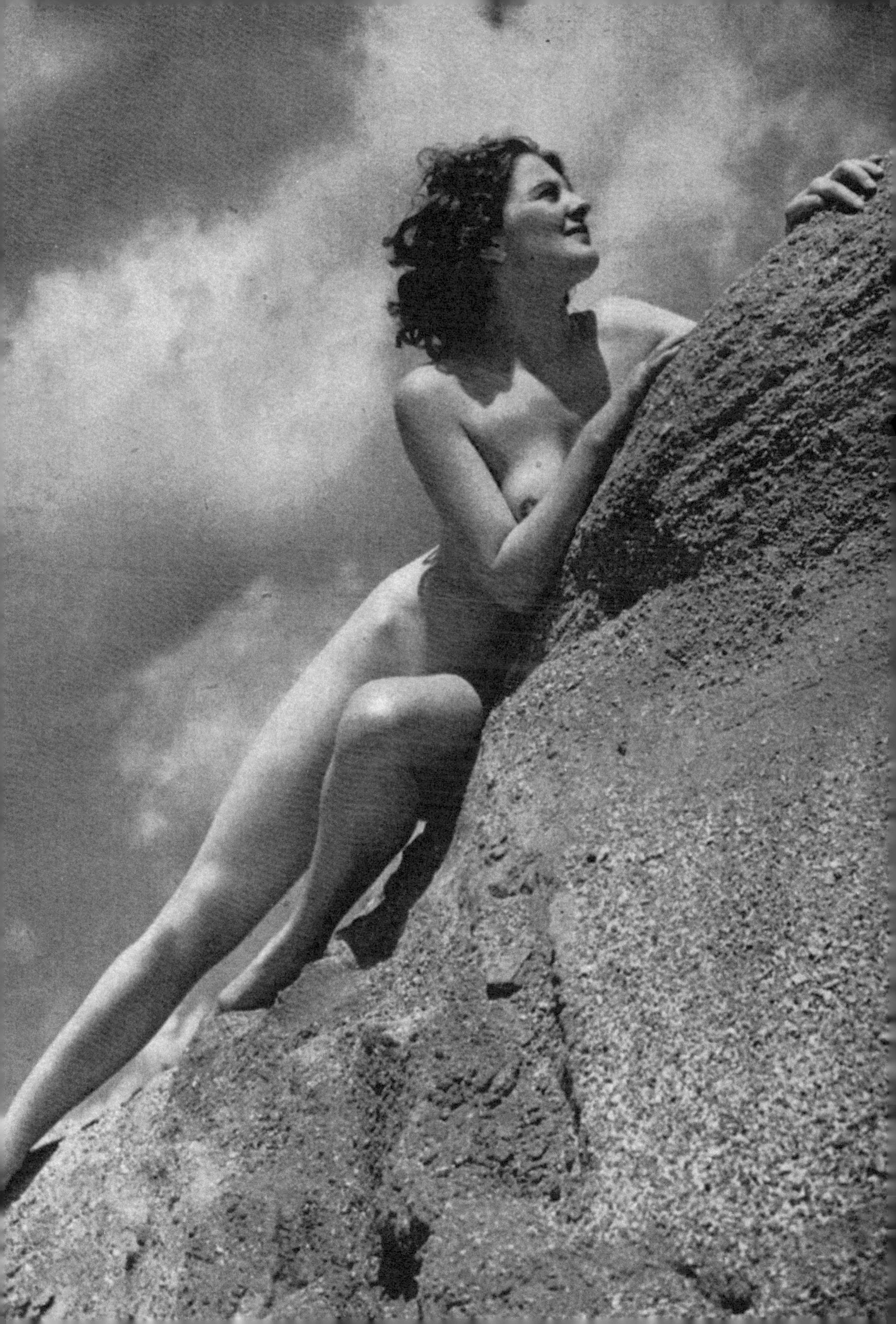

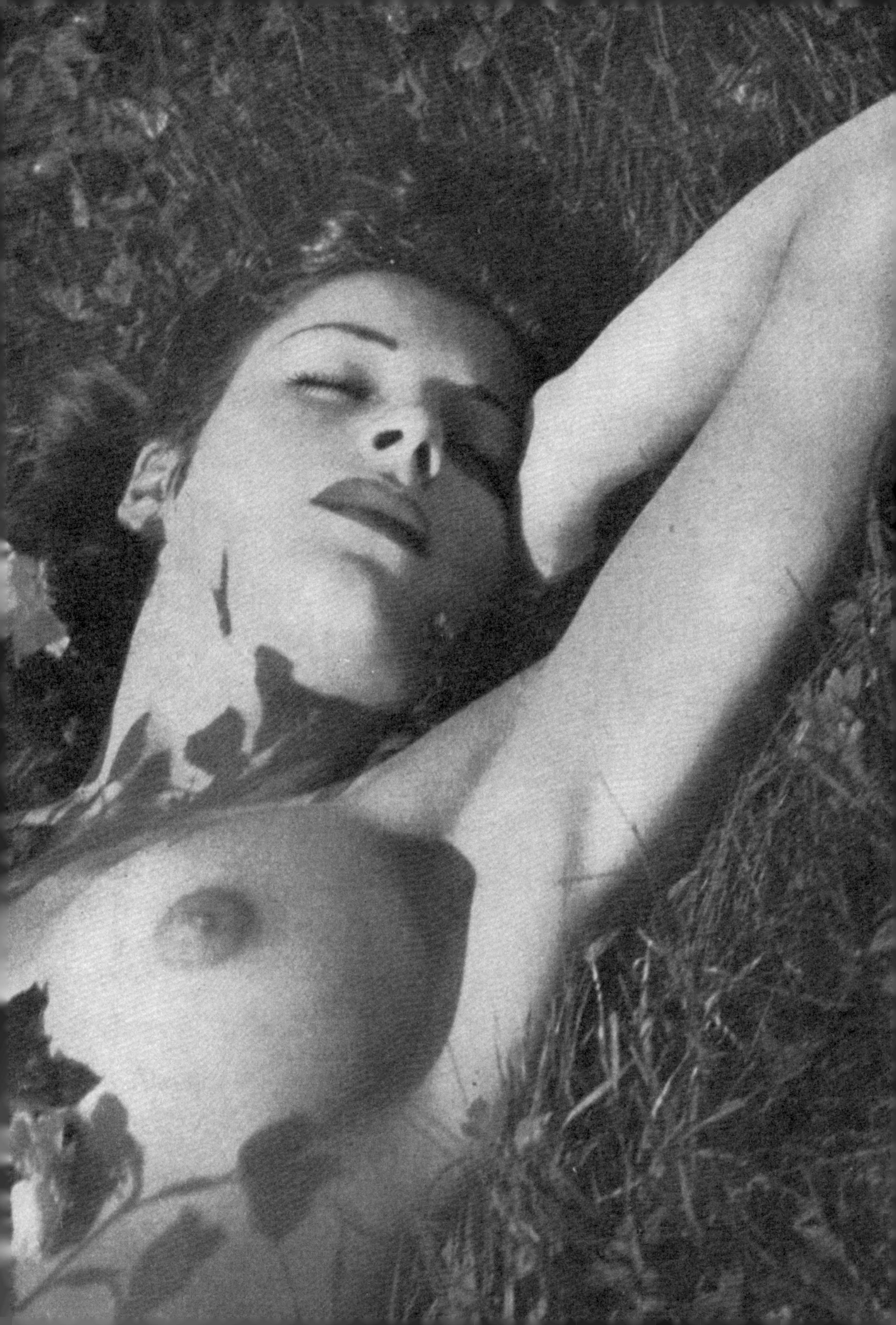

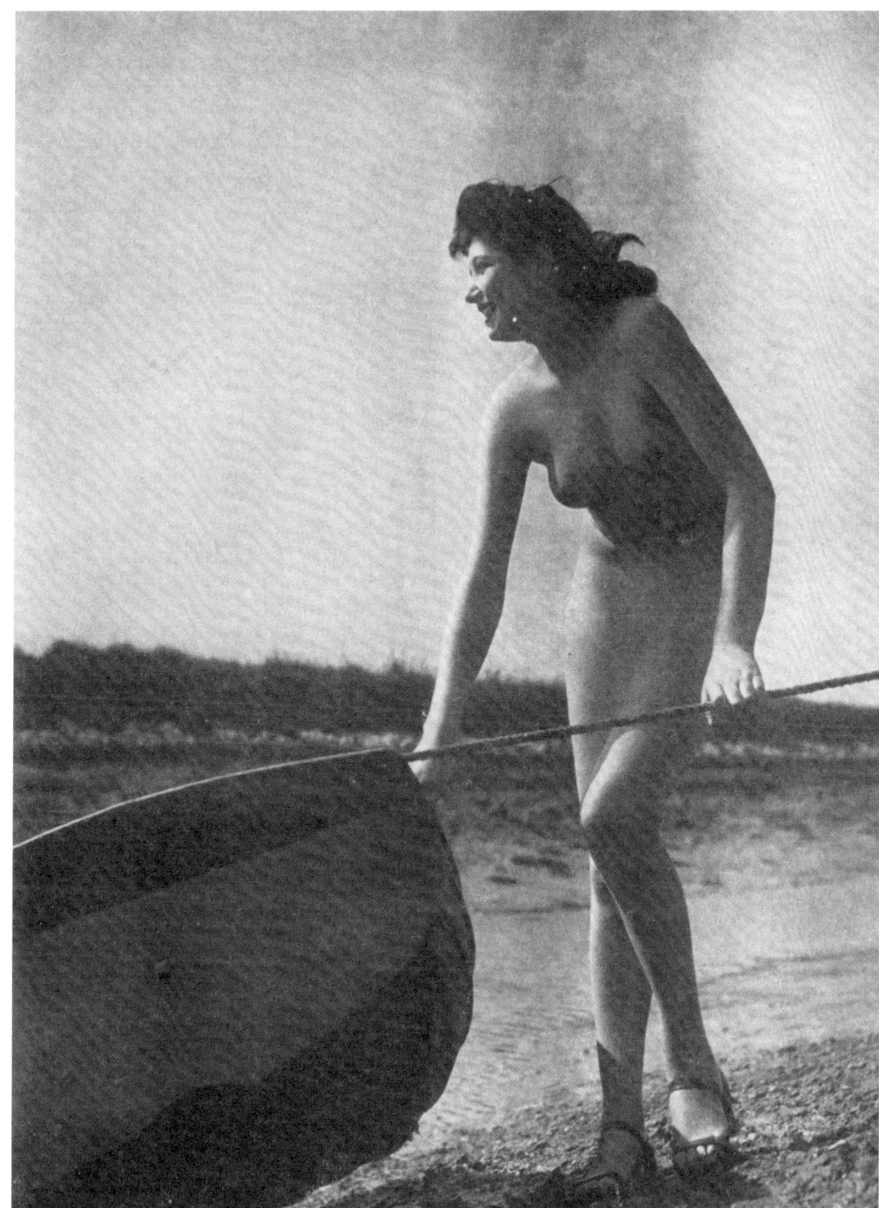

Left - Roye's wartime book, *The English Maid*, used the context of asbestos suits and gas masks to show nude model bodies. These, he argued, represented national ideals of nature, beauty, and freedom.

Right - To appear in print legally in mid-century Britain, nude photographs had to be carefully posed or "retouched" so public hair and genitals were not visible. This treatment could be heavy-handed.

TEARING DOWN PIN-UPS

The authors of the Mass Observation study noted, "We didn't use the phrase 'pin-up girl' in this investigation but willy-nilly that was what we were investigating."[29] Although printed images of undressed women have a very long history, the phrase "pin-up", meaning a cheap printed photograph of a partially dressed, sexually desirable woman, only entered the *Oxford English Dictionary* in 1941. Not coincidentally, this was the same year that the US entered the Second World War. That the pin-up is inextricably linked with American culture is a fact observed by many.[30] French film critic André Bazin, for example, writing an etymology of the form in 1946, claimed that like other American industrially made pleasures, the pin-up was "manufactured on the assembly line".[31] He went on to characterize it as "chewing gum for the imagination", implying it was cheap, sweet, consumable, and disposable.

Appraisals in the British naturist press also characterized pin-ups in the context of anti-American attitudes at mid-century, which positioned Hollywood glamour as brash and showy in contrast to home-grown attractions. The Betty Grable pin-up, for example, adorned in sequins and feathers, with heavy make-up and studio lighting, was perceived in the Mass Observation experiment to be too artificial and excessive; the terms used to describe Roye's photograph, by contrast, evoked simplicity and vitality. Roye's photograph was characterized as a pin-up in *Picture Post* but in *The Naturist* the same image served to illustrate the nudist cause; its outdoor element enabled it to inhabit both positions. Following Bazin's metaphor, if British naturist imagery could be likened to food, rather than chewing gum for the imagination, its parallel would be the brown bread advertised in 1940s naturist magazines: healthy, wholesome, and good for you.

The suggestive nature of the pin-up in a skimpy two-piece bathing suit was seen by many naturists to be the very antithesis of their honest, natural, or even non-sexual project. Many opposed the artificial production of sexual allure, and morally outraged articles decried pin-ups alongside chorus girls, strip tease, and stage nudity. British anthropologist Geoffrey Gorer provided a critical analysis of burlesque performance in his 1937 book *Hot Strip Tease and Other Notes on American Culture*, which was assessed favourably in the naturist press. The reviewer summarized the entertainment as "a mass-produced dream of tired and lonely men".[32] Douglas Stewart, author of several

British naturist books, stated in 1940 that "nothing could be more repugnant to the sincere nudist than this crude exhibitionism, that takes place nightly in packed theatres and cabaret shows". Naturism provided "an outset for the obviously bottled-up sexual instincts of the audience who frequent these places", he argued. "It removes the veil of suggestiveness and false glamour from the naked body, without which stage nudity has no appeal."[33]

At odds with the wider culture, where pin-up magazines and strip-tease performances were expanding rapidly and enjoying success as new forms of popular leisure, naturists took a highly moralistic position. Their response may have been genuinely felt but it was also invested in the need to separate what naturists did from other displays of flesh. They could not risk the reputational damage of being spoken about in the same breath as nude shows and sexualized models. Individual naturists, including a 17-year-old boy, born and raised in the movement, reflected on the inadequacies of glamorous imagery. Unlike his peers, he claimed to have no preoccupation with sex: "My room-mates cannot understand why I have no interest in their pin-ups of nearly-naked film stars and bathing beauties. The only pin-ups decorating my wall", he added primly, "are photographs of my mother and the Queen."[34]

If Americans were blamed for gaudy inventions such as strip-tease and pin-ups in the eyes of the British naturist, the 1948 Kinsey report *Sexual Behavior in the Human Male* confirmed their sense of moral superiority. The study showed high levels of pre-marital sex and the use of prostitutes among American men, which British naturists reported with disgust. "Does anyone think that those people have any right to accuse nudists of immorality?" the regular contributor "Woodsman" asked *The Naturist*.[35] British naturists repeatedly asserted that they maintained "a stricter code than most non-naturists would care to be held to".[36] Clubs would not tolerate what was described as "indecorous conduct".[37] Another warned, "Any hint of looseness means termination of membership."[38] Magazines insisted naturism was "a wholly purifying experience".[39] The chorus asserted again and again the status of clubs as "above suspicion" and noted that "nudist resorts have never been cited in the Divorce Court".[40] Finally, "venereal diseases are never, and never have been, the result of nudism".[41]

The Kinsey report reflected American practices, and it was speculated that British moral "standards are much higher".

However, Woodsman noted, "no one has ever attempted a similar examination of the sexual habits of the British people" to corroborate this claim.[42] In fact, following Kinsey, Mass Observation undertook the first random sample survey of sex in Britain, commissioned and serialized by the *Sunday Pictorial*, a newspaper with a readership of more than 10 million.[43] Sex and its scientific analysis was on the nation's minds and in its newsstands in the late 1940s and early 1950s, and although many wished to characterize Britain as sexually restrained and Americans as lax, the evidence revealed a different picture. Aspects of sexuality traditionally presented as "perversions"—including extramarital sex, masturbation, and homosexuality—were in fact shown to be more common than had been previously thought.

In the moral context of naturist magazines, however, even if casual sexual behaviour was becoming more common in Britain, it didn't mean that it was right. Certainly, it should never be associated with the cause. Mid-century British naturists proclaimed that their practice was a sexual corrective that created "healthy" bodily attitudes. Naturism was both "a moral necessity" and a cure. "If the practice of naturism were to become general," some claimed, "a good three-quarters of our sexual troubles would disappear forthwith."[44] Sexologist Norman Haire characterized nudism as a "harmless channel for the deflection of urges which might otherwise manifest themselves in a manner harmful" and even suggested that convicted "Peeping Toms and Exhibitionists" could be reformed by being "sentenced to regular attendance at a Nudist Camp".[45] What was covered by "sexual troubles" and "urges", however, included a multitude of practices.

Masturbation, for example, was regularly alluded to as a "bad habit" to be defeated in the advice pages of mid-century naturist magazines, in keeping with wider attitudes of the period.[46] Magazines denied any relationship between the naked bodies they depicted and erotic desire. Anyone who perceived naturist photographs as sexually stimulating must be at fault. "The true naturist regards his nudity as something unaffected and natural, simple and open", one contributor asserted in a debate on sexual morality. "This, or a proper photographic representation of it, should have no provocative effect—except, perhaps, to a sex-mad mind, which will, in any case, find vice in the most innocent subject." When counter-arguments were made—that "it is well-known that there are traffickers in nude pictures"—which acknowledged that photographs of naked bodies could have sexually stimulating effects, other naturists rejected the claims as unthinkable. "Those, whatever they are, aren't genuine naturist pictures. There is nothing surreptitious about the display of genuine naturist illustrations," the respondent retorted. Naturist photographs "do more to encourage a clean view of nudity than all the morality talks in the world".[47]

The sexual stimulation of naked bodies in camps was repeatedly denied, and a few cautious articles addressed "the commonest problem" of erections. In 1933, an author in *Health and Efficiency* who said he had undertaken interviews with about 2,000 club applicants and found that a commonly shared fear among men was that "in a mixed nudist gathering they will involuntarily exhibit physical signs of sex excitement". He asserted: "There is not the slightest ground for this fear. No case of such excitement has ever been known in the history of the British Sun Bathing League," and, he emphasized, "all reputable societies" found the same.[48] When the subject was tackled again two decades later, would-be nudists were again reassured: "The kind of embarrassment you have in mind simply does not happen in the circumstances of a sun club. What makes chaps worry about it is the popular tendency to associate nakedness and sex and the exploitation of nakedness or partial nakedness in a 'glamorous' way; it leads to an unfortunate association of ideas." The author insisted: "If nakedness was, instead, associated with bathing, and athletics, and personal hygiene, in fact, in the naturist way, people would just lose this 'complex'." When an incredulous follow-up was posed: "Do you mean to say, this problem never arises at all?" the more experienced nudist concluded, "It can only be caused by the presence of unclean thoughts. I do not believe they can arise in a sun club, but if ever there was such a case I suppose the chap concerned would automatically be shown the door."[49]

A central problem, however, was that naturists made these assertions in magazines that were fronted by material that fit the descriptions of glamorous pin-ups—*The Naturist* featured young women in bathing suits on almost every cover—and which were back-ended by advertisements selling exactly the suggestive pictorial material that was positioned as the enemy. Naturist authors complained that "naked poses [...] much in vogue at the present time on our music-hall stages" were "deliberate pandering to an unhealthy

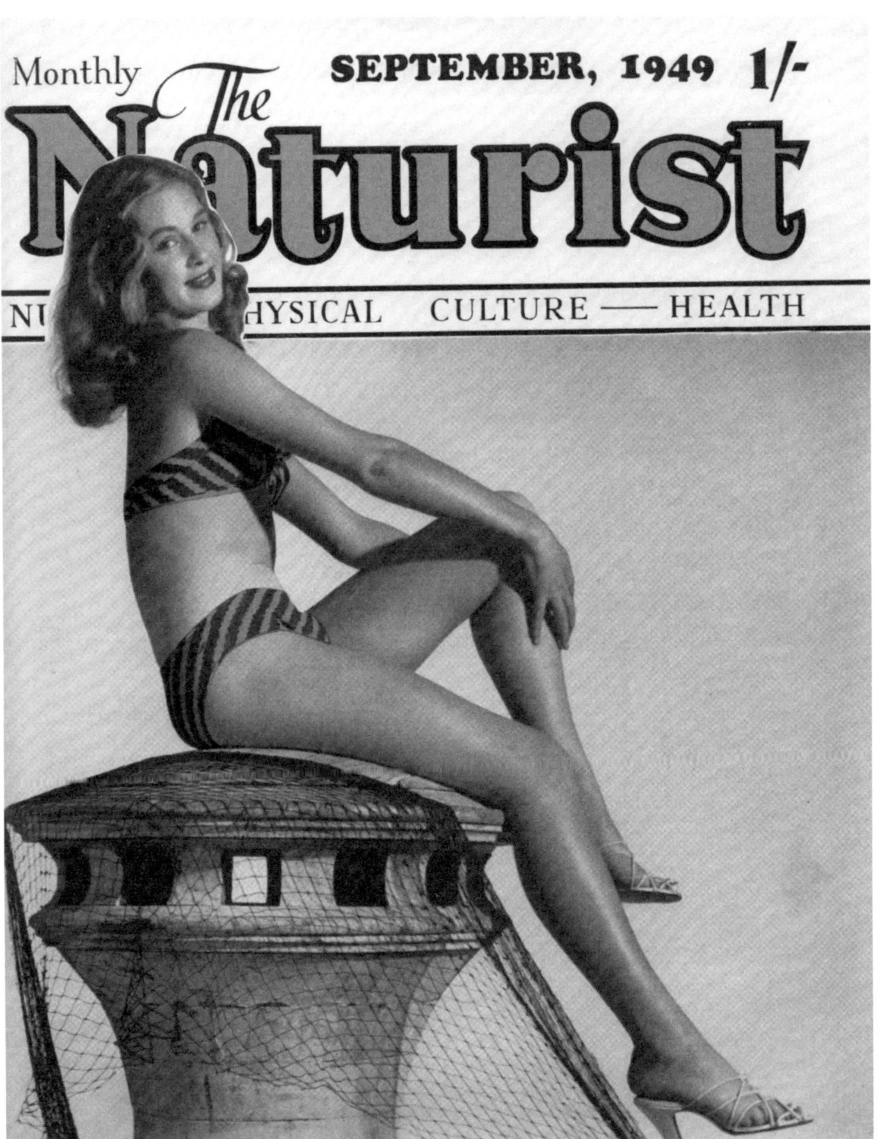

The Naturist magazine covered a wide range of physical health matters in its articles, but its illustrations were almost always of young women, nude or in swimwear.

and unnatural attitude towards the human body". Similarly, they complained that "'Art Albums' of nude photographs, highly priced so as to make them appear more desirable, are assured of a ready sale in the less savoury bookshops".[50] Yet the same "naked poses", "art albums", and, indeed, the very same naked stage performers, were pictured and sold in naturist magazines. The enemy was hiding in plain sight. What was more, these were not imported problems to be laid at the door of Paris or Hollywood; they were British products and services.

Naturist purity had been a strict guarantor of respectability at the beginning of the movement but in the face of changing post-war attitudes to sex, the moral position grew harder to hold. Nude photographs of attractive women were what kept naturist publications commercially afloat. The magazines were described in 1945 as "the shop window of the movement" but they sold images and ideas to a much wider range of readers than practising naturists.[51] The bestselling naturist magazine was said to have 100,000 readers per issue by the end of the 1940s, even as naturism was declining in popularity.[52] The consumption of naturism's image was much more popular than participation in its practices. A 1946 survey of "several hundreds" of visitors to a popular non-naturist holiday camp including "civil servants, motor mechanics, business managers, musicians, professional footballers, postmen, waitresses, typists, clerks [and] servicemen on leave" found 57 per cent of men and 60 per cent of women to be firmly against naturism, with a further 15 per cent of men and 8 per cent of women to be "doubtful".[53]

Even among enthusiasts, it was reckoned in 1946 that there were, at best, "about 3,000 naturists in a population of 47 million", with only 35 camps surviving the war and most with fewer than a hundred members. Here, again, there were national distinctions. Britain was "very clothes conscious as well as a small country". The author Rex argued, "We cannot expect the mass conversion of the public into Naturist enthusiasts." American nudism, by contrast, was said to be expanding, but the relative conditions of post-war prosperity shaped national differences: "Not only have the USA immeasurable advantages in the plentifulness of land and larger population, but America is still a country conditioned by adaptability to new methods and ideas. We cannot compete", he concluded, "with the USA in Naturism any more than we can compete with it in the quantity of its engineering production."[54]

FOR CONNOISSEURS

As British markets for nude photography boomed, one of the key locations in which images circulated was in publications aimed at "art connoisseurs". These works, often highly priced and described in terms that connoted luxury, taste, and class, conferred high-art status on the nude even as they were sold through the naturist press and featured the same images, photographers, and models. Mid-century naturist magazines generally sold at a mere shilling apiece (roughly £1.50 in today's money) and were thus widely affordable. *The Naturist*'s illustrated books sold at prices upwards of a still-modest three shillings and sixpence (around £5). Art albums, by contrast, often styled as "de luxe", presented nude photographs on heavyweight paper, with lush production values, at prices up to 36 shillings (£60).

One example was the 1942 book *Eve*, produced by Anthony Peacock with an introduction by D. G. Johnson, editor of *Health and Efficiency*. Peacock was a regular contributor to the photographic press and was proud to have been the first photographer to gain accreditation by the Royal Photographic Society via a portfolio of nudes in 1942. For the naturist press, he provided photographs for "art supplements", judged amateur photography competitions, and advised prospective nude photographers on style and technique.[55] While he was an active naturist and took accomplished photographs of both sexes in camps, *Eve* depicted only professional female models who, a columnist in *Sun Bathing Review* reassured readers, "became naturists for the day".[56]

Peacock had strong feelings about what constituted a successful image, and "impersonality" was key; any other approach would sully the picture and thus render its subject merely "naked" rather than the more lofty and artistic "nude". This subtlety marked the difference between what he called "a sorry fiasco of a chorus girl with no clothes on" and "the impersonal loveliness of a nude in a perfect setting".[57] Morally and aesthetically, he asserted, "work should be attempted and judged on the highest plane".[58] Peacock's disinterested language and his active position in the naturist movement, not to mention the accolades he received from the Royal Photographic Society, sanctified his book morally and aesthetically for the naturist press, where it was advertised as "an exquisite album of sixty-six nude studies of beauteous womanhood". The word "studies" suggested scholarly investigation, while its production "on fine art paper" removed it from associations with the crude, cheap, and tawdry.

John Everard's 1951 *Artist's Model* was the most ambitious book in this mould in mid-century Britain, including some 1,200 photographs of mostly female nudes. It was also the most highly priced.[59] Its respectability was reinforced by the accreditations of both Everard and Charles Simpson, the author of the extended introduction. Simpson had been a member of the Newlyn artist colony in Cornwall since the 1910s, and by mid-century had exhibited nearly 50 landscape and nature paintings in Royal Academy shows. Everard was a member of the British Institute of Professional Photographers but had not been to art school—he was self-taught, and was formerly in the Royal Air Force—but he emphasized that the purpose of the book was educational: "It caters for the needs of the young student in art, the professional artist, the sculptor and perhaps even more than anyone else, the professional artist and the layout man."[60] To this end, the book included a range of poses ostensibly intended to display anatomy of different kinds, from different angles, to be used for reference, as if in a life class. Some dressed figures—for example male pole vaulters and female models in New Look fashions—were included alongside close-ups of body parts, especially hands, in relatively diverse line-ups including a mature male gardener grasping a spade and an older woman knitting. Children (undressed) and men (partly dressed) were, however, depicted far less than young naked women, who took up 83 pages. Men, mostly in sporting poses wearing posing pouches, took up only 15.

"The introduction to *Artist's Model* is as important as the illustrations," Everard noted.[61] For those in doubt that photography could be art, Simpson established that Everard's technique was "nearer to that of a painter than a photographer. Perhaps I should say sculptor," he stated, "for his broad rendering of modelling and planes, his frequent portrayal of parts of a figure, such as a torso, was strikingly suggestive of the art of sculpture, rather than mere photographic representation." Art historical language was used throughout, as Simpson praised "the formal and monumental boldness" of Everard's personal vision. Simpson provided historical context by comparing the book to Eadweard Muybridge's *The Human Figure in Motion* (1901), which comprised detailed photographic sequences, including of nudes in movement, and had a major influence on turn-of-the-century painters. Everard, however, "had never heard of them".[62] A particular innovation in *Artist's Model* was the use of a turntable on which naked

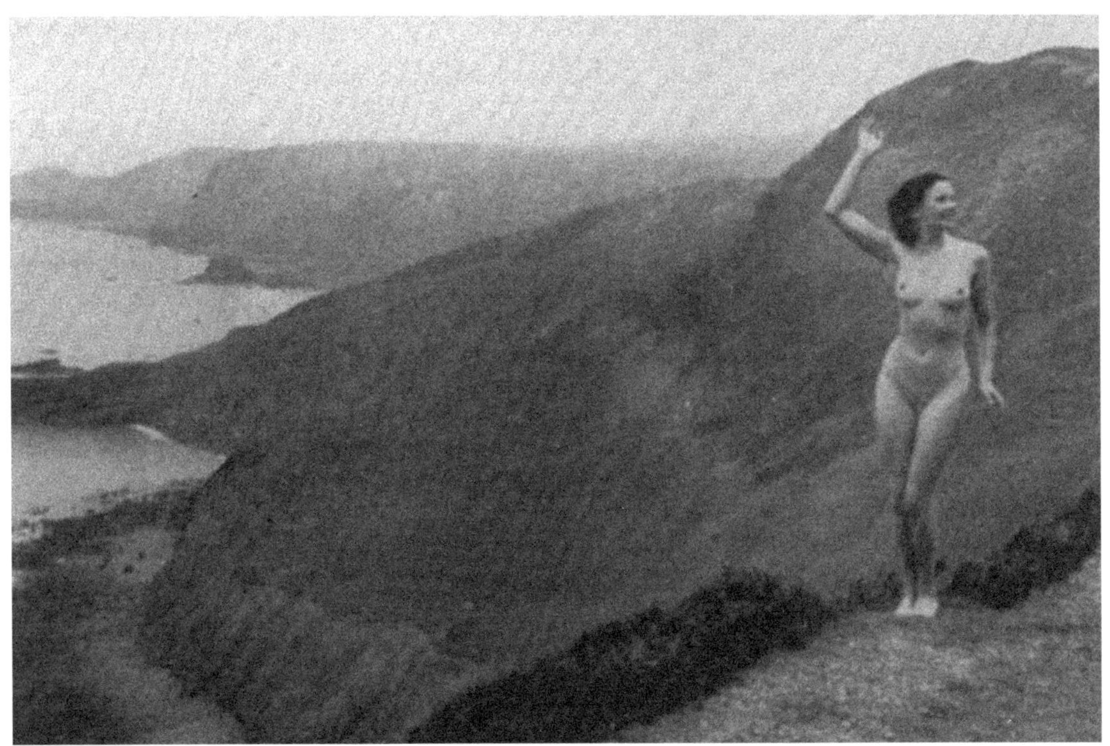

Anthony Peacock
was a prolific
photographer for
naturist publications.
His technical and
compositional skills
made him the first
nude photographer to
win accreditation from
the Royal Photographic
Society.

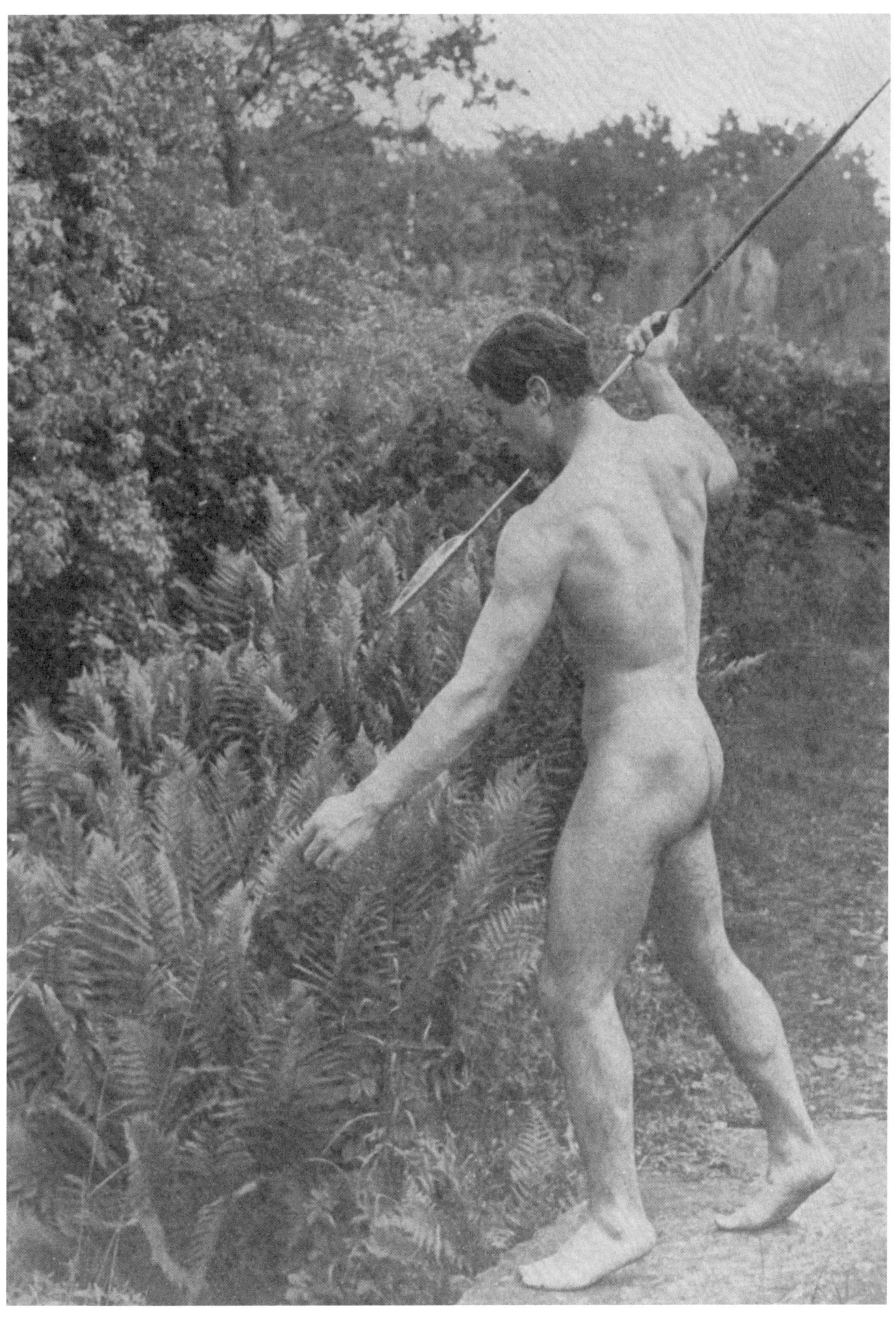

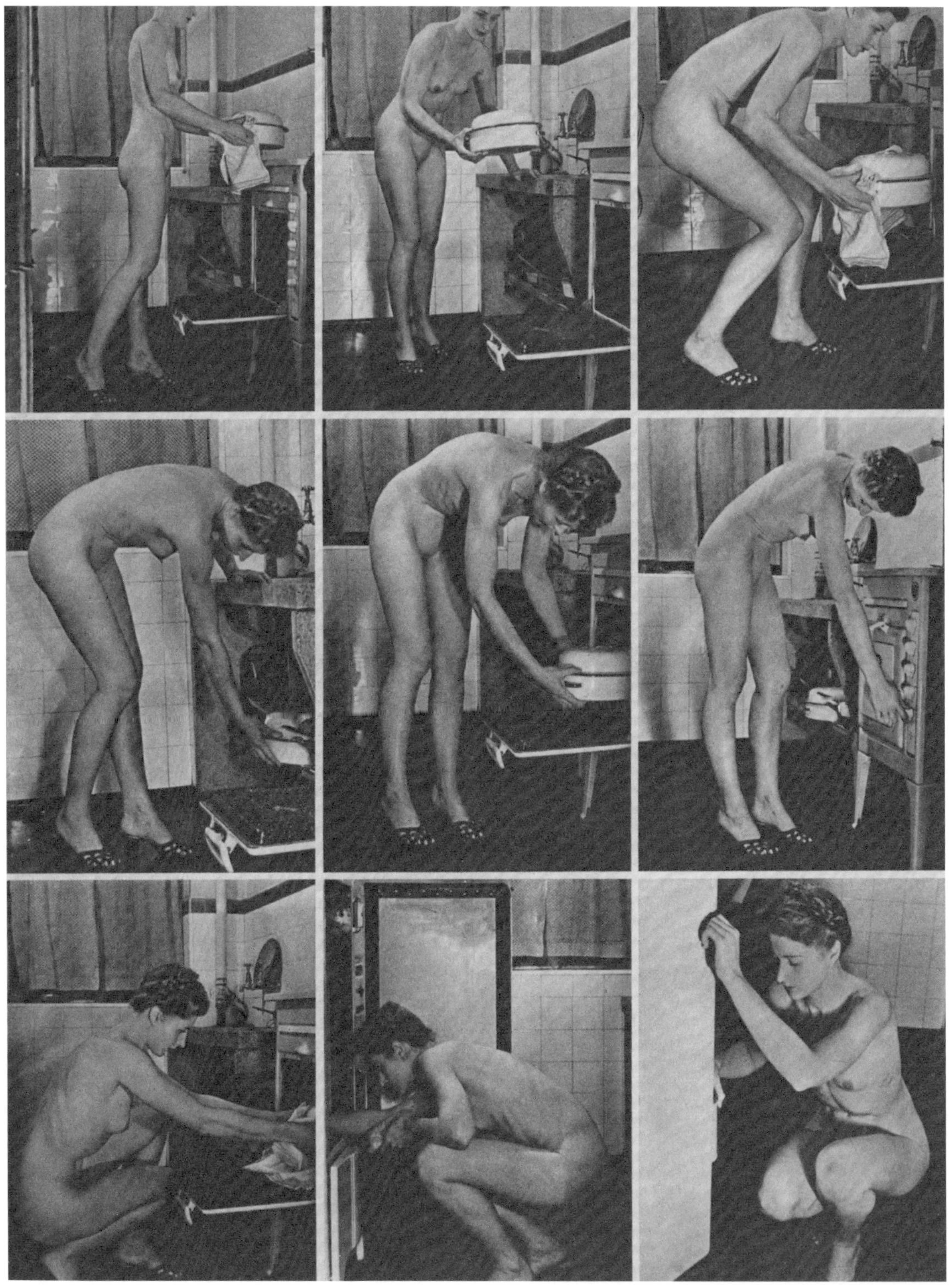

122

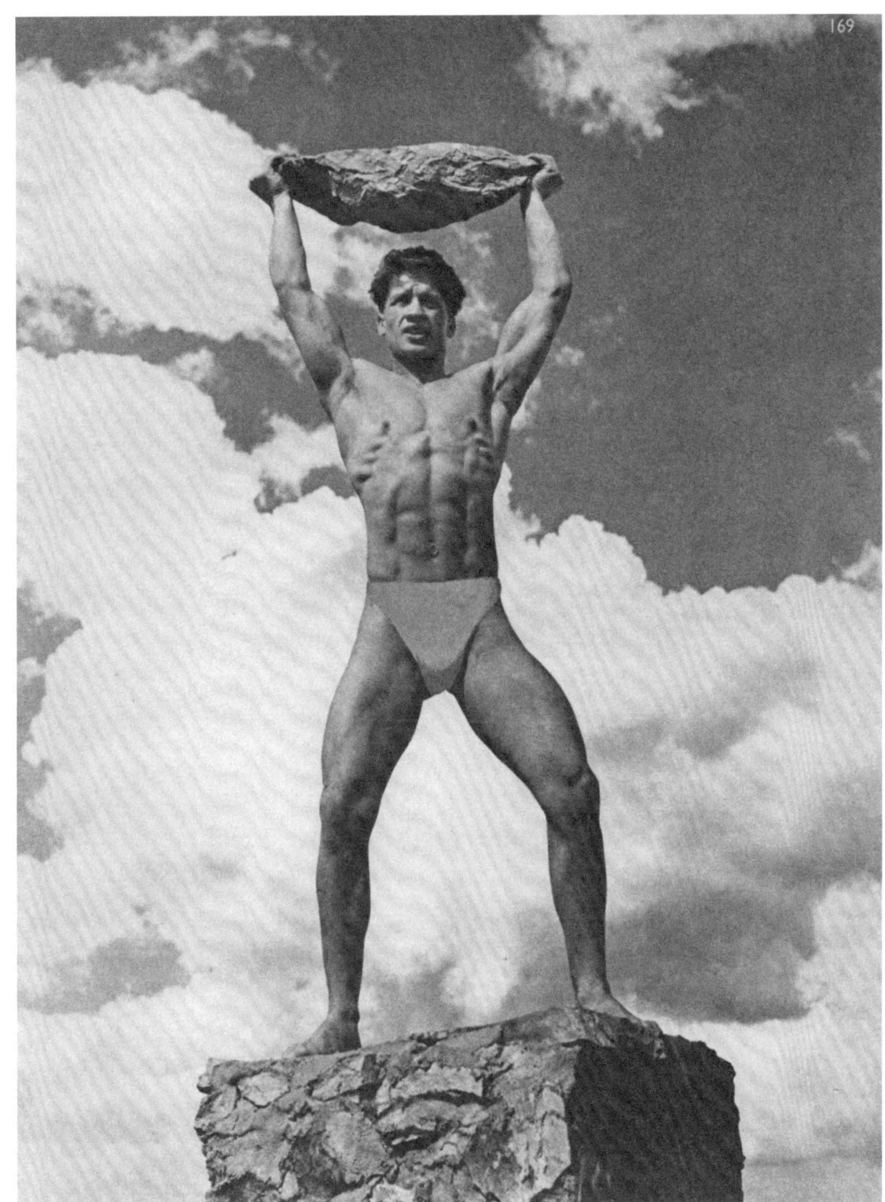

Nude publications could be legally justified if they provided source material for art students. John Everard's artist model book series in the 1950s included indoor and outdoor photographs of nude women and children alongside partially dressed men.

female sitters were moved by 30 degrees for each sequential depiction. The purpose was said to show the varying effects of light and shade from different angles. The result, however, also provided a filmic frame-by-frame sequence that enabled the viewer to consume, in turn, every angle of a woman's body. Although the book does not mention it, a longer history for *Artist's Model* could also be located in 19th-century *académies*, which represented the earliest legal nude photographs in Paris, and which also claimed to serve artists in want of live models. But these too, with their poses, props, and framings suggestive of erotic intent, seemed to be more than academic.[63]

Simpson explained Everard's photographs in relation to historic art even when the scene was decidedly modern. A photograph of a naked woman on the telephone in a series of reclining positions might suggest, to some, an intimate conversation. Simpson ignored the telephone and instead stated that "a reclining figure on a horizontal base has been one of the noblest themes of great statuary in the past", with the Parthenon and the Sistine Chapel drafted into his defence. A section dedicated to "occupational poses", that is, naked women cooking and cleaning, caused interpretive issues. Simpson confessed that this section "is not one in which it is very easy to write a critical essay from the point of view of composition or even the artistic qualities of the photograph". Referring again to the 1901 study *The Human Figure in Motion*, he admitted: "Among the hundreds of photographs of the female figure in his book, Muybridge did not include a sequence of a woman drinking tea." The photographs found in this section, he expected, would provide commercial artists with inspiration for "designing advertisements for various female requisites and lingerie".[64] While they could indeed serve that purpose, they also suggest other perspectives. Photographs, for example, showing a woman removing stockings and suspenders in slow sequence are vignetted to create peephole views. Other images show women observed, seemingly unaware, with mop, broom, and duster, naked but for high heels. No men cook or clean in the nude in domestic settings. Instead, they grapple with rocks and toss spears in the wilderness, albeit with underpants painted on for legal protection.

Everard's "sane vision" and "vigorous outlook" was praised by Simpson as a corrective to two bugbears. The first was to the "naive and unimaginative" photographs, conventionally and awkwardly posed, of "the sun bathing magazines", to which he was, in fact,

124

a regular contributor. The second was to artistic modernism, of which Simpson was no fan, and whose aesthetics naturist magazines also regularly decried as monstrous. The modernists, not mentioned by Simpson by name, but usually encapsulated in the period by the paintings of Pablo Picasso and the sculptures of Henry Moore, were said to display bodies as "victims of elephantiasis, as the relics left by famine, or, like a cinema film that jumps the sprockets, as a dancing confusion of features and limbs that have forsaken order for chaos".[65] Everard's skilful photographs, embodying enduring conventions of beauty and nature, were, he believed, the antidote; they evoked the best of modern technique while holding to a classical ideal. The Royal Photographic Society, however, disagreed. As the central arbiter of professional photographic art in Britain, it reviewed the book in its journal and found the photographs "pictorially unattractive and, in many cases, crude".[66]

A sequel, *Second Sitting*, was produced by Everard in 1955. The gender split was even greater, with 127 pages dedicated to images of nude women, compared with 31 of men (clothed), and children (nude). "Occupational Studies" continued to be peekaboo, showing women in the bath and shower. As in the previous volume, the photographs reinforced gender roles. "Outdoor Studies" of naked women saw models lying in wheat or dancing in the woods. Everard argued, "Photography of the male model calls for a completely different approach to the subject," as had Peacock before him. "The most natural method of portrayal of the male form is statuesque and in semi-classical poses, with nature's original interpretation of the male as the leader, the fighter, the gatherer of food and the hunter, glorifying in his strength."[67] There were chiaroscuro female nudes in studio settings, sometimes with come-hither facial expressions but with easels drawn around them to underscore artistic intent. Other photographs featured a cross-hatch treatment, imitating engraving techniques to emphasize artistic finish. Over 50,000 copies of Everard's first two books in the series had sold by the time *Sculptor's Model: Third Sitting* was produced in 1956. The format continued, with men in briefs in outdoor wrestling scenes and naked women as classical allegories carrying ceramic vases.

AN IDEAL ART

In mid-century Britain, drawing from the model was a staple method in art education, and art history continued to draw on a classical lineage in painting and sculpture. The nude remained a central subject in art theory and practice, even as modernist practitioners experimented with new styles. In the years that Everard was producing his photographic model books, new scholarly analyses were emerging, most particularly in Kenneth Clark's 1956 book *The Nude: A Study of Ideal Art*. As the preeminent art historian in Britain at the time, a former Director of the National Gallery and Chairman of the Arts Council, Clark's words were widely read and referenced, including in the pages of the naturist press. Charles Sennet, the author of several books about naturism, said that although "naturists do not go to our various resorts to contemplate the nude from the artistic point of view", practitioners were "grateful to men like Sir Kenneth Clark who remind the world that the nude is neither freakish nor immoral".[68]

Clark's book, from the outset, framed his subject as more than nakedness—the state of being without clothes—locating it instead as a transformed and idealized image. Rather than a direct transcription of the body, his artistic nude was transcendent and thus carried "no uncomfortable overtone". Clark was contemptuous of ordinary bodies, such as "the shapeless, pitiful model" found in life drawing rooms. Instead, he was interested in perfected forms. This meant that Clark was ambivalent about photographic nudes, which were, to him, relentlessly real. He conceded that photographers could select pleasing models and "can tone down and accentuate by retouching. But in spite of all their taste and skill," he reflected, "the result is hardly ever satisfactory to those whose eyes have grown accustomed to the harmonious simplifications of antiquity. We are immediately disturbed by wrinkles, pouches and other small imperfections which, in the classical scheme, are eliminated."[69] Photography as a high art form, despite more than a century of effort by photographic campaigners and practitioners, was still not fully consecrated in mid-century Britain. Clark's appraisal of photography's failings in the face of the nude, as art's pre-eminent subject matter, showed its continuing instability.

Sexual feeling was addressed in the book, but in the elliptical and universalizing tone of voice typical of the patrician art historian of the period. "Since the earliest of times the obsessive unreasonable nature of physical desire has sought relief in images," Clark noted obscurely. At the same time he insisted that a good nude should be appealing to the body as well as the eye, arguing: "No nude, however abstract, should fail to arouse in the spectator some vestige of erotic feeling, even although it may be only the faintest shadow—and if it does not do so, it is bad art and false morals."[70] Too much sex appeal, on the other hand, would disrupt the delicate border between art (engaging the eye and mind) and pornography (engaging the body).

Clark's book divided nudes into male Apollos and female Venuses, as per the mode of naturist publications. The former were associated with activity and character and the latter with grace and beauty. Female nudes depicted by male artists were understood by Clark to communicate universal and timeless values, rather than being the product of social and cultural circumstances, informed by power and desire. Women's bodies simply have "smoother transitions", Clark argued, and therefore for the artist, comprise more "satisfying geometrical forms, the oval, the ellipsoid and the sphere". They are "plastically more rewarding". This, of course, did not refer to all bodies. In an uncharacteristically plain-spoken statement, Clark noted that there are "more women who look like a potato than like the Cnidian Venus". Taking this observation one step further, he claimed his taste was a universal truth: "Every time we criticise a figure, saying that a neck is too long, hips too wide or breasts too small, we are admitting, in concrete terms," he asserted, "the existence of ideal beauty."[71]

This ideal particularly pertained to youth, which was contrasted with "the deplorable body of the middle aged female". Although Clark was a major supporter of modernism's challenge to conventional artistic vision, this did not extend to subject matter, to which the Ancient Greeks should be turned to for guidance. For them, "to draw from a misshapen model would have seemed [...] incomprehensible and revolting".[72] Clark, who wrote the book when he was 51, shows a similar repulsion for older women's anatomy to that found in the contemporary naturist press. Similarly, like Clark, the predominantly middle-aged male contributors and editors remained dressed in photographs or, more usually, stayed completely out of view and escaping scrutiny.

While naturists asserted that their practice was a "way of life" rather than an art form, and while Clark's argument seems to render the photographic nude as a contradiction due to its unforgiving realism, his book gave naturist magazines justification for their photographic choices. *Sun Bathing Review*, for example, observed that *The Nude*'s authority and substance was "a tribute to the importance (in these days we need not add the respectability) of the subject". Clark's argument, that without a design scheme "the nude is embarrassing", provided a riposte to those who sneered at the use of professional models in naturist photographs. In the imagery of the naturist magazine, the reviewer argued, idealized styling, bearing, and posture were equivalent to "the artist's design".[73]

HOUSEWIVES AND BEAUTY QUEENS

While young and slim women dominated naturist imagery, women of all shapes, sizes, and ages participated in the post-war naturist community. Membership continued to be strongly male-dominated—a concern described as "the greatest brake on progress against which Naturism has to battle"—and there were regular naturist press articles entitled "Women Won't be Nudists" and "My Wife Won't Join".[74] Reasons given included the lack of club comforts and fundamental suspicions of the sexual motives of men. Nonetheless, some women regularly attended and even co-led clubs.

Newsagents and booksellers reported in the early 1950s that it was rare for women to buy naturist magazines, so efforts were made to make them more appealing to potential women readers.[75] Editors did this by aligning the practice to what they saw as female concerns, including appearance. "If only women would realise that Naturism is the greatest aid to fitness and physique," one caption to a nude photograph in *The Naturist* read, "many more would join the clubs."[76] Women were directly addressed by post-war naturist advertising including promotions for Tampax tampons—a mid-century innovation that solved the issue of how menstruating women could fully disrobe in an era of cumbersome sanitary belts and pads—as well as treatments for period pain and the menopause.

In addition, women authored articles and books on a range of naturist themes, especially its gendered benefits and risks. Some post-war female authors, like their male counterparts, used pseudonyms, others, however, including those who the magazines called "celebrated authoress" June Hope Kynaston and "distinguished woman journalist" Anne Seton, were regular named contributors. In a 1953 article entitled "The Ladies—God Bless 'Em!", illustrated

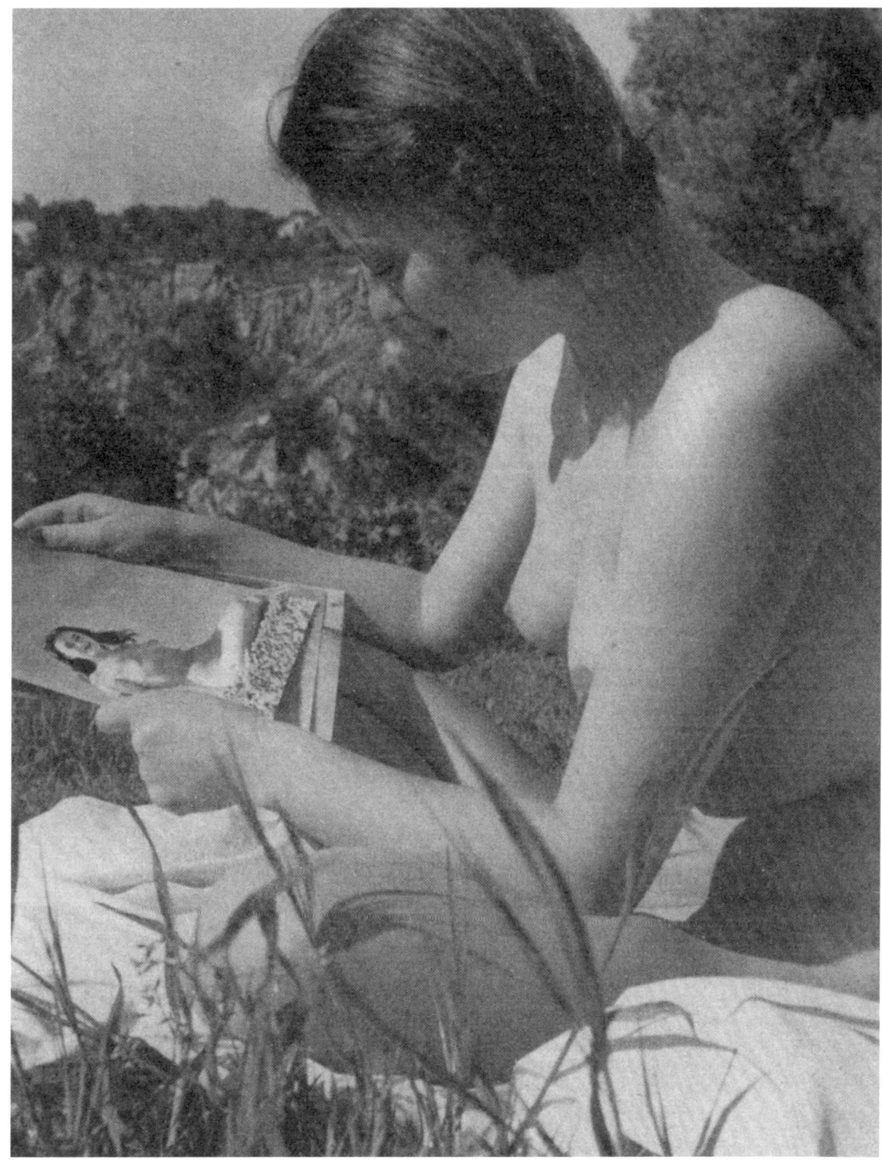

with a photograph of a bent-over naked young woman, *The Naturist* patronized even as it celebrated. "Time was where naturist journalism was almost a male prerogative," they noted, "but now we welcome contributions by more women."[77]

Female authors were not necessarily offering a more generous view to their fellow women. Post-war writers struck a strikingly different tone to the egalitarianism of early gymnosophist philosophy and nudism's pre-war feminist pioneers. Kynaston, for example, who appears outside of naturism to have been both a Christian and a believer in fairies, wanted to harness the power of nudism as a moral corrective to social deficiencies, including those that she saw as particularly feminine.[78] Among the stock characters she planned to improve with a naturist treatment was "the little plump woman who admires a fine figure, and is very body conscious. She goes to all the local films which display scantily dressed females." Recognizing women's interest in looking at the bodies of other women, Kynaston argued, "I would like to see her interest herself in the nudist pictures of the magazines instead of always the films." Kynaston presumably thought that bodies stripped of glamour would provide a wholesome alternative to the fantasies offered by Hollywood movies, although the types of models pictured made this unlikely.

Prescribing homegrown vegetables instead of her preferred "buns", Kynaston hoped that naturism would make this hypothetical woman more "diet-conscious". While she undoubtedly thought of her prescriptions as remedies for health and harmony, in the context of a magazine that advertised both weight loss and weight gain products alongside bust creams claiming to produce "lovely curves", Kynaston's guidance sounds more like what would now be called norm policing and fat shaming. She also believed that naturism would benefit the modern independent woman, or as she describes her: "the sophisticated damsel who struts around in her husband's trousers, stands legs akimbo, throwing back her bleached head while she puffs cigarette smoke into the air". Kynaston sneered, "I'd like to rip the masculine trousers off her legs-akimbo, and tell her to stand like a woman. I'd like to make her a nudist, for nudism puts the emphasis on deportment." She argued that wearing "no clothes" is "far more becoming to a woman" than wearing trousers.[79]

Seton was *The Naturist*'s agony aunt, advising on health, sex, and club etiquette, and an assistant editor to the magazine during the 1950s. In addition, she was the author of two books on naturism, *Pool of Enchantment* (1950) and *Garden of Eden* (1952), with the latter particularly recommended for any man to give to a "doubtful wife".[80] Seton revealed little of herself in her writing and even less of herself in photographs. A correspondent once asked if she was one of the beautiful young women illustrating her columns. She responded that she was not; readers would be disappointed if they saw her. Examining the role of women in naturism, Seton perpetuated gendered expectations of the time. "There are jobs which only men can do successfully," she argued, such as "the hard work of preparing the club site, chopping down trees, erecting signage—and there are equally important jobs at which women excel: the preparation of food, looking after children, providing the decorative touches which add colour to an otherwise drab pavilion."[81]

Despite this fixed positioning, she was positive about the potential of nudism to rehearse a more equal world. "Women", she argued, "are taking an ever-increasing part in occupations previously reserved entirely for the masculine sex, and there can be little doubt that both men and women can gain in understanding and outlook from this happy and natural mingling of the sexes." At the same time, Seton acknowledged that women were held to a much higher moral code, and their reputation or "honour" was a fiercely protected asset. Putting it more plainly, she asked: "Does an unmarried girl cheapen herself by allowing her naked body to be observed by men who may be complete strangers to her? Is communal nudism an invitation to unmarried men to get a cheap thrill by observing naked women?"[82] In Seton's estimation—even amid conventional assumptions of monogamous heterosexuality—better knowledge of bodies could lead to better marriages. In this position, she reflected the wider changes of the period, where modern marriages were increasingly based on expectations of mutuality and companionship, and where "the facts of life" were understood to be essential to informed preparation.[83] Other female nudists felt the same, with articles describing the practice as a "marriage-saver". Housewives were advised, for example, by "Pandora" that the invigorating effect of taking off their clothes could offset domestic drudgery: "You will probably soon find yourself feeling more energetic and better able to cope with post-war life."[84]

As well as fears about sexual impropriety, women's reluctance to join the naturist movement was frequently explained in relation to anxiety about appearance. Naturism was thus regularly claimed to improve attractiveness, not only by a fashionable tan and the bodily benefits of exercise but also by some unlikely assertions. A 1953 article, for example, in the "Beauty Bureau" section of *The Naturist* by Elizabeth Brooks, promised that for those who were "scraggy", "relaxing in the nude will help to put on weight". A previous article in *Sun Bathing Review*, on naturism's positive effect on obesity,

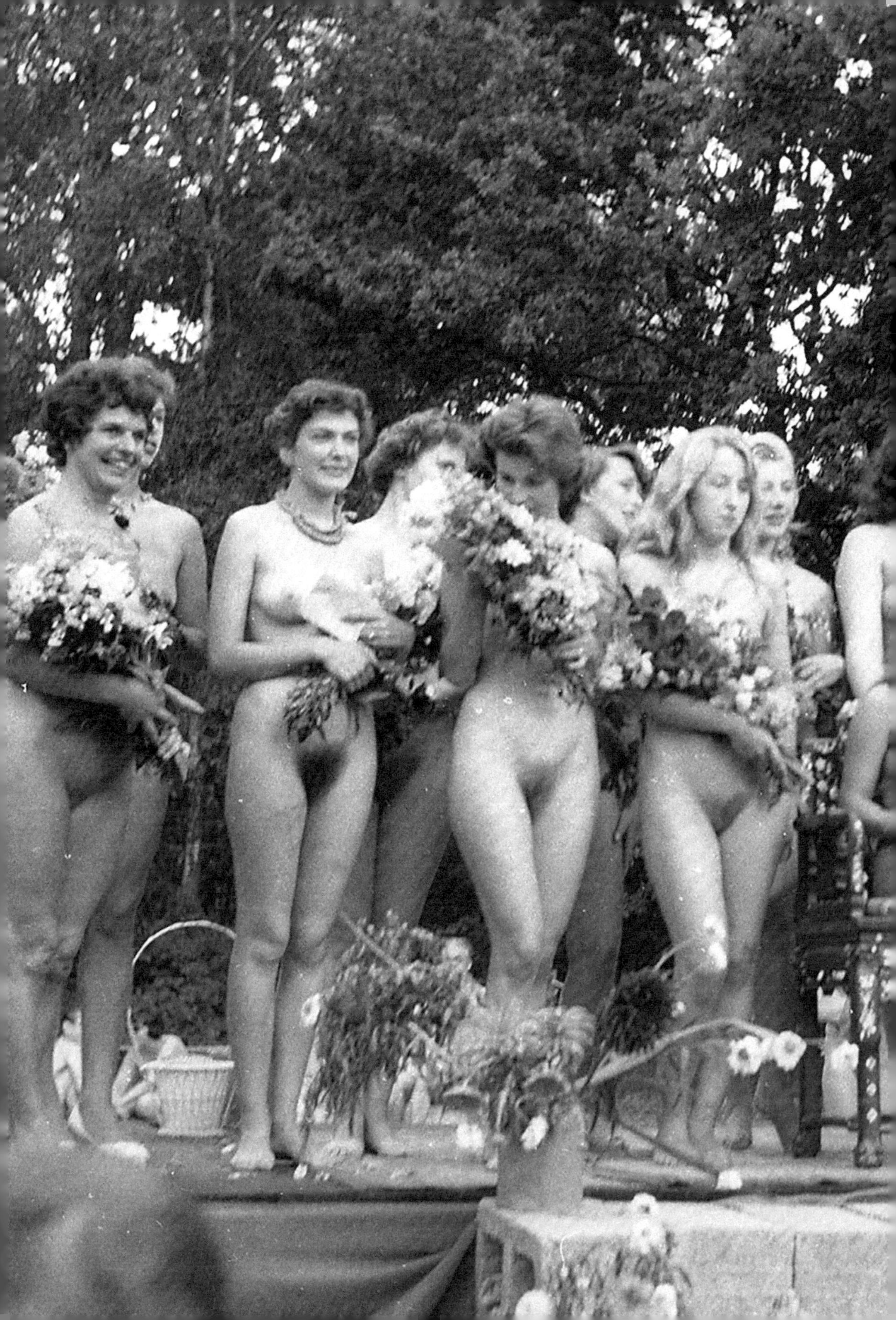

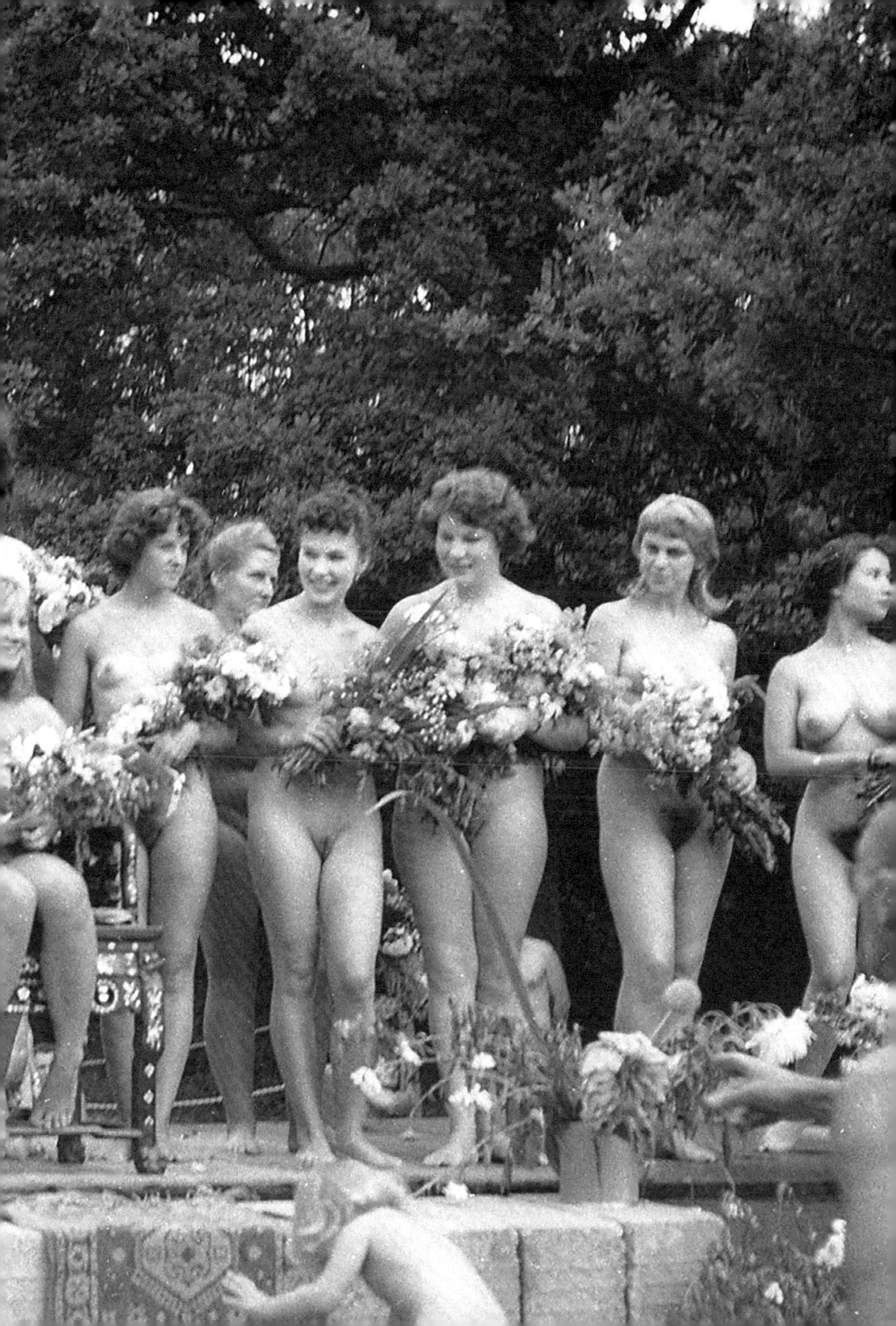

however, promised exactly the opposite.[85] In the midst of these competing claims, practising naturists such as Lynda M. Pyle of the North Kent Club offered reassurance to "the housewife who may be 'figure-conscious'": "don't be deterred if your measurements don't happen to coincide with those of the Venus de Milo. You won't be the only one!"[86] These inclusive encouragements were, however, contradicted by club practices, such as post-war naturist beauty pageants, which clearly indicated that bodies could be ranked as winners or losers.

From the late 1940s, Spielplatz hosted an annual beauty queen challenge known as the Venus competition. It was distinguished from conventional pageants by its requirement that competitors display naked "poise and deportment" rather than dressed "trappings and decorations".[87] Poses, performed in the open air on a plinth covered with a Persian carpet, were allegorical and mythological, including "Stargazing" and "Renunciation". The result, however, was always a young and slim set of contenders and a crowned and enthroned winner.[88] Although there was obvious delight taken in the event by both competitors and organisers, there were moral debates in the naturist press about the value of these activities. As one female contributor put it, "I don't see why we shouldn't recognise and applaud exceptional beauty when we see it. On the other hand, we mustn't forget that this feature must be kept to a minor aspect of the Naturist Movement."[89] Vanity had originally been part of what naturism was meant to counter but appraising bodies remained central. Pam Colbourne, another of *The Naturist*'s female journalists, advised, "A girl need not mind being openly 'observed'—especially if it is with obvious admiration."[90] Post-war publications admitted that there was some truth in the joke that there is no such thing as a blind naturist.[91] Looking was permitted if neutral; as the Spielplatz brochure put it, "It is just as pleasant to look upon well-kept human bodies as upon fine horses, racehounds or birds on the wing."[92] Like many naturist writings, however, these positions often assume a male viewer and a female subject. When women did the looking, different debates arose.

Women journalists reflected on how naturist magazines might appear to female readers. Elizabeth Somers, for example, a regular contributor to *Health and Efficiency*, imagined the following scenario: "Suppose one's husband comes home one night with a copy of a naturist magazine and suggests with admirable casualness that you and he try it. Just how does one react?" In her reckoning, for this imagined first-time reader, "she'll study the photographs very carefully, probably the single studies most carefully at first—with some very private mental comparisons between their figures and her own. When she has finished looking at the photographs (and we can be quite sure that she will look at them more than once), she'll probably be wondering what it is all about."[93] While the purpose of the article was to persuade "sensible women" to "have a go", it acknowledged that women would be likely to approach naturist material self-critically rather than neutrally; idealized imagery hardly helped. Any idea that a woman might look at images of other women with any type of sexual interest went unmentioned; it was simply beyond the pale.

What of women looking at naked men? The subject was barely acknowledged, though a rare statement was made by Mervyn Oakdale, author of *The Mystery of Naturism*. "The legal view is that the sight of a man without clothes is an affront to a woman," he said. However, he conceded, "Women today are very unlike the timid, whimpering, fainting creatures whom the male novelists of another age were wont to convey."[94] In the cautious context of post-war naturism, this euphemistic writing was as close as British naturists dared to get to acknowledging women's sexual appetites.

While most models in the naturist press remained unnamed, there were some significant exceptions.[95] Dorothy Macaskie, co-founder of Spielplatz with her husband Charles, regularly appeared in Spielplatz literature and the wider naturist press, often wearing nothing but her trademark pearls and a hostess sash to show her position as the club's matriarch. Her daughter, Iseult, born 1932, was also regularly photographed in the naturist press, including throughout her childhood. While images of children had been included in the early naturist publications to underscore its family focus, the aesthetic appraisal of her body struck a very different tone. An article from 1950 in *The Naturist* appraised photographs of Iseult up to the age of 17. The author of a book on Spielplatz asked, "Is Iseult the most-photographed nudist girl in the world? Most people think she is. Most people think she deserves to be. We are inclined to agree."[96]

As women with a platform, Dorothy and Iseult were consulted on naturism's value to their sex. As propagandists, both were inevitably enthusiastic but they also expressed some caution, not least as to how a woman could be appropriately naturist and discard the material world of femininity. Dorothy admitted in 1956 that women do not usually take kindly to naturism straight away; she noted that they often compare themselves unfavourably with naturist models and, she added, "Women love clothes, and they feel unhappy if their clothes are taken away for a prolonged period."[97] Iseult, despite being born naturist, was anxious to show that she was fully socialized and had not been "brought up as some kind of freak"; as such, she emphasized how much she adored "pretty clothes", even wearing a swimming costume on holiday. Her father complained, "Sometimes I think that no woman is ever at heart a true nudist." Dorothy made a counterclaim: "Of course every woman loves clothes. I do myself. But it is only the true nudist who can get the full value from attractive clothes, because she is not a slave to them."[98]

SUBJECTS AND OBJECTS

One of the most visible women in post-war naturist photographs is Pamela Green, who now has a cult following.[99] As, variously, an artist's life model, cabaret dancer, member of Spielplatz, photographic cover model for *Health and Efficiency* and *Sun Bathing Review*, and a regular subject for photographers Stephen Glass, Bertram Park, Yvonne Gregory, and John Everard, as well as being one of the most widely pictured mid-century British glamour models for pin-up photography and striptease film, Green traversed all of the domains that naturist writers tended to morally segregate, revealing their interconnection and their interdependence. As a trained artist as well as a striking model with a dancer's deportment, she produced as well as starred in nude publications.

Green began modelling for artists in 1948 when studying Fashion Drawing at St Martin's School of Art in London (now the illustrious art and design school Central Saint Martins). In 1949 she joined Spielplatz in pursuit of an all-over tan and in 1950 won its Venus competition. In the same years she was working as an underwear model and as a nude showgirl in the Follies at the Prince of Wales Theatre, London. There she met George Harrison Marks, a bespectacled jobbing photographer with a beatnik style and a small live-in studio in Soho, a bohemian area of the capital well-known for the production and sale of sexual material. By the end of 1953 they were living and working

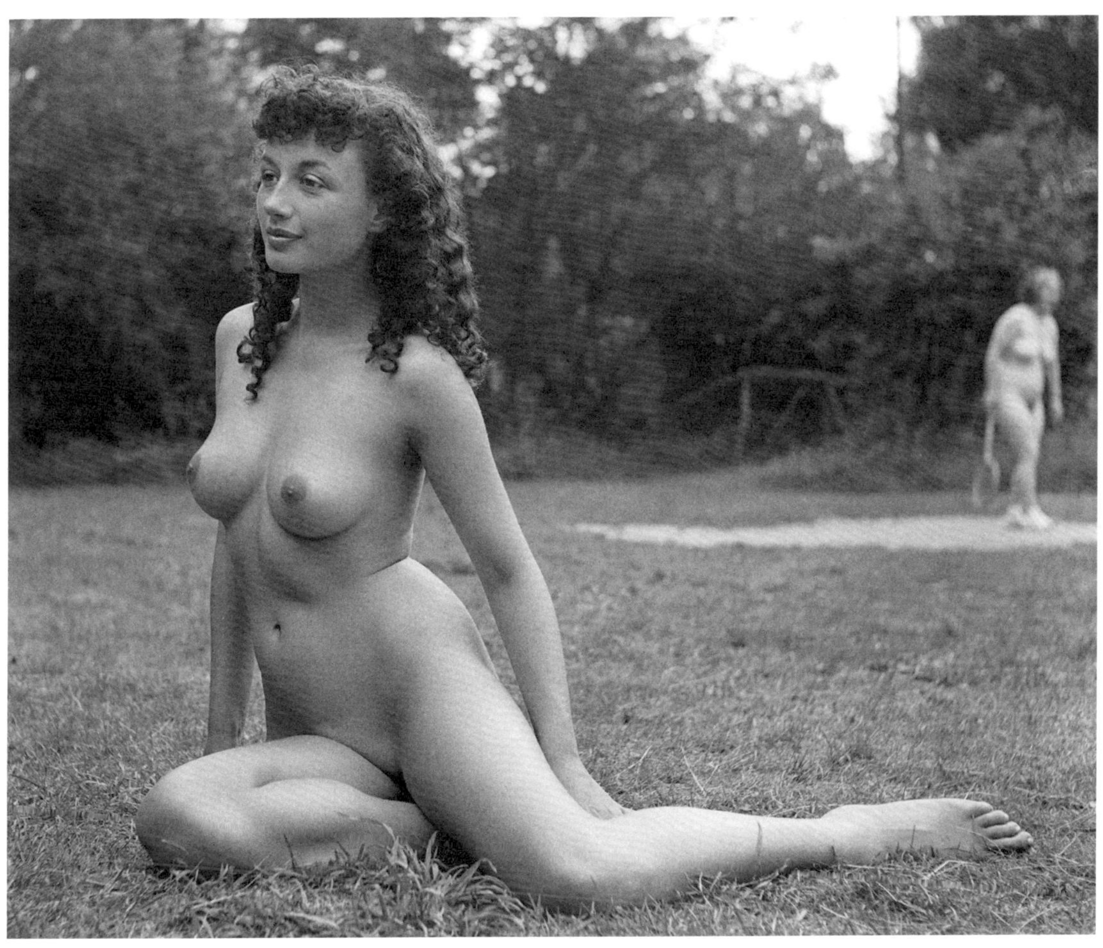

Stephen Glass was a regular naturist photographer. Many of his images were taken at Spielplatz nudist camp, including this one of young model Pamela Green. His framing and focus avoids the larger, older woman in the background.

together, producing glamour photographs for local bookshops and, subsequently, running a thriving Soho photographic gallery and a mail order business providing magazines and books, calendars and slide sets, 3D photographs and 8 mm films to feed the decade's expanding market for depictions of young women posed in lingerie in indoor "glamour" settings as well as nude in outdoor "naturist" style.[100]

Green was the model for many of these productions, including as the sole focus for Harrison Marks's 1955 book *Pamela: A Portrait in 58 Studies*, which included dramatically lit studio nudes, naturist-style outdoor nudes, and highly sexualized glamour shots. In addition to modelling under her own name, she also took on a range of alternative guises to cater for different fantasies, donning a long auburn wig over her short brown hair to become a fictional Parisian model called

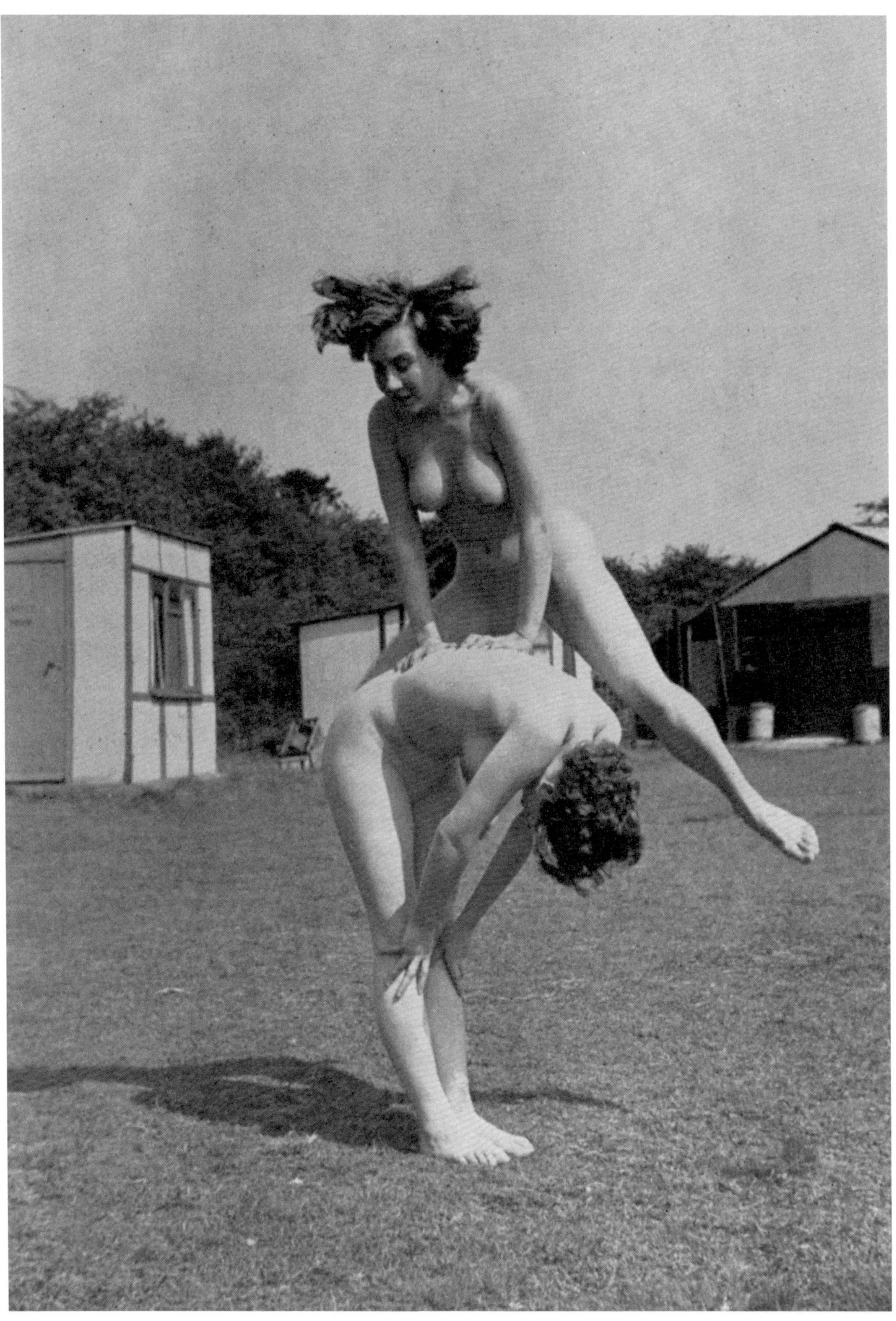

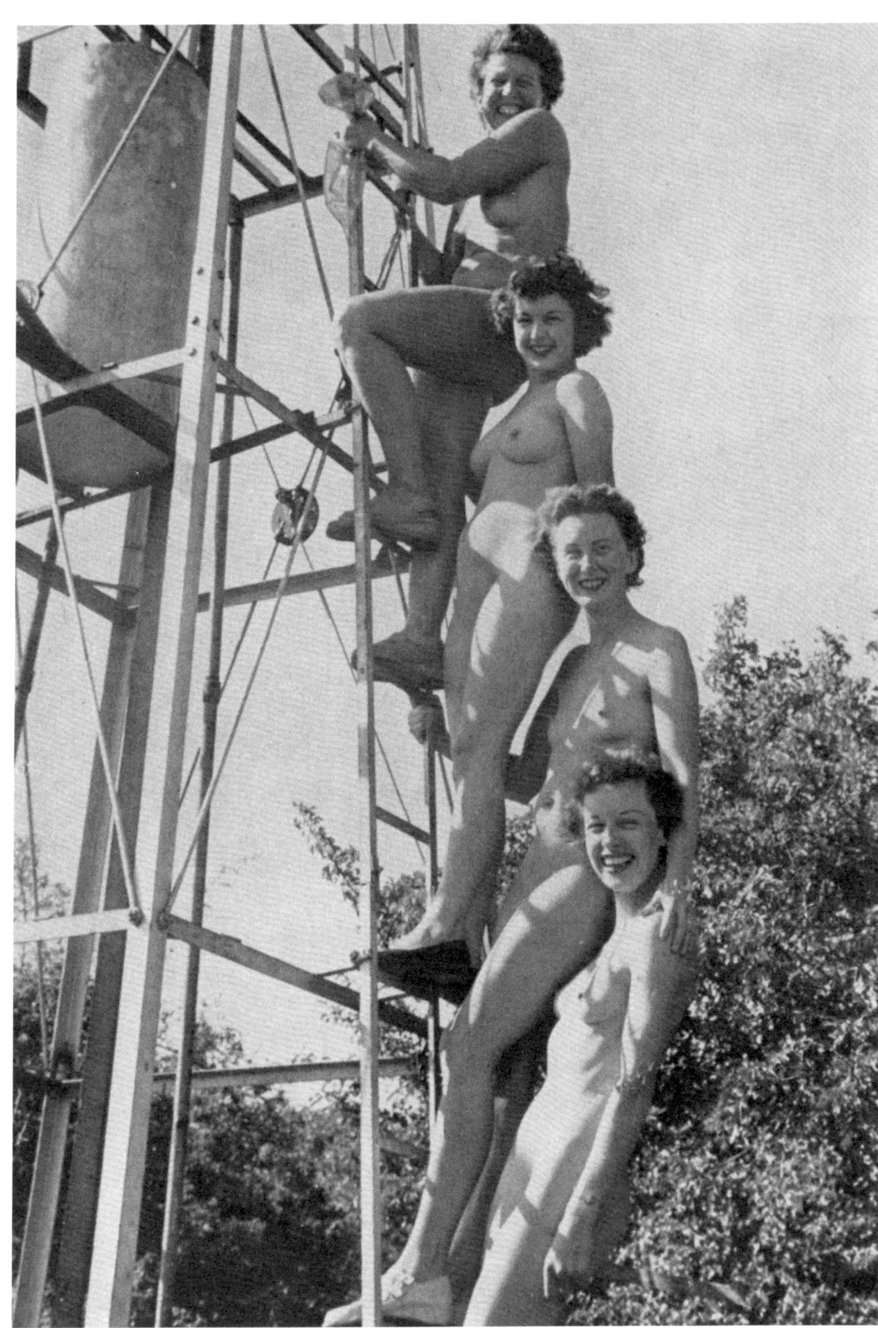

Colin R. Clark was a member of the Royal Photographic Society and an attendee of many naturist clubs. His lively mid-century photographs show the range of ages, sizes, and shapes among members.

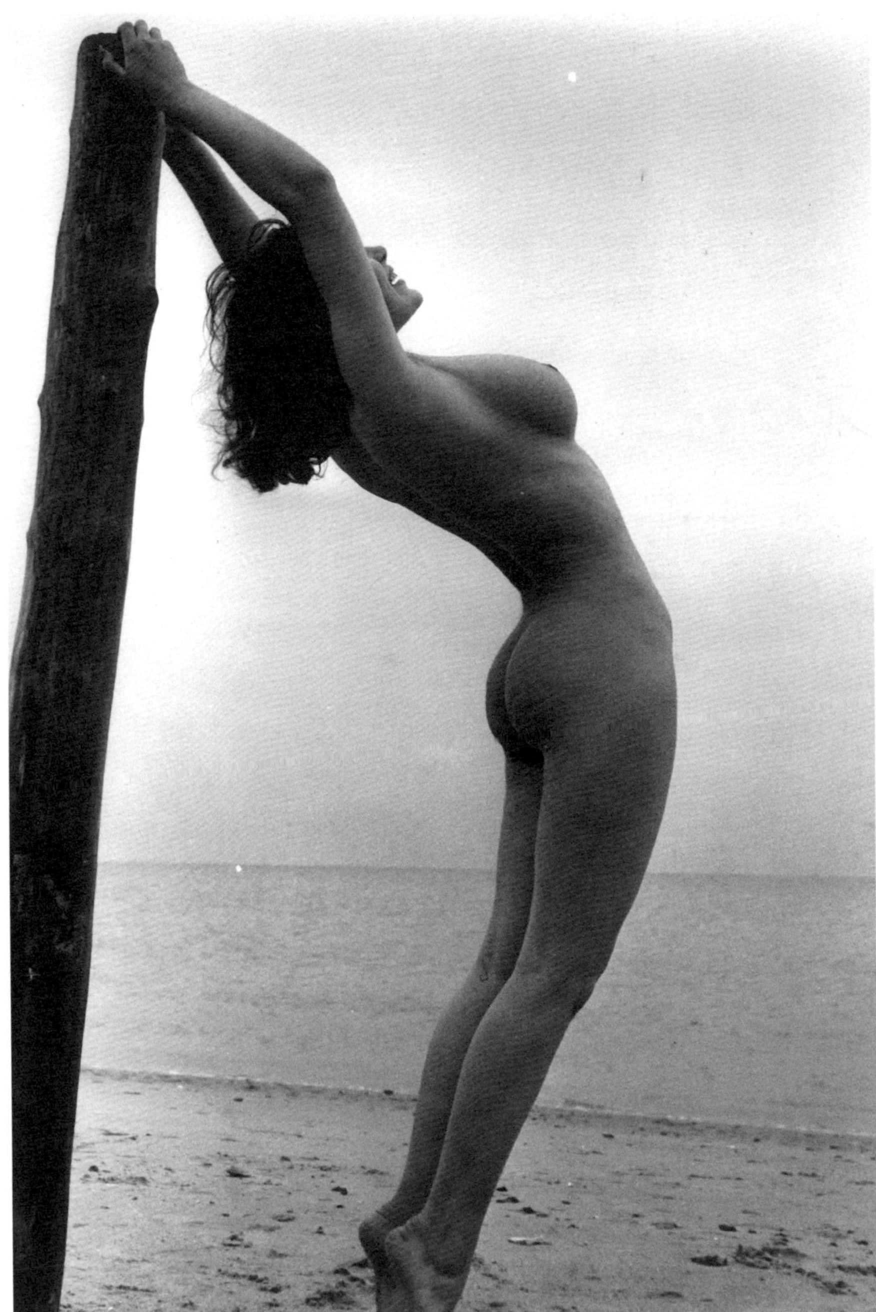

Eva Grant was a rare female nude photographer who not only provided photographs for 1950s naturist publications but also produced her own magazine of sexualised female nudes, *Line and Form*. A former model, Grant ran a busy photographic studio providing instruction for amateurs.

Rita Landre, and putting on blackface to become the spurious so-called "Eastern" Princess Sonmar Harricks (an anagram of Harrison Marks' name). In addition, she painted studio scenery and sewed costumes, selected and choreographed models, retouched pubic hair from photographic negatives for legal necessity and, with Harrison Marks, selected prints for publication. Although the business carried his name, Green undertook much of the labour and, even after they parted ways at the end of the decade, Harrison Marks credited Green for setting him up and starting it all.[101]

Green's active roles on both sides of the camera in the creation of photographs for mass market titillation cannot be neatly accommodated into the rigid moral landscape of naturist discourse in the 1950s. Showgirls and partially dressed glamour models were positioned as the murky shade to naturism's bright light; pin-up producers with their base intentions were the moral enemy of naturism's high-minded purity. Cheaply manufactured pocket-size pulp magazines were the cultural abject of the high-end expensive art volumes, yet Green appeared in them all. Green in naturist guise at the seaside, in the woods, and at the naturist club may have been styled as "Beach Maiden", "Beauty Unadorned", and "Sculptor's Model" but in the same years she was bending and pouting in a different set of poses and for a different set of publications, wearing nylon negligees, fishnet stockings, and satin corsets in leopard-print-draped boudoirs in Soho studios.

At the same time, Eva Grant, a former glamour model turned glamour photographer, similarly crossed borders. Grant had begun modelling for swimwear pin-ups for amateur photographers to supplement her income but found she could earn more in an hour than in a week as a student nurse. She found modelling boring, however, and grew more interested in a role behind the camera.[102] As a photographer, she sold outdoor nudes to *Health and Efficiency* in the mid-1950s but also supplied more suggestive photographs for cheap pin-up magazines while producing her own pocket-sized publication, *Line and Form*, under her publishing imprint Photoform. In addition to modelling and taking photographs, Grant acted as a nude model agent, ran a busy central London studio providing instruction for aspiring nude photographers, and penned advice articles for photographic magazines.

In these, she detailed what was distinctive about being a female nude photographer. "It helps break down that innate suspicion", she said, "that lurks deep down in the heart of every young girl when she stands unclothed, for the first time, in the presence of a strange man." In addition, she noted that having been a model herself gave her "tremendous advantage" in reaching a successful result, which was a "combined effort" produced by "a true bond between the two persons either side of the camera".[103] This team approach presented a rather different viewpoint to some mid-century male photographers who considered mastery of the nude to be a measure of virility.[104] By the end of the decade Grant was selling work on both sides of the Atlantic. British photography magazines called her "one of the most expert and experienced woman glamour photographers in the business" and in the US she was described as "the world's foremost female figure photographer".[105]

FLIMSY BOUNDARIES

Just as models traversed different territories, there was no clear water between naturist and non-naturist photographers in 1950s magazines. One 1955 issue of *Health and Efficiency* magazine offers a typical example of cross-fertilisation. Groon, grasping a crop of grass, was the subject of an outdoor nude in a dry-stone-walled field by Harrison Marks in a photograph entitled "In the Warm Sun". The front and inside feature nude women at the seashore photographed by Russell Gay, another leading British glamour photographer of the era, who was once described as a "curve prospector".[106] Gay founded the 1950s pin-up magazine *QT: The Best of Beauty* and launched the career of the popular model Sabrina (Norma Sykes from Stockport), marketed as a busty British "blonde bombshell", before he went on to establish prominent 1960s British pornographic magazines *Knave* and *Fiesta*.

Articles in this 1955 sample issue include dry reading about replanting rhododendrons and repairing pavilions from the Federation of British Sun Clubs, including the evocatively titled Shangri-La club in Lancashire, the Arcadian Fellowship of Billericay, and the Sun-Folk Society of St Albans. Articles expound naturism's benefits to body and mind, emphasizing that "naturists are clean-minded people. In a world full of smutty jokes, sordid themes for novels, plays and music-hall acts, and every kind of suggestive exploitation of sex, a sun club stands as a kind of oasis."[107] In a further article in the same issue, Wallace Arter, an early gymnosophist and a 1920s attendee of the first English nudist club, appraised changing attitudes to nude photography. He reflected that booksellers can sell "nudes to schoolboys" by pleading in court that "pictures of nudist camps" can be seen on any bookstall. Arter complained, "The Naturist movement is linked, in the mind of the public and, apparently, the Law, with any form of nakedness." He asked, "Can we get any satisfaction from being 'bracketed' with some of the near-the-line pin-up rubbish which is on sale?"[108]

Whether they liked it or not, or knew it or not, British naturist publications in the mid-1950s were part of a continuum of models, photographers, and advertisers who traded in naked bodies as part of a rapid boom in commercial print culture and shifting patterns of taste. Pictorial periodicals as a whole had grown from a circulation of 26 million in 1938 to more than 40 million in 1952.[109] Cultural critic Richard Hoggart, writing in 1957, saw the huge growth of pin-up, glamour, or "cheesecake" photographs as "the most striking visual feature of mid-20th-century mass art".[110] Reviewing the previous 15 years, he stated: "Pin-ups used to be, and still are, standard decoration for servicemen's billets and the cabs of lorries; but now, whether we will or no, we are assaulted by them."[111]

The mid-1950s mass-circulation magazines that Hoggart described as "small picture-monthlies", costing around a shilling and frequently depicting, as he put it, "a pleasantly English-looking chorus girl from Scunthorpe, tricked out unconvincingly in silk pants and brassiere", precisely characterized the glamour magazines developed by Harrison Marks, Russell Gay, and others from the mid-1950s.[112] With colour covers but black-and-white photographic interiors, they sold cheek-by-jowl with naturist and amateur photography magazines in high-street newsagents and bookshops. Glamour magazines were deliberately designed to be sexually alluring but they also conveyed enough innocence to be sold by the most mainstream of retailers. In London's Soho in the 1950s, by contrast, specialist independent bookshops also sold pin-up pictorials, nudist magazines, and nude art books, but in these locations they were merely the front-of-house window dressing for a lucrative and furtive backroom trade in more raw material. For those who knew what to ask for, there were hardcore photographs and explicit typescript publications for sale depicting copulation in all its forms: straight and gay, flagellation and bondage, fetish and beyond. While some of these hardcore photographers recruited their models from 1950s nudist clubs, their secretive,

143

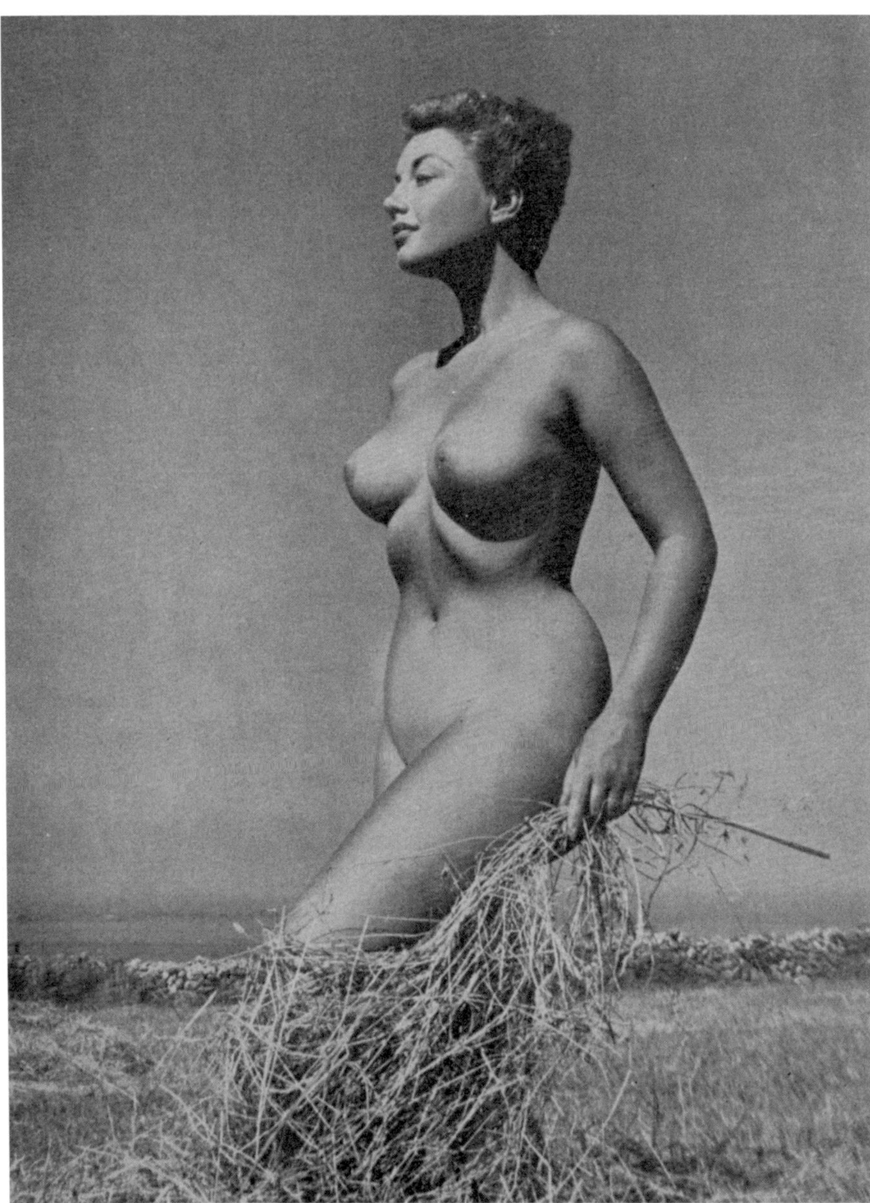

George Harrison Marks and his business and romantic partner Pamela Green were key figures in glamour photography production in mid-century Britain. As photographer and model, they jointly produced material for naturist and erotic destinations alike.

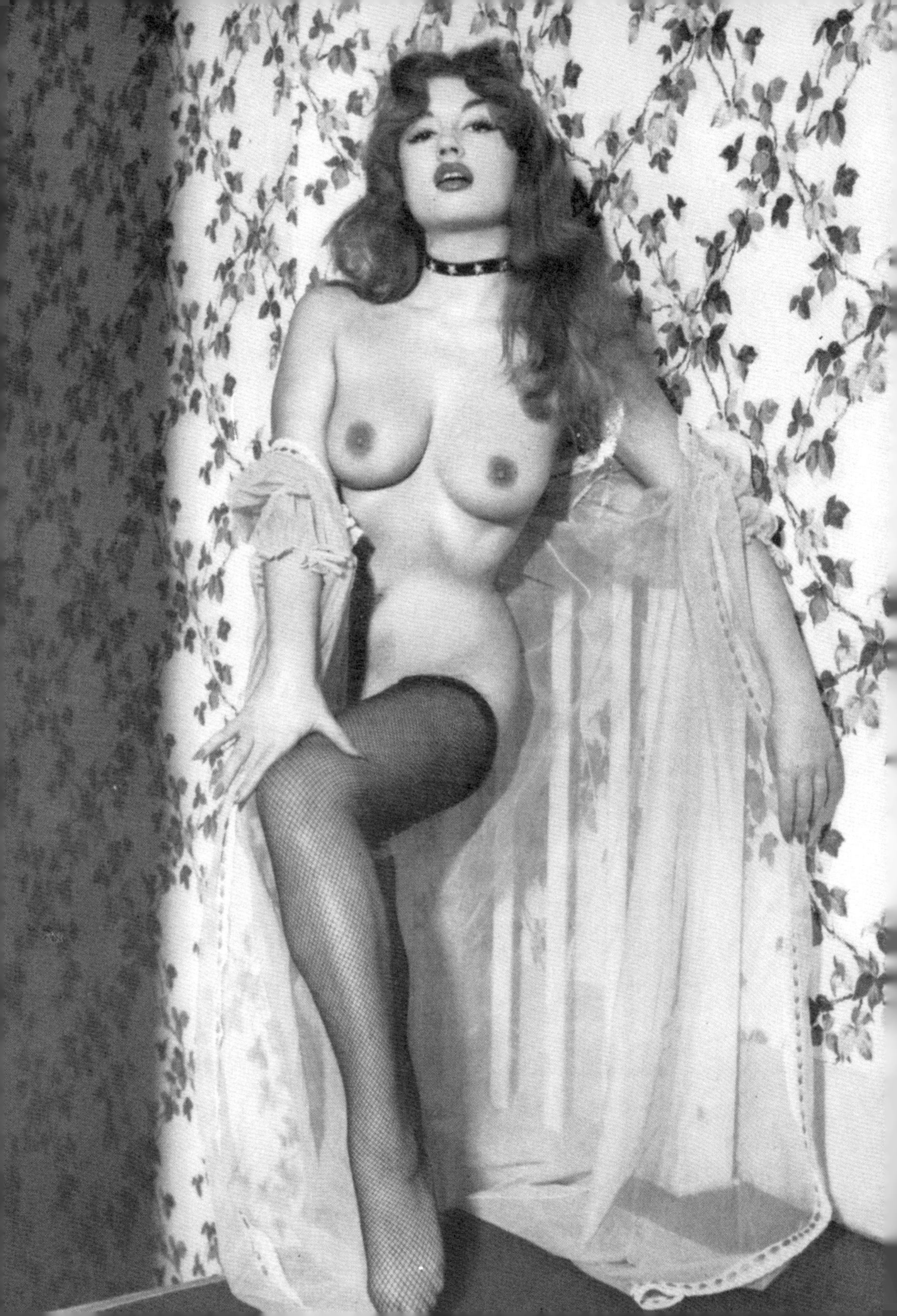

under-the-counter end products stood apart, spatially and culturally, from the popular pin-up and naturist publications sold in the open air.[113] Morally and legally, however, the lines were less clear, as will be shown.

THE GREAT LEVELLING

The 1950s were still marked by acute class-consciousness in Britain but structural changes and improving material conditions resulted in some traditional class divisions becoming less pronounced. This included educational reforms that made selective schooling and university education more possible for many, alongside significant urban redevelopment, the building of new towns, and the provision of new council housing.[114] Hoggart was a product of some of these changes. From an impoverished upbringing in Leeds, he had received an educational scholarship and became the first member of his family to receive a university education. From his own perspective, these social upheavals, alongside the coming of mass media, commercial pop culture, and cheap American imported pleasures, posed a threat to the traditions of authentic British working-class life. The titillating photographic magazine embodied this. Its readers, he bemoaned, were "exchanging their birthright for a mass of pin-ups".[115]

Commercial newsstand magazines were expanding audiences for nude and semi-nude photography at the same time as nudism was recording a broadening of membership from its founding days when it was an elite group. In the 1930s, "it was rare to hear from a nudist who belonged to the 'working classes'", the editor of *The Naturist* asserted. The maturity of naturism meant "a great levelling", in his reckoning, and he was proud to boast a post-war readership that now included "farm-hands, factory workers, clerks, shop assistants, Service men and women, as well as from the professional and leisured classes".[116] The normalisation of naturism in the post-war period was demonstrated by a shift in attitudes and practices from the intellectual and artistic interests of the early days, with its vegetarianism, expressionist dance, and rhythmic exercise, to a mid-century naturist culture where British clubs offered, for example, darts and pie suppers.

Ingeborg Boysen, a prominent German naturist, noted how faithfully mid-century British practitioners brought their "old accustomed manners and habits from the everyday world" to the clubs, including smoking and wearing make-up. She pointed out: "Continental naturists don't stop washing, combing, cutting their nails and caring for their appearance, but they don't set too much store by artificial methods and preparations. They care for themselves by physical culture, by water, air and light, and not by powder, brilliantine, perfumes and cosmetics." She warned British naturists to remember that naturism's purpose was healthy life reform "and you can't do that simply by throwing off your clothes and sitting with a pipe in your armchair!"[117]

As British naturism developed its own identity and found security in endurance, some members cautiously critiqued the longstanding puritanical claims of those who argued that the practice was high-minded. They confessed that they did not sit about in discussion of lofty subjects. In a 1953 article entitled "Why Don't We Tell the Truth?" a naturist author volunteered: "As a rule, my conversation is pretty puerile, ranging around my job, films and plays, beer, cigarettes, and women." He wanted naturists to admit that they too felt self-conscious when naked and that sexual attraction did not evaporate when one enters a club. "People talk and behave in exactly the same way, and do precisely the same things," he observed, reasonably. "They enjoy the same pleasures except that they have an additional one—nudism. It neither raises nor lowers their morals, nor affects their outlook on life."[118] As the 1950s progressed, British naturists rationalized and standardized the practice away from accusations of eccentricity, to render it as an equivalent to, as one author put it, "breeding canaries or collecting horse-brasses or carving model boats".[119]

CLASS AND TASTE

Despite this purported shift towards a more egalitarian culture in nudist clubs, class remained a prevailing factor in discussions about the morally "good" nudes of naturist publications and the base inclinations of other portrayals. Naturist nudes, in the consensus of the period, should be wholly unclothed, pictured outdoors in sunshine, and communicate health with athletic bodies. Their negative opposites would be taken in a studio setting, in artificial light, and would include suggestive garments and voluptuous figures. How the model was shaped, how the camera was angled, and how the gaze was engaged could be all that kept photographic categories morally apart.

These flimsy demarcations were a tightrope for a nude

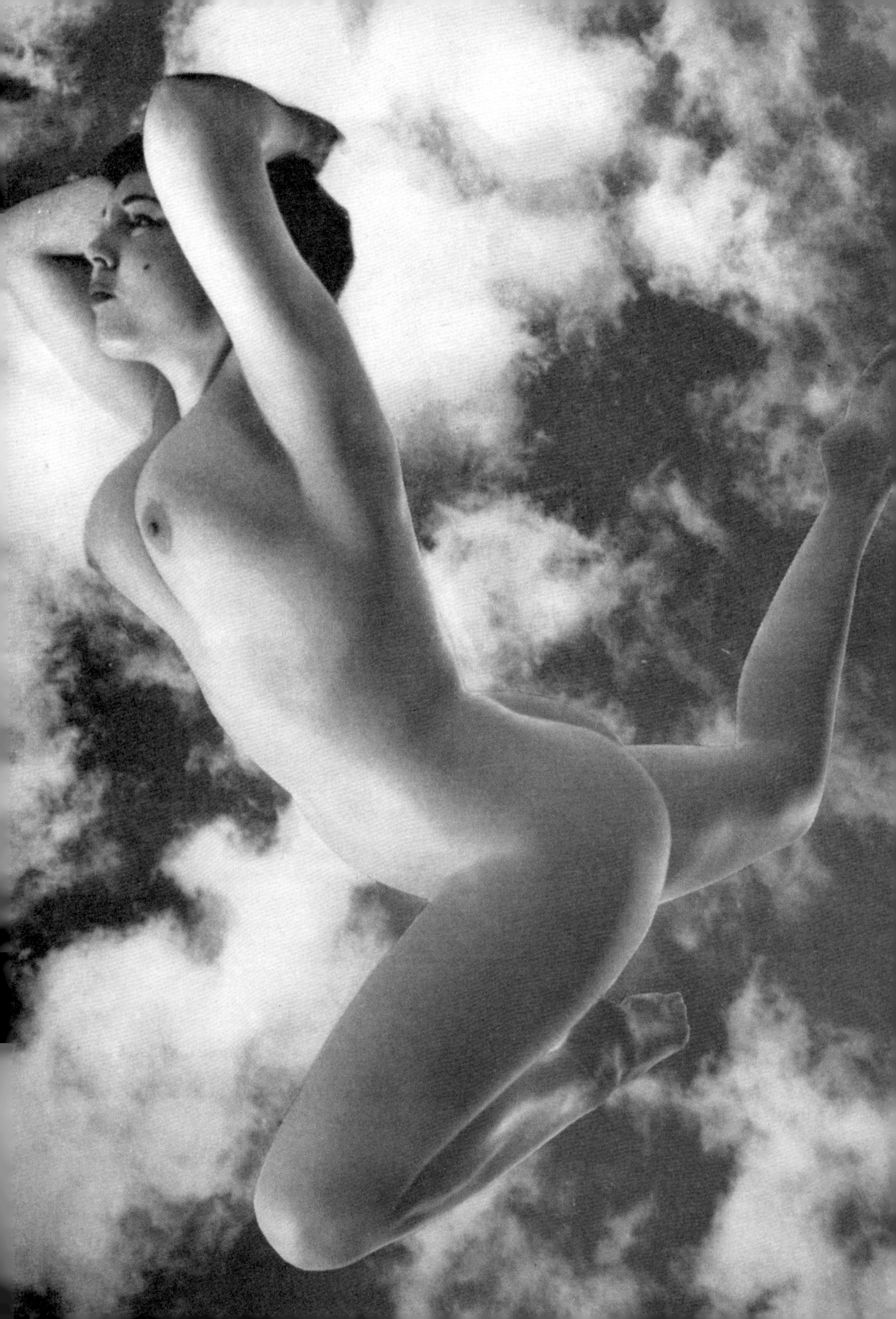

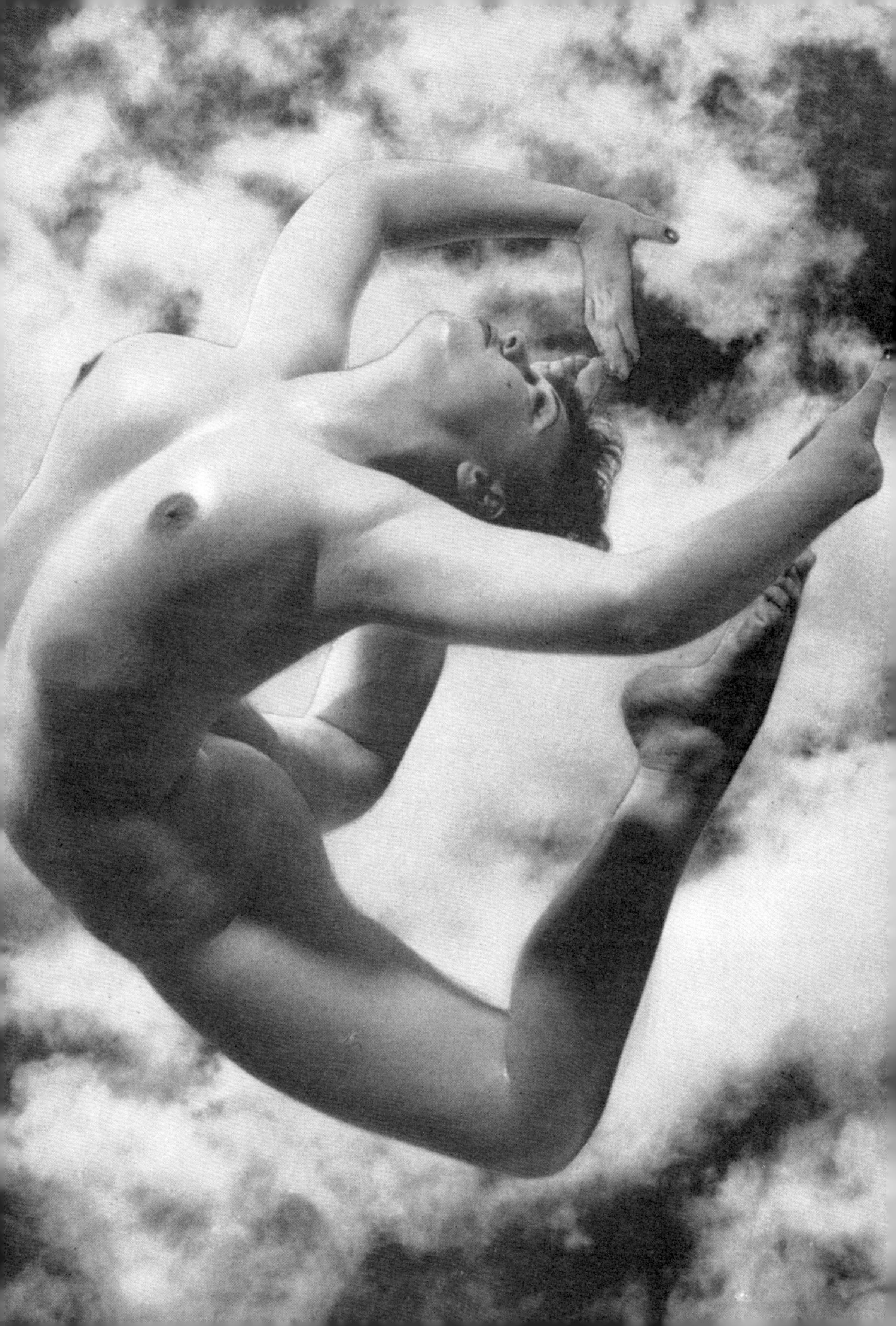

photographer to walk, and class was often conjured to secure moral superiority. Roye's work, for example, was regularly discussed in terms of his unassailable good taste; reports also emphasized his refined manners as well as his wealth. In 1955, the *Sunday Pictorial* gushed about his "magnificent four-storey Georgian house in Belgravia", his "well-cared for hands", and his "immaculately tailored grey worsted suit". Ever the gentleman photographer, dressed in a bow tie and "sipping a dry sherry", his aristocratic manner secured his respectability even as he produced what the magazine called "saucy snaps".[120] Roye always emphasized the importance of social standing in constructing a worthwhile nude. His models, he insisted, were a better class of woman. "I find that lack of breeding often expresses itself in a gracelessness of movement and a want of symmetry," he stated. "Most of my girls have come from better-than-average backgrounds, and an amazing proportion have been daughters of clergymen."[121]

Other articles by male photographers of "figure studies" betrayed class judgements. Photographer Ken Greenwood, for example, writing in the magazine *PhotoART*, ostensibly an independent illustrated guide to amateur photography but mostly a means to sell photographic nudes under Roye's ownership, stated: "Unless I have a really first class model I am not interested in taking any figure shots. I feel that many of the so-called models would have been better employed and better advised if they had stayed behind their counters and typewriters." He complained of such subjects, "There is nothing worse than to see nude studies of figuratively speaking imperfect models who—unfortunately—are all too often featured in some magazines. There is an unpleasant tendency towards out of proportion, outsize busts and undue emphasising of other anatomical parts. This is not art," he concluded, "it is bawdyism."[122]

The baseless connections made between "imperfect" body shapes and humble social standing echo eugenicist ideas about fitness and social superiority, while the moral connections built between so-called vulgar imagery and vulgar culture—evoked in the phrase "some magazines"—show how cheap content was associated with immorality on the part of the model and the viewer. The differences between categories were partially economic: cheap magazines were assumed to display low morals, and expensive publications were seen to display elite good taste. These were values that money could buy. Despite this, as a cheap pocket-sized vehicle for pin-ups

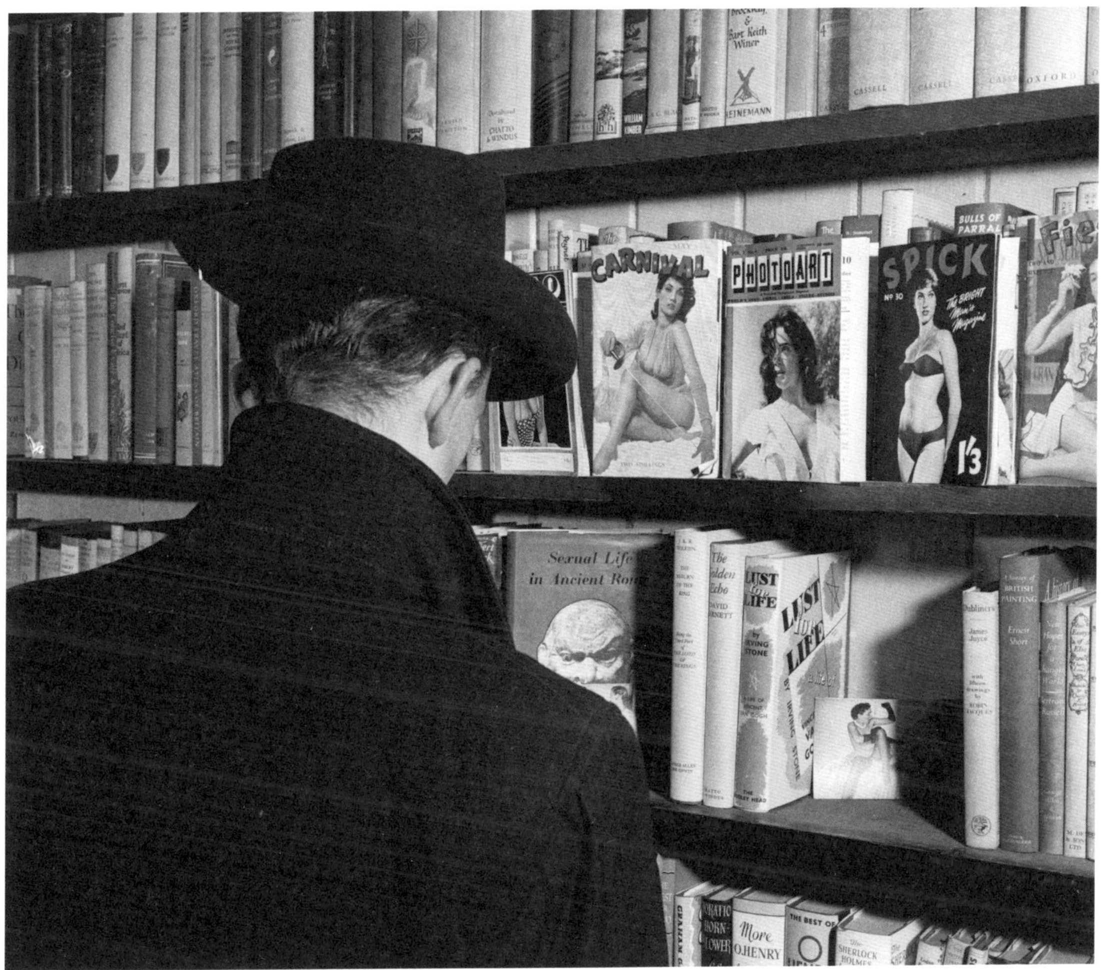

Above - Although each asserted their moral differences, pin-up publications, guides for amateur photographers, naturist magazines, and nude art books all sold side-by-side in Soho bookshops.

Previous spread - Harrison Marks developed a series of highly lucrative photographic endeavours in the 1950s, including nude and glamour prints, slides, books, and magazines. These pseudo-outdoor nudes for his *Kamera* magazine show his adaptability to innovate across all nude genres.

and nudes, *PhotoART*, no matter how strongly it emphasized its ambition through capital letters in its title, was sold alongside the very magazines it claimed to oppose in the public areas of 1950s Soho bookshops.[123]

Meanwhile, as cheap pocket photography magazines looked down on their rivals, they were in turn looked down upon by exclusive periodicals, such as the esteemed journal of the Royal Photographic Society, whose members undertook nude "figure photography" only under the very strictest of moral terms. As one member stated, "I try as hard as possible to suppress the sex element and I try not to make the sort of pictures that would interest the monthly journals intended for men, which publish that sort of work under the guise of art." Aware of how his hobby could be perceived, the author used his wife as a guarantor of virtue, stating that if she didn't like it, he wouldn't do it. "The only advice I can give to anyone who is thinking of this kind of work is to examine your conscience very closely as to the reason you want to do it," he concluded.[124]

GUIDES FOR THE PERPLEXED

Abundantly illustrated articles on how to take nude photographs peppered the pages of post-war naturist magazines, glamour publications, and all levels of the photographic press at a time when amateur photography was an expanding and largely male-dominated leisure activity. The cheapest illustrated magazines with the lowest production values, produced under artistic names like *Photo Studio: Camera Art for the Connoisseur* and *Art Advertiser and Studio News*, discussed the apparent complexities of producing such photographs and provided technical specifications for the best camera, film, and settings. They claimed to advance "the artistic study of the figure" even as their photographs of voluptuous nudes with dirty feet and bruised flesh, taken in squalid studios or roughly superimposed onto rural backgrounds, lacked technical and aesthetic merit.[125]

How-to guides reveal the reasons, aside from access to nude models, why amateur photographers might want to enter this arena. Pin-ups were described as a way for photographers to "pin down fortunes" in the more legitimate instructional *PhotoGuide* monthly magazine in 1957. A "seemingly inexhaustible market" was replacing former lucrative aspects of commercial practice, such as formal studio portraiture.[126] By the late 1950s, *PhotoART* noted that "glamour photography is today a vast business—an industry on a formidable scale, whose top prizes, in terms of monetary rewards for its most successful exponents, make small beer of Prime Ministers' salaries".[127] In the same period Roye claimed to have sold nearly 2 million photographic books. Harrison Marks was making £1,500 a week (equivalent to £30,000 in today's money) at the height of his success.[128]

Dubarry was the fanciful French-sounding *nom de plume* of the more prosaically named John D. Underwood Barry. As a published nude photographer, he provided guidance to mid-century readers of *The Naturist* looking to take up the practice. As a professional keen to assert his own skills, he was dismissive of amateur attempts, even as some of his own efforts were amateurish. His 1942 volume of studio nudes, *Venus through the Lens*, for example, describes a lamp constructed from a lightbulb and a biscuit tin.[129] "So many people have the idea that one has only to stick a pretty girl up against a tree or rock, and say 'Smile, please'. All too often," he complained, "a study in the nude is nothing more or less than a snapshot of the photographer's wife without her clothes on, or lease a hired glamour-girl, coyly pretending to be a sun-bather, and whose lily-white limbs and dazzling torso are, like the negative, exposed to the light for one reason only: to exploit the commercial angle." Despite writing in the pages of a naturist magazine, he warned against using naturists as subjects. He sneered, "intellectuality is not effective, pictorially". Dubarry avoided professional models, whose poses and expressions, he felt, communicated boredom. He recommended instead a compliant and unselfconscious beginner, characterized as "more anxious to please". Meanwhile, "self-assertion, a dominant nature, and an over-active brain on the model's part are antipathetic to the best work of this nature. Rather", he recommended, "a gentle and amiable personality, with a complacent simplicity of mind."[130]

Dubarry was not averse to artificially improving aspects of the model's appearance in ways seemingly antithetical to naturist principles, from thinning eyebrows with tweezers to using cosmetics to cover "freckles, minor scars, strawberry-marks, moles, pimples" from the "pitiless and exaggerative eye of the camera". However, he warned that "not all types of minor disfigurement are susceptible to correction by make-up. Rigid operation scars, for example, will defy any attempt at concealment." Settings were also discussed:

"Any recognised article of bedroom, bathroom or drawing-room furniture is very out of place in the treatment of the nude. Such backgrounds should never be conspicuous or sharply defined as to distract attention from the main subject. It must be subordinated", he noted, in the name of artistic abstraction.[131] Despite this, his domestic nudes were regularly interrupted by encroaching armchairs and skirting boards.

Gordon S. Malthouse, editor of *Miniature Camera World*, also advised naturist photographers to consider their backgrounds, complaining in *Sun Bathing Review* that scruffy camp scenes with bottles of milk and handbags in the frame were a betrayal of the movement's ideals. The magazine regularly carried advertisements for his publication, and Malthouse clearly saw a means to create a secondary set of consumers among nudists with cameras. Candid camp photographs, he argued, were monotonous and "suggest only wearisome acres of flaccid flesh". He compared them unfavourably with the posed and purposeful nude photographs "exhibited in the photographic salons and in the pages of physical culture journals". He was particularly critical of naturists depicted at ease in "ridiculous shoes and socks", not only on aesthetic grounds but in the contradiction of these items to the principles of the cause, which he saw as the pursuit of healthy hardihood. Where photographs fail, he argued, "the movement fails".[132]

Malthouse's perspective embodies the central conflict between nudist image and experience. The scruffy scenes he despised were the actuality of camps; the flaccid flesh, its ordinary members. While he wished to see hardy heroes at one with the rugged landscape, the reality of barefoot camp life would not be gods and goddesses but middle-aged nudists gingerly picking their way through bracken. Ideal photographic subjects should not be old or fat or caught engaging in any non-heroic emotion or activity. Nudists could not slouch and snack or be bored and tired before the camera.

By the early 1950s, *Sun Bathing Review* recognized the centrality of photography to the movement by evoking a "biting description of a nudist" as "a man wearing nothing but a wrist-watch, sandals and a camera".[133] C. S. Frost, writing in *The Naturist*, observed with some suspicion "the number of males that wield cameras of all types and descriptions at the sun clubs". In a 1952 article complaining of "photographic fiends", he described visiting a club with female friends, only to be "pestered" by "unattached" men "asking for permission to

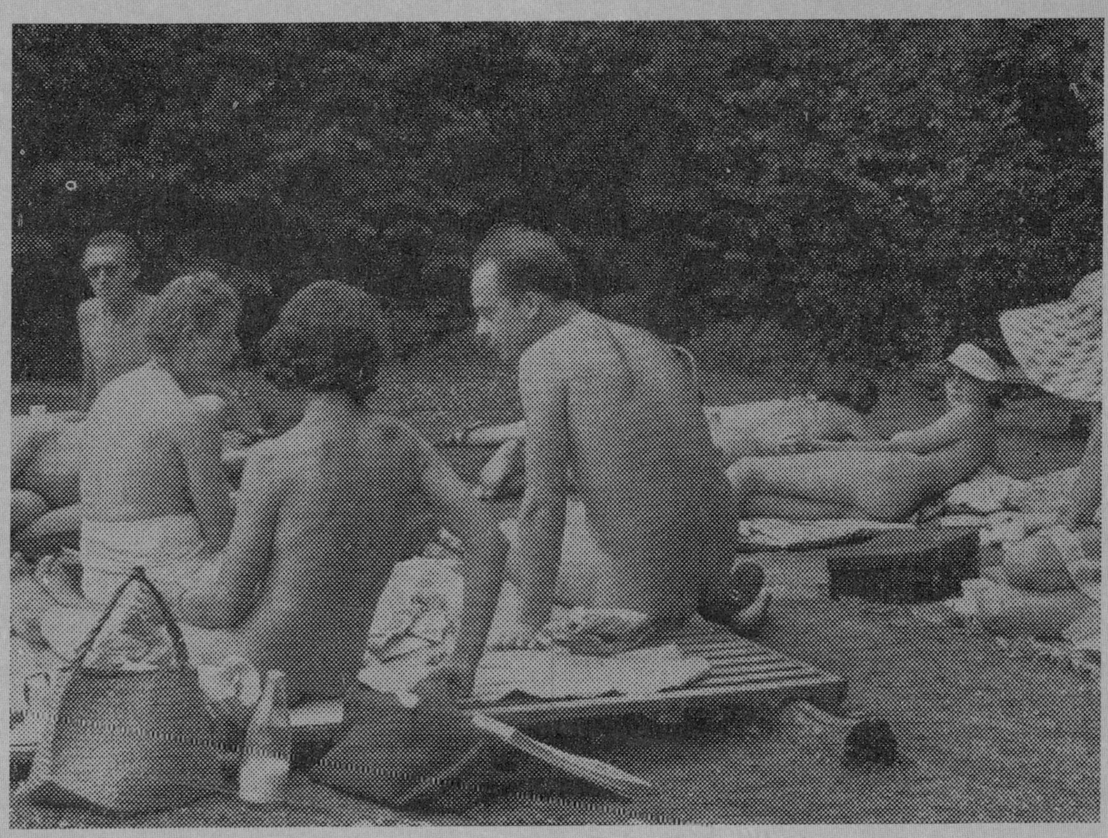

Nude photography and photographs of nudists and were not one and the same. Advice guides for aspiring photographers warned that candid images of relaxed camp scenes, such as this one, created negative impressions of a movement based on idealism.

photograph the ladies". To test the photographers' credentials, he asked them to display their work, and found "these pests produce albums which all bear a marked similarity of subject. No male studies appear in their collections. All the photographs are of young females with their backs to a wall or tree, as artistically posed as a carcase of mutton in a butcher's window." As further condemnation, Frost noted that such photographers seldom produced their own prints so their technical skill "is absolutely nil; which gives rise to doubt as to the ultimate purpose of these pictures". Their presence, he regretted, had led to a camera ban in many clubs, which meant "bona fide" naturists cannot make "mementoes of their sun club visits for the family album".[134] The most preferential circumstances for an authentic naturist photographic practice was for it to be undertaken by naturists in camps, where it could be, as a Royal Photographic Society member put it pithily, "of the nude, by the nude, in the nude, for the nude".[135]

Seton addressed criticisms of the naturist camera in *Garden of Eden*. "Because many naturists are also photographers," she began, "it is suggested in some quarters that naturists like to take these pictures of other people in the nude for some unsavoury motive. It has even been levelled as a serious criticism of the movement that interests in such photographs is 'unhealthy' and that, if nudists are as unaware of nakedness as they maintain, there would be no point in taking pictures." Her conclusion: naturists "take photographs of one another because they wish to capture the spirit of a happy moment, and the fact that they are all naked at the time is of no importance whatsoever". The consequence was that there could be no objection to nude periodicals. "If a naturist—who is, after all, more keenly aware than most of the importance of a healthy body—chooses to photograph a fine specimen of it; and if other naturists like to see that picture published in their own journal—what more natural? It would indeed be hypocritical if we pretended to despise it."[136]

Naturist advice to amateurs on how to photograph nudes was moral as much as it was aesthetic and technical. A playful 1952 antiguide showed, in its inverted attitudes, the expected norms. "Your First Nude Study: How Not to Set about it" began with advice on obtaining a model: "You may ask your sister, who will laugh her fool head off! You can ask someone else's sister. This is much more fun, because the reactions of individuals are unpredictable." Other jokes included model payment: "This is to be avoided where possible. Ask her if she will take a cheque," the author stated, while acknowledging that this should only be done when there was no money in the bank. He surmised, "Perhaps the best way is to ask her to wait outside a public house while you cash a cheque, then beat it hell for leather out the back door!"[137] The article's tone was satirical, but it pointed to real abuses found throughout the period, from lack of fair payment to cases where amateur photographers impersonated famous professionals to convince women to undress.[138]

In both amateur photography publications and sexually charged glamour magazines, advice about naturist-style nude photography offered tips on avoiding the police and cajoling uncomfortable models. An article in the flimsy and mostly illustrative periodical *Photo Studio* considered the implications of an intemperate climate. The unnamed author noted the value of a car for British photographers: "The model must have somewhere to undress in some comfort, and it may rain as it usually does." The legal problems with taking "figure photographs" on public commons or in forests were warned against: "Some members of the public will be offended and will report you to the police. You may be charged." Instead, acting like the photographic fiends that nudists complained about, photographers were advised, "If you can get the cooperation of your local sunbathing club then you will have nothing to worry about." Models' needs were cursorily addressed: "Don't ask her to wade through a nettle bank. The more athletic type of model is always better for open-air photography," it was observed; "she is not so likely to be scared by insects".[139] Similarly, an article entitled "The Nude Outdoors" in *PhotoART* offered advice on the art of persuasion, claiming that getting a model to do what you wanted was "a matter of applied psychology". Flattery helped but models were not fools: "All women can see through the bogus and spurious man and recognise the sincere and conscientious artist when they meet one."[140]

Harrison Marks also published articles such as "How to Take Glamour Studies" in his own 1950s pin-up periodical, *Foto*. As one of the most prolific and high-profile photographers of sexualized images, it is striking that his advice on photographic nudes, including those taken outdoors, closely echoes the moral and aesthetic guidance of naturist magazines from the period. He acknowledged, "Unless one is a professional of some repute, most models are not keen to work for you. This", he deflected, "is due to the glut of trashy magazines on sale today. I have seen some that make the slightly crude pictures of girls in pin-up underwear their selling point. Naturally", he noted, "figure models fight shy of posing for photographers unless they are sure that the pictures taken are decent straightforward studies and will not appear in undesirable booklets." He recommended cups of tea and a pet cat in the studio to ease models' troubled minds.[141]

Despite being a prominent producer of precisely these "undesirable booklets", Harrison Marks's advice was modest and moral. Like others, he noted the presence of "a couch, or some such piece of furnishing", would be interpreted "as a bed, and as such will lower the tone". Working outdoors could neatly avoid this hazard: "Your backgrounds are the finest, and money can't buy them, and your lighting, properly handled, will give you the purest tones that it is possible to obtain." Harrison Marks's guidance for the commercial production of naturist-style nudes notably addresses the style merely as a market fraction rather than a morally superior form; each style simply served a specific aesthetic and sexual preference. For those wishing to take glamour photographs, Harrison Marks gave parallel advice on making nipple pasties for models using cardboard, sequins, and glue.

When Clark wrote his art history of the ideal nude, he located its peak in the first hundred years of the classical Renaissance, during which time, he said, "there was no concept, however sublime, which could not be expressed by the naked body, and no object of use, however trivial, which could not be the better for having been given human shape". In his estimation, in 1956, "such an insatiable appetite for the nude is unlikely to recur".[142] At the time of Clark's writing, however, another peak was established. The post-war publishing boom created new markets for nude consumption from cheap glamour magazines to expensive art albums and amateur photographic literature. These new forms overlapped directly with naturism's commercial print culture and shared its audience, subjects, and photographers. Naturists evaluated the nude photographs that appeared in these publications, but they were not the only ones doing so. Surveyors also included the police.

3

Testing the Boundaries

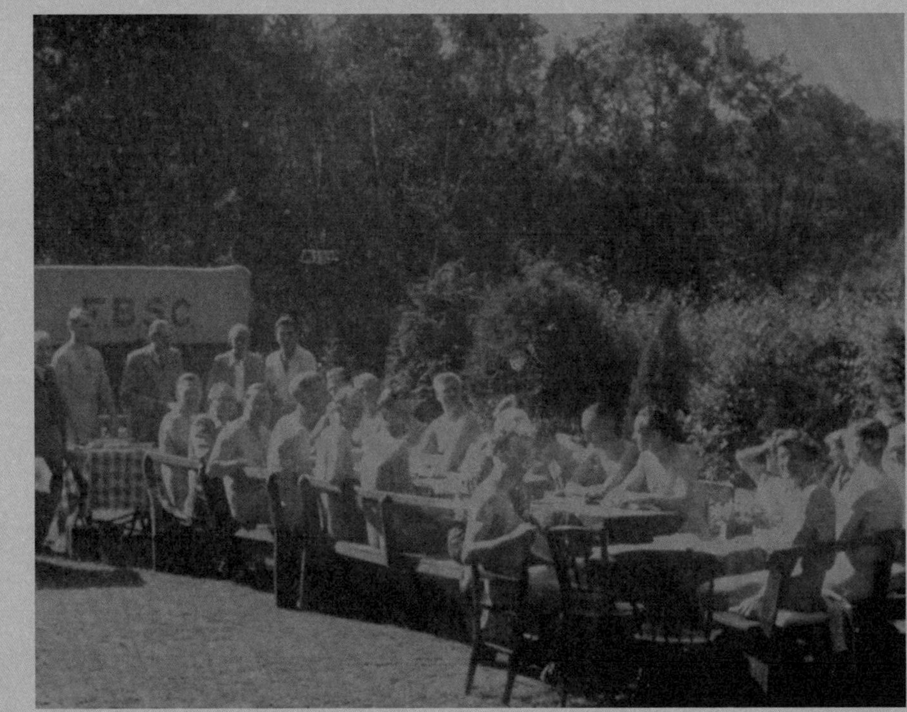

A nudist camp somewhere in England: British Naturism pennants flutter along railings trimmed with barbed wire. A notice-board is pinned with rules for the site. Folding sun loungers in psyche-delic prints are pulled up alongside plastic picnic tables strewn with sun tan oil, mosquito repellent, flasks of cocoa, and European travel brochures.

Previous spread – Post-war naturist clubs were often organized around committees, with annual general meetings, formal agendas and published policies. These structures signalled seriousness, but naturist bureaucracy was off-putting for some.

When George Harrison Marks advised amateur photographers on matters of nude technique in the 1950s, he cautioned, "It is your judgement in positioning the model whether the finished results will be artistic or otherwise."[1] This brief assertion, so fraught with legal and moral tensions, prompted what Harrison Marks described as "a deluge of letters", each asking for clarification on a key question: "When does a pin-up or a nude study become indecent?" Harrison Marks hedged the issue with general guidance about making sure that there was "no suggestion of crudity" by checking the model is "tastefully arranged".[2] His elliptical language betrayed that his own ability as a photographer hung precariously on his "artistic" status, and was thus on the right side of the law. Matters of indecency shaped what could be sold over or under the counter, on public newsstands, or in bookshops' backrooms, and the borders between stylistic and moral categories were tightly policed.[3] The pornographic "otherwise", as Harrison Marks well knew as one of its principal producers, was a wide territory and a matter of endless debate, including by government ministers, censors, and judges.

The earliest nudist magazines in Britain carefully acknowledged and met legal constraints about what they could picture even when they didn't agree with legal principles. The 1857 Obscene Publications Act had been originally established to prosecute works of pornography, but as both obscenity and pornography were concepts that depended on the eye of the beholder, for over a century the law required fresh debate in each case.[4] Lord Chief Justice Cockburn's 1868 definition of obscenity endured, as that which could "deprave and corrupt those whose minds are open to such immoral influences and into whose hands a publication of this sort may fall".[5] This was vague at best. Frankly written sexology books, including those by the nudist-endorsing Havelock Ellis, had been victims of legal censure at the turn of the 20th century, especially when aimed at a general rather than medical audience, but from the 1930s a new raft of legal prosecutions included material directly produced for and consumed by nudists.

For the curious nudist or potential convert, mail order companies offered a direct and convenient means of buying texts that might otherwise prove hard to find or prompt embarrassment in a bookshop. One large-scale West Country supplier, Economy Educator Service, which advertised in the Christmas 1936 edition of *Health and Efficiency*, offered nudist titles by Merrill, Gay, and Welby, with loan and payment plan options for cheap supply. In the late 1930s and early 1940s, Economy Educator Service also advertised "Leading Naturist Art Books" in *The Naturist* and *Sun Bathing Review*. Via double-page spreads they sold volumes by Park and Gregory, Everard, Bird, and Roye alongside sexology and anthropology by Magnus Hirschfield and Bronislaw Malinowski, and practical information about family planning. All who ordered received a free copy of Reverend Norwood's founding text, *Nudism in England*.

The style of Economy Educator promotions in the naturist press where, for example, an advertisement for the book *Sex Satisfaction in Marriage*, with the word "Sex" emphasized in the largest and boldest text, appeared next to Roye's females nudes, undermining the claim that sexual desire and non-sexual naturism were categorically separated.[6] As the distributor's promotions were less than discreet, the National Vigilance Association, which considered these efforts "objectionable", alerted the police. In 1942 the managing directors of Economy Educator, Ralph and Lilian Clemoes, were arrested. By this time they employed a staff of 14 and kept an extensive stock from three-shilling booklets to 33-shilling encyclopaedias, including a range of at-least-borderline pornography including the flagellant *Pleasures of the Torture Chamber* and *A History of the Rod in All Countries*.[7] The prosecution found that while customers needed to testify that they were over 21, there was no means to corroborate that they were telling the truth. As such, supply of these materials was a criminal offence and the directors were imprisoned for six months.[8]

A challenge of the Economy Educator case was that none of the books advertised, including those on naturism, had been subject to individual obscenity prosecutions. The variability of obscenity depended on a range of factors, including "circumstances of publication", that is, the location and method of how material was promoted, displayed, and sold.[9] In this case, the juxtaposition of naturist books with printed matter that crossed a pornographic border caused a kind of pollution; their collective distribution shaped how the material was perceived. In addition, contemporaneous police reports confirmed that nude photographs were not, in themselves, obscene, although "partially dressed females" in "suggestive poses were definitely indecent".[10] In many cases, indecency related to the visibility of sexual organs and pubic hair. Naturist publications had been posing and retouching photographs for protection against this charge since their inception. Where prosecutions occurred due to the publication and distribution of so-called "integral" or unretouched nude photographs in the 1950s, however, obscenity's uncertain boundaries were revealed anew.

In 1958, the Metropolitan Police Commissioner reported to the Select Committee on Obscene Publications that the customer lists "normally found in mail order businesses appear to consist of names of male persons only", and when arrested for possession of obscene photographic material, men usually claimed to have purchased them "in connection with their anatomical and/or art studies".[11] Prosecuted individuals sometimes lived in small English towns where the direct purchase of under-the-counter material would otherwise prove hard to access. John C, for example, a painter and fitter of Biggleswade, Bedfordshire, was reported to have ordered nude photographs of women as he was "fond of sketching", but later claimed their unretouched quality struck him as "vulgar" and he had decided they were "entirely unsuitable". Nonetheless, he ordered more. Amateur photographer Thomas B, a clerk in Buckingham, was found in possession of unretouched photographs, which he said he had ordered for montage. He also owned magazines, including *Paris Pin Up*, *Sex Appeal*, *Showgirl*, and *Eyeful*, showing the overlapping domains of the art nude and the glamour press.[12] The illegal status of unretouched photographs equally affected all circulating nude images, and magistrates prosecuted naturists on the same grounds in the 1950s.

Arthur Hodgson, General Secretary of the British Sun Bathing Association (BSBA), a body established in 1943 to represent the collective interests of naturist clubs, and to which dozens were affiliated, was found guilty in 1951 of supplying large quantities of international unretouched naturist magazines that were not beholden to the same laws. The official BSBA position was that sales of such material "can bring nothing but discredit to the whole movement and jeopardise the existence of our own British journals". Nonetheless, the president ran a busy mail order service until the offending materials were seized at customs. "Viewing them with due consideration to the claims of art and physical culture," the London magistrate stated, "I am forced to the conclusion that they offend against modesty and delicacy."[13] The outcome was a major embarrassment to a movement courting respectability. A letter to *The Naturist* from the president of a Devon naturist group claimed the case "besmirches the reputation of all the clubs which are connected with that body", while the magazine's editor reflected on differences in international publishing, especially in material that shared naturism's name but not its morals. Foreign magazines should take care that their content was above suspicion, he warned; indeed, they "would be wise to make their connection with the genuine nudist movement a little less obscure". British publishers should be reminded that "lack of retouching is the final straw that breaks the magistrate's back. We may regret this fact, but we must accept it as representative of the general public's attitude to nudity today."[14]

NOT OBSCENE

Photographers for the naturist press were aware of the legal strictures; their livelihoods depended on staying inside their boundaries. Eva Grant, for example, headed off any possible issues by employing a lawyer to sanction her photographs for public circulation by stamping and signing on the back: "I have examined this print and it is / is not in my opinion obscene, questionable or exceptional in any way and is / is not fit for general publication."[15] Others were less willing to toe the legal line. Roye had long been frustrated with the regulations, and made public play with what he saw as their hypocrisies in his 1942 publication *Phyllis in Censorland*. The cover design was a colourized photograph of burlesque dancer Phyllis Dixey, the so-called British Queen of Striptease, naked on a tiger-skin rug but with her breasts and genitals concealed by the blue pencils of the censor. Its contents comprised nude and near-nude photographs of the cabaret dancer by Roye, accompanied by mocking verses by a writer concealed behind the name of the Greek comedy muse, Thalia.[16] Each poem pilloried the position of those who sought to protect public morals while enjoying the privileged pleasures of surveillance.

Roye, always commercially savvy, reissued his 1942 book during the mid-1950s when the seizure of printed material on obscenity grounds was at a new high. The 1951 Conservative government oversaw a period of escalating destruction orders and extended punishments in the period when cheap magazines were booming. The desire to contain them led to a protracted legal power struggle.

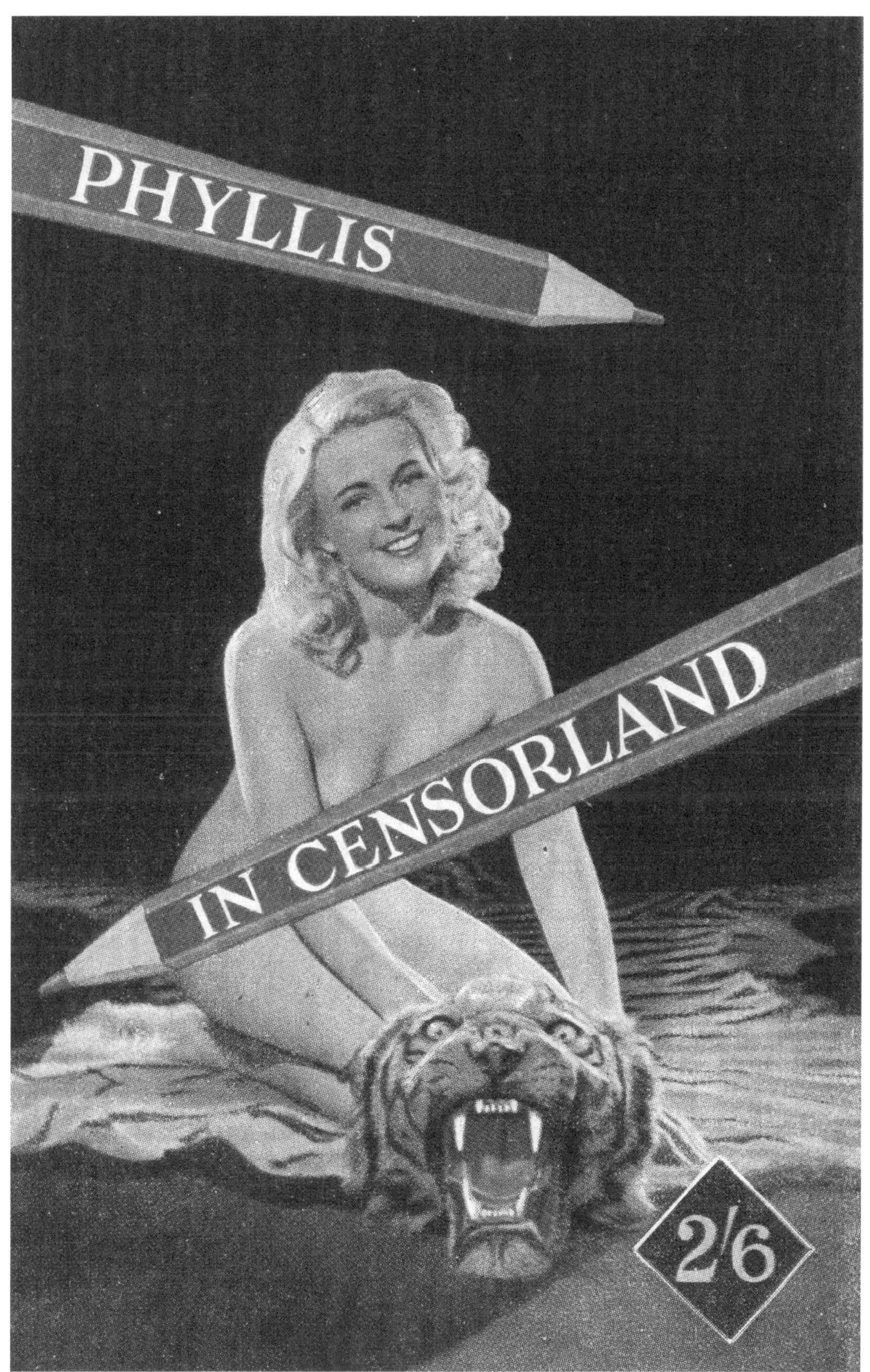

Nude photographs in mid-century Britain were subject to legal censure about which body parts could be shown. Roye produced mocking publications challenging the moral basis of these decisions.

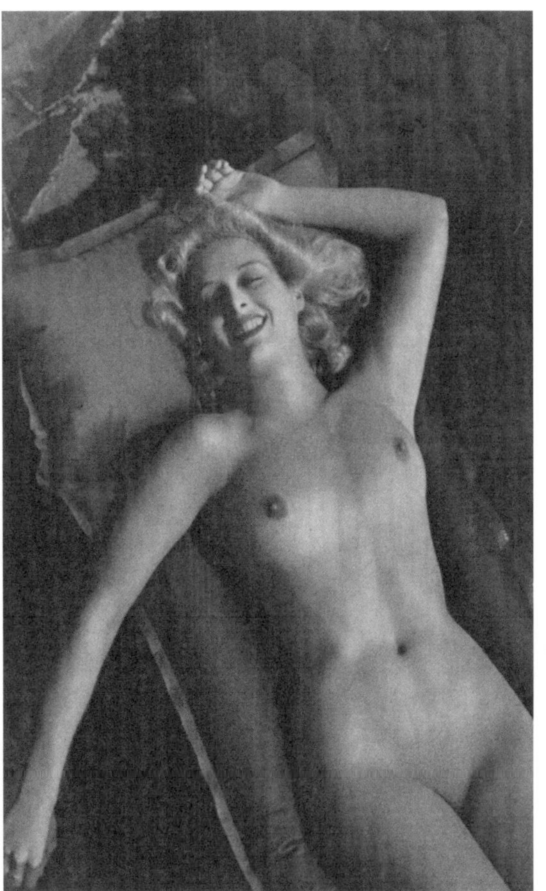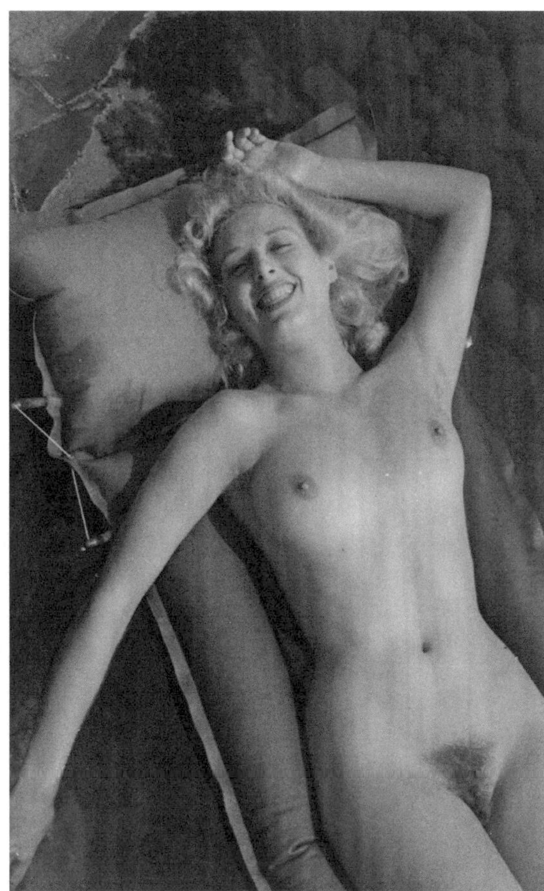

Roye had published photographs of showgirl Desirée Cooper in naturist publications since the 1940s, 'retouched' for legality. In the 1950s he challenged British law by publishing "unretouched" prints, showing pubic hair, leading to his arrest on obscenity charges.

In 1954, for example, around 167,000 books and magazines were seized and imprisonments ranged from three to 18 months.[17] The hundreds of annual prosecutions included the production and supply of material previously considered benign, such as comic seaside postcards. In their enthusiasm to uphold public morals, some magistrates ordered the destruction of eminent literary works including Boccaccio's 14th-century *The Decameron*, leading to widespread ridicule about the lack of cultural knowledge among law enforcers.[18] Roye critiqued the laws in his publications but his photographs were also caught up in them. In 1953, Norwich police seized 462 books from booksellers in the city, including *Romance of Naturism* with an art supplement by Roye, and his 1942 book *Desirée*, comprising dressed and undressed photographs of showgirl Desirée Cooper, which had previously featured as covers and illustrations in *The Naturist*. Roye's publishers intervened and as a result, he claimed, his books were the only ones saved.[19]

The following year Roye combined forces with Vala, an innovator in technical stereoscopy, to produce a series of "Stereo-Glamour" illustrated publications. Each pocket-sized edition came with a pair of paper 3D viewing glasses. Advertised equally in the back pages of naturist, glamour, and amateur photography magazines, the pamphlets promised an unprecedented viewing experience dubbed "roundedness In space". Advertisements claimed: "Everyone interested in photography, and stereoscopic photography in particular, will derive every satisfaction from these superb stereograms." The promotions listed the technical benefits, but the obvious pleasure, coyly suggested in the term "*every* satisfaction", was in the photographs' immersive erotic dimension, especially when the images featured jutting breasts and foregrounded legs. *PhotoART* sniggered, "The pictures are not only outstanding—*they stand out* too!"

British film star Diana Dors was the subject of one of Roye's 3D books. Described by *PhotoART* as "Britain's Number 1 Glamour Girl" and as "the only real challenge" the country could offer "in the field of International Blondes", Dors, née Fluck, traded on a Marilyn Monroe-style image with platinum curls, fur coats, and diamonds. Her overt sex appeal was qualified for national audiences who might find her too "commercial". Her "flamboyant publicity and near-vulgarity" was defended as a moderate domestic product: "The sum total of what La Dors has to offer the British audience would be mere Sunday School

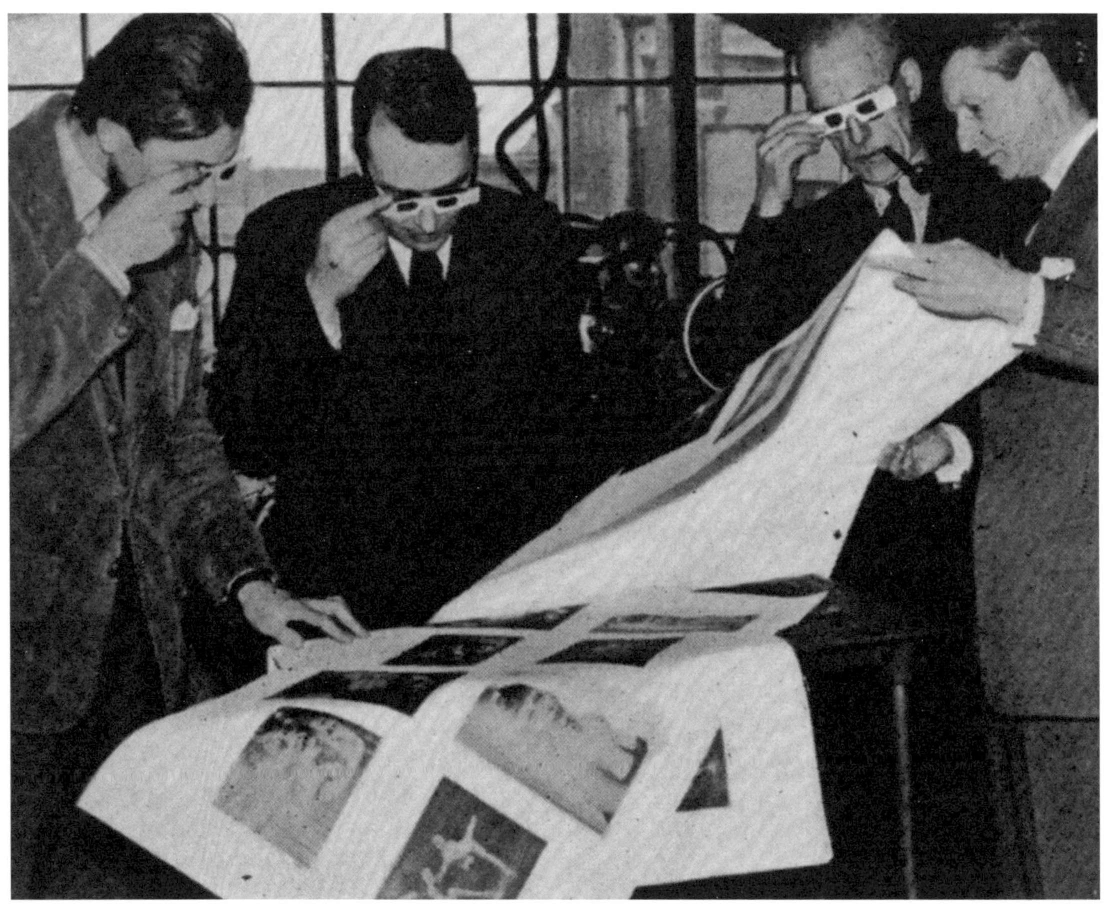

The male gaze:
Roye (on right, without
glasses) produced an
immersive series of 3D
pocket sized pamphlets
in the 1950s featuring
nude and partially
dressed showgirls
and film stars.

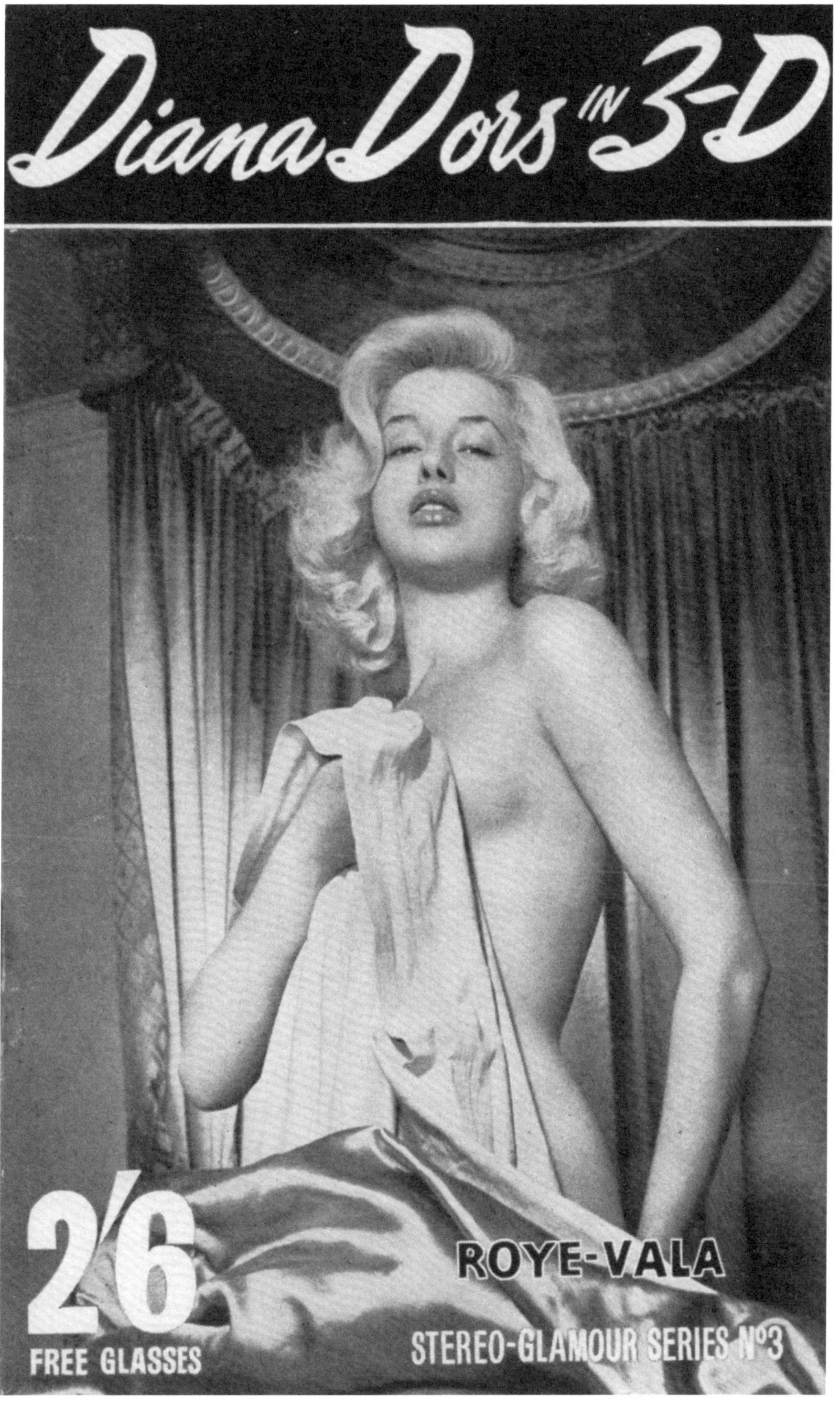

Diana Dors IN 3-D
2/6
FREE GLASSES
ROYE-VALA
STEREO-GLAMOUR SERIES N°3

stuff to the great American male."[20] National anxieties aside, Dors regularly appeared *déshabillée* in photographs in the mid-1950s, including some by Roye, who depicted her in luxuriant poses on a synthetic animal pelt and in 18th-century-style stays on a palanquin. His 3D portraits of Dors, styled as "captivating, curvaceous", were described as "the most intimate photographs ever published."[21] Proving their appeal went beyond Britain, Roye sold his Dors prints to the newly established American magazine *Playboy*, already famous for its nude Monroe centrefold.[22] The sexual potential of *Diana Dors in 3D* brought the publication before the magistrates, following a 1955 raid on a Halifax bookshop. In the final judgement, however, Roye's production was designated "not obscene".[23]

Emboldened by his legal successes, Roye continued to push his luck and, in 1958, launched a private subscription series of un-retouched nudes under the title *Unique Editions* via his Camera Studies Club, through which he published and sold mail order copies of his books and prints and distributed *PhotoART*. Repurposing earlier negatives, including those previously included as retouched illustrations in *The Naturist*, the unmarked, buff-covered volumes each comprised four photographs of nude female models with visible pubic hair, carefully interleaved between tissue pages that conferred both art value and a sense of revelation.[24] While the content included naturist-style nudes in rural environments, including those that had been elsewhere cleared of obscenity charges, the photographs attracted the attention of the law when they were found in the possession of a subscriber. The police then seized over 1,000 copies of the publications from Roye's studio and called him to court.[25] The case provides an illuminating snapshot of legal and lay attitudes to nude photographs at the end of the 1950s.

DIRT FOR DIRT'S SAKE

Roye's prosecution coincided with propositions to revise the Obscene Publications Act in 1957 and 1958. Following public derision when acclaimed historic and literary works had been seized, the changes, confirmed in 1959, exempted from prosecution material with literary or artistic merit. The nude was singled out for mention in parliamentary discussions about the problem of defining corruption, as "it can be used for lectures, such as those [...] given by Sir Kenneth

Clark, to provide inspiration for the painter or photographer or, on the other hand, be degraded for the purposes of the pornographer's wares".[26] The need for revision was based partly on the need for greater precision but also to deliver greater prosecuting powers, not least as "the trade in suggestive photographs" was said by government ministers to be "growing rapidly year by year".[27] Although the government argued that it was "easy to tell the difference between the Song of Solomon and a collection of salacious photographs", the problem was the evaluation of material in between.[28] Lord Birkett, a barrister and Liberal Party member, gave evidence to the Select Committee on the proposed revisions, stating, in a striking turn of phrase: "I want art for art's sake, even with some imperfections, to come in, but dirt for dirt's sake to be prosecuted and thrown away."[29] It wasn't easy to legally distinguish the aesthetically edifying from the morally corrupting, especially in the case of nude photographs capable of stimulating sexual desire, regardless of the makers' or publishers' purported intent.

Roye used the nebulousness of legal definitions to support his cause, believing "so far as photography is concerned" that the police should "go after the back-street characters, posing as 'photographers' and using bovine females as 'models', and leave the serious, reputable photographer free to move with, and even lead, the ever-changing climate of public opinion".[30] In representing an alternative to these enemies of taste, Roye's class and the body shapes of his tall, slim models represented respectability. He reiterated that his subjects were "sincere, decent girls of character and charm, who under no circumstances would allow any departure from good taste in connection with any photograph in which they appeared". To position himself as a modernizer and liberator, he added: "Remember, if someone had not led the way, women would still be wearing swimming costumes that covered their bodies from ankle to chin."[31]

In Roye's two sessions in court—the second required as the first jury could not agree a verdict—he positioned himself in the avant-garde, aesthetically and culturally. Retouching, he argued, was a sacrifice of "artistic integrity". He told the court, "I decided that the time was appropriate to publish a book free of mutilation by retouching and I had a feeling of satisfaction that I was once again breaking new ground in my profession." His defence lawyer, James Burge, argued that "standards had changed since 1868, when pictures of

Venus, in the Dulwich Gallery, had shocked Londoners; and it would be unrealistic to say that, in 1958, a photograph of a woman without clothing was an obscene thing".[32] Roye's case was built on supposedly superior aesthetic value and his high professional standing, and he laid on thick his former employment as a wartime photographer for the Ministry of Information and his worldwide reputation, as well as his claims to have broken records for photographic book sales at over 2 million. Why would he risk his whole career, "for the sake of—*perhaps!*—gaining a few extra sales from people to whom, frankly, he would not like to sell his works anyway"?[33] Roye's customers were surely select connoisseurs and not mere masturbators.

Roye claimed in court that nudes were only "a very small part of his work" and said he was a landscape photographer who never produced "sexually exciting or salacious" photographs. On this basis, he was acquitted.[34] He wasted no time in turning his victory to his advantage, reissuing *Unique Editions* and also producing *Unique Verdict*, a self-serving account of the trial. Readers were invited to consume the images and "judge for themselves whether they consider the Police should be occupying their time with this sort of thing or would be better employed trying to arrest the present mounting waves of crimes of violence".[35] *Unique Verdict* included letters of support Roye had assembled in his defence. The endorsements were similar to repeated claims long made for the public benefit of viewing nude photographs in naturist contexts, including that sex crimes would be eliminated, and Victorian prudishness would be overturned. The photographs' unretouched "natural" status offered additional protection by distinguishing them from the synthetic "artificiality" of pornography.

Clark was evoked by one supporter. "Only on Sunday a prominent art critic of BBC Television emphasised that only truth in representation makes a picture worthy of consideration as a work of art," they stated, while observing that Roye's unretouched nudes were morally superior because they showed natural bodies. "There are certain types of publication which I do regard as indecent, where nudes are posed and lighted in an obviously unnatural manner," the author conceded. These were, however, "blatantly suggestive in intention".[36] Roye stated that his prosecution "interested men and women of all callings, classes, faiths and nationalities".[37] The gender of specific endorsers was

Right - British 1950s 'blonde bombshell' film star Diana Dors poses nude in Roye's studio on a satin-draped bed complete with toy leopard. A smartly suited Roye adjusts the lights.

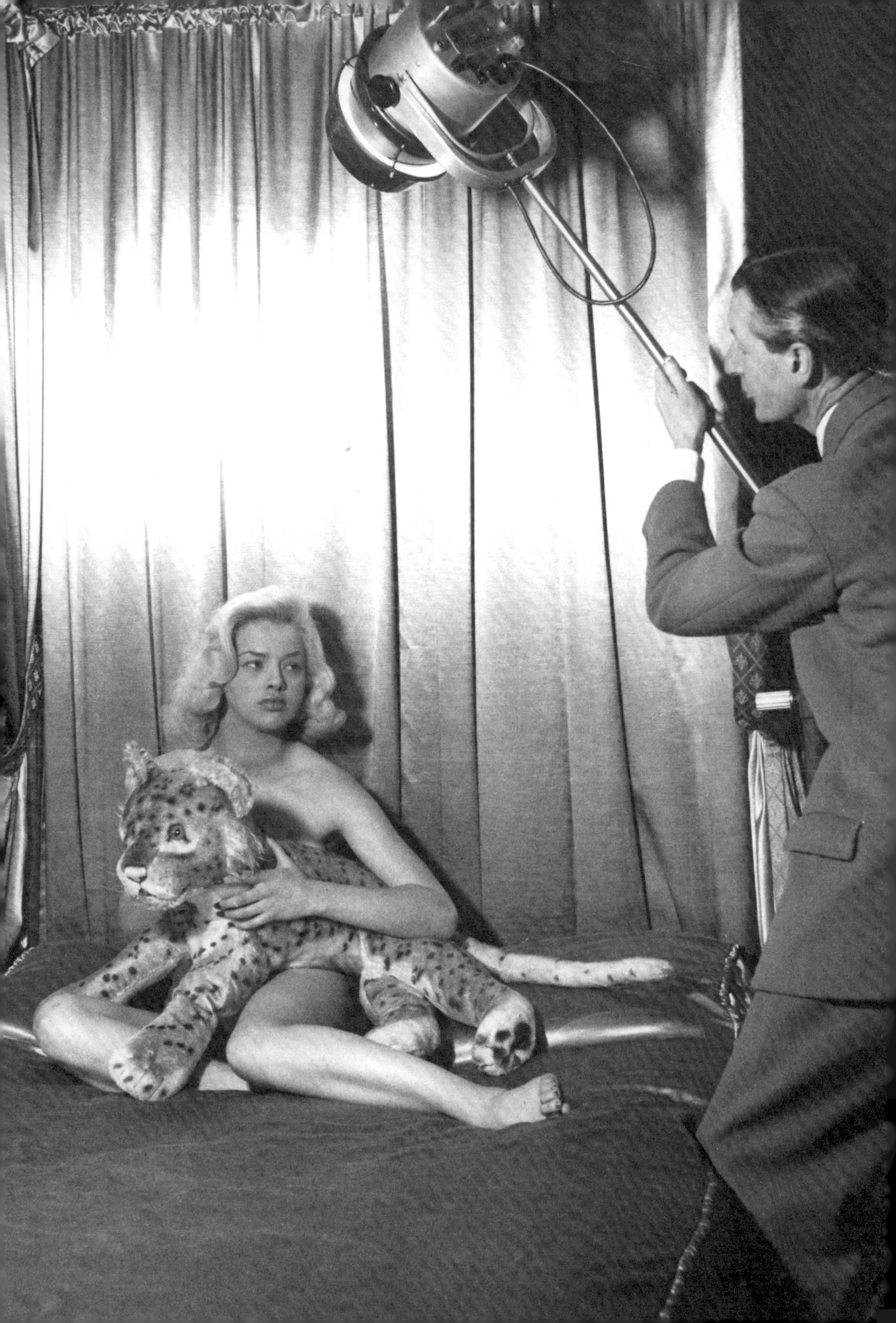

not given but their content indicates many were written by men, especially when they refer to "the great social problems of sex education and our responsibility to women and children", which would be solved by regarding "the human body as something natural, beautiful and, above all, wholesome".[38] As laudable as this sentiment might be, in Roye's case the public need for openness and bodily display seemed to only apply to nude and nearly nude young women.

Several of his supporters argued for the value of displaying "beauty", perceived to be an abstract absolute that was inherently feminine and morally improving. As one put it, through the consumption of beauty in "decent artistic photographs and paintings, the seeker of knowledge, which is everyone in turn, would gain it in the right way". As a result, "obscenity would become revolting to all, obscene publications would lose their market and thus disappear, and our daughters would be able to walk about more freely without the fear of being molested".[39] Ugly bodies, by this logic, created an ugly society, while beauty was spiritually elevating. Another supporter insisted, "There is nothing to be ashamed of in a beautifully developed female figure. How could God's best work be evil?" The author repeated one of naturism's central planks: "I am firmly convinced that it's only the semi-clad illustrations in contemporary magazines [...] which are responsible for the waves of juvenile delinquency which are sweeping the world."[40] Roye's champions were seemingly unaware that the noble artist of beauty and nature and the photographer of "semi-clad" sexualized studio portraits were one and the same. If they did know it, they would not be wise to say so in a mid-century court of law.

ENTERTAINMENTS OF DOUBTFUL CHARACTER

British nude photographers in the 1950s used filmic techniques to intensify and animate the erotic experience of still photographs, from Everard's sequential poses and the imagined depths of Roye's 3D imagery to slideshows by Harrison Marks, which enabled glamour models to be projected life-size through home projection equipment. By the end of the decade, the nude moving image rendered these techniques outmoded, as feature films, sanctified by claims to naturist authenticity, began to be produced for public screening, causing new naturist anxieties about the visual representation of their movement. *Nudist Paradise*, filmed in 1958 and released in 1959, was the

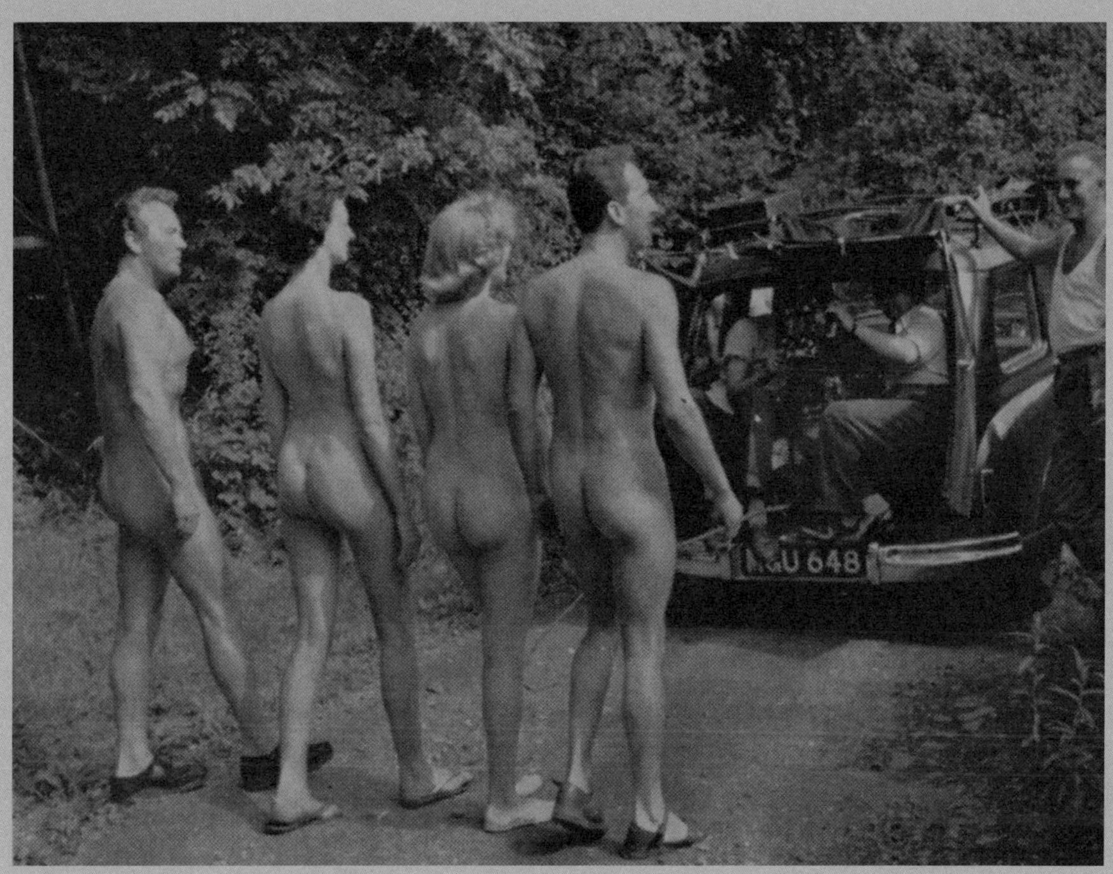

Nudist Paradise, 1959,
the first British fea-
ture film to include
naturism, was shot at
Spielplatz camp but
its central stars were
professional actors
rather than practising
naturists.

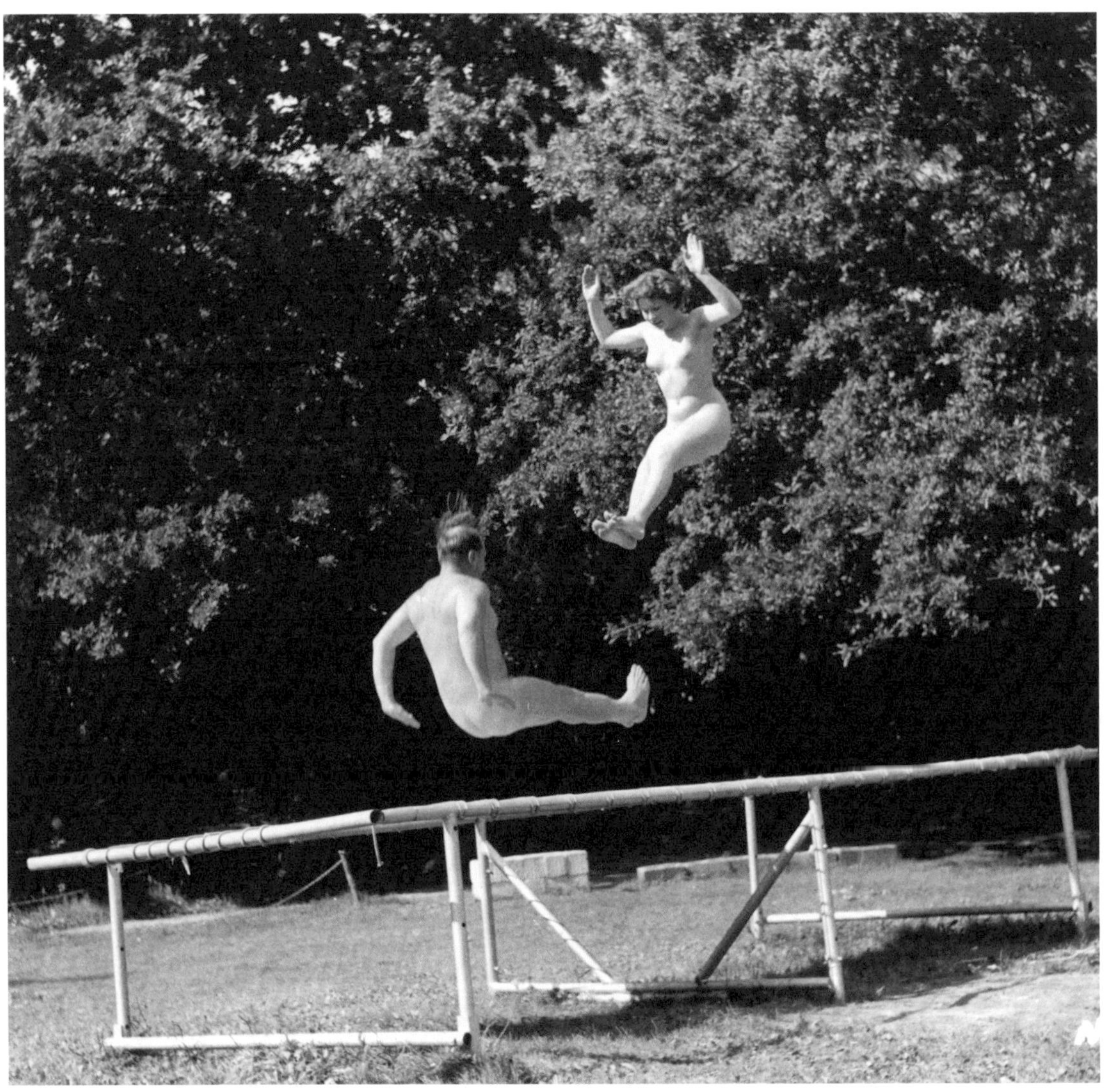

While outdoor exercise
had long been a staple
of club activities,
naturists complained
that scenes in the film
Nudist Paradise showed
bouncing flesh for
erotic appeal.

first British film of its kind. An hour-long scripted drama, shot partly on location at Spielplatz, and with lead parts played by professional actors, it included cameos from Dorothy, Charles, and Iseult Macaskie. The Venus competition featured in the storyline, which saw an American art student fall in love with a beautiful British woman who happened to be a nudist; he joined her at camp and became a convert. Despite the flimsy premise of the transatlantic love story, it was initially championed as history-making by naturists who hoped its propaganda about the improving virtues of disrobing would promote their cause to a wider audience.[41] Its reception was not as expected. *The Naturist* observed that a queue of 100 men formed outside a cinema at 3 p.m. in the afternoon when it was showing.[42] They also regretted the "dubious company" the film kept as it toured the country alongside "a torrid film about love in the jungle".[43]

Sun Bathing Review rightly reported that releases claiming to be naturist were proliferating as a convenient means of bypassing punitive regulations about showing nudity on screen. Soon after their initial excitement, naturists reflected, "Who would have thought that there would come a time when one would find it difficult to get away from nudist films?" Some, they noted, "are thoroughly depressed by them".[44] *The Naturist* in 1960 argued that it was time for a reassessment: "Anybody who has observed the character of the audience on these occasions can be in little doubt as to the motives of the impressionable gentlemen there to be found. It is exactly the same audience that patronises entertainments of a more doubtful character elsewhere in London. To these gentlemen, naturism on the screen is simply an inexpensive form of strip tease." The author of the article, frustrated by naturism's trivial treatment, was especially distressed by a scene in *Nudist Paradise* that included "prolonged bouncings on the trampoline".[45]

In the last years of the 1950s, George Harrison Marks and Pamela Green, Soho's glamour power couple, were conducting a roaring trade in the clandestine sale of short silent 8 mm striptease and "stag" films for home projection, under the Kamera label of their pin-up magazine, often featuring Green in a range of sexual guises. As the redhead Rita Landre she attracted the attention of celebrated British film director Michael Powell, who recruited her to appear in his X-rated 1960 feature *Peeping Tom*, in which she played a nude model who met a grisly end at the hands of the film's sadistic protagonist, a soft-core pin-up photographer-filmmaker based in Soho. Among the real world of Soho photographers and filmmakers, Harrison Marks's experience and model contacts made him the perfect candidate to direct a major nudity feature financed by Michael Klinger and Tony Tenser, the owners of Compton Cinema Club, Soho's first private members' sex cinema.[46] Erotic films were widely produced in the 1950s but could only circulate furtively through private channels, including the advertisements in the backs of glamour magazines and Soho bookshops. Naturism provided the first public opportunity to release the nude moving image from the shadows and hold it up to the light.

Naked—As Nature Intended featured Green as one of a group of young women who holiday to Cornwall and discover the joys of naturism at a camp (actually Spielplatz), ultimately discarding their clothes. Green's longstanding relationship with Spielplatz would have helped secure the club's backing for the film, but she acknowledged its weak plot and lack of script.[47] Inevitably, its nude content attracted huge attention, and it ran in cinemas for 18 months. *Naked—As Nature Intended* joined a boom of British quasi-naturist releases in 1961, often featuring naturists in the cast and using naturist camps as locations. They included *Some Like it Cool*, shot at Sheplegh Court naturist site, and *Nudes of the World*, whose plot saw international beauty queens descending on an English club. The latter was advertised in *Health and Efficiency* as featuring "13 gorgeous girls and a cast of over 70 naturists" on a striptease-style poster.[48]

Aside from Green, the films' stars were mostly glamour models with no connection to naturism. Practising naturists complained of actors' inauthenticity, like the professional photographic models before them. Ernest Stanley, the elder founder-leader of the North Kent naturist club, said, "Filmmakers want to use clubs as settings but then bring models who state on record 'I only did it because I was paid; I wouldn't dream of joining a club'." Titillating scenes, he added, "raised naturist eyebrows".[49] Naturism's moral case for sun, health, and bodily liberation, however, proved ripe for appropriation.

Others complained of the films' deceptions on different terms. As one put it, the naked "lovelies" prominent on the posters signalled what the films were really about. Promotional material certainly revealed sexual motivations in both image and text, which lingered over the bust, waist, and hip measurements, or "vital statistics", of female characters.[50] Rather than a lack of realism, however, this contributor expressed regret about the shortcomings of real-world naturist women: "It would be wonderful if those gorgeous creatures were really found on show at any of the naturist clubs in our experience; and it is possible, I suppose, that a few gullible males will, as a result, join the lengthening queue of would-be bare bachelors in the hope of feasting their eyes on forbidden delights. If so," he stated, "I fear they're in for a bitter disappointment."[51]

The Federation of British Sun Clubs wrote an open letter to the British Board of Film Censors at the end of 1961 stating that "in common with the growth of strip-tease clubs", there has been a "considerable increase" in British films "under the title of 'nudist', which have little resemblance in either action or characterisation to the activities of the true naturist or nudist movement and its members". They asserted: "We formally register our protest that by the passing or tacit approval of such films, even for restricted showing, harm is being done to a growing and genuine health movement whose main membership is made up of ordinary families." Among their complaints included the inclusion of drinking scenes—none of the federation clubs allowed alcohol—and the showing of luxury premises that bore no relation to the threadbare reality of club amenities.

More pressingly, they were concerned about the "persistent use of implication and innuendo in both dialogue and action which only serve to emphasise the sexual rather than the health-seeking undertone of these films", combined with "excessive and unnecessary photographic emphasis on the nude female body in particular". They offered to provide an FBSC Certificate of Approval for films deemed "factually representative of modern naturism".[52] No reply was recorded but John Trevelyan, Chief Censor, later stated, "We know perfectly well that the people who make nudist films do so for commercial sex exploitation." However, he went on to argue that naturism could serve a purifying function in the emerging British sex film industry for both producers and censors when he said that these types of films could be kept "within reasonable bounds" if they had to "put up the pretence of advocating naturism".[53]

British film censors approved pseudo-naturist films for general release in the late 1950s and early 1960s but not without careful consideration and, in some cases, cuts. Producers were aware of what

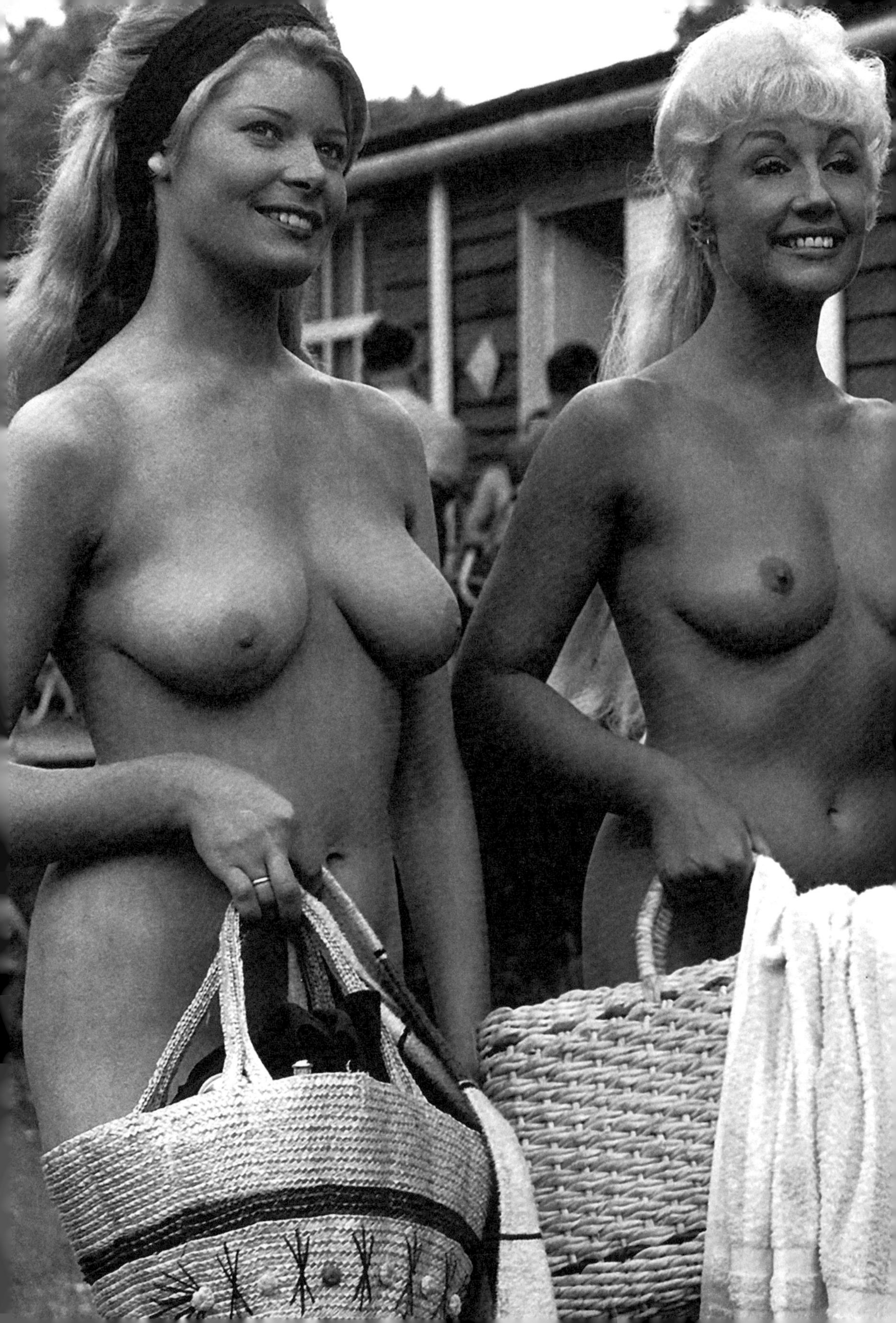

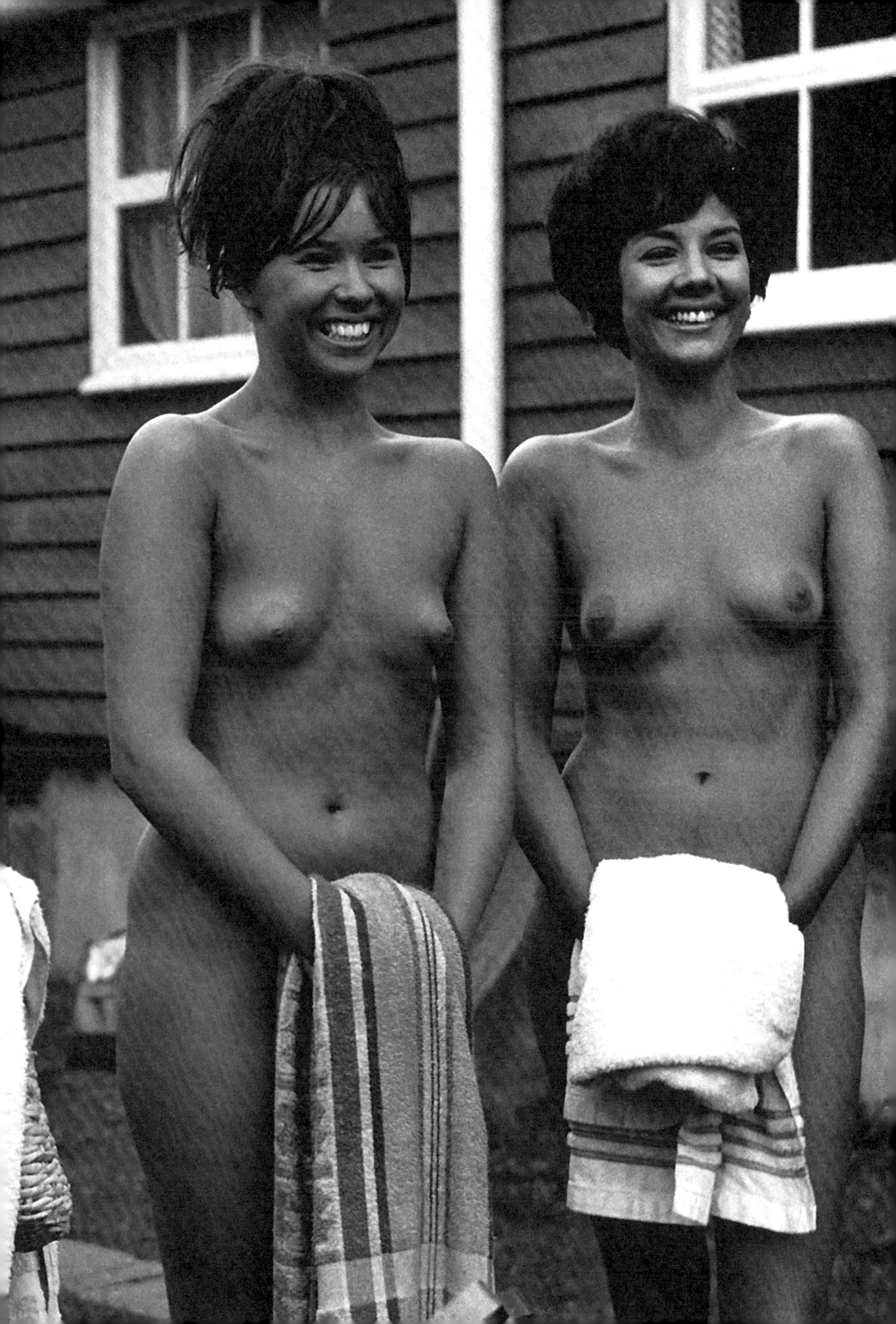

might get their films pulled so they moderated scenes by shooting bodies at a distance and screening genitals with fencing, furniture, or tactically placed props. Green recalled that during the filming of *Naked—As Nature Intended*, a gust of wind blew up her dress and revealed "a lot more than a glimpse" of her G-string. The footage was rejected by the production manager as "not the sort of shot that would go down well with the Naturist Movement".[54] Another scene, involving Green towelling her wet and naked co-star Jackie Salt, was also eliminated in advance as too risqué. The intended opening scenes, showing Green and the actor Petrina Forsyth at home, in towel and negligee respectively, ostensibly planning their holiday route as flatmates, was included in the director's cut but was rejected by censors who thought it implied lesbianism. The representation of homosexuality was not banned in British cinema in the period but, from the censor's point of view, Trevelyan felt "the subject was one that would probably not be acceptable to the British audience".[55] Homosexuality, and the changing laws and attitudes around its discussion and practice, was also of rising concern to the naturist movement.

A TYPE WE CANNOT AFFORD TO ADMIT

Although several prominent early naturists are known to have had same-sex relationships, from Roland Berrill, one of the 1924 founders of Britain's earliest nudist club, to Jan Gay and Eleanor Byrnes, the respective author and illustrator of the influential 1933 book *On Going Naked*, the subject was taboo in mid-century naturist circles, just as it was in larger British society.[56] Homosexuality was rarely addressed in early naturist publications, and when it was, it was treated hurriedly, elliptically, and dismissively. A rare example can be found in a 1947 column in *Health and Efficiency*, where the author considered a possible solution to dealing with the excess of single men who were excluded from joining naturist clubs under the dominant "couples only" rules. He suggested "men only" clubs could be established as an alternative. As a result, he received eager correspondence from "many young men" who said they would prefer "a rough-and-tumble affair which reminded them of Service life" as an alternative to the genteel net sports, table games, and tea times that comprised usual nudist club activities. However, he regretted,

"Among the letters I received were a few from men who are of a type we cannot afford to admit into Naturism. I have replied to each one and, as might have been expected, I have received a good deal of abuse for my pains."[57]

The topic was also addressed in a 1949 issue of *Sun Bathing Review* that elsewhere reflected on Kinsey's *Sexual Behavior in the Human Male*, where 37 per cent of the American respondents had reported some experience of homosexual activity. Here, too, the author did not mention homosexuality by its name, but in his "Viewpoint on Men's Clubs", he made it clear that he deplored the proposition: "The segregation of the sexes is diametrically opposed to the tenets of nudism as we know it. For men to band themselves together in naked companionship with others of their own sex is to isolate themselves completely from the relationships of which we all stand in need. In discarding one inhibition," he stated, "they may acquire a worse."[58]

By the early 1950s homosexuality began to be addressed by the British press more broadly, particularly as high-profile prosecutions included well-known cultural and aristocratic figures, from the actor Sir John Gielgud to Lord Montagu of Beaulieu. Homosexual acts between men had been illegal in Britain since 1885 but the morality crackdown of the 1950s had seen prosecutions rise dramatically, and by 1954 over 1,000 men a year were imprisoned for crimes relating to homosexuality. Despite the more public discourse, attitudes were mostly hostile in the period, with homosexuality characterized as perverted "unnatural practices", to borrow a phrase from Conservative MP Cyril Black.[59] Calls for understanding and decriminalization were limited to a few progressive voices.

As naturism had been aligned at its founding with a broader set of social reform agendas, with key members participating in ventures such as the Federation of Progressive Societies and Individuals, established 1935 and later renamed the Progressive League, the debates reached the naturist press.[60] In 1954, for example, the formal affiliation of the Progressive League with the British Sun Bathing Association came up for discussion. The editors of *The Naturist* noted with alarm that the League's campaign for revision to the homosexuality laws would "come to be associated with naturism, and thus cause naturism to be misunderstood by the general public". The editor argued that the time had come to break the link between naturism and progressive causes. The two had drifted apart in the intervening decades: "The League is not a naturist organisation, though it approves of naturism in theory. It is pledged to secure reforms in many other spheres far remote from naturism."[61]

The editorial prompted rare naturist discussion on the subject, which was illustrative of a strand of conventional medical discourse about homosexuality in Britain at the time; that is, it was an unfortunate psychological condition from which some people suffered and from which they might be cured. One correspondent clarified that the Progressive League did not wish to condone homosexuality but aimed "to reform the treatment of homosexuals who are not criminals but sick people who need a different and more humane treatment that a criminal prison sentence". L. T. Minchin, chair of a naturist club and a Progressive League member, made his case: "Nearly all enlightened people feel that the present legal penalties for male homosexuality are barbaric and outmoded. By general consent," he observed, "they are ineffective as a deterrent." Finally, a Liverpool nurse wrote to defend homosexuals against a naturist who described them as animals. "Some of these patients (yes, patients) are the brightest and most brilliant of men," the correspondent concluded. "I am ashamed to belong to a movement which harbours such narrow-minded, sordid-thinking individuals."[62]

In the later 1950s the British government's Wolfenden Committee undertook a formal process of evidence-gathering on homosexuality from medical professionals, police, magistrates, lawyers, and clergy, alongside a small group of elite homosexual men in public life. The resulting report, published in 1957, recommended decriminalizing private homosexual acts between consenting adults over 21.[63] The process and outcome attracted a tremendous amount of press attention and reached naturist periodicals. "Strix", a regular contributor to *Sun Bathing Review*, noted in 1958: "Inevitably, the Wolfenden Report has come into the picture, not because 'anything to do with sex immediately interests nudists', as a critic once sneered, but because we are unconventional, unorthodox and are receptive of new ideas." He clarified: "Men and women who are rebellious enough to become nudists are more than likely to be unprejudiced when some departure from generally accepted standards of behaviour is being considered."[64] This open-minded view, however, was not unanimously shared.

A *Health and Efficiency* article entitled "Odd Men Out", inspired by further parliamentary discussion about putting Wolfenden recommendations into practice, attempted to summarize in 1965 "what organized Naturism's attitude is to homosexuals in the fold". Despite the guise of a dispassionate authorial voice, the author Robin Black felt "repelled" by the "disturbing" fact that "there are many, many thousands of homosexuals, and in the very nature of things, some of them are naturists". He knew of three men-only naturist clubs; each had been terminated "when it was found that they attracted homosexuals". He surmised: "The 'queers', always under threat from the existing law, were on the look-out for some more secure place where they could meet others of their kind." While it was surely true that an ostracized minority would want to seek out a community, naturist or otherwise, Black had little sympathy, using naturism as an ideological weapon to sexually discriminate, segregate, and shame. "Naturism is something so natural, so much of the open air, and so much for normal people," he claimed, "that that the odd men out will always be a tiny minority who will, law or no law, keep so much under cover that their impact will be negligible."

As part of his discussion, Black recalled that one of the "veterans" of the naturist press had been approached "on several occasions" by male readers who asked for "revealing" photographs. "In several instances he was even sent specimen snapshots showing exactly what was required, with explanatory letters." Black added, as an afterthought, "something that cannot be avoided. There are homosexual women." With no evidence or example, he concluded, "I do not consider that they are likely to be attracted to the Sun Clubs, or stimulated by pictures of naked females."[65] Lesbians had no public voice or dedicated space in mid-century naturism. A female correspondent wrote to *The Naturist*'s agony aunt in 1958 to ask after women-only clubs; the terse response was that there were none.

THE "LESS-CLOTHED RACES"
What British naturism was and who it was for came under heightened scrutiny in the 1950s and 1960s in a period of mass immigration, violent racism, and changing colonial relations. British naturists had repeatedly evaluated the national superiority of their own practices in the 1930s and 1940s, drawing contrasts with the

187

intellectual tendencies of their European neighbours and the differing tastes of American colleagues. Magazines in the 1950s provided round-ups of practices internationally; these show that formal naturism was largely observed in Europe, North America, and Australasia, with occasional endeavours in colonial locations with white British expatriate populations, such as South Africa. British naturists had little to say about and even less direct experience of undress outside the Anglosphere, where they tended to draw on exoticized stereotypes and racist assumptions.

As we have seen, early British exponents believed nudism to be a simple and healthy cure to a social problem afflicting urban populations suffering an excess of cultural sophistication.[66] As naturist author Michael Rutherford had put it, "the hectic atmosphere of our civilisation, with its noises, petrol fumes, the shrieking of advertisements, the background blare of the radio, the competition and concentration of earning a living" was the problem.[67] The solution was to cast off the trappings of modern life, including clothes, as a direct method of getting back to all that had been lost. The remedy's success was measured by the result that, as Douglas Stewart asserted, "modern naturism" was spreading to every "civilised" part of the globe. The contradiction in these statements was stark: naturism was both an antidote to civilization and an index of it.[68]

The generalized non-European "savage", in the language of early naturists, could be a source of envy. They believed that that this imagined figure offered a model to correct social ills: "The mingling of the sexes in the nude is the solution to all the sex-problems that have ever plagued civilized man. Primitive peoples in hot climates where clothes are not needed", it was commonly claimed, "have no sex problems."[69] The "less-clothed races" were also said to have no pain in childbirth and better digestion.[70] At the same time, a monstrous other was also evoked to illustrate the illogicality of English dress, where "ladies who regard with horror the savage women's habit of putting bars and rings of metal through a hole in her nose", as prominent philosopher C. E. M. Joad put it in 1933; nonetheless, English women wore rings and high-heeled shoes that crushed the flesh.[71] These reversals were meant to show that "societies untouched by European culture" were parallel and the so-called civilized society was bound by "taboos as strange and illogical as any self-imposed by the savage".[72] These were inversions and comparisons that, even when presented in positive terms, were based on ignorance and insult.

Some naturists who had overseas postings in the Second World War gained perspectives on what were described as the "less civilised parts of the world".[73] In an article that attempted to praise "other people's clothes" through observations brought by war travel, Commander J. H. Bowen stated that "where people regard clothing from simpler and more fundamental aspects", they were "healthier, cleaner and better off in consequence". His assessment of dress, from Bengal and Masai to Malta and Yemen, was admiring and patronizing at once, but was intended to provide reflection for the "bogged down" bodies of England.[74] Other international naturist reports included a Royal Navy seaman, "put ashore" on an island in the Manus in the North Pacific, who regularly went naked on the beach. He envied "the natives", who were "fine muscled fellows", "clad only in loin cloths".[75] Another contributor who had lived in East Africa was impressed by the "unremarked" exposure of women's breasts and the dignity of men's naked dance.[76] These were practices from which the British, with their "vaunted Western progress and applied intelligence", should learn.[77] Some naturists hoped that Britain was losing its "island outlook" through these international experiences, and creating "strong links of sympathy and understanding", but all accounts, even when full of praise, were othering, and in many cases, objectifying.[78]

This was particularly the case in relation to skin colour in a movement devoted to "beautifully-bronzed bodies" but whose British practitioners were all assumed to be white.[79] Every aspect of nude photographic guidance used white skin as its measure for exposure and lighting, even while early naturism was based on revulsion towards skin that had not been exposed to the sun. Medical practitioners who endorsed light therapy argued that non-tanned skin signalled ill-health, and naturists eagerly followed them, claiming "ordinary human skin is pale, anaemic, atrophied". This "ordinary", however, was also assumed to be white. Its "deadish white" state was likened to "grass which has been covered by a plank".[80] Browned skin signalled liveliness and the true natural state of being dressed in the sun. "The pigmented sun bather", heliotherapist Sir Henry Gauvain stated, "no more gives the suggestion of nudity than does an unskinned animal. Non-pigmented he appears naked; pigmented he no longer appears nude."[81] Conversely, for those who opposed nudism, especially among those who saw it as unnatural and foreign,

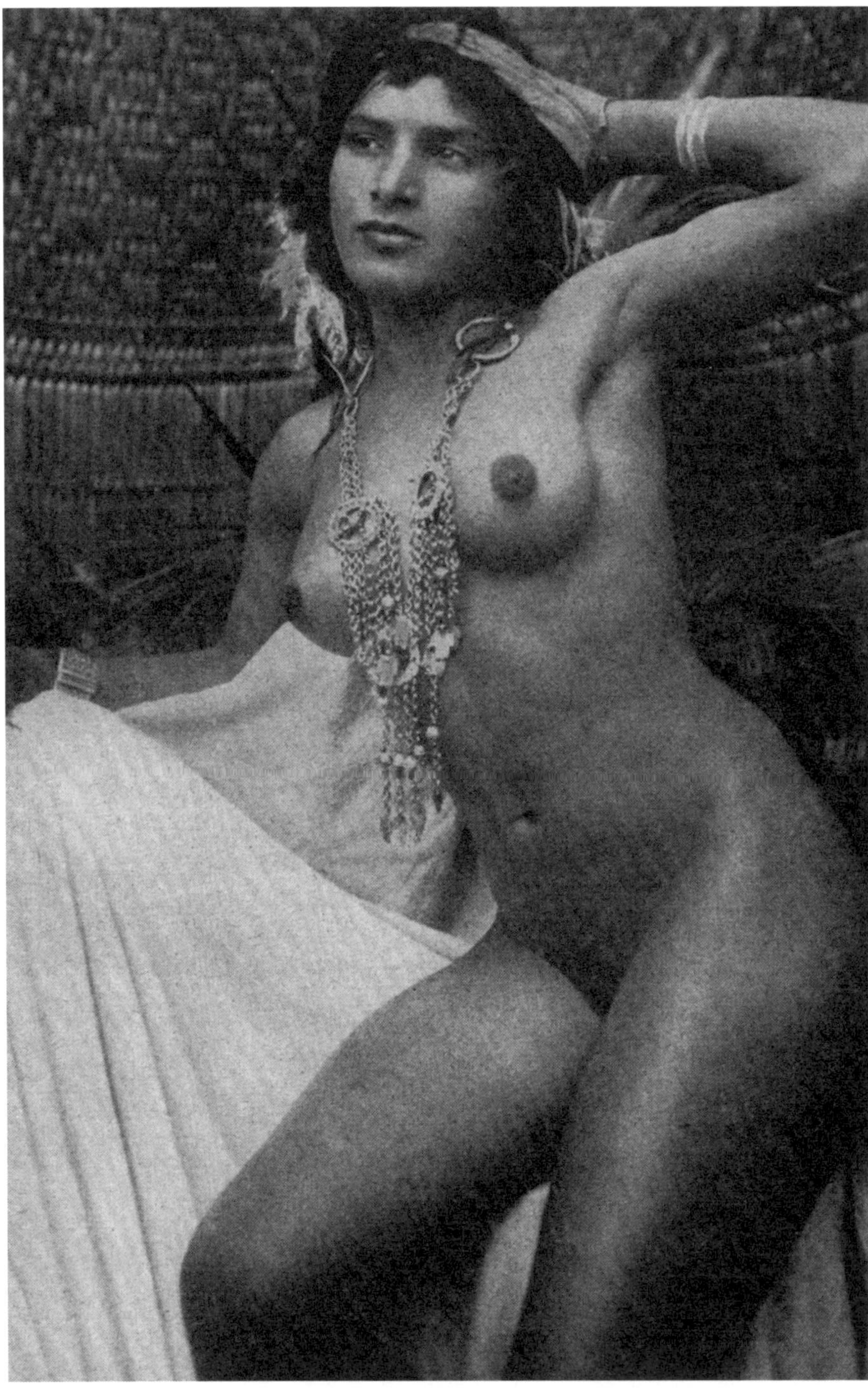

Women's black and brown skin was exoticized and eroticized in British mid-century naturist magazines. Illustrations invited aesthetic appraisal and accompanied racist and primitivist discussions.

whiteness was a merit. A 1936 correspondent to the *Daily Mirror* objected to nudism because "white races were certainly never meant to expose themselves in this way".[82] In the *Cornish Times*, a 1938 reader asked, "Can anything be more disgusting and senseless than a party of sunbathers trying to change their natural colour? It is to be wondered that they dare do such a thing; God could smite them as black as jet in less than a moment, and no amount of washing would ever get it off."[83]

TIMELESS "TYPES"

Black and brown models rarely appeared in early naturist photographs, and when they did, they were exoticized. Just as naturism provided a moral alibi for the consumption of images of naked white flesh in the 1930s, parallel ethnographic publications provided an alibi for consuming photographs of naked black and Asian bodies. *Nudes of All Nations* was produced in 1936 by Routledge as a follow-up to Park and Gregory's book *Sun Bathers* and was framed as a comparative study of "racial types". A book of photographs of sexualized young naked women, it began with an "English" subject, taken by Walter Bird, and moved through a showcase of international models, often posed in studio locations, but with some taken outdoors where "the tropical background lends added interest". Most photographs were given geographical titles to indicate their location, but some models were labelled in the racialized language of the time as Quadroon or Mulatto. The opening essay used the terminology of anthropological classification to discuss skull, jaw, and nose shapes, hair textures, and skin colours to reinforce white supremacy. The book was intended to be a celebration but it reiterated norms even as it deviated from them. "Those who imagine that beauty of face and form is a monopoly of the white races of Europe", it noted, "will be surprised at the exquisitely graceful proportions of people on whom they are accustomed to look down as primitive, uncivilised, even animal."[84]

Occasional naturist magazine articles in the 1930s and 1940s, such as "Beauties of Three Races: White, Yellow and Black", offered pseudo-anthropological contrasts as a means to show topless photographs of women from China and Rwanda alongside photographs of the "typical Anglo-Saxon girl".[85] Their texts often refer to "we British" and reproduced clichés, calling Africa the "dark continent" and

191

claiming that the "Near East" (Tunisia, Egypt, and Libya) is characterized by "ferocity", "pillage and brigandry".[86] The accounts denigrate the "strange-looking" appearance of "natives" while also appraising women's black and brown bodies in lascivious terms, described as "broad-hipped and full-breasted to propagate their species".[87] Young women were called "dusky beauties" and shown amid woven blankets and ceramic pitchers as the timeless "types" of early 20th-century photo-postcards from North Africa produced by Europeans for tourist markets.[88] These photographs, in particular, were repurposed from *Nudes of All Nations* and appeared again in John Everard's 1955 book *Oriental Model*, which showed the results of his cargo-ship travels across Asia in pursuit of naked "Far Eastern beauties", again mostly described in anthropological terminology. Everard's publication, according to his wife Jane, demonstrated the English photographer's triumph over international conditions of "prudery", which included "tribal taboos, the colour bar, the centuries-old Roman Catholic prejudices of the Philippines, the self-conscious nationalism of such countries as Indonesia, [and] the Moslem tradition of veiling and purdah".[89]

PINK-AND-WHITE SUN-LOVERS

British naturists in the 1930s and 1940s tended to view matters of skin colour in relation to what they perceived as foreign others. In the 1950s, more politicized discussion about skin colour and race emerged in naturist magazines. During this decade, the wider contexts of racial discrimination in Britain could not be kept out of the Garden of Eden fantasy. Naturists needed to address colour prejudices and restrictions of their own. Shifting immigration patterns and race-related conflict in Britain in the mid-1950s focused attention closer to home, including to the exclusive and sometimes exclusionary white naturist circles. In 1956, *Health and Efficiency* reported that "a young man now living in this country" had been refused admission to several naturist clubs "because he is coloured".

Robin Black, the article's author and regular nudist magazine contributor, acknowledged the wider context, stating, "It may very well be that with the steady influx of coloured folks in the past few years we shall have to investigate, discuss, and formulate a policy." As it stood, naturist clubs had no such thing. The article gathered a quick

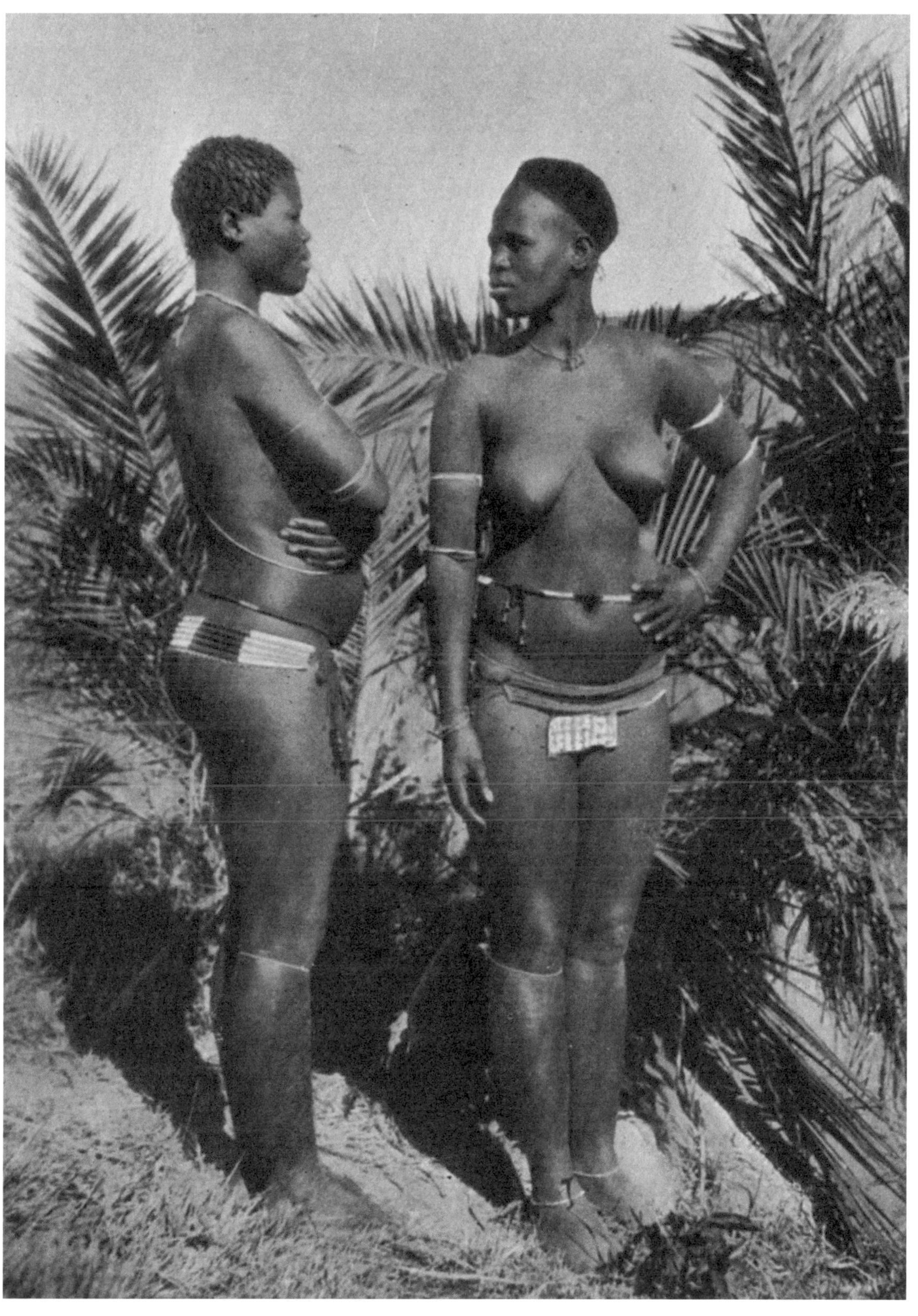

193

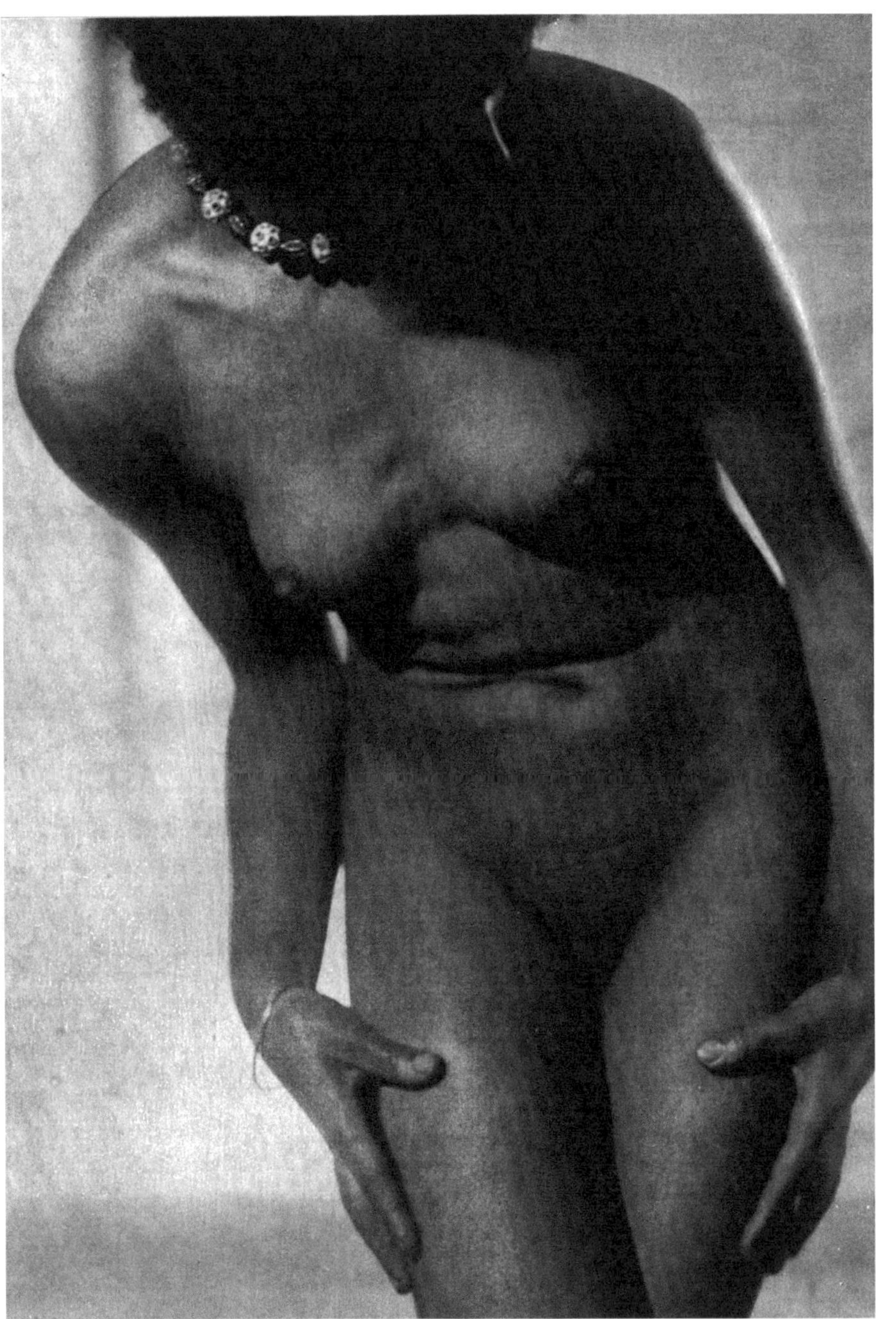

Bertram Park and Yvonne Gregory had depicted a more diverse range of ethnicities in their female studio nudes in the 1930s, but their sun bathing publications only featured white women.

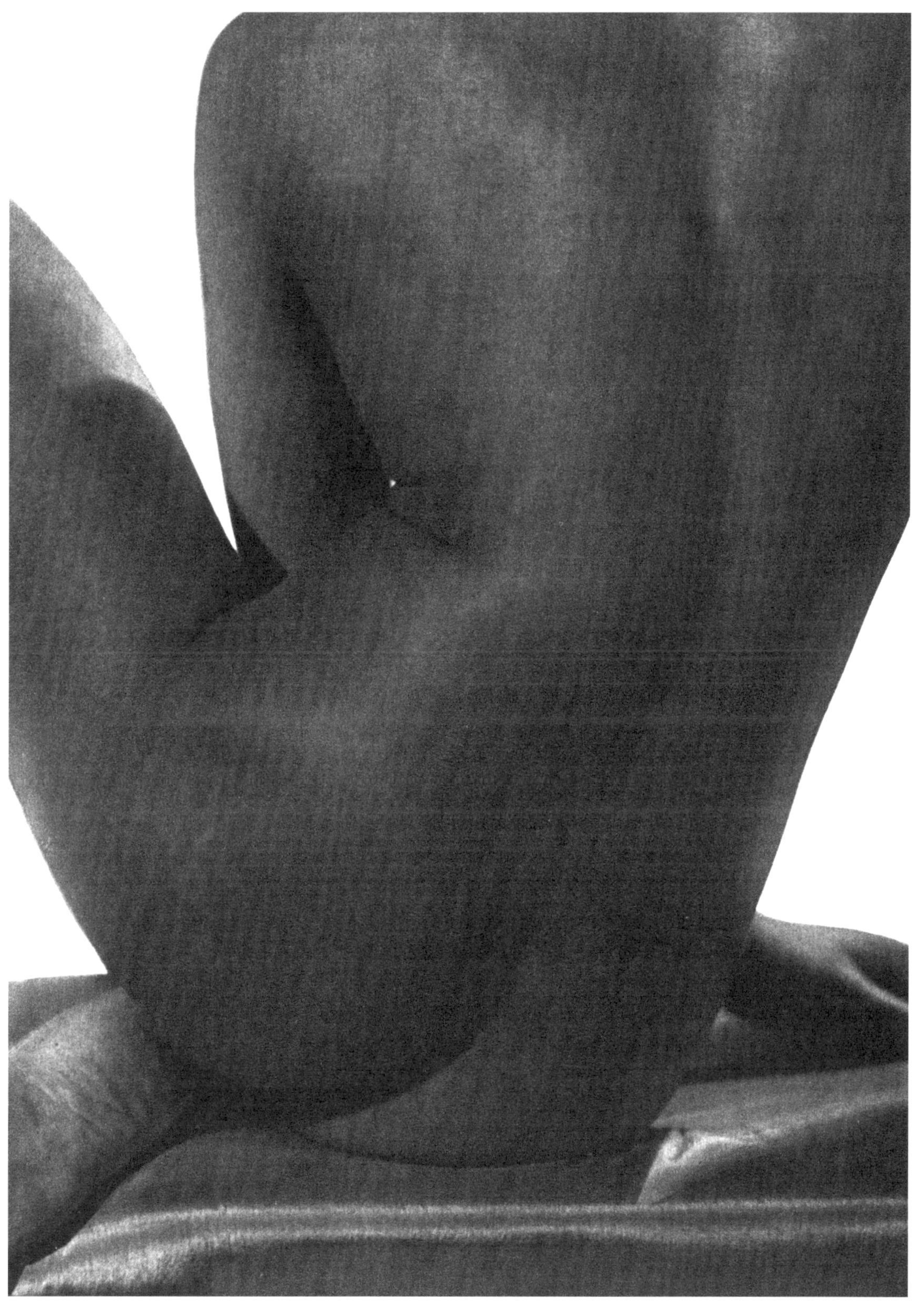

survey of club attitudes to "coloured nudists". This showed that applications from people of colour were few. One had an Asian couple on their list but another indicated that black applicants would need committee consideration in case white members objected. The author summarized, "There are many naturists, in most clubs, who would not give a whole-hearted welcome to a coloured man." His personal conviction was that this was wrong but he nonetheless defended clubs' autonomy.[90] As was the norm, the article was accompanied by photographs of all-white bodies.

As labour shortages in Britain underpinned the post-war wave of West Indian migration, by the mid-1950s London Transport was one of several major British companies recruiting directly from Barbados.[91] As a result, bus and rail services in the capital became a focal point for black labour. "There was a new face on the Piccadilly Tube the other morning," a 1958 article in *The Naturist* noted, "a smiling, dusky face set off by a smart London Transport uniform. And the face was yelling at the top of its voice: 'Mind the doors, please!'" To the article's author, the sight of such "coffee-coloured girls" working on the London Underground was welcome as long as they knew their place. He worried: "What happens when the coloured people begin to infiltrate into classes and professions which were previously the prerogative of only the 'intelligentsia'? What happens when white people find their jobs being taken over by the new breed of dusky Britishers?"[92]

These concerns reflected wider racist anxieties, but there was a naturist implication. "The occasional entry of a dark-skinned couple into our pink-and-white community of sun-lovers", the author stated, "is regarded as delightfully refreshing. But, friends, how are you going to feel if you are the only pink-and-white skins in a membership of dark brown bodies and thick lips?" His speculation was that it could be positive, if "the advent of coloured folk in our midst makes us look again at our puny, sun-starved bodies and resolve to do something about them". The final observation, that "coloured people will be accepted easily and naturally into our activities" if they looked like the "dusky maidens" adorned with shell jewellery and hair flowers in the article's accompanying photographs, was less progressive.[93]

In 1965, *Health and Efficiency* echoed this claim that "coloured men and women" were tolerated in Britain "so long as they are willing to take on the less popular forms of work", but the author also

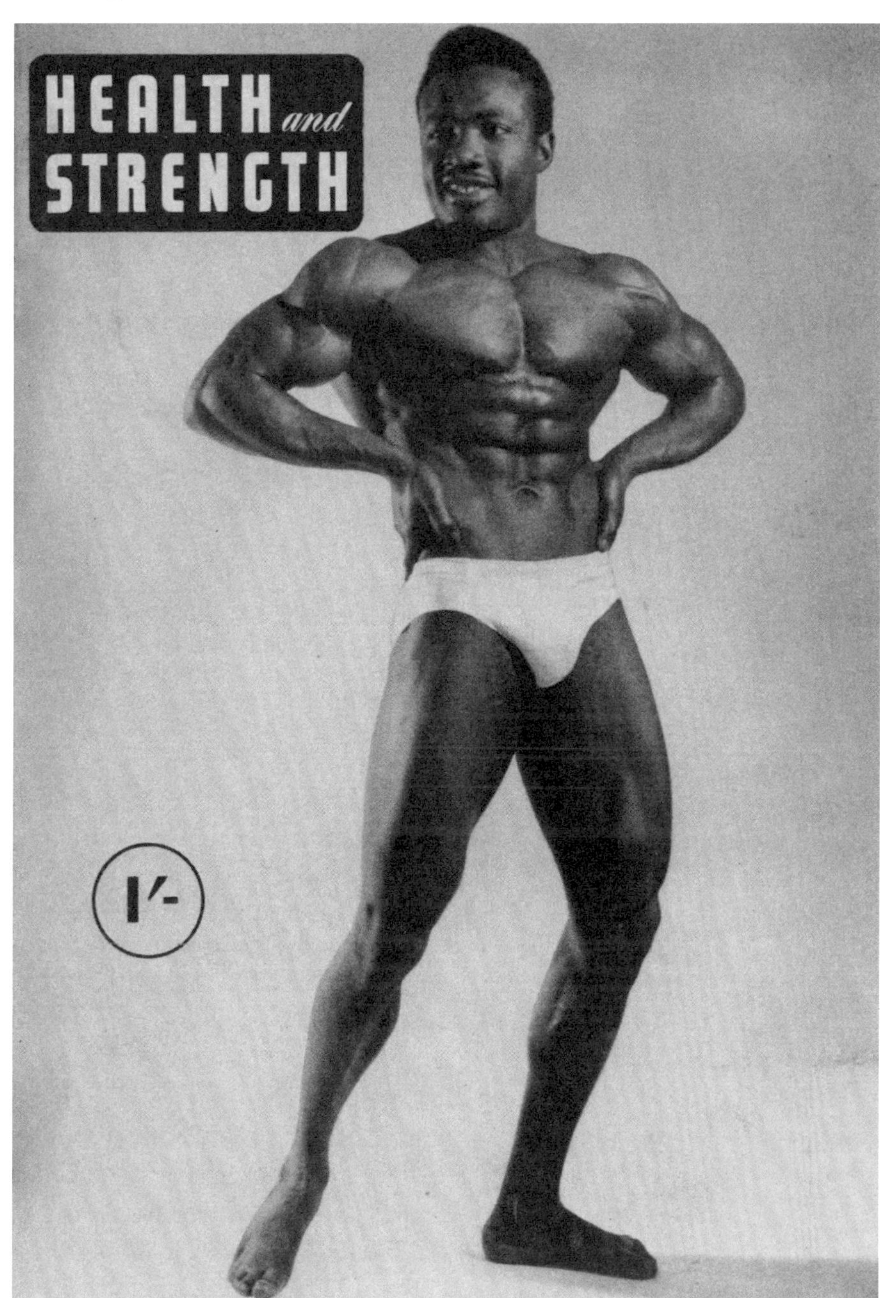

Bodybuilders, nude and dressed in skimpy posing pouches, appeared in physique and naturist periodicals alike. Models covered a wider range of ages and ethnicities than naturist magazines, following the contours of the international competition circuit.

suggested that "the naturist movement throughout the world has it within its power to play an active and notable part in breaking down the barriers of racialism wherever they exist. It can do this", he argued, "by letting it be known as widely as possible that in naturism at least, all are equally welcome, no matter what the colour of their skins." In the same year that the article was published, the Race Relations Act made racial discrimination a crime in Britain.[94] In a naturist context, racially discriminatory British clubs, "Sunny Pepys" suggested, should be barred from the International Naturist Federation. He suggested following New Zealand: "They are proud to have in their club Maoris, Chinese and Polynesians, along with all the other races that go to make up their community. They accept people for what they are; not how they look." Despite its progressive basis, the article took an us-and-them perspective: the inclusive attitude was "a belated acknowledgement of our regret that it was our missionaries who forced them to dress up in foolish western clothes".[95]

In the same year, *Health and Efficiency* published two nude photographs of black subjects, and received an enraged letter in response from a naturist claiming to speak on behalf of many about people of colour in the movement. The editor, Leslie Bainbridge, took the opportunity to reaffirm naturism's philosophical basis, as he saw it, as "complete acceptance". He argued, in unwitting contradiction of some of the movement's founding exclusionary aims, that "the bond of union is common social nudity and not social status, profession, creed and colour". He referred to contemporaneous civil rights protests in the US, which enabled him to segue to his pet subject, that of photography and obscenity. Bainbridge was keenly driving his magazine towards greater explicitness in depiction. As a nude photographer, bodybuilder, and former Mr Universe, as well as an editor of more sexualized illustrated magazines, he revelled in the increased visibility of nude bodies, and he tethered his interests to wider calls for social and sexual emancipation.[96] Quoting *American Sunbather*, Bainbridge argued that the obscene was, in fact, "that which shows the police dogs being unleashed on the Negro demonstrators in Birmingham". Bainbridge went even further, summoning the "lewdest" pictures of all to make his point. More obscene than all the tawdry products of the smut industry, he said, were "the pictures of Dachau, the ovens, and the grotesque pile of human corpses".[97]

NEW PLEASURES OF LOOKING

By 1960, *Health and Efficiency* was the last of the first wave of British naturist magazines, having incorporated *Sun Bathing Review* in 1959. *The Naturist* ceased production at the start of the decade.[98] *Health and Efficiency* was owned at this time by Man's World Publishing, which also produced *Man's World* magazine. As a pocket-sized publication of male physique photography established in 1953, *Man's World* had expanded progressively to incorporate other physical culture magazines, including *Body Sculpture* and *Modern Man*. Later in the decade it would merge with rival pictorial publication *Health and Strength*, established 1899.[99] *Man's World* in the early 1960s was as full of images of eroticized, posed, and muscled male bodies as *Health and Efficiency* was full of idealized females.

They shared not only an editorial team but also a design style and many of the same advertisements, in many cases supplied by the same publisher. While there were depictions of a wider range of ages and ethnicities than naturist magazines—following the contours of the international bodybuilding competition circuit—the key difference was audience. If *Health and Efficiency* was overtly heterosexual, *Man's World* and similar "physique" magazines, as they were known, were covertly homosexual, and their appeal to gay men at the time is now widely acknowledged.[100] Physique magazines figured large in the visual imaginations and personal collections of prominent queer men in pre-liberation Britain, from playwright Joe Orton to artist David Hockney.[101]

As already shown, when British naturist magazines first emerged in the 1930s, their visual content included both sexes. As the decades went on, naturist magazines only included women on their covers, and images of men were sidelined within. Physique photography competitions for men continued into the early 1950s but magazines regularly reiterated that "natural" outdoor photographs with an emphasis on "beauty of physique rather than muscularity" were wanted.[102] Photographs of men performing formal poses and displaying highly worked bodies were discouraged. What should stand in its place, however, was never clearly specified, and without further direction, readers continued to submit photographs with a bodybuilding aesthetic.

By the 1960s, in parallel, the photographs in physical culture magazines were dominated by flexed, hyper-masculine bodies in the briefest of briefs in dramatically lit studio shots populated with Greek

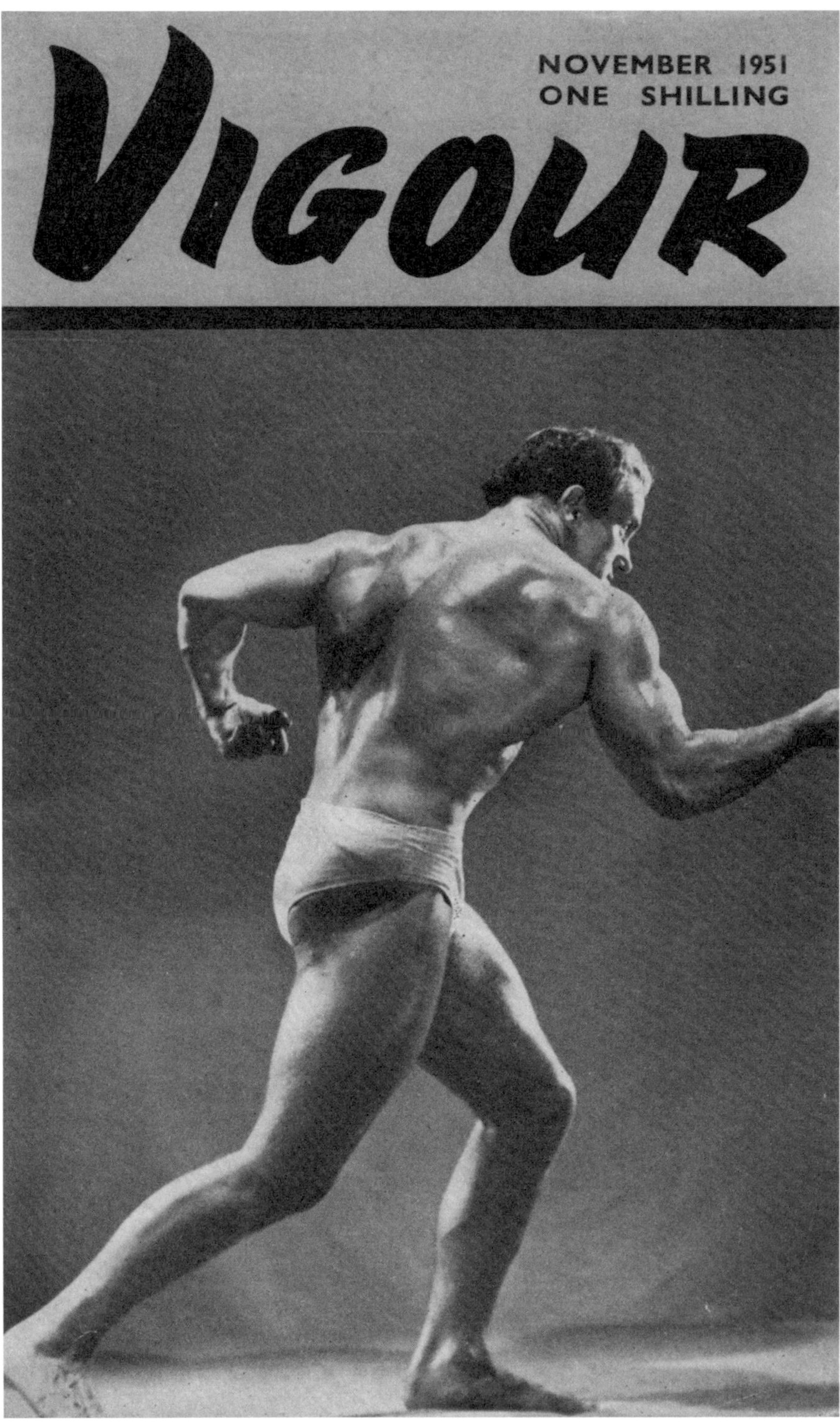

Left - Physique magazines were mostly men-only spaces but they shared their publishers, advertisers, photographers, and models with naturist magazines. Their appeal to homosexual men in pre-liberation Britain is widely acknowledged.

Right - Physique photographers used studio and outdoor settings to depict health and strength. Models included Sean Connery, who posed for artists and was a competitive bodybuilder in the 1940s and 1950s before he found fame as an actor.

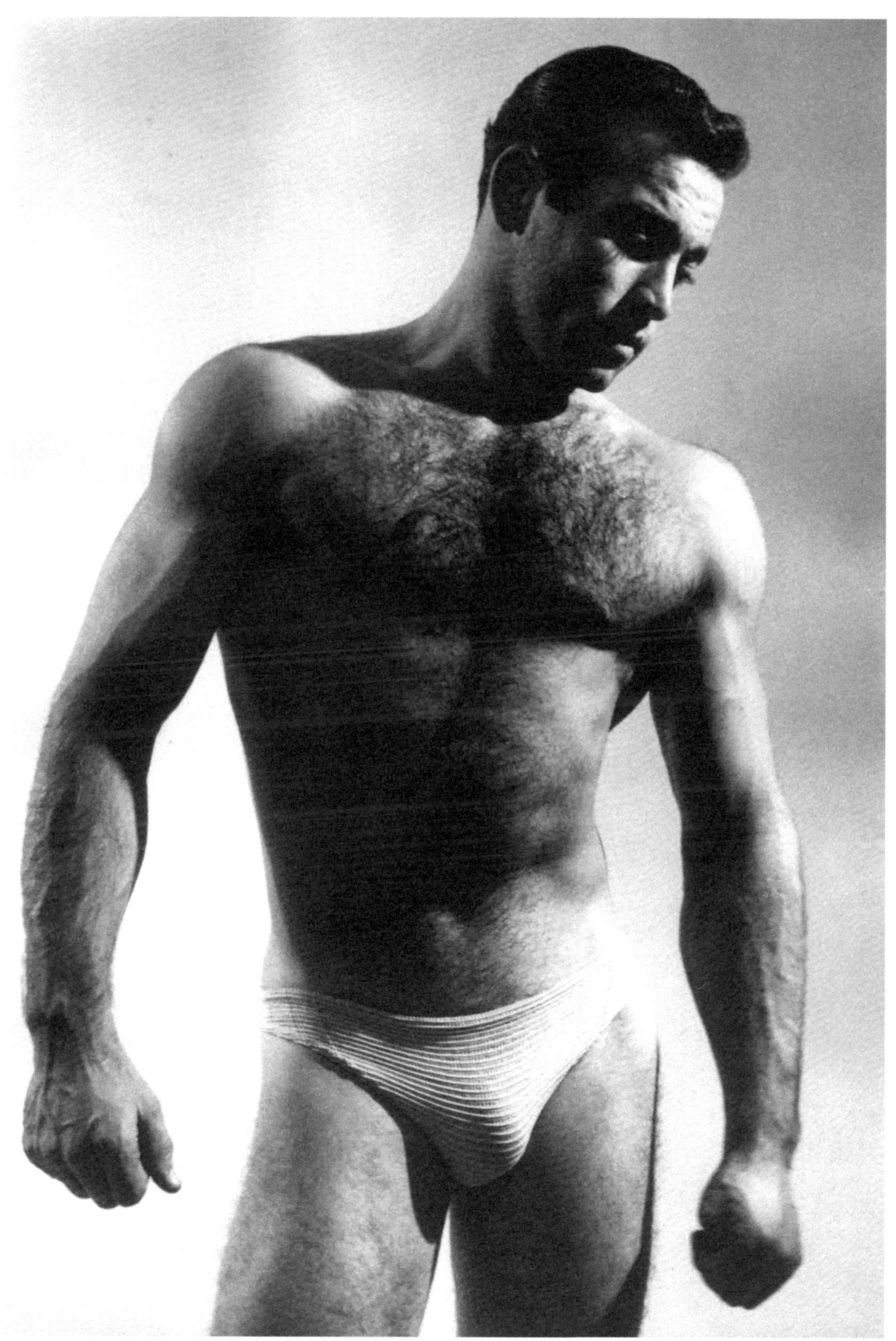

201

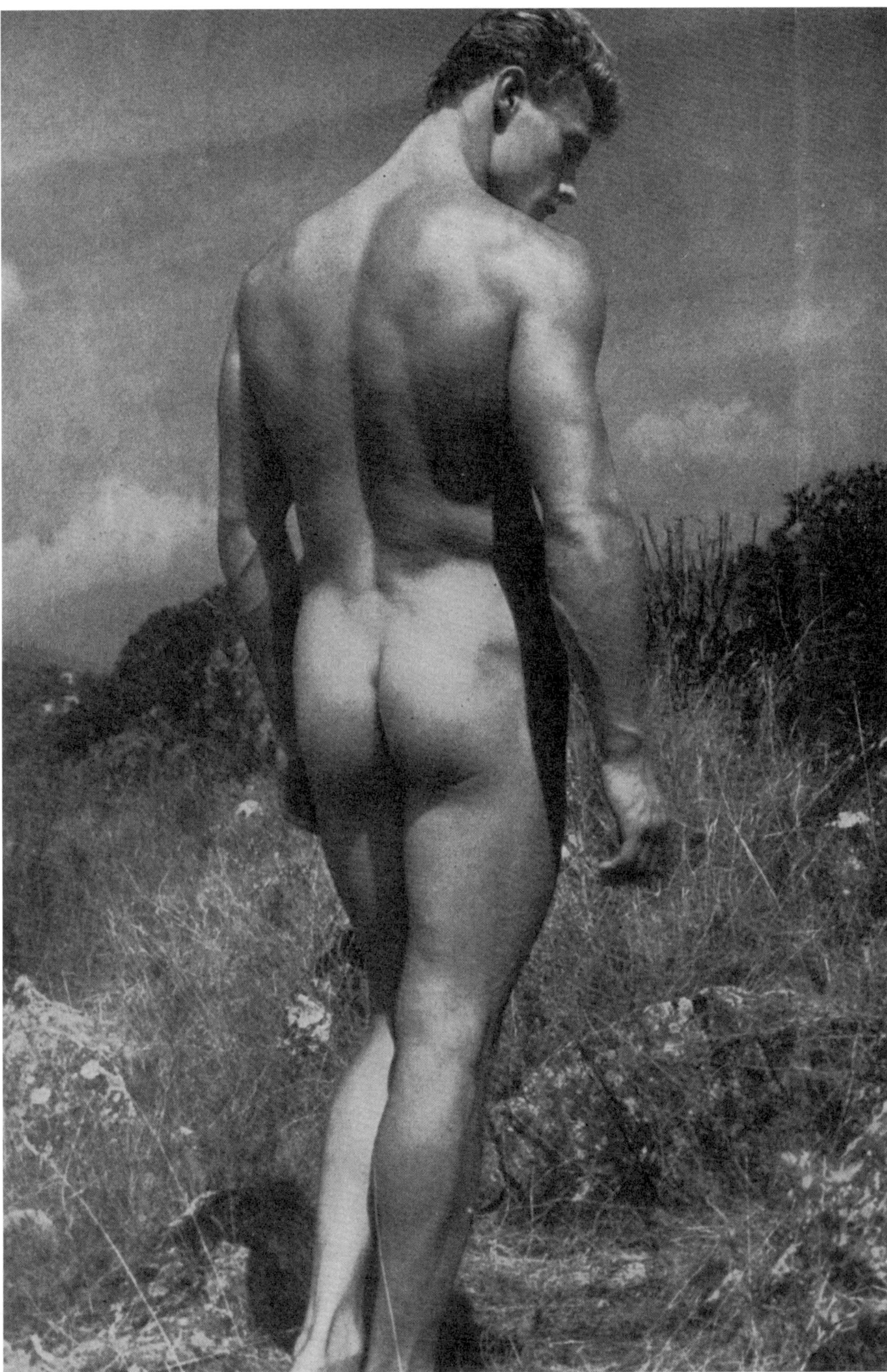

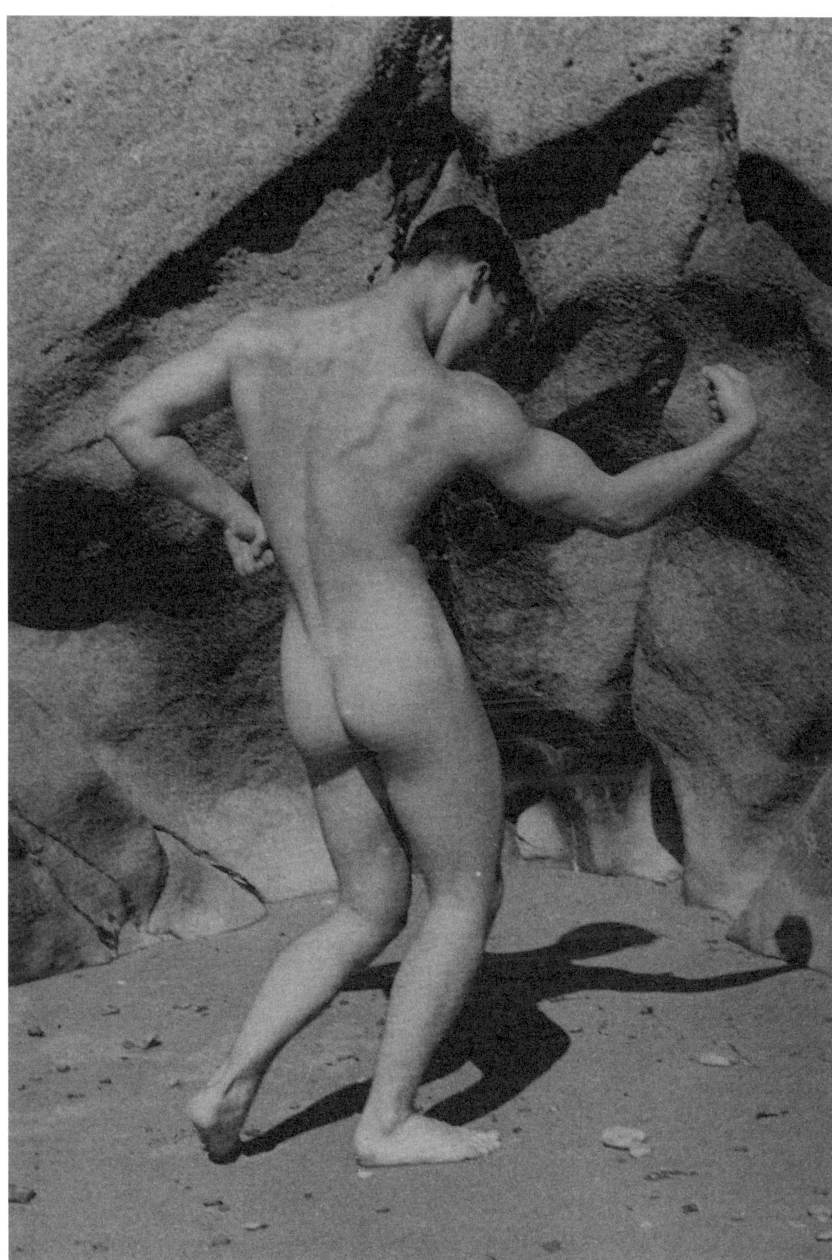

Left - Male nudes, heroic and coy, frequently featured in naturist magazines, although they were always fewer in number than female nudes. In the context of changing public attitudes to homosexuality from the 1950s, their homoerotic potential worried some homophobic naturists.

Right - Vince (Basil "Bill" Green) was the most prolific British post-war photographer of muscular men. He published in naturist and bodybuilding magazines. From the 1950s he ran a business designing and making posing pouches and, later, tight-fitting menswear.

columns and heroic props. The magazines provided a clandestine space where sexual material could be circulated and sexual networks built through reader photography competitions, mail order book and print sales, and so-called "discreet" photographic processing services. These mirrored many of the services provided by naturist and photography magazines targeted at heterosexual men, from baldness remedies to the erectile correctives euphemistically styled as "mighty tonics" for "gland treatment" and "loss of virile tone".

While they addressed different audiences, there was striking visual overlap between this line of bodybuilding imagery and naturist culture, and depictions of muscular men by photographer and bodybuilding judge Gregor Arax, for example, appeared in both *Health and Efficiency* (naturist) and *Health and Strength* (non-naturist). Perhaps the most significant crossover between nudist and physique magazines is the inclusion of material by Vince of London, otherwise known as Basil "Bill" Green. As the preeminent studio photographer of male physique imagery in mid-century British magazines, his partial nudes were, like others, curtailed by the legal requirement to conceal genitals. Green could not easily find suitable posing garments for men, so improvised by cutting down women's Marks & Spencer knickers until they were "very slick" and "very brief" on his male models.[103] In 1950 he experimented with making his own designs, and was overwhelmed with demand; he consequently shut down his photographic studio and turned full-time to fashion production, first selling posing wear but later expanding into a wider range of mail-order garments for men, mostly advertised in theatrical and health magazines, including naturist publications, before opening a shop that served queer communities in London and seeded the famous Carnaby Street fashion revolution.[104]

Throughout the 1950s and 1960s, naturist magazines advertised clothes for erotic exhibition that ran contrary to their editorial chastity. Women could choose from sheer swimming costumes with "high thigh cut legs" or "Pagan" bikinis in leopard skin pattern. Men had the greatest options via Vince or his young protégé, John Stephens, trading as Domino Male, including "short shorts" in leather-look and zebra print, "the world's most daring sunbriefs", and "sheer luxury 20 denier nylon" or flesh-coloured "featherweight" trunks with side rings fastenings entitled "Naturiste".[105] The inclusion of these items disrupted the assertively heterosexual and even the neutral non-sexual

204

messages of the articles and suggested different pleasures of looking and being looked at.

Promotions for men's jock slips, jock straps, loincloths, and G-strings had been a part of naturist publications from the earliest days of the movement. In Hans Surén's 1924 *Man and Sunlight*, the author wore a discreet black garment of this kind to enable front views as he demonstrated exercises; a pattern for its home construction was given at the rear of the book. Early advertisements in naturist magazines sold similar garments as "supportive" medical products protecting against "rupture", with medicated, iodized inserts. By the 1950s, as emerging European naturist beaches stipulated that clothing be worn when leaving the designated site, a new garment called *le minimum* was created to provide the briefest of coverage, merely a triangle and tapes.[106] Some naturists described the garment as "ugly and suggestive", claiming that its inclusion would turn *Health and Efficiency* into a titillating *Paris-Hollywood*-style pin-up magazine. To its defenders, it was merely an expediency for photographing men who "have to be retouched with a much heavier hand than females before they can be depicted for publication, and no-one will deny that the result is even more ghastly".[107] The garment was said to be more "natural", though this claim was undermined by its availability in a flashy, gold lamé finish.

THE N-PRESS
As has been discussed, naturist magazines' editorial and advertising had long been in contradiction. From the earliest days there was an antagonism between the virile and heroic reader addressed by the articles and the imperfect reader addressed by the promoted products that together imagined a short, ageing, overweight, bald, impotent man, lacking in confidence, who needed to buy the treatments, services, and equipment to correct his many physical and mental ills. In the 1930s *Sun Bathing Review* had recognized the damage that commercial content of a "doubtful nature" could do to the reputation of the movement, which comprised "the right kind of people" who were "beyond reproach". They made full-page statements about their selectivity, observing that "advertisements more surely than any other feature colour a magazine and define its standard, scope and tone".[108]

By the 1960s these claims seemed quaint as advertisements grew ever more sensational and the fit with the pious sermons of the articles grew ever more awkward. In addition, throughout the 1960s, covers of *Health and Efficiency*, now the main public voice for naturism on the newsstands, became more obviously sexual. The models that posed in swimwear on the magazine covers began to overflow their bikini tops and tug suggestively at their bikini bottoms. Inside the nudist magazines, expanding photographic pages of young female nude models bending and reclining with sultry gazes and pouting lips were juxtaposed with reduced space for club news, printed in fonts too small to be easily read. This was a contrast too far for some readers. In 1964 a magazine was established for a new organization that aimed to represent more authentically what club-attending naturists wanted and needed.

British Naturism was to be the mouthpiece for a new unified body, the Central Council of British Naturism, which brought together two former consortia, the British Sun Bathing Association, established in 1943, and the Federation of British Sun Clubs, established in 1953. Each represented a cluster of clubs, each had its own constitution and committee, and each ran its own newsletter. In 1064, following years of discussion about wasted energy, the new conglomerate represented over 70 clubs and 1,000 individuals and formed a united front to promote shared causes and to attack common enemies.[109] The organization's title was carefully chosen. Nudism was popularly understood as a term, but it was formally rejected in favour of naturism in 1964 in an attempt to protect a movement dedicated to sun and health from the increasing glut of nude media with pornographic intentions. Many of these productions, however, called themselves naturist to borrow the movement's moral and legal protection; the word was freely used and widely abused.

From the outset, *British Naturism* addressed the problem of the movement's press, including an address on the subject by Erik Holm, President of the International Naturist Federation, which brought together organizational leaders from across the world.[110] "Naturist magazines are nearly as old as the movement itself", Holm noted, and "it was only with the appearance of one or more journals devoted to the naturist idea that the movement made any progress at all, in any part of the world". The importance of these forums was worth remembering, he said, for those who are "fed up to the teeth with naturist publications and are consequently prepared to throw everything connected with them on the bonfire". The problem was encapsulated by what Holm called the "absolutely scandalous periodicals issued in the name of naturism" that had put "the good standing of the movement [...] in serious danger". These magazines, which had "no more to do with naturist ideas than the flowers that bloom in the Spring", attempted to communicate legitimacy by including club news in their pages, giving the impression of an official relationship to the movement.[111]

His accusations named no names but the illustration of what he called the "N-press" showed a range of international illustrated nude magazines with variations of sun, health, and nature in their titles, including *Health and Efficiency*. Moral debate about magazines had been an annual anxiety at international naturist gatherings since their establishment in Britain in 1951. These annual events took place in a different member country each year and included formal lectures on aspects of naturist policy and practice alongside communal nude sports, nude social events, and meals for nudists of many nations. Discussions about the public face of naturism became more urgent as cheap illustrated magazines boomed across the continent. In 1956, for example, the President of the German Federation said that "the abuse of pictures" was such a problem that he would prefer publications to go without them than suffer misrepresentation. Holm had argued at the time that "the text was more important than the photos" but admitted "without model pictures there would be no sales to the general public".[112] By 1964, this relaxed attitude was gone. Holm asserted that "critical discrimination" needed to come between "muck and filth on the one hand and confident cultural endeavour towards sincere naturist goals on the other". He proposed that "every naturist organisation in every country" should set up approval committees: "No picture which has not been previously released by the Committee on the grounds that it was either non-aesthetic or unedifying should be printed."[113]

A European Voluntary Picture Control Board was established to this end, comprising continental members of the International Naturist Federation. Its first concern was with "integral male studies" in recognition of the known homosexual appeal of photographs of men "in statuesque pose". *Health and Efficiency* received news of "this censorship board" with incredulity, and worried it would cross

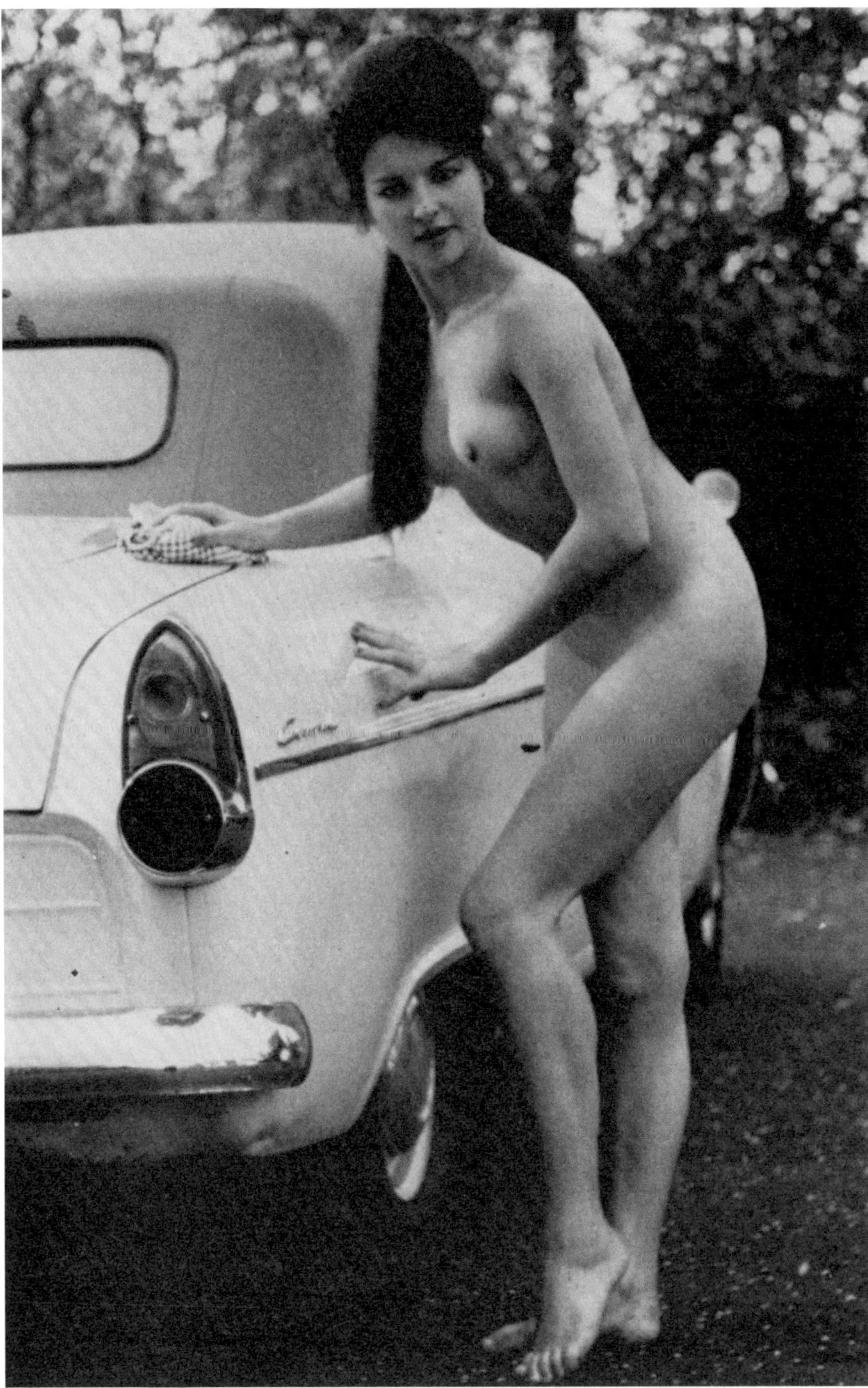

Naturist magazines in the 1960s continued to show nude bodies in camp maintenance, but their use of glamour models became increasingly obvious. The inclusion of a tree or a wheelbarrow could be all that distinguished a naturist nude from an erotic nude.

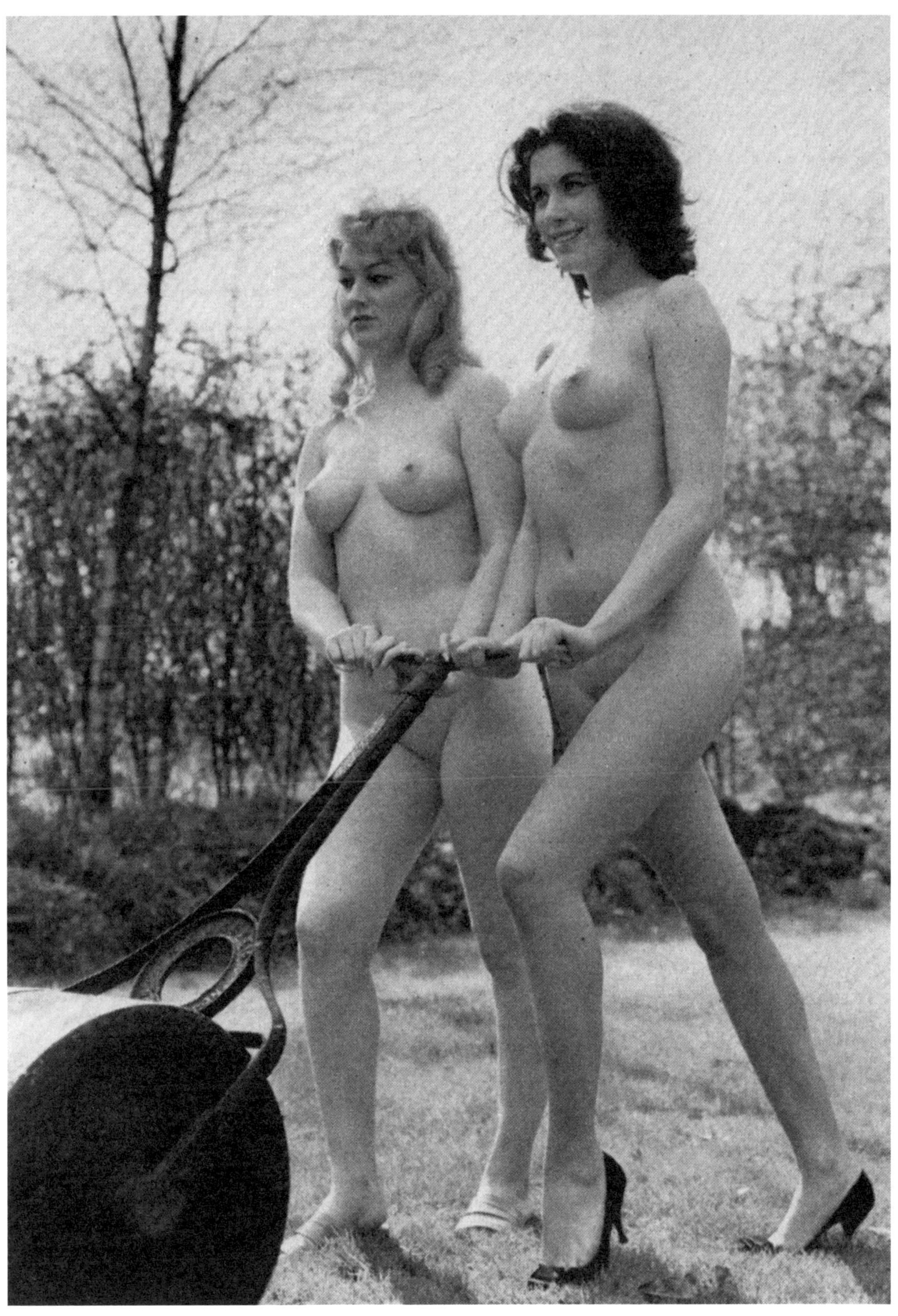

the English Channel. "Prudery has assumed the mantle of authority," the editor complained. "What will come next? A control on what the good naturist should read?"[114] In any case, the scheme proved unworkable. Commercial magazines operated outside the need for club approval and were expanding internationally at a rate beyond any voluntary control committee. Also, if police and parliament had struggled to evaluate the subjective boundaries of the aesthetic and the edifying, why would naturists be better arbiters? Thirty years of argument had shown that there was no consensus on what constituted an appropriate naturist image. British naturists were increasingly hostile to the commercial naturist press but they also recognized its utility. Research by the British Sun Bathing Association had shown that 64 per cent of men and 40 per cent of women first become interested in naturism through magazines. While the majority of naturists said they rarely read them once they were members, naturist publications constituted the single largest motivation for joining a club.[115]

Powerless to censure imagery that appeared elsewhere, *British Naturism* went it alone, producing its own photographs for its covers and contents, comprising mostly unposed scenes of camp life, including what had long been requested: depictions of a cross-section of naturists including the very old to the very young in mixed-gender family groups undertaking everyday club tasks. The paunchy and the bald were seen alongside the perky and the hairy. Pubic hair and genitals could be shown as the magazine was distributed to private members only; this subscription model also meant that no advertising was required. Clubs and federations had previously produced their own local publications, but *British Naturism* aimed to speak for the movement as a whole. The result was an authentic account of the realities of club life in a minority organization, little different from any other, and consequently as unremarkable. With no public-facing agenda and no need to attract commercial sales, the conversations focused on internal matters relating to membership fees and annual general meetings, mosquito cream, and the best kind of flask to keep cocoa warm at camp. The homely contents were more amateur parish newsletter than glossy magazine, especially once the money to produce a professional finish dried up and simple sheets of typescript had to suffice.

For some naturists, this was the organ they had long wanted, representing the movement as it was experienced. For others, especially in the context of a decade where cultural norms and conventions were being profoundly challenged, the product was flimsy, old-fashioned, and symptomatic of a wider problem. A complainant to *British Naturism* argued that the movement had become dull and domestic: "with very few exceptions", he said, it had "changed little in habits, outlook and activities during the past thirty years". The problem was that "nothing much happens apart from undressing and playing silly games. Naturism", he concluded, "has become respectable." While this was the outcome that many wanted, the comfort and security of an ageing movement was warned to have nothing to offer the young.[116] The author was not alone; many critical members in the 1960s claimed naturism was a moribund movement failing to connect with the radical new spirit of the times.

NATURIST YOUTH

Naturism's enduring search for reputability had seen it develop a formidable code of conduct since its earliest days of home visits and probing questionnaires, as has been previously noted. Vetting was seen as necessary protection against "the vulgar curiosity of sensation-seekers", safeguarding standards against any "lunatic fringe", but in the 1950s single membership requests still needed to come with the endorsement of an applicant's spouse, and under-21s needed the written permission of both parents.[117] The cumulative effect of self-imposed regulations, however, came to be perceived as joyless and restrictive in a period of greater informality. By the late 1950s, naturists could be expelled from camps for being divorced or for swearing.[118] Clubs had autonomy to impose their own rules, including where clothes could be worn and photographs could be taken, and what kinds of contact was permissible between members—no nude dancing and no piggy-backs in the pool, for example.

The regulatory culture was acknowledged in *British Naturism* in a cartoon where two naturists note, "It will be a great day when the movement finally gets rid of the concentration camp atmosphere," at a club entrance surrounded by barbed wire and signs declaring "No Alcohol, Members Only", and a timetabled Work Programme.[119] While the comparison was grotesque, it showed how the organizational structures of naturism were viewed by many, especially as the wider culture was beginning to let its hair down and traditional authoritarian

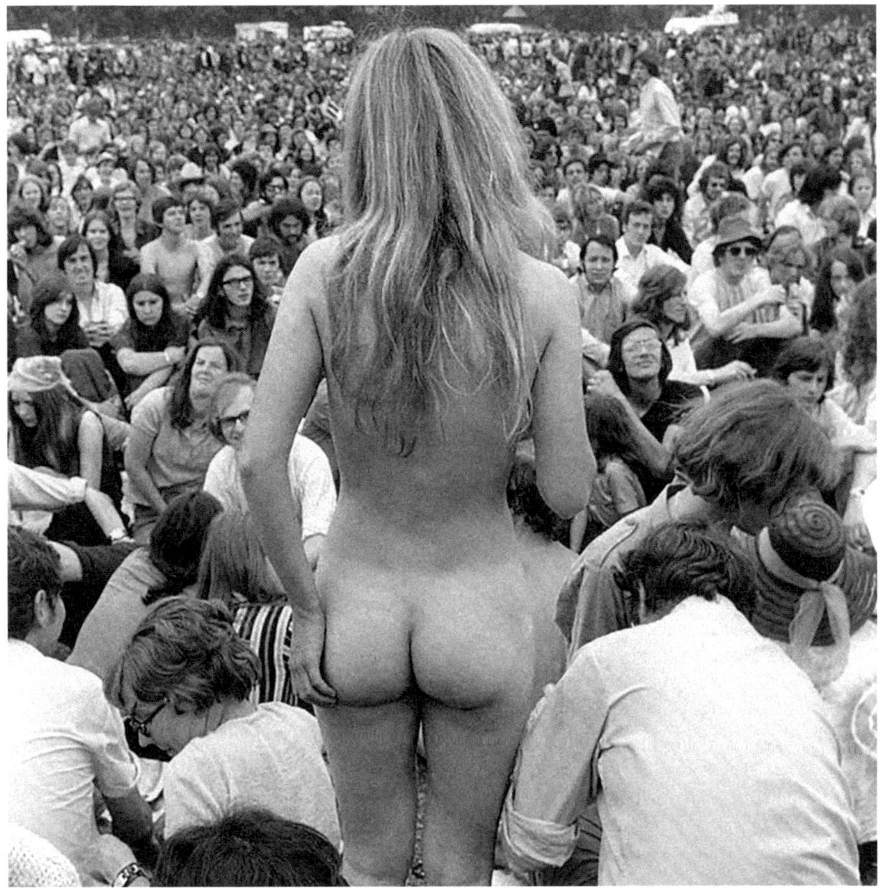

structures were increasingly questioned. With formalisation into federations and councils came increased bureaucracy. As one correspondent to *Health and Efficiency* put it, "I am fed up to the gills with club Nudism. I have met some very fine people in the camps and have had some good times, but for the most part I have found snobbery, prudery and a terrible sense of shame to say nothing of the terrible bore of rules, regulations, by-laws, resolutions, elections, petty politics, ninety-nine per cent of which do not mean a thing."[120]

Naturists could see the increasing acceptability of nude bodies in the wider culture, and recognized that they were losing monopoly on the territory.[121] British naturists, for example, were holidaying abroad in European resorts that welcomed naturists, and secluded British beaches were being tentatively used as unofficial sites for nude bathing without any need for personal checks, membership cards, or subscription fees. In the same years that British youth cultures in art and music were breaking new ground, and hippies were casting off clothing and sexual inhibitions at outdoor festivals as part of their countercultural rebellion, naturists wondered why young people were not attracted to their clubs. Even those who had been brought up in the movement tended to defect in their teens. The author "Sunny Pepys" summarized that young people were "bored by the almost religious air of dedication that attends so many of our activities, the Ark-like pairing of the sexes, the vicarage tea-party type atmosphere, the feeling on a chilly day that though we may not be enjoying it very much, it is doing us a lot of moral good as we watch the goose-pimples proliferate".[122] The numbers were devastating: the Naturist Youth of Great Britain organization comprised only 30 members in 1967 in a country with a population of 55 million that was undergoing a cultural youthquake.[123] Naturism was always a minority pursuit but young members were especially thin on the ground. A few hippy youths were pictured in the magazines, combining their naturism with folksy beards and banjos, but young people were simultaneously characterized by older members as too adventurous, and therefore likely to find naturism dreary, and too casual, and therefore be put off by its formalities. Naturists had long warned, "Young people are not flocking into the camps now, and unless they begin to do so soon, the official nudist movement may discover what it feels like to be dead from the neck upwards."[124]

Naturism, in fact, was never a young person's pursuit in Britain, although its visual culture always emphasized youth in both its models and its moral messages. The movement's middle-aged-and-up founders expressed worries from the start about the lack of younger members. In 1933, British nudists regretted that, unlike the Germans, whose nudism was closely aligned to its youth movement, "the younger generation are not as strongly represented in our nudist camps as they should be". There were high membership fees to produce and long distances to travel to sites, but there was also a dismissive attitude about young people's commitment: "a considerable proportion" of younger people were said to lack the "moral courage, independence of outlook, or seriousness of purpose" that were seen to be requirements of nudism.[125]

A survey of the ages of naturists in the early 1950s found the average to be around 40.[126] As teenage subcultures began to emerge

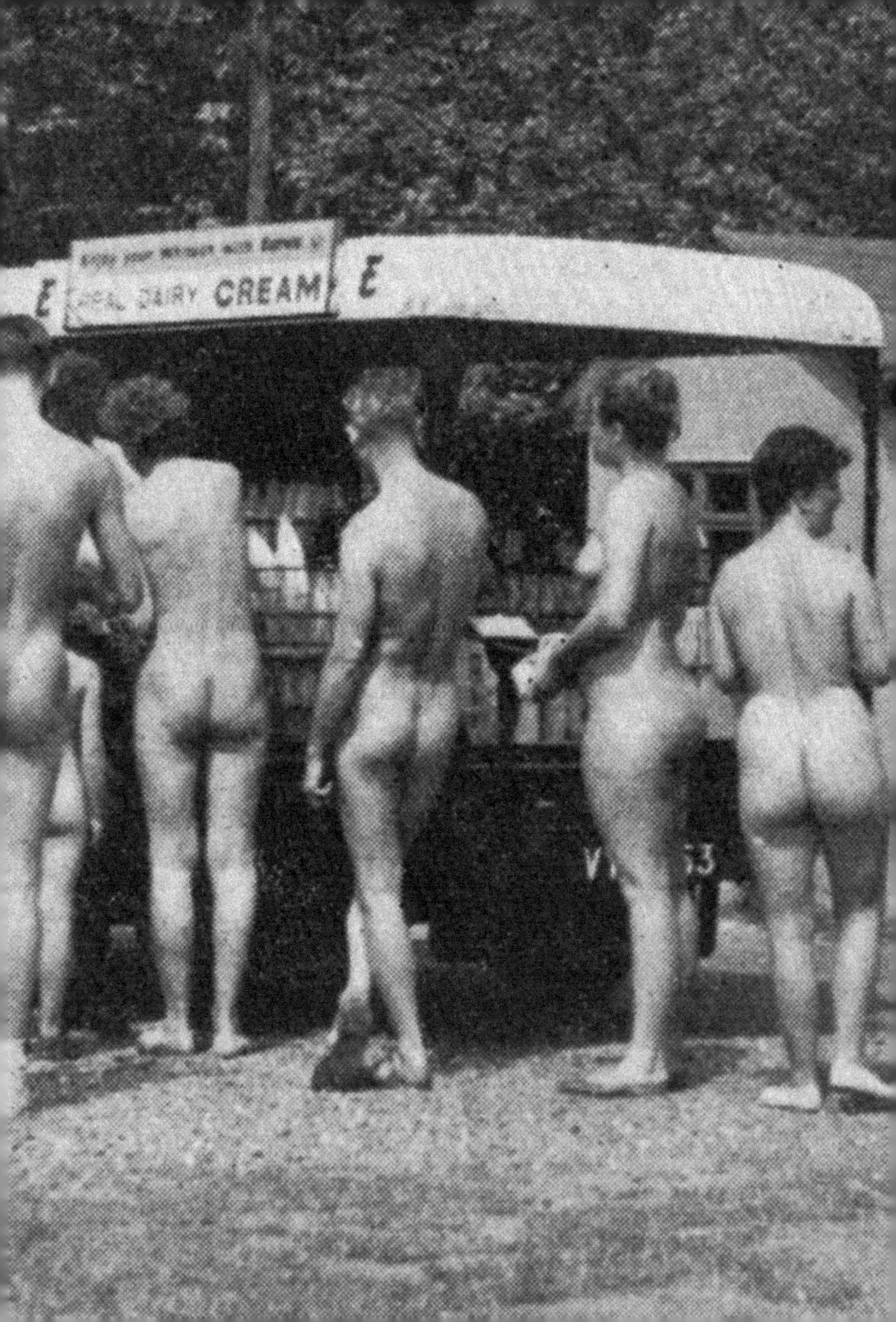
E
REAL DAIRY CREAM
E

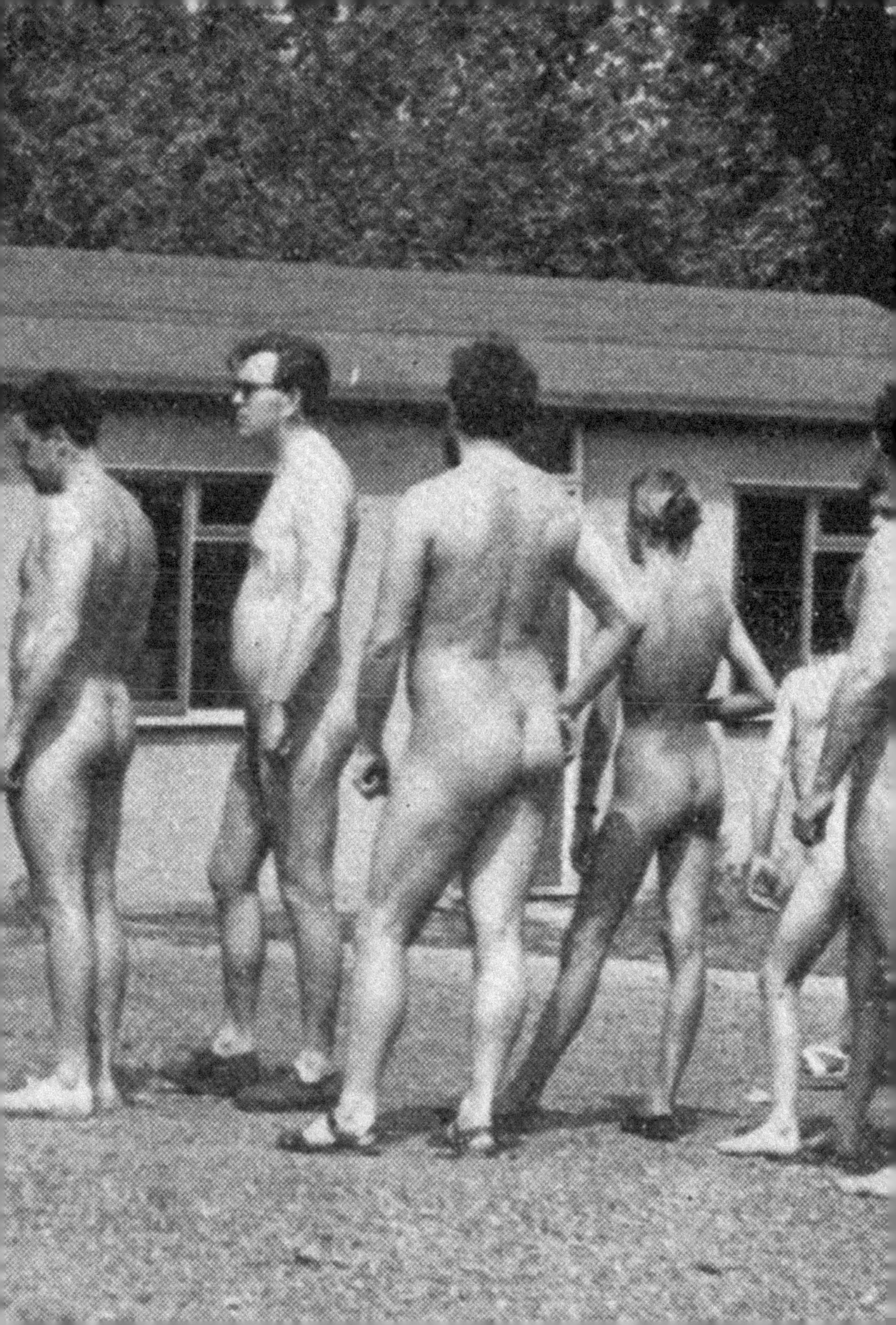

mid-decade and youth culture became an engine for social change, naturists worried about how to compete with rival interests. A 1957 article, "Why not Rock 'n Roll for Nudists? Naturism and the Younger Generation", argued that "naturist activities must parallel closely the activities which non-naturists of the same age group normally engage in". How this should be done was never satisfactorily resolved. With some desperation, nudity was argued to be appropriate to rock 'n' roll's "jungle" dances.[127] In 1962, *Health and Efficiency* suggested that youth delinquency, epitomized by the Teddy Boys subculture, described as "deck chair dragging, obese, heavily shod, overdressed", could be cured by a dose of naturism. The author asserted: "We encourage all delinquents to take off their clothes, for what better way to render them harmless, no pockets for flick knives, bicycle chains or any other type of hardware, and who knows, once they acquire clean and healthy bodies, their minds may grow likewise." For an urban gang culture characterized by loud music, quiffed hair, and sharp suits, this seemed an unlikely medicine. It was clear that older naturists were wildly out of touch with younger generations.

In the late 1960s, as the naturist movement aged and dynamic new youth culture flowered, several founding members' deaths were observed, including the Macaskies. Members worried: "What will happen when the last of our pioneers is taken from us?"[128] The do-it-yourself spirit of the founders was also in decline. Members noted changing camp expectations. With affluence rising in Britain more broadly, commercial environments, including live-in chalets, sit-down meals, and back-to-back organized entertainments for the whole family, such as Butlin's holiday camps, were "attracting a large slice of the pleasure-seeking population".[129] Could naturist venues compete with the facilities at these new destinations? Some argued that better amenities were needed in place of what was more customary: "sagging chairs, a miscellany of cutlery and chipped crockery which club members have ejected from their homes". A naturist who was also an accountant argued in his club magazine that camps needed to be run more like profit-making golf clubs: "Leisure time and spending are increasing," he argued, and "the days of self-build pioneer huts and locally dug latrines are over".[130] Others agreed that they had "no intention of joining a club in order to slosh around in the mud all winter" and then "spend most of the summer [...] digging a swimming pool".[131] Building a culture from scratch was no longer attractive to middle-class naturists who wanted relaxed holidays amid comfort and luxury. Such improvements, it was argued, would make naturism "acceptable to more people, and drag naturists out of their present mental and physical ghettoes".[132] British naturism in the 1960s was also competing with cheaper European travel to warmer climates in both temperature and temperament. Unless changes were made, naturist spending would inevitably go abroad at "the much-publicised Continental resorts".[133]

THE QUEEN VERSUS ETHELRED JEAN STRAKER

Jean Straker, a middle-aged photographer with a Soho studio and gallery, became an unlikely figurehead for late-1960s counter cultural campaigns for "Freedom of Vision". Straker argued, in the context of wider declarations of human rights, that the right to look was as important as freedom of speech. His efforts to liberate the nude photograph attracted young hippies and university students, while also uniting anti-censorship politicians, lawyers, artists, publishers, and naturists.[134] Since the early 1950s, Straker, a former photojournalist, had earned his income from the use of his photo-graphic studio for nude sessions. Amateur photographers in groups could take images under his direction, or simply observe the teaching and, of course, the nude models. Straker's studio was one of many offering commercial nude and glamour tuition in the period, as seen in copious advertisements in amateur photography magazines, but his was highly popular, attracting some 10,000 visitors per year. [135] It was also highly distinctive. Straker's idiosyncratic approach to instruction can be seen in photographs taken in his studio in the mid-1960s by Magnum photographer David Hurn. In some, Straker, a balding middle-aged man with a remaining shock of wiry hair, gestic-ulates in his underpants as he explains his process amid young nude models. In others, packed groups of formally dressed men with hand-held cameras—apparently comprising "judges, parsons, scientists and engine drivers"—jostle for photographic views of an undressed woman.[136]

Established in 1951 as the Visual Arts Club, and later renamed the Academy of Visual Arts, from 1961, Straker's venture was posi-tioned at the heart of Soho's nightlife. Open from noon until 10 p.m.,

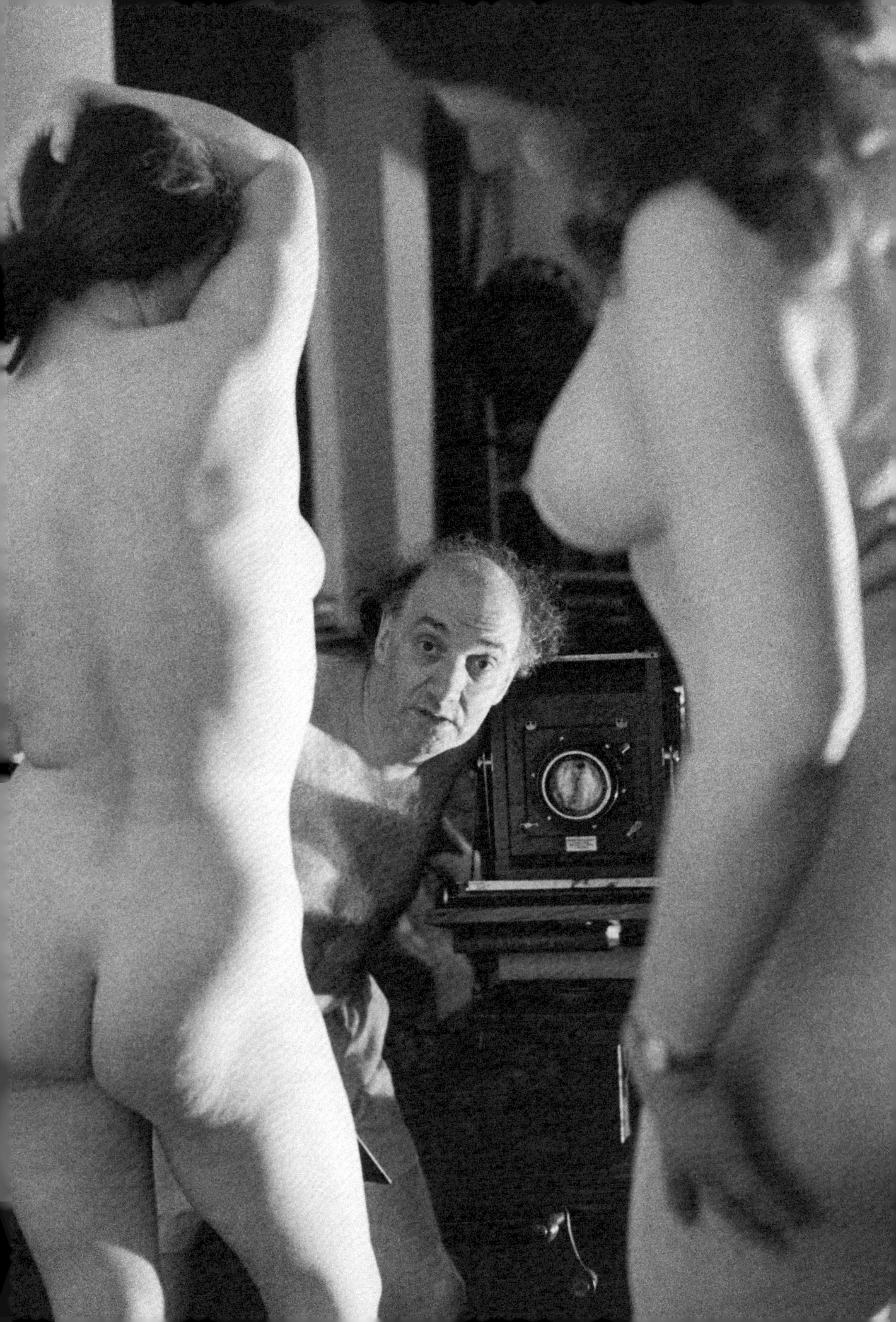

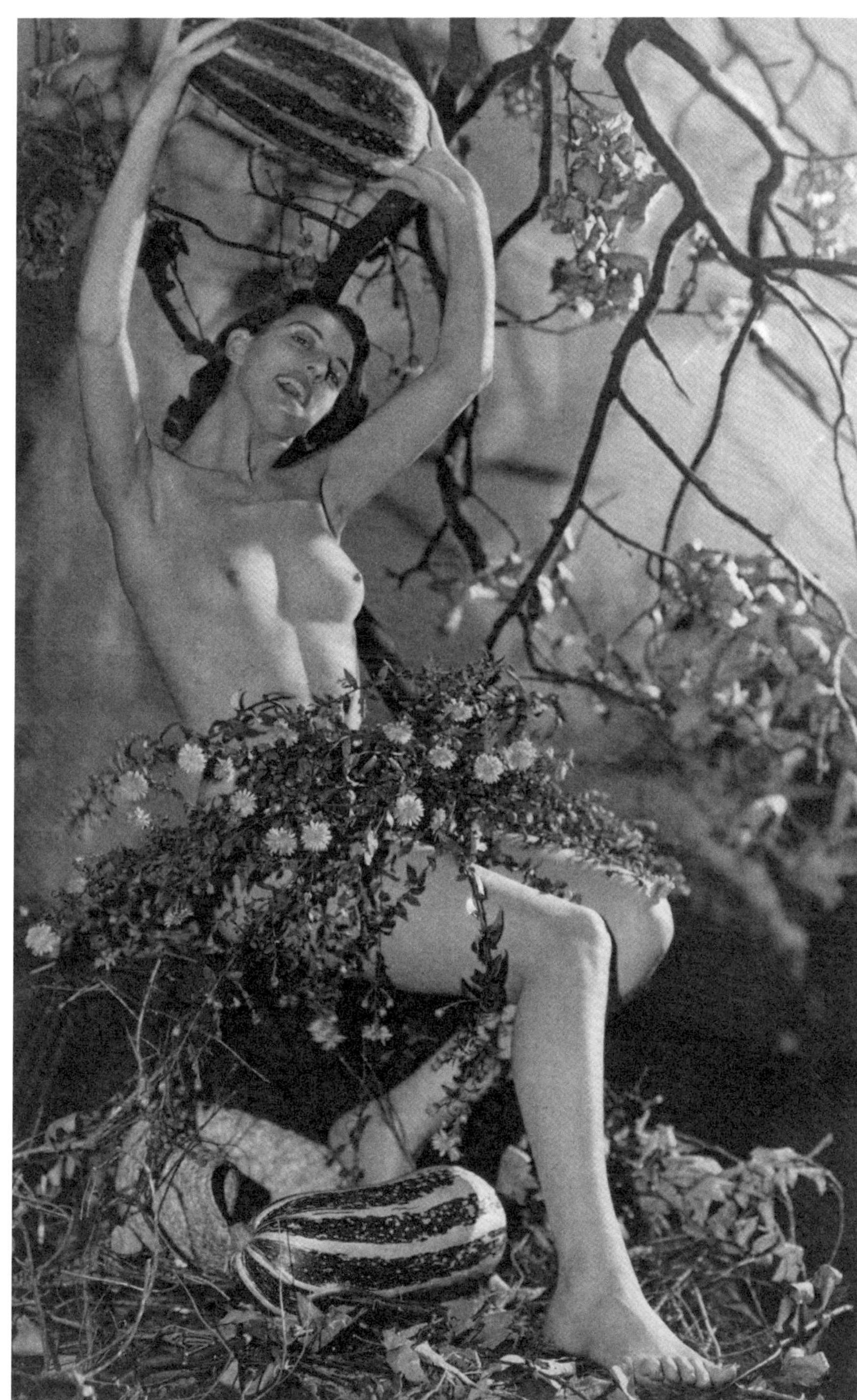

Left - Photographer and educator, dealer and litigant, Jean Straker's anti-censorship campaigns of the mid-1960s united artists and publishers, hippies and lawyers, naturists and university students.

Right - Straker's 10,000 nude photographs, available for purchase via his Soho gallery, ranged from the artistically surreal to the pornographic, including fantastical settings and staged sex scenes.

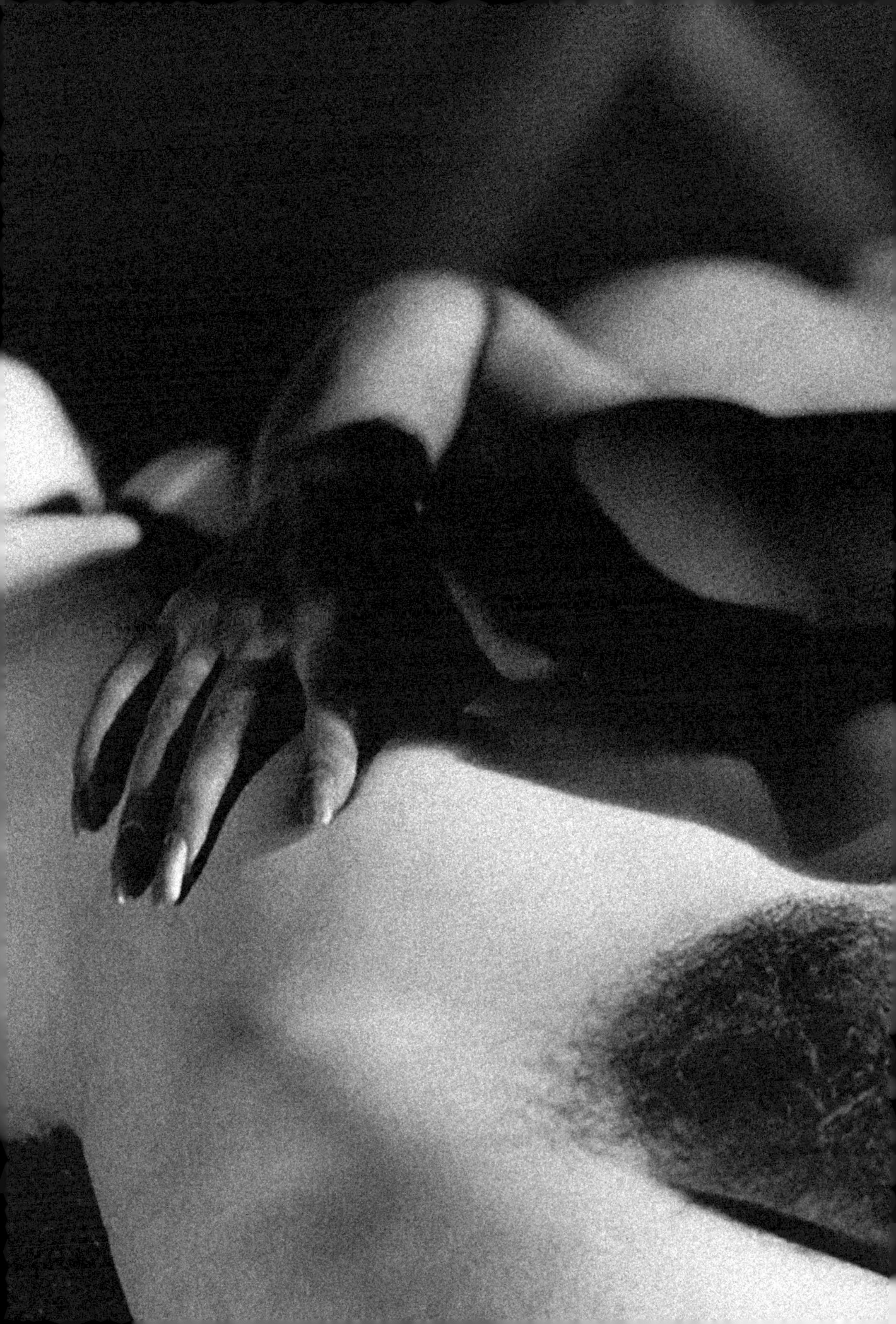

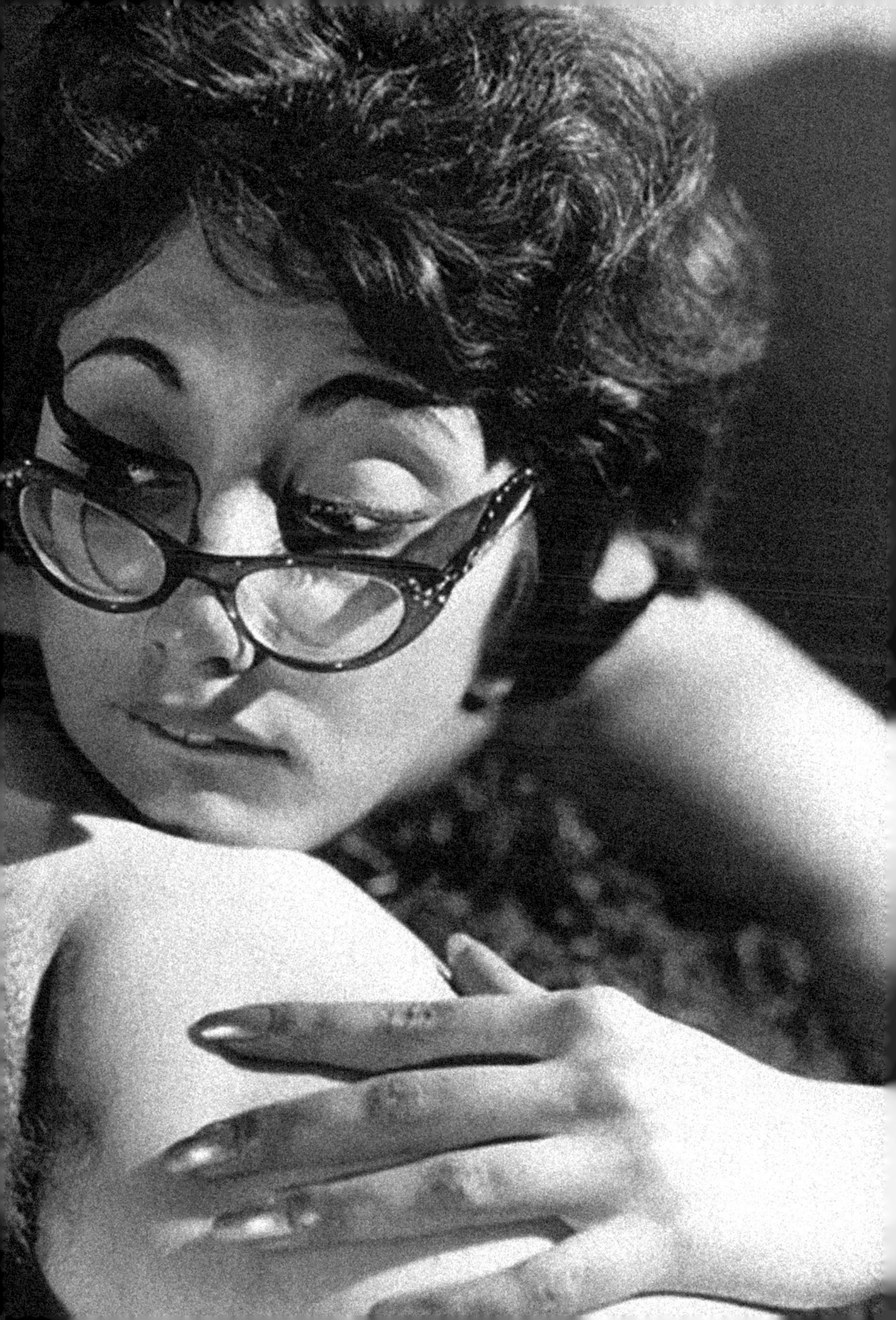

five days a week, it provided an exhibition venue for the sale of his prints and a platform for the photographer to lecture on art and, latterly, on censorship, as he clashed repeatedly with the law. [137] In 1958, Straker produced a book of photographs with his own dressed image on the cover, his large-plate camera pointed at an unnamed female nude.[138] Including photographic pastiches of classical paintings alongside experimental lighting treatments and eclectic improvised settings, *Nus de Jean Straker* was a curious hybrid of art historical, surrealist, and erotic references, with his exclusively female models variously arrayed among looming shadows, dustbin lids, cellophane, chicken wire, and vegetables. Published in three languages, the book secured positive reviews from artistic luminaries including Kenneth Clark but showed only a small and sanitized selection of Straker's nude output, which extended to some 10,000 examples. His wider work included close-ups of breasts, buttocks, and vulvas in isolation, formal experiments in nude photomontage, and an extensive series of what he called "cross-cultural nudes", comprising women of diverse ethnicities in simulated lesbian group sex scenes.

The full range of Straker's work could be viewed and ordered for purchase via his permanent *Femina* exhibition of prints, established in 1955 above his Soho studio, and, for clients further afield, via his mail order library. In his advertisements for these services, Straker described the female nude rapturously as "a microcosm of the forces which play upon the mind and emotions of the creative person". His studies offered, he claimed obscurely, "not only a sense of affective perception but also a source of unimpaired anatomical evidence".[139] This latter aspect referred to a genre of Straker's own creation, "gynaecographic studies", that is, detailed images of women's bodies, including genital close-ups.[140] Despite Straker's attempt to dignify his photographs with a scientific-sounding neologism—he claimed they served important clinical purposes—his work drew the attention of the police in a series of prosecutions. These seeded Straker's commitment to anti-censorship, which he communicated not only through the naturist and photographic press but also, latterly, in the colourful psychedelic pages of the countercultural magazines *Oz* and *International Times*.

The first case was brought when police raided his Soho Square premises in 1961, which were advertised by the street sign: "Jean Straker. Photographer. Fabulous Nudes. 5 Shillings. First floor." They

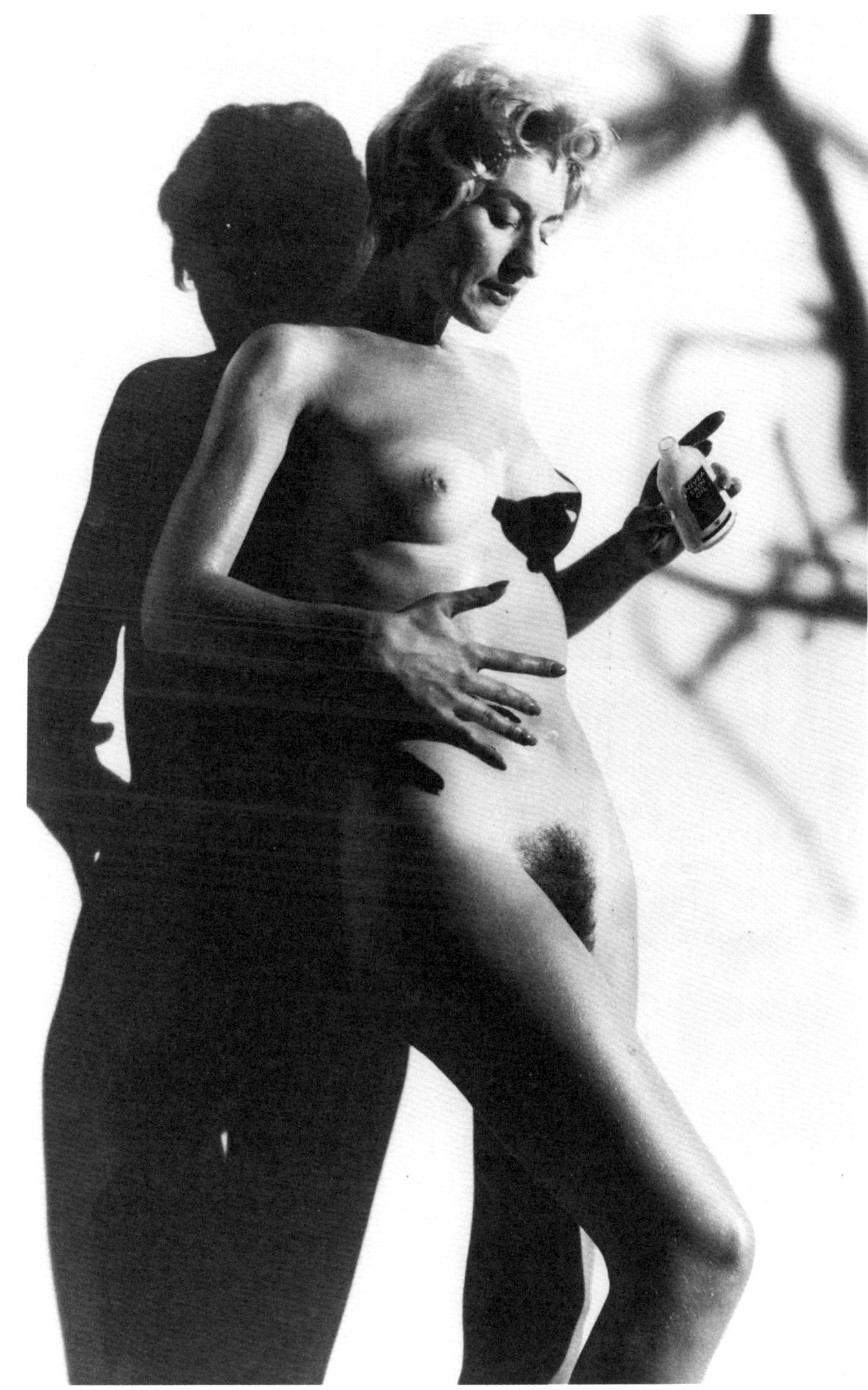

Right - *Sun Worship*
depicted naturist
subject matter but
controversially showed
the model's pubic
hair. In 1958, Straker's
photograph was
seized by police under
obscenity law. In 1967,
the same image was
published without
penalty by Oxford
University.

Previous spread
- Gynaecography was
Straker's name for
female genital close-up
photographs. The
scientific-sounding
title provided clinical
justification for his
production of detailed
crotch shots.

seized 233 display cards and 1,615 negatives, of which the majority were deemed to be obscene material, depicting women's pubic hair or sexual organs, intended to be "reproduced for gain". In 1962, in the High Court, Straker defended himself and proved to be a thorn in the side of the prosecution, quibbling about the semantics of every definition used in the accusation: his site was not an exhibition; the material was for reference and not for sale; the photographs comprised artistic expression and scientific information rather than obscenity.[141]

In his daily petitioning letters to magistrates and in transcripts from his trial, Straker mocked the police for their search, observing that "their zeal exceeded their jurisdiction" and concluding, "They know little about art, less about science, and, it seems, hardly more of law." He also mocked the Metropolitan Police Photographic Department, where a detective inspector who was also a member of the Institute of British Photographers produced prints from the offending negatives for the case; Straker found their technical quality "atrocious".[142] Highly informed about the 1959 Obscene Publications Act, which had updated the existing law to protect works of artistic and cultural value, Straker confidently reminded the court, through his eloquence as a litigant, of their moral obligation to "uphold and license the freedoms of expression of the artist". He stated that it was "no longer in the power of any magistrate to use a relegated heritage of authoritarian orthodoxy to lay down rules as to how a photographic artist should portray female anatomy or arrange a woman's limbs".[143] Using his trial as a soapbox, he declared, "Many things which used to be unrespectable are now respectable; many things which society used to think right are now considered to be wrong. Yesterday's truth often becomes tomorrow's falsehood."[144]

Straker contended that the seizure of his material would harm the country, causing financial losses to the Treasury and impediments to international trade if his negatives remained impounded. His photographs were in high demand everywhere, he claimed, including by American urological journals, which required "close and clear views of the female reproductive organs".[145] Despite pleas for the value of his work to art, science, truth, and the nation, Straker lost the case and was fined £150 (about £5,000 in today's value). In 1965 he was prosecuted again, this time under the Post Office Act, for circulating "indecent" photographic nudes as part of his ongoing international mail order trade. Combining his wounded pride with his legal knowledge, Straker assembled a 1966 London "teach-in"—using the hippie argot of the time—on "Censorship in the Arts". This brought together in debate a psychiatrist, a publisher, a lawyer, an art historian, a former censor, and a model.[146] Two longstanding naturists were also included: educationalist Norman Sheppard and Jack Gray, leader of the Naturist Youth of Great Britain and part of the cast of the film *Nudist Paradise*.

All speakers argued for the value of representing bodies truthfully and factually. While there was public scepticism that Straker's photographs were artistic—prompting some loud heckling from the floor—there was wide support for the open-minded principles of naturism for cultivating healthy bodily attitudes. The alignment of opinion about the censorship debates brought together naturists and Soho photographers—previously morally segregated—around a common cause. Anti-censorship naturists argued for the value of bodily visibility in all its forms: at home, in public, and in magazine media. Gray stated, "There is nothing that I wouldn't let my children see; they can ask me or my wife anything and they will get a straight answer. The eldest saw their mother when she was pregnant at home and at the sun club—and they've all been brought up to accept human bodies as they are, and humanity for what it is."[147] An unnamed female attendee worried that the abolition of censorship would lead to the increase of titillating pictures of women in magazines, but Gray argued that if a pornographic magazine such as the newly launched *Penthouse* could be permitted, then naturists should have "the right to show what goes on in a sun club".[148] Current rules, he argued, made it impossible to show "a wholesome uncensored picture of the human body".[149]

Straker was aware of the wider shifts in public attitudes to bodies and sex, especially among the new generation, and he wrote up his anti-censorship thoughts for a countercultural audience in *International Times*, linking his own prosecutions to better-known cases, including the 1966 confiscation of paintings and prints featuring male and female genitals by American pop artist Jim Dine from the Robert Fraser Gallery at the centre of the Swinging London scene.[150] The following year he photographed free love and body-painted young people attending the Festival of the Flower Children, a "three day non-stop happening" at Woburn Abbey, Bedfordshire, and he made the news as Oxford University's student magazine, *Oxymoron*, published one of his unretouched female nudes.[151] Entitled *Sun Worship*, the subject was ostensibly a nude sun bather applying sun lotion under the shadow of a tree, although it was in fact shot indoors in Straker's studio. The print had been part of a body of photographic material seized by police in a raid in 1958, but in 1967 it was published with the authorization of the university's proctor and escaped prosecution, illustrating the changing times.[152] Straker was lauded by the all-male editors of the hippie publication *Oz* for his "fight for freedom". Between articles on Mick Jagger's drugs bust and sex hook-up advertisements, he positioned Freedom of Vision as part of a radical new moment in cultural and sexual liberation, aligning himself with youth who, he said, are "discovering their own psychological and sexual maturity" in contrast with "moronic adults".[153]

PERMISSIVES AND PURITANS

Naturists had long fought for the public acceptance of nudity but they had conflicted attitudes about how this was unfolding as part of a wider set of permissive social moves. Naturists, for example, barely accepted alcohol in camps; the use and endorsement of recreational drugs would have been beyond the pale and was never discussed publicly. In 1967, *British Naturism* quoted *Life* magazine in America, which stated that nakedness "seems suddenly to have achieved acceptability [...] It might even be safe to say that it has become a sort of social concept, a valid rather than invalid part of our culture, among a great many segments of society which would have rejected it two or three years ago." As a result of these winds of change, the naturist Bob Peters was certain, "the opportunities for naturist expansion are as never before. The climate of public opinions, is favourably inclined to properly controlled social nudity providing is well presented." During this unprecedented permissive moment, however, he felt naturists were "protectionist of the status quo" even though they no longer had "any peculiar possession of the nude state to protect".[154]

Naturists, it is true, were mostly too busy arguing among themselves to take advantage of changing attitudes. The disputes played out between warring magazines. *British Naturism*, representing the movement's organized and more conservative club culture, was

226

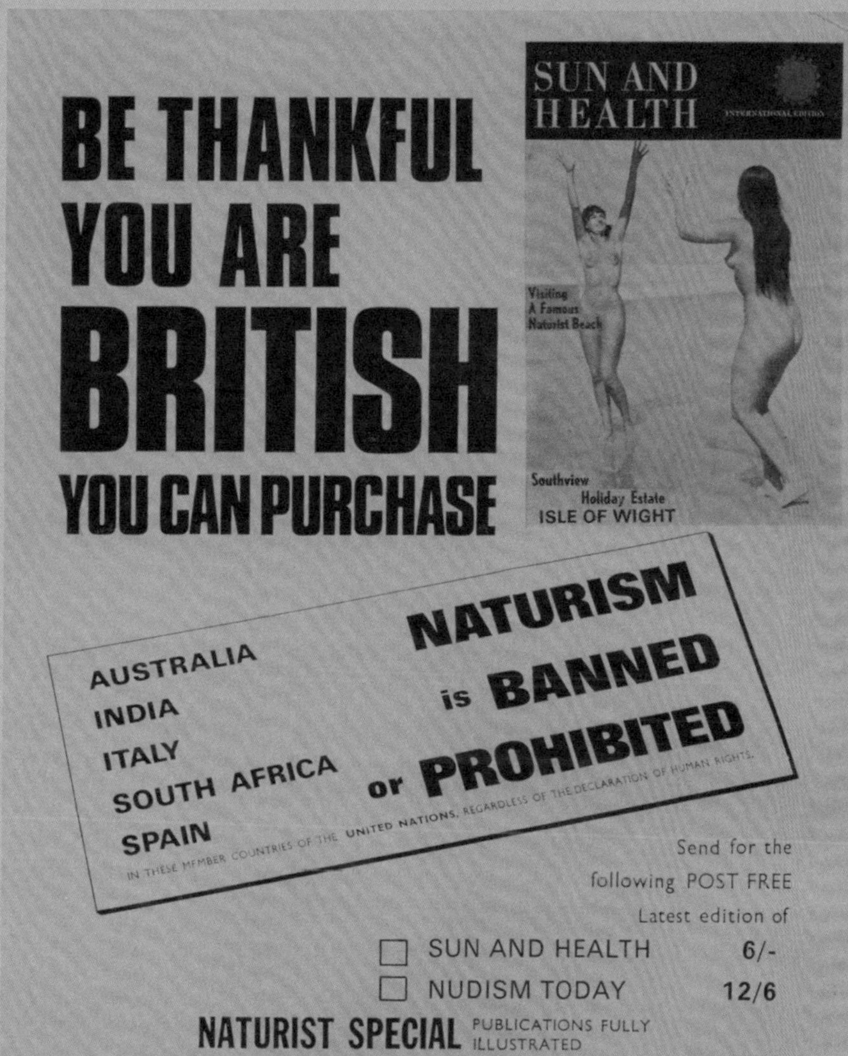

Britain was positioned as a site of permissiveness in naturist magazines by the end of the 1960s, in contrast to censorious attitudes to nude bodies, in public and in print, in other countries.

appalled that the more hedonist editor of *Health and Efficiency* said naturists took their clothes of for reasons of "sensuality", but in the same period the long-stated health basis of their movement was also in dispute.[155] The first discussions of a link between sun exposure and skin cancer began to emerge in the pages of naturist magazines in the 1960s, and members also observed poor health practices in camps where children ate sweets for breakfast, adults smoked, and personal hygiene after using the toilet was, apparently, minimal. These dirty details tended to get left out of the idealized descriptions provided in most narratives, but this naturist brought Arcadia, Eden, and Paradise down to earth. "The only requirement of Naturism seems to be a will-ingness to undress—provided it isn't too cold! Hardly a sufficient philosophy", the complainant griped, "on which to base a health move-ment."[156] If social nudity was not to be connected to sex but was also no longer based on cultures of social reform, fitness and self-improve-ment, what was it to become?

As naturists fought to redefine their movement at the end of the decade, *The Guardian* newspaper characterized the dispute as a split between "the hedonists and the disciplinarians, the radicals and the conservatives".[157] The old guard, embodied by the elders of *British Naturism*, were certain that the movement had nothing to do with permissiveness, which they saw as licence rather than liberation.[158] In this position, they were typical of the larger society. According to Geoffrey Gorer's 1969 survey, *Sex and Marriage in England Today*, "England still appears to be a very chaste society."[159] A quarter of men and two-thirds of women were virgins at marriage, and 20 per cent of men and 25 per cent of women married the first person they had sex with.[160] Despite the media promotion of a swinging society, rumours of a national sexual revolution seem to have been greatly exaggerated.

For naturists who saw themselves as boundary-breakers on the hedonist side, such as *Health and Efficiency*'s editor Bainbridge, the conservative practitioners were puritanical and wore their naturism "like a hair shirt".[161] In the end, it was in fact body hair that would be the breaking point. By the end of the 1960s, *Sun and Health* maga-zine, the British inheritor of a defunct American naturist title, was openly selling unretouched nude photographs via its mail order ser-vice, which also distributed international "natural" magazines. In full-page adverts in photography and countercultural periodicals alike, they proclaimed "Be Thankful you are British". The new breed of naturist magazine positioned the nation as a bastion of freedom, with detail added that naturism was banned in Australia, India, Italy, South Africa, and Spain. The books and magazines they sold featured "giant enlargements of fully detailed, unretouched artistically executed nudes" that are "excitingly alive, in contrast to usual pale, static studies of posed figure models". The implication was that traditional naturism and its depiction was dull and unnatural. The order form required purchasers to sign an agreement that its supplies "will not be passed to other than bona-fide Naturists, or those sympathetic to the movement, nor will I permit the magazine or photographs to be misused".[162] "Misuse" presumably meant use for sexual purposes, despite the promotional emphasis on bodily detail, enlargement, and animation.

As shown, photographers taken to court in the 1950s and 1960s argued against what they saw as the illogical establishment stance that the human body was obscene and illegal. In fact, British police and magistrates were careful to distinguish between going naked on a beach (possibly indecent) and the production of explicit visual material for sexual stimulation (legally obscene).[163] Regardless, the idea that an external agent should not be allowed to decree what was ultimately a subjective personal matter gained increasing traction. Both new pornographers and naturist magazine editors took advantage of the shifting attitudes to nudity and sex at the end of the decade. The British softcore "girlie" magazine *Mayfair*, for example, predicted "a nude new year" in 1969 and revelled in the acceptance of public nudity manifested in women's naked bodies in advertising and art.[164] The most popular film in 1969 at the British box office, *Carry On Camping*, began with a clip from *Nudist Paradise* and was premised on the comic potential of the naturist club as a site of sexual satisfaction.[165] Public nudity hit the mainstream, but what could be seen and shown was still legally and morally uncertain. Naturist Jack Gray, for example, was prosecuted for importing unretouched magazines in 1969 even as parliamentary questions were raised about whether the case should have been pursued, given how much nude material was available in the public domain.[166]

Health and Efficiency entered the fray in the late 1960s, with a stealth campaign to see what was possible to show legally in the magazine's photographs. At the end of the decade an occasional unretouched image appeared in the readers' section, protected by the alibi that a stray photograph could have slipped through the screening process, and that amateurs were, in any case, less likely to mind the guidelines about concealing or retouching pubic hair. Selected professional photographs followed suit, wisp by wisp. Emboldened by the publication of an unretouched and unprosecuted centrefold in *Penthouse* in April 1970, many magazines jumped on the bandwagon. By the end of the year, *Health and Efficiency* went "natural". A triumphant editorial in December 1970 declared it was "Time to Change the Image" and to usher in an era of unadulterated pubic hair and genitals.[167] In the same year, Straker closed his photographic studio and retired to rural Sussex where he bought a historic abbey to use as a base for "an experiment in social nudity".[168] His long campaign to show unretouched nude photographs in the public domain, without fear of prosecution, had succeeded.

Meanwhile in the wider culture of the press, *The Sun*, relaunched in November 1969 by Rupert Murdoch as a popular newspaper "opposed to Capital Punishment, apartheid, racism and the Vietnam War, and in favour of the permissive society", included a photograph of a "birthday suit girl" to mark its first anniversary, launching its long-running feature, the topless Page Three Girl.[169] In its first iteration, model Stefanie Khan was pictured naked, in profile, sitting in a meadow. The newspaper's editors consciously modelled the photograph on the "wholesome naturist genre of *Health and Efficiency*" rather than a more directly pornographic style; its outdoor rural location enabled it to appear "breezy not sleazy".[170] Over five decades, naturist nudes, with their associations of fresh air and family, had used foliage to provide cover for naked bodies. By 1970, the same approach was adopted by the country's most popular newspaper, which used these healthy associations to present topless young women as a kind of national tonic.

In these new contexts, the naturists who had originally positioned themselves as pathbreakers were accused by others of being prudes. Ever tangled in their own contradictions and conflicts about health, sex, and morality, by the end of the 1960s they had helped pave the way for a world that they now didn't fit into, and saw their ideas and images going in directions they didn't expect. Their name and their claims were appropriated, their founding intentions had drifted, and their continuing earnestness was ridiculed. As a final insult, their efforts went unrecognized: "*We* were the hardy pioneers who took all our clothes off long before the mere idea of a body in the buff could be projected with as much freedom and vigour as we find today at pop festivals, in papers and magazines, on screens and stages," *Health and Efficiency* complained. "The permissives of 1970 are not even grateful."[171]

THE PINK WARS

By 1970, the battle to show more flesh was complete. Largely fought by male photographers over the bodies of women, what were colloquially called "the pink wars" had been won.[172] British naturist magazines, like pornographic publications, had long argued for the need to show women's "natural" nudity, meaning pubic hair. Once this was possible, the next step was to show enlarged close-ups of women's wide-parted legs. For some, this was a betrayal of naturism's status as a non-erotic naked practice, but for others, like the boundary-pushing editor Bainbridge, who led the change, the models posing in 1970s magazines were more "genuine" naturists than any other. Professionals were unafraid to display every part of their body equally and without hypocrisy: what could be more fitting to moral openness than a close-up photograph of a vulva?

Bainbridge railed against what male photographers were expected to do with a woman's body before the viewfinder, that is, "to rave about the cropped and abstract design of detached breasts and loins and the texture of skin. He is left with only two choices," he complained to a London camera club in the 1970s, "producing pictures of living statues or busying himself with geometric pattern." His sexualized alternative was, however, shouted down by photographers and naturists who accused him of producing pornography.[173] Along with Murray Wren, regular *Health and Efficiency* photographer in the 1960s and Bainbridge's successor, naturism's new image was a necessary update to the coy and artificial styles of yesteryear. For Wren, the ideal image was one that communicated women's carnality, showing, for example, "a sexually defiant female challenging all who may so view her to try their luck if they dare. By the canons of naturist photography", he admitted, this kind of image was "no naturist photograph. It is an erotic picture."[174] The line between the sexual and non-sexual nude had long been hard to define on magazine pages that concealed and denied. By the 1970s, there was no longer a border to police. Explicit imagery came out from under the counter and could be displayed on the coffee table.[175]

As *Health and Efficiency* ran more obviously sexual content in imagery, its adverts in the 1970s made their intentions ever clearer, with promotions for penis enlargers, vibrators, and lingerie to "bring back excitement to your marriage", and Adam and Eve dating centres. Articles still delivered advice but now it was, for example, on "finger fucking" rather than physical culture.[176] The sexual strategy initially paid off commercially—the magazine moved to a fortnightly schedule as sales exceeded 110,000 per issue.[177] But there were downsides. While it claimed to be "truly representative of the principles and philosophies of British Naturism", there was little to distinguish the magazine from its pornographic bedfellows, leading the magazine to a financial precipice later in the decade.[178] *Penthouse* and *Mayfair*, for example, could boast rival sales figures of 400,000 per issue by the mid-1970s. Full-colour and four times the size of the still-monochrome naturist magazine, they did not need to conceal their pornographic purpose behind complex alibis.[179] Interestingly, some porn magazines adopted an approach similar to early naturist periodicals by including articles by public intellectuals—including Sir Julian Huxley, one of naturism's founding supporters—between photographic spreads.[180] *Health and Efficiency*, meanwhile, described itself in the early 1970s as "the fount of nudist thought" but its textual content became increasingly vapid with its philosophical origins long gone.[181] To retain a relationship with its core demographic, the magazine included an "Official Bulletin" claiming to be from naturism's governing body, but organisation members strongly opposed its 1970s degeneration into "a sex therapy-girlie mag".[182]

Institutional opponents of the newly sexualized naturism, however, had their own issues. Ageing and inward-looking, the movement's elders acted as if the changing world could be ignored. *British Naturism* in 1970, for example, was inspired by watching the Miss World competition on television to institute a "Miss British Naturism". David Archer advised his readers, assumed to be all male: "All you need is a photo of a pretty girl in your particular club or region. She can be your wife, girlfriend or just a fellow member. Get her written permission on the back of the photo and state her Christian name only, and what club she is a member of." A selection of "the prettiest" was to be voted on in the magazine.[183] Miss World 1970 was the same event where Women's Liberation activists had stormed the competition with placards proclaiming, "We are not Beautiful, We are not Ugly, We are Angry!"[184] Behind their club fences, naturists were slow to notice the raised voices of a growing body of women who were tired of being judged solely on their appearance, naked or otherwise. The wider cultural emphasis on depictions of women as sexual beings was increasingly recognized to have more to do with helping men feel better about their use of pornography than the liberation of women.[185]

NEW WAYS OF SEEING

The new visibility of sexualized bodies of nude women across all aspects of the press, television, and advertising was addressed in *British Naturism*, which recognized, by 1972, that "half-naked women" boosted product sales but it also noted that they could reduce women to "sex-objects". With a fresh spin on early nudists' feminist theories, naturism was again the remedy: "if nudity were generally accepted, and the female body thus elevated from the category of 'improper' to that of 'natural'", women would be perceived as people rather than bodies. By this logic, feminists were naturism's natural allies, and members were directed "to recruit as many Women's Liberationists as possible into sun clubs". The author predicted: "Together Women's Lib and naturism could fight the continuing degradation of women's bodies, and the accompanying contempt of them as persons."[186]

The objectified female body in popular culture was also drawing critical attention by writers and artists who were developing a powerful body of visual critique. In 1972, Marxist art critic John Berger authored a four-part BBC television series and book, *Ways of Seeing*. This mounted a major counterpoint to Clark's enduringly popular art historical exploration of the nude. Dismantling the disinterested position and mystifying language of art appreciation, Berger posed a new politics of looking in a world of widely reproduced imagery, juxtaposing contemporary 1970s magazine nudes with highly consecrated nude painting, and drawing provocative parallels between the two. He noted how the popular visual culture of the contemporary nude relied on the mythic, poetic, and artistic strategies of high art for its legitimation. Little had changed since the claims of Everard and

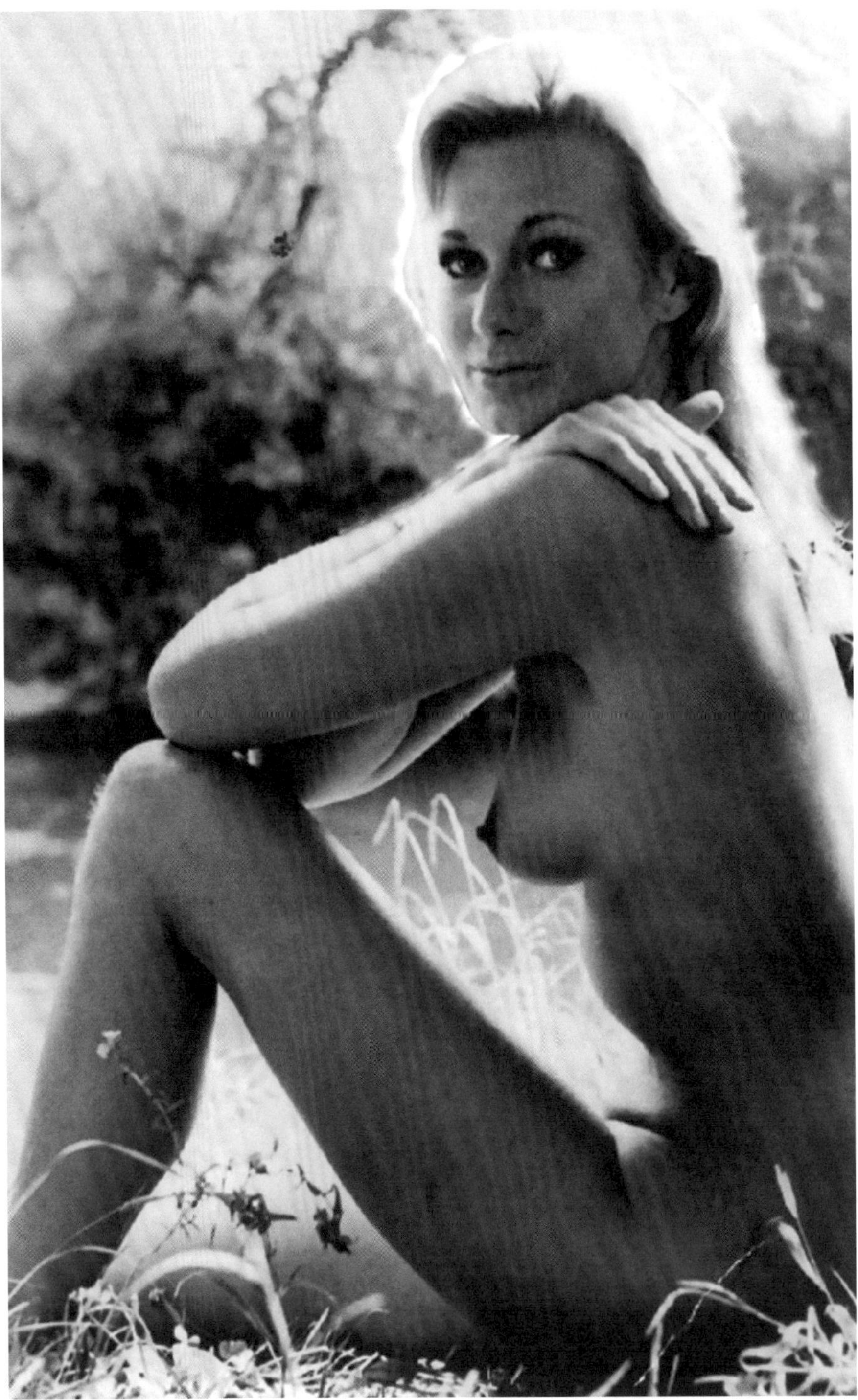

By 1970, photographs of young women's nude bodies were fully incorporated into British mainstream media. Naturism's longstanding claims for freedom and family respectability were used to justify the daily sale of female nudes in *The Sun*'s Page Three Girl feature.

others in the mid-1950s.

By the mid-1970s, advertisements using artistic justification still ran in the page of *Health and Efficiency*, but now that adult bodies could be freely shown, art was used to justify the sale of images of naked children in publications offering "charming pre-teen boys", for example, via titles such as *Just Kids* and *Young Rascals*. The publications promised "superbly printed publications packed with a remarkable collection of unretouched, unaltered pictures depicting the naked human body, male and female, in completely authentic form". The photographs, the advertisements claimed, "are especially suitable for professional and amateur artists who find it difficult to obtain young living models".[187] The new border war in the 1970s was the age of consent, both inside and outside naturism.[188]

One of Berger's most influential statements is that women watch themselves being looked at and internalize their own objectification. This, he argued, "structures the consciousness of many women. They do to themselves what men do to them. They survey, like men, their own femininity."[189] Feminist art criticism of the 1970s worked to name the male gaze—through the work of film scholar Laura Mulvey and others—and to dismantle gendered hierarchies of looking.[190] Feminist artists presented new visions of the body as subject rather than object, underpinned by oppositional motives. British photographer Jo Spence and collage artist Linder, for example, tore up the photographic pages of 1970s magazines to create and restage new, alternative views of women, with Linder's work featuring cut-apart Harrison Marks images of Pamela Green.[191]

Articles in radical British 1970s photography periodicals, such as *Camerawork*, scrutinized popular visual practices. Some asked why women might want to analyse glamour and nude photography when it had been used to objectify women. The feminist response was that "in order to challenge dominant representations, it is necessary first of all to understand how they work, and thus where to seek points of possible productive transformation". Examining mainstream images of women, feminists asserted, might "teach us to recognise inconsistencies and contradictions within dominant traditions of representation, to identify points of leverage for our own intervention: cracks and fissures through which may be glimpses of what might in other circumstances be possible".[192] Yet using an image of a nude to disrupt the norms of the nude was—and continues to be—fraught with challenges. "It is a subtle

235

abyss that separates men's use of women for sexual titillation from women's use of women to expose that insult," art critic Lucy Lippard famously noted in 1976, surveying the preponderance of new feminist art made about women's naked bodies.[193]

In 1971 a new photography gallery opened in Great Newport Street, London, announced as the first in Britain dedicated to the subject. In fact, the Photographers' Gallery was just a few streets away from the Soho nude photographic galleries of Harrison Marks and Straker of the 1950s and 1960s. With a much wider remit, however, the Photographers' Gallery covered a much wider range of genres for a much wider range of purposes. Yet when it exhibited *Self Impressions*, featuring seven female photographers making self-portraits including nudes, the feminist magazine *Spare Rib* asked: "Why the predominance of female nudity? The media continually confronts people with images of naked, passive females."[194] The complainants asked, "Why have these photographers held on to the usual stereotypes?" Some argued that women were reclaiming their naked image but agreed that "photography is loaded with sexist associations".[195] A survey of amateur photography magazines of the 1970s confirms this. Female nudes featured in every issue; women's naked body parts sold products in advertisements addressed to men, and photographic companies ran regular beauty contests. Finally, it seemed that the visual culture of naturists looked little different to the wider photographic culture; its normalization had been achieved.

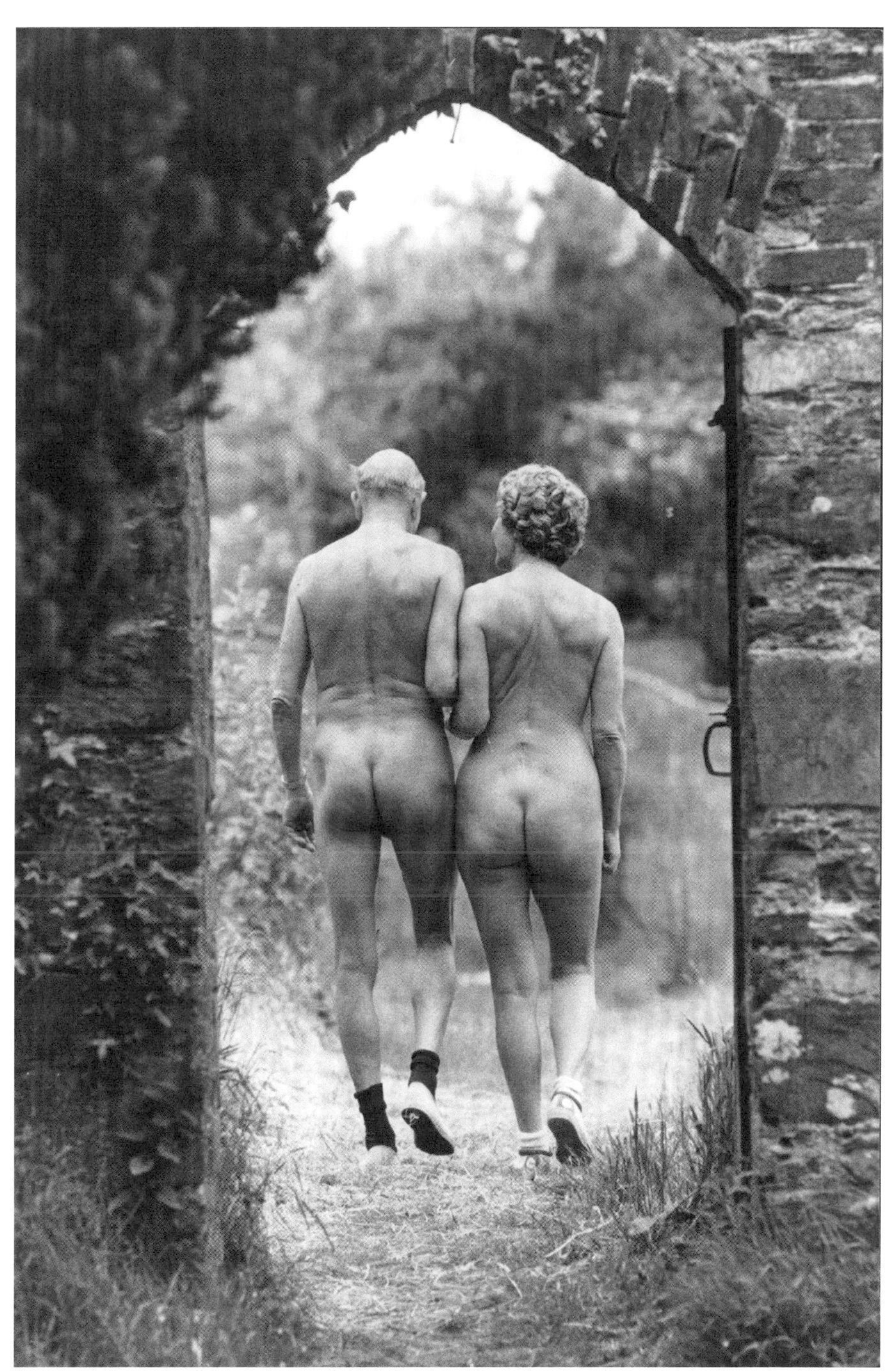

After weathering half a century of cultural change, by the 1970s nudism in Britain had matured.

Taking in the View

In 1946 Michael Rutherford addressed "historians of the future" in his field guide to the subject, entitled *British Naturism*. He predicted that scholars will consider the practice "among the significant and important happenings of this, the 20th century". He wrote: "If our grandchildren can say of us, as they grow up to a sane acceptance of their own bodies: 'What was all that fuss about concerning Naturism in the 1940s?' we shall have done our part."[1] As the historian addressed by Rutherford, it has been my ambition in *Nudism in a Cold Climate* to assess that fuss and to appraise naturism's historical value.

As a devotee, Rutherford was certain that naturism would have a transformational social effect on future populations. His fellow early enthusiasts shared his faith even if their prophecies were fantastical. John Langdon-Davies understood the future of nakedness—the title of his 1929 book—to be inevitable on every high street.[2] Those who wished to reform dress to its most extreme end imagined that garments would ultimately cease to exist; nudism was the progressive outcome of design evolution.[3] Other founding nudist authors who took a more moderate line foresaw that broader bodily acceptability would come with reason and patience. William Welby, for example, asked in 1935, "Has Nudism a Future?" He anticipated that, over time, "the Government may well issue Nudist bathing beaches at seaside resorts".[4] This came to pass in England in 1979 with the first local authority-instituted naturist beach at Brighton.[5]

A VIEW FROM THE MILLENNIUM

Nudism in a Cold Climate has focused on the 50 years from the 1920s to the 1970s, a period that captures the dramatic change from founding secretive practices to the full visibility of nude bodies across all aspects of British culture, inside and outside naturism. Another 50 years has passed since the end of the story, with enough having happened to fill another book or more. Naturism in Britain has not gone away, and its print and visual culture has endured. *Health and Efficiency* magazine, for example, remains in print 120 years after its founding, albeit under a slightly changed name; *British Naturism*, as both an organization and magazine, still flourishes.

To what extent has nudism achieved the ambitions of its founders? Have its contradictions and controversies been resolved? Scholars who study 21st-century naturists note that contemporary practitioners "are more inclined to describe their practice as a source of personal relaxation, freedom or esteem". In Ruth Barcan's research for *Nudity: A Cultural Anatomy*, for example, her interviewees denied any social reform agenda, describing the practice as a lifestyle. Few were happy with the idea that nudism might be a philosophy, and they denied any relation to socialism, vegetarianism, or anti-materialism. One stated: "It's something I like doing, and that's it."[6]

This shift from early-20th-century social cause to early 21st-century lifestyle can be mapped against naturism's changing identity in the pages of its magazines. With health quietly dropped from the naturist agenda and the historic meanings of efficiency long lost, *Health and Efficiency* became abbreviated to *H&E* then *H&E Lifestyle* by the end of the 20th century. Enthusiasts argued that naturism was merely an activity and that "there is no such thing as a 'naturist movement'".[7] In the years around the millennium, a period of intense self-scrutiny, naturists reflected on the purpose of the practice. Critical contributors felt frustrated by a lack of change. "With a new century and a new millennium only a year away," one asked in 1999, "why do British naturist clubs continue to operate as if they were in a time machine stranded in the 1950s?"[8]

Naturism's continuing emphasis on "families and couples" was still said to conceal discriminatory attitudes to sexual orientation behind its "secrecy and high walls".[9] Members who joined in search of open-minded company noted conservative and homophobic views in the sauna.[10] While naturist magazine advertisements contained queer contact ads and gay gyms, naturist practices could be less inclusive; a 1999 case saw a lesbian couple's application to join Manchester Sun and Air Society subject to "emergency" committee scrutiny, unlike heterosexual applications, ultimately leading to its rejection.[11] Some members called for greater tolerance, describing naturism as "staunchly heterosexual", fearful, and bigoted.[12] A contributor to *Sunlovers*, however, an independent magazine, argued in 2000 that naturism is "not suitable for many gay men".[13] Queer culture, in the eyes of this anonymous author, was perceived to be sexually adventurous while naturism was non-sexual.

The debate about whether naturism was a libido stimulant or suppressant continued to rage at the turn of the 21st century.[14] Some clubs embraced their sexual potential, running erotic party nights for singles with private rooms and fully stocked bars. Advertisements in naturist magazines offered "escort" and swinging services, cock rings, and Viagra; clothing for sale included "sexy satin" lingerie for women and "studwear" mankinis for men. While some of these services were supplied by external businesses, premium rate phone lines provided directly by naturist magazines offered advice including "Threesomes—Are they Worth It?" and "How to Live with Large Breasts". Videos advertised for sale included "Sexercise" tapes and films catering to particular sexual tastes, such as "Shaven Angels". After years of campaigning to view body hair, some naturists organized around the opposite cause, establishing "Smoothie Clubs" and a specialist magazine for shaved bodies, *The Nudest Nudist.*

Other videos on the subject of "Family Naturism" sold moving images of naked children to naturists. One film entitled "Happy Birthday Petra" was said to include footage of "Petra's friends as they help her celebrate her 10th birthday". The advertisement came accompanied with a note: "We apologise but we were not allowed to run an ad that included images which showed nudist youth."[15] Using language that implied they were victims of an illogical oppressor, the advertisement acknowledged the changing and contradictory laws, where images of naked children could not be shown in print but could still be supplied by mail order. These advertisements appeared in naturist magazines alongside anxious articles that showed that the long-cherished family nature of naturism was under a fresh spotlight in a changed cultural context. Child protection concerns, and subsequent legislation about the photographic depiction of children, followed high-profile cases in the late 1990s, when British public figures had naked photographs of their offspring seized when they took their films to be developed.[16] Naturists read this as a restraint on their family freedom, but it is obvious that some advertisements were supplying material by and for paedophiles at the turn of the century. As with earlier editions of naturist magazines, the problem could be laid at the door of the advertisers rather than the editors, but advertisement and editorial were in dialogue on facing pages; each reinforced the other.

Other previously unmentionable subjects came out into the open at the turn of the century, such as masturbation, in articles entitled "Give Yourself a Hand" by *H&E*'s "psychosexual guru" Petra Vallance, who noted its positive, rewarding, and therapeutic qualities.[17] Nicholas Whittaker had been a reader of naturist magazines since 1972, when he found a copy of *Outdoor Leisure*, edited by Leslie Bainbridge, on the top of a friend's wardrobe. He fondly recalled "the first flush of erotic pleasure" when viewing the magazine as a teenage virgin, and admitted, "We know that lots of people buy *H&E* for the supposedly 'wrong' reasons. They always have." He asserted that naturism was "big enough not to feel threatened by a few men buying it for a wank".[18] The mixed intentions of naturist magazines' readership was longstanding, but the language used to describe it had dramatically shifted.

Photography continued to be both a subject for discussion and a product for sale. Specialist processing services were offered by Charlie Simonds, a photographer for naturist magazines since the 1960s whose mother had been a naturist photographic model in the 1940s.[19] Simonds provided international photographic holidays where, judging by the illustrations, mostly older portly naturist men photographed professional young female models. Whether photographing nudes in the nude was egalitarian or a means to bring photographers' and models' flesh together was discussed in letters pages, which continued enduring disputes about naturism's "girlie" image and its exclusions.

Just as photographers were regularly nude themselves, magazine editors and contributors were now pictured unclothed. Pseudonyms and concealed identities were a thing of the past. In 1998, *H&E*'s mission statement read: "We think bodies are wonderful! And everyone has a right to enjoy a naked lifestyle whatever their ages, size or sexuality. We reflect the wonderfully diverse ways people take pride in their bodies and whatever nudity means to them." Comparing end-of-the-century *H&E* to its less commercial rival, *British Naturism*, however, showed that the former still emphasized buxom young female models over the mixed ages, genders, and sizes who populate naturist clubs.

In response to a complaint about idealized imagery from a 45-year-old woman who said that she had "obvious scarring" and felt intimidated by the visual messaging, *H&E* published a photograph of a smiling male naturist with a tattooed and amputated arm to show that all were welcome.[20] A 1999 article, however, "Are We Just Body Snobs?", confessed that "those with disabilities are being largely ignored". A British Deaf Naturist Club, for example, established in the 1990s, complained that it had been refused recognition by the Central Council of British Naturism. After interviewing those with direct experience of both naturism and disability, the conclusion was drawn that, nevertheless, "a naked environment is generally more tolerant than a clothed one".[21] The wider world is discriminatory and naturism operates within it.

Other historical exclusions were considered anew. "As naturists, we pride ourselves on a philosophy of freedom and tolerance", a magazine contributor stated in 1997. "Why is it, then, that the majority of naturists are middle-class, white heterosexuals?" In an article accompanied by nude photographs of an unnamed black glamour model, the author recounted racist comments overheard in clubs.[22] A 2005 article posed a similar question, showing little had changed: "Why are there no black, Asian or Arabic naturists?" The author said, "We are not racists—that's unthinkable," and found cultural reasons for the omission. The editor added that she had only received "three or four" photographs of "non-whites" out of hundreds of readers' submissions in ten months, and none had been sufficiently technically accomplished to publish.[23]

Once female pudenda could be freely shown, there were new bodily terrains to be conquered. One correspondent counted 37 erect nipples on women in one edition of a naturist magazine in 2004, and asked for an equivalent number of erect penises. The editor responded that unless readers wanted every issue to be positioned "on the highest of top shelves" then there could be "no erections and no overtly sexual body clinching".[24] Naturism was subject to new legal constraints about visibility, including the 2003 Sexual Offences Act, which threatened to criminalize nudity in public places.

At the turn of the century there were 20,000 members of British Naturism as an organization, and 20,000 readers of the leading naturist magazine.[25] The numbers were half those of the 1930s but earlier demographic patterns continued. The unequal gender balance also continued to be a talking point, with too many images of women and too few female members noted. Naturist magazines, however, were increasingly led by women, with five out of six female editors at *H&E* (now called *H&E Naturist*) since 1980. In the present day, women have leading roles in organized naturism, but they continue to be less visible on the ground. "More men attend events, visit beaches and Naturist holiday resorts making it appear that Naturism appeals more to men than women," a 2020 summary by *British Naturism* noted. A fresh campaign was launched to find the reasons why.[26]

NEW NUDE MILLIONS

100 years after the 1921 conversations that tentatively suggested that a British nude culture might be possible, historical echoes resound but differences are also apparent. Current covers of naturist magazines show embracing bodies, black and white (and even some with blue hair).[27] Naturism in the present day is aligned to new contemporary causes and agendas; it is more environmentally friendly than wearing clothes, is good for those with Asperger's syndrome and for better mental health overall. Physical health is no longer prominently promoted, although naturism is still said to be improving in a general sense of feeling nice and being relaxing. Bodies across genders and ethnicities, dis/abilities, sexualities, and sizes are all visible. Ages are more expansively represented, although rightly, for reasons of legal protection, no under-18s now appear. The perfect body image may not have disappeared but naturist magazines and clubs no longer enforce it through shame and disgust.

Meanwhile, in the wider culture, new agendas in nude representation, such as Free the Nipple, stake similar claims in their calls for gender equality and freedom from censorship on social media. These debates are not strictly naturist but practitioners have skin in the game. Like earlier campaigns against the photographic retouching of genitals, campaigners see illogicality in the characterization of women's bodies as sexual and offensive when male toplessness is legal and neutral. These causes are championed by Rutherford's imagined grandchildren, although they do not live among the "sane" attitudes to nudity that he hoped for back in the 1940s. Unlike earlier campaigners against retouching, it is now young women leading the Free the Nipple charge, creating the philosophies and controlling the conditions of consent, such as who can be seen and by whom (in Britain, on nude protests, the request is that women are photographed by female photographers only).[28] Another key difference is that the huge numbers of participants in these campaigns debate the right to be nude without the need to build an alternative society or even a clubhouse to do it in.

In 2011, *British Naturism* commissioned a national survey of public attitudes, sampling over 2,000 respondents in over 150 locations. From the 6 per cent who identified as nudist or naturist, they extrapolated that there could be nearly 4 million practitioners in the country.[29] Ten years on, however, organized naturism in Britain remains small: merely 8,000 members and 100 clubs.[30] The nude pursuit, as a formal membership activity, is a minority interest even as nude visual culture attracts endless attention. In some ways, naturism has achieved its historic ambitions, as clubs were originally seen by some as a means to an end Langdon-Davies argued in 1932 that nude organizations need only exist until it was possible to go about "with nothing on but shoes and sunshade". As he put it, "I dispense with clothes whenever I can, but I do not need a secretary and a treasurer to help me."[31]

As I have shown, much ink has been spilled over the last century about what nudism is, what it should be called, who it is for, and what it should look like. For millions in the present day, it has cast off its philosophy and is losing its bureaucracy. The latest official definition is that naturism in Britain is simple. It is nothing more than "the practice of going without clothes".[32]

End Notes

INTRODUCTION

1. A full range of primary sources consulted can be followed through the references but key periodicals include *Health and Efficiency*, 1920s–1970s, *Sun Bathing Review* 1933–1959, *The Naturist* 1937–1960, and *British Naturism*, established 1964.
2. Attributed by Julian Strange to "a famous author" in "On Meeting the English", *Sun Bathing Review*, Autumn 1936, pp. 118–120.
3. A 1939 survey, for example, of the 27 clubs in Britain, included only one in Scotland and one in Wales. "Nudism Must March On", *Sun Bathing Review*, Winter 1939, pp. 136–137.
4. Prudery is seen as an English characteristic, for example, in "Wake Up England!", *Sun Bathing Review* 1:1, Spring 1933, pp. 3–4. The few mentions of Northern Irish nudism relate to its condemnation by religious figures, see for example "Nudism the Doom of the World", *Western Daily Press*, 5 November 1934, p. 1. Naomi Michison provides an English view of Scottish nudism, informed by Protestantism, in "Tabu in the Highlands", *Sun Bathing Review*, Autumn 1946, p. 51. Pseudo-anthropological writing in Roye's series on English, Welsh, Scottish and Irish "maids" relates to nudes supposedly from these locations and the text perpetuates national stereotypes; *Maids: Thirty-Two Camera Studies of the Nude by Roye* (London: Elstree, n.d. c.1947).
5. Nudity shifts in meaning according to history and geography. The naked state is more of a sign of universality than a universal experience. See Ruth Barcan, *Nudity: A Cultural Anatomy* (Oxford: Berg, 2004).
6. Annebella Pollen, *Mass Photography: Collective Histories of Everyday Life* (London: I.B. Tauris, 2015).
7. Strix, "The Passing Scene: Nudist Matters Mostly Controversial", *Sun Bathing Review*, Summer 1951, p. 44.
8. Annebella Pollen, *The Kindred of the Kibbo Kift: Intellectual Barbarians* (London: Donlon Books, 2015). The Kindred of the Kibbo Kift and the English Gymnosophist Society, which founded England's first nudist club, shared members. Gymnosophy was described as "closely in line with Kibbo Kift ideals" in a letter by Zex (Rex Wellbye) to *The Flail: An Independent Kibbo Kift Magazine* 5:1, Autumn 1927, pp. 200–201. "How it all Began", *Sun Bathing Review*, Autumn 1949, p. 72, includes Kibbo Kift among originators. Kibbo Kift "provided more than its share of recruits for the first clubs"; Strix, "The Passing Scene", *Sun Bathing Review*, Winter 1951, p. 94.
9. Lisa Tickner, "The Body Politic: Female Sexuality and Women Artists since 1970", *Art History* 1:2, June 1978, p. 239. For excellent feminist analysis of female nudes, see Lynda Nead, *The Female Nude: Art, Obscenity and Sexuality* (London: Routledge, 1992).
10. Mrs Grundy is a fictional character who first appeared (offstage) as a character in the 1798 play *Speed the Plough* by Thomas Morton, where she represented the spectre of public disapproval. She was a popular figure in Victorian literature especially in relation to the fear of sex. "Mrs Grundy is a prude who carries this fear and hatred to the stage of more or less organised interference with other people's pleasure" says Peter Fryer, *Mrs Grundy: Studies in English Prudery* (London: Corgi, 1963), p. 19.
11. Nathan Scott Epley, "Pinups, Retro-Chic, and the Consumption of Irony" in Laura Saarenmaa, Kaarina Nikunen and Susanna Paasonen (eds), *Pornification: Sex and Sexuality in Media Culture* (Oxford: Berg, 2007); Ryan Moore, *Sells Like Teen Spirit: Music, Youth Culture, and Social Crisis* (New York: New York University Press, 2010).

CHAPTER 1

1. Charles Macaskie, founder of Spielplatz nudist camp in Hertfordshire referred to his site as "virgin jungle" in Charles Sennet, *Nudist Life at Spielplatz: The Story of a Modern Experiment in the Art of Living, with an Art Supplement of Photographs taken at the Hertfordshire Nudist Resort by Stephen Glass* (London: The Naturist, 1956), p. 4. The Sun Bathing Society, one of the earliest of nudist societies in Britain, described its activity as "Active Sun and Air Bathing" in an advertisement in *Sun Bathing Review: Journal of the Sun Societies* 1:1, Spring 1933.
2. There were isolated instances of British nudism before the 1920s, for example in the "sun bath" practices of the radical social circles around the gay socialist poet and social reformer Edward Carpenter from the 1890s, and even a small club of three members, the Fellowship of the Naked Life, inspired by Carpenter's example, established among British Raj officials in 1891–1892 in Bombay by C. E. G. Crawford. For wider context on Carpenter, see Sheila Rowbotham, *Edward Carpenter: A Life of Liberty and Love* (London: Verso, 2009).

3. For context see Richard Overy, *The Morbid Age: Britain and the Crisis of Civilization, 1919–1939* (London: Penguin, 2009). For context on the ambivalent attitudes of interwar nudists towards civilization, see Ruth Barcan, "Regaining What Mankind Has Lost Through Civilisation: Early Nudism and Ambivalent Moderns", *Fashion Theory* 8:1, 2004, pp. 63–82.
4. The phrase "diseases of darkness" was used repeatedly in Caleb W. Saleeby, *Sunlight and Health* (London: Nisbet, 1923).
5. Lens, "Modern sun-worship: I: Its creed", *New Statesman*, 24 September 1921, pp. 670–671; Lens, "Modern sun-worship: II: Its history", *New Statesman*, 8 October 1921, pp. 10–12; Lens, "Modern sun-worship: III: Its high priest and his temple", *New Statesman*, 15 October 1921, pp. 42–43; Lens, "Modern sun-worship: IV: Its rewards and warnings", *New Statesman*, 22 October 1921, pp. 71–72. For details on Saleeby see Ine Zweiniger-Bargielowska, *Managing the Body: Beauty, Health and Fitness in Britain 1880–1939* (Oxford: Oxford University Press, 2010).
6. Caleb W. Saleeby, *Sunlight and Health* (London: Nisbet, 1923), p. 12. For context on interwar sunlight and health see Tania Anne Woloshyn, *Soaking up the Rays: Light Therapy and Visual Culture in Britain, c.1890–1940* (Manchester: Manchester University Press, 2017).
7. *Health and Efficiency* was originally underpinned by eugenic ideas about personal improvement, fitness and "efficiency" in the face of perceived national "degeneration". For many years the magazine contained an introduction claiming it was founded in 1899 or 1900 but the current editor has located its origin to 1902. Following major editorial redirections, the magazine continues, dedicated to naked lifestyle, as *H&E Naturist*.
8. Correspondence in *Health and Efficiency*, October 1921, p. 336, and April 1922, p. 146, quoted in Peter Fryer, *Mrs Grundy: Studies in English Prudery* (London: Corgi 1965 [1963]), p. 223. H. D. Byngham (also known as Dion or Dionysus) was a journalist for health periodicals in the 1920s, a member of the British Society for the Study of Sex Psychology and an active member of the progressive pacifist educational group, the Order of Woodcraft Chivalry. See Derek Edgell, *The Order of Woodcraft Chivalry 1916–1949 as a New Age Alternative to the Boy Scouts* (Lampeter: Edwin Mellen Press, 1992); Annebella Pollen, "The most curious of all queer societies? Sexuality and Gender in British Woodcraft Camps, 1916–2016" in Kenneth B. Kidd and Derritt Mason (eds), *Queer as Camp: Essays on Summer, Style and Sexuality* (New York, Fordham University Press, 2019), pp. 31–50.
9. Flang has been identified as Harold Booth. Zex has been identified as Rex Wellbye (by my reckoning likely to be Reginald Wellbye of the Sociological Society, contributor to *The Sociological Review* on subjects such as "Sunlight and Sociology" in 1924, member of the British Society for the Study of Sex Psychology, enthusiastic cyclist and author of several guidebooks on touring). Thwang has been identified as Roland Berrill, who was an enthusiastic member of British woodcraft organisation, the Kindred of the Kibbo Kift, and a founder member of Mensa. See Annebella Pollen, *The Kindred of the Kibbo Kift: Intellectual Barbarians* (London: Donlon Books, 2015). Moonella is widely suspected to be the novelist Ursula Bloom. See accounts of the earliest days of nudism by Philip Carr-Gomm, *A Brief History of Nakedness* (London: Reaktion, 2000); Barbara Croom, *Five Acres Country Club: 80 Years of Naturism* (St Albans: Five Acres, 2007); Michael Farrar, "Chong, Flang and Moonella", *British Naturism* 92, Summer 1987, p. 23; Nina J. Morris, "Naked in Nature: Naturism, Nature and the Senses in Early 20th Century Britain", *Cultural Geographies* 16, 2009, pp. 283–308.
10. Zex [Rex Wellbye], "The Freeacres Scheme", *The Flail: An Independent Kibbo Kift Magazine* 5:1, Autumn 1927, pp. 200–201. Now known as Five Acres Country Club, the site still provides naturist facilities in 2021.
11. Advertisement, New Gymnosophy Society, *Nomad* [Kibbo Kift Magazine] 9:2, February 1925, inside cover.
12. N. F. Barford was the founder of the Sun Bathing Society, first mooted in 1927 and formally inaugurated in 1929. He was the founding editor of its journal, *Sun Bathing Review*, 1933. See "How it all Began", *Sun Bathing Review*, Autumn 1949, p. 72. Barford's contributions are analysed in "Looking Back: Alec Craig Reviews Sun Bathing from his Childhood Days", *Sun Bathing Review*, Autumn 1935, pp. 86–89.
13. "Nudist Societies in Great Britain", *Health and Efficiency*, June 1933, p. 185.
14. Nesta H. Webster, *The Socialist Network* (Aylesbury: Boswell, 1926), pp. 122, 134.
15. "Sun Bath "Riots" at Lake Side", *Daily Express*, 30 June 1930, p. 11; "Sun Bathing War", *Times* and *Guardian* [n.d., n.p.], illustrated in Adam Clapham and Robin Constable, *Naked as Nature Intended: A Pictorial History of the Nudists* (London: Heinemann, 1982), p. 44; "Sun Bather Prosecuted", *Times*, 20 September 1933, p. 7.
16. Hans Surén, *Man and Sunlight* (Slough: Sollux, 1927). For more on

Appendix

Surén, see Nina J. Morris, "Naked in Nature: Naturism, Nature and the Senses in Early 20th Century Britain", *Cultural Geographies* 16, 2009, pp. 283–308.

17. For further reading on nudism in Germany: Michael Hau, *The Cult of Health and Beauty in Germany: A Social History, 1890–1930* (Chicago: University of Chicago Press, 2003); Chad Ross, *Naked Germany: Health, Race and the Nation* (New York: Berg, 2005); Karl Toepfer, *Empire of Ecstasy: Nudity and Movement in German Body Culture, 1910–1935* (Berkeley: University of California Press, 1997); John Alexander Williams, *Turning to Nature in Germany: Hiking, Nudism, and Conservation, 1900–1940* (Stanford: Stanford University Press, 2007).

18. The cradle phrase is from Michael Rutherford, *British Naturism* (London: The Naturist, 1946), p. 54.

19. Iseult Richardson, *No Shadows Fall: The Story of Spielplatz* (Scarborough: Coast and Country Naturist Publications, 1994); Sennet, *Nudist Life at Spielplatz*. Spielplatz continues in 2020 as a naturist club with Iseult, daughter of the founders, still resident.

20. Prices were not often published in early nudist camp advertising but were available on application as part of the approval process. Costs in the 1930s and 1940s seem to have been relatively modest, judging by advertisements in nudist magazines. A club's brochure might be typically one shilling, the same as the price of a nudist magazine (roughly £1.50 in today's money). The price to pitch a tent for the night began at two shillings (£3). Annual memberships ranged from 10 to 20 shillings (£15 to £30) with differential prices for women (cheaper) and men (more expensive).

21. Details taken from Richardson, *No Shadows Fall: The Story of Spielplatz* (Scarborough: Coast and Country Naturist Publications, 1994) and *A Confidential Chat about Spielplatz* (St Albans: Spielplatz, 1948).

22. Langdon-Davies [1897–1971] was a Quaker, conscientious objector, and an advocate of progressive and pacifist causes. His principal legacy was as the co-founder of Plan International, the refugee children's charity, in 1940.

23. John Langdon-Davies, *The Future of Nakedness* (London: Noel Douglas, 1929), pp. 9, 29, 35, 59.

24. Jan Gay, *On Going Naked* (London: Noel Douglas, 1933). Gay was born Helen Reitman. Her lesbian partner Eleanor Byrnes (Zhenya) was the book's illustrator. Gay was a German-born, US-based author whose European investigations led her to establish a New York nudist club in 1933. Gay was also an influential researcher of female homosexuality or "sex variants". See Brian Hoffman, *Naked: A Cultural History of American Nudism* (New York: New York University Press, 2015), pp. 79–80.

25. Frances and Mason Merrill, *Among the Nudists* (London: Noel Douglas, 1932), p. 192.

26. Parmelee [1882–1969] was a Turkish-born American and a prolific author on sociology, anthropology and criminology; see Don C. Gibbons, "Say, What Became of Maurice Parmelee Anyway?", *Sociological Quarterly* 15:3, Summer 1974, pp.405–416.

27. Havelock Ellis, Introduction, Maurice Parmelee, *Nudism in Modern Life: The New Gymnosophy* (London: Bodley Head, 1942 [1929]), p. 2.

28. Parmelee, *Nudism in Modern Life*, p. 16.

29. Parmelee, *Nudism in Modern Life*, pp. 36, 37, 43, 44, 50.

30. Parmelee notes that he consulted one Dorothy Baldwin on the text for "a woman's point of view", *Nudism in Modern Life*, p. 7.

31. Parmelee, *Nudism in Modern Life*, p. 75, 84, 158, 179.

32. Clarence E. Norwood, *Nudism in England* (London: Noel Douglas, 1933), pp. 10–11, 44.

33. By my deduction, the author attended the 1933 Sun Bathing Society summer conference at Bedales School.

34. *In a Nudist Camp! (Somewhere in England) or The Naked Truth* (Glasgow: Scottish Protestant League, 1933), pp. 8, 9, 13, 20, 24.

35. Advertisement for *Gymnos*, *Sun Bathing Review* 1:4, Autumn 1933, p. 37.

36. Key contributors include Byngham and Major Theodore Faithfull, a former veterinarian, an author of experimental works of psychology and the head teacher of the nudist Priory Gate School. See Annebella Pollen, "The most curious of all queer societies? Sexuality and Gender in British Woodcraft Camps, 1916–2016" in Kenneth B. Kidd and Derritt Mason (eds), *Queer as Camp: Essays on Summer, Style and Sexuality* (New York, Fordham University Press, 2019), pp. 31–50.

37. "What We Stand For", *Gymnos* 1:1, February 1933, p. 3.

38. "Dr Bracht's Famous Decree", *Gymnos* 1:1, February 1933, p. 14; "Herr Göring's Decree", *Gymnos* 1:3, April 1933 p. 14.

39. "Our Friends in Germany", *Gymnos* 1:5, June 1933, p. 3; "Latest News from Germany", *Gymnos* 1:5, June 1933, p. 14.

40. "What We Stand For", *Gymnos* 1:1, February 1933, p. 3.

41. *Gymnos* closed in 1934 and was incorporated into *Illustrated Sun Bathing News* in an explicit attempt to help nudism appeal to "the average man—and his wife—and his family". "Editorial: We Begin Again", *Illustrated Sun Bathing News: The Official Organ of the Gymnic Association of Great Britain* 1:1, Spring 1935, p. 3.

42. "Policy of the *Sun Bathing Review*", *Sun Bathing Review* 1:1, Spring 1933, back page.

43. Advertisement, *Sun Bathing Review* 1:3, Autumn 1933, p. 35.

44. J. H. Badley, H. P. Bibby, Vera Brittain, Elizabeth Sloan Chesser, Stella Churchill, A. E. Coppard, J. C. Flugel, Robert Gibbings, Norman Haire, Winifred Holtby, Laurence Housman, W. Hope-Jones, Julian S. Huxley, C. E. M. Joad, A.C. Jordan, Margaret Mayo, Naomi Mitchison, Beverly Nichols, A. Rollier, Dora Russell, G. Bernard Shaw and Kathleen Vaughan, "Sunbathing", *The Times*, 18 March 1932, p. 10. The artists, authors, pacifists, physicians, sexologists and feminists in this list present an impressive roll call. Many were also involved in wider pressure groups, including the Federation of Progressive Societies and Individuals and the World League for Sexual Reform.

45. "Our Appeal in *The Times*", *Sun Bathing Review* 1:1, Spring 1933, pp. 19–20.

46. For a fuller discussion of the dress theories and practices of early nudists, see Annebella Pollen, "Utopian Bodies and Anti-fashion Futures: The Dress Theories and Practices of English Interwar Nudists", *Utopian Studies*, 28:3, 2018, pp. 451–481.

47. Haydn Brown, "The Psychology of Nudism", *Sun Bathing Review* 1:7, 1933, pp. 77–78; Caleb W. Saleeby, *Sunlight and Health* (London: Nisbet, 1923), p. xix.

48. Clarence E. Norwood, *Nudism in England* (London: Noel Douglas, 1933), p. 32.

49. H. Robini, "Total or Partial Nudity", *Gymnos* 1:8, 1933, pp. 21–22.

50. Cedric Belfrage, "Naturism Transforms a Nation", *Health and Efficiency*, February 1934, p. 42.

51. Albert Ebor, "The Future of Gymnosophy", *Gymnos* 1:2, 1933, p. 14.

52. Clarence E. Norwood, *Nudism in England* (London: Noel Douglas, 1933), p. 32.

53. J. C. Hale, "Undress and Redress: An Appreciation of the President's Article in *New Health*", *Gymnos* 1:8, 1933, p. 20.

54. Laurence Housman, "Our Letter File", *Sun Bathing Review* 1:2, 1933, p. 34.

55. Clifford Coudray, "Hiking a La Nature", *Health and Efficiency*, October 1931, p. 86.

56. Maurice Parmelee, *Nudism in Modern Life: The New Gymnosophy* (London: Bodley Head, 1942 [1929]), p. 90.

57. For eugenics in the period, see Lucy Bland and Lesley A. Hall, "Eugenics in Britain: The View from the Metropole" in Alison Bashford and Philippa Levine (eds), *The Oxford Handbook of the History of Eugenics* (Oxford: Oxford University Press, 2010).

58. W. Hope-Jones, "Eugenics and Sun Bathing", *Sun Bathing Review* 1:1, 1933, p. 11.

59. Arnold Pickin, "Commonsense Dress", *Health and Efficiency*, June 1935, p. 192; W. S. Sparkes, "Without Clothes: A Fantasy", *Gymnos* 1:12, 1934, p. 17; "A Summer School Described", *Sun Bathing Review* 1:2, 1933, p. 8.

60. Clarence E. Norwood, *Nudism in England* (London: Noel Douglas, 1933), p. 33; George Bernard Shaw, "On Excessive Clothing", *Sun Bathing Review* 1:2, 1933, p. 5; "Thirty Years On", *Illustrated Sun Bathing News* 1:1, 1935, p. 32.

61. W. S. Sparkes, "Behold the skin! It must be of some use" *Gymnos* 1:11, 1933, p. 8.

62. Maurice Parmelee, *Nudism in Modern Life: The New Gymnosophy* (London: Bodley Head, 1942 [1929]), p. 187.

63. Laurence Housman, "Our Letter File", *Sun Bathing Review* 1:2, 1933, p. 34.

64. "Some Views of Mr. C. E. M. Joad", *Sun Bathing Review* 1:2, 1933, pp. 5–6.

65. For fuller details of dress reform in the period, see Annebella Pollen, "'The sartorial rebirth of man'? Reconsidering the promise of the Men's Dress Reform Party, 1929–1937", *Vestoj: The Journal of Sartorial Matters* 7, 2016, pp. 59–68. The Men's Dress Reform Party, established in 1929, had as its Honorary Secretary Dr Alfred C. Jordan, CBE, a London radiologist of international reputation; its Chairman was Saleeby. Berrill, Byngham and Flugel were key members.

66. Eric Gill, "Nudism—A Natural Reaction from Industrialism", *Health and Efficiency*, April 1935, pp. 111–112.

67. Maurice Parmelee, *Nudism in Modern Life: The New Gymnosophy* (London: Bodley Head, 1942 [1929]), p. 124.

68. W. Hope-Jones, "Eugenics and Sun Bathing", *Sun Bathing Review* 1:1, 1933, p. 11.

69. Eric Gill, "Nudism—A Natural Reaction from Industrialism", *Health and*

Efficiency, April 1935, pp. 111–112.

70. George Ryley Scott, *The Common Sense of Nudism* (London: T. Werner Laurie, 1934), p. 48

71. See, for example, Scott, *The Common Sense of Nudism*; J. C. Flugel, *The Psychology of Clothes* (London: The Hogarth Press, 1950 [1930]).

72. Arnold Lane, "Prudery's Veil on the Sun", *Health and Efficiency*, October 1931, p. 81.

73. Maurice Parmelee, *Nudism in Modern Life: The New Gymnosophy* (London: Bodley Head, 1942 [1929]), pp. 120–121.

74. "Nudism is Not Just Sunbathing: It means Exercise and Effort", *Health and Efficiency*, September 1933, p. 310.

75. "The Wealth of Mountain Health—in Britain", *Health and Efficiency*, July 1934, p. 252.

76. Although many illustrations are uncredited in early British nudist publications, photographs of German nudists in German landscapes taken by German photographers Kurt Reichert and Gerhard Riebicke were reproduced and their style imitated. There is little detail provided about precisely how these were attained but early British nudists had close relationships with pre-war German practitioners and magazine producers. For more on German *nacktkultur* photography, see Ulf Erdmann Ziegler, *Nackt Unter Nackten: Utopien der Nacktkultur 1906–1942* (Berlin: Pawlak, 1992).

77. "Correspondence", *Gymnos* 1:1, June 1933, p. 19.

78. "Planks of Nudism", *Gymnos* 1:1, February 1933, p. 1.

79. For definitions of obscenity in the period, see Harry G. Cocks, "Saucy Stories: Pornography, Sexology and the Marketing of Sexual Knowledge in Britain, c.1918–70", *Social History* 29:4, November 2004, pp. 465–484. Prominent nudist anti-censorship campaigners include Alec Craig, author of *The Banned Books of England* (London: Allen and Unwin, 1937), and George Ryley Scott, author of *Into Whose Hands? An Examination of Obscene Libel in its Legal, Sociological and Literary Aspects* (London: Gerald Swan, 1945).

80. Gibbings [1889–1958] founded the Society for Wood Engravers in 1920, and ran the Golden Cockerel Press, 1924–1933, a fine printing press that produced Eric Gill works. Gibbings was described in his obituary as "always a devoted sun bather"; see "An Appreciation of Robert Gibbings", *Sun Bathing Review*, Spring 1958, pp. 9–10. He featured in early nudist magazines, for example "Famous Artist at Sun Bathers' Holiday Camp", *Health and Efficiency*, October 1931, pp. 78–79.

81. *Sun Bathing Review*, 3:9, Spring 1935, p 7

82. Charles Simpson, *Photography of the Figure in Colour and Monochrome* (London: H. F. and G. Witherby, 1938), p. 55. Simpson was a Royal Institute-anointed painter who wrote on nude photography for *Health and Efficiency* in the 1930s and the introduction for John Everard's *Artist's Model* (London: The Bodley Head, 1951).

83. Bertram Park OBE [1883–1972] was a founder member of the London Salon of Photography in 1909 and contributed photographs to the Paris *International Salon* of Nude Photography, *1933*.

84. Alan Warwick, "Introduction", in Bertram Park and Yvonne Gregory, *Sun Bathers* (London: Routledge, 1935). For Park and Gregory's publications, see Jay W. King, *Past Masters of the Nude* (London: Wolfbait, 2020).

85. Bertram Park and Yvonne Gregory, *Sun Bathers* (London: Routledge, 1935), p. v.

86. Charles Simpson, *Photography of the Figure in Colour and Monochrome* (London: H. F. and G. Witherby, 1938), p. 67.

87. Bertram Park, "Nudity Knows No Falsehood", *The Naturist* 1:8, July 1938, inside cover.

88. Bertram Park and Yvonne Gregory, *Sun Bathers* (London: Routledge, 1935), p. v.

89. Bertram Park, "Photography of the Nude", *Sun Bathing Review* 3:10, Summer 1935, pp. 54–56.

90. Park and Gregory photographs appear in many nudist publications in the 1930s, with and without credit, including in William Welby's series of illustrated books *Naked and Unashamed: Nudism from Six Points of View* (London: Thorsons, 1934) and *It's Only Natural: The Philosophy of Nudism* (London: Thorsons, 1935). Their later publication, *Eve in the Sunlight* (London: Hutchinson, 1937) also features only outdoor nudes.

91. John Everard [1898–1964] was the pen name of Edward Ralph Forward, a self-taught photographer who sold prints to newspapers and illustrated periodicals from the 1920s. *Adam's Fifth Rib* (London: Chapman and Hall, 1935) was the first of Everard's books of nude photographs. Walter Bird [1903–1969] was a commercial photographer for magazines from the 1920s; *Beauty's Daughters* (London: John Long, 1938) was the first of a series of mid-century nude publications. See Jay King, *Past Masters of the Nude* (London: Wolfbait, 2020).

92. The "naturist nude" or "naturist-style nude" is my preferred phrasing. Contemporaneous magazines sometimes spoke about "outdoor nudes". Shaffer has suggested that "environmental nude" could encompass photographs in naturist publications, photographs of naturists and photographs of environmental activists; Marguerite S. Shaffer, "On the Environmental Nude", *Environmental History* 13:1, January 2008, pp. 126–139.

93. "Comments on Illustrations", *Sun Bathing Review*, Spring 1938, p. 23.

94. "Sunk Without Trace", *Sun Bathing Review*, June/July 1936, p. 62.

95. P. S. Robson, letter to the editor, *Sun Bathing Review*, Autumn 1936, p. 133.

96. Letter to the editor, *The Naturist*, April 1940, p. 92.

97. "Register of Models", *Sun Bathing Review*, Autumn 1937, p. 94.

98. Colin Smithson, "Getting the Best Out of Your Sun Bathing Snaps", *Sun Bathing Review*, August/September 1936, pp. 110–111.

99. Advertisement for P. C. D. and P. Service (Private and Confidential Developing and Printing Service), *Sun Bathing Review* 1:2, Summer 1933, inside back page.

100. Alec Craig, "Naturism and the Law", *Health and Efficiency*, December 1938, pp. 428–429.

101. Monthly physique competition, *Health and Efficiency*, October 1955, p. 17.

102. "More Men Wanted", *Sun Bathing Review*, Early Summer, June/July 1936, p. 61.

103. Letter to the editor, *Sun Bathing Review*, August/September 1936, p. 103.

104. Alec Craig, Letter to the editor, *Illustrated Sun Bathing News* 1:2, Summer 1935, p. 28.

105. Letter to the editor, *Sun Bathing Review*, Summer 1937, p. 58.

106. Letter to the editor, *Sun Bathing Review*, Summer 1937, p. 57.

107. Woodsman, "In Defence of Models", *The Naturist*, November 1939, pp. 360–361.

108. Sun Bathing Society membership application, *Sun Bathing Review* 1:2, Summer 1933, back page insert.

109. Subscription prices at Five Acres club in the 1940s are double for single men. Barbara Croom, *Five Acres Country Club: 80 Years of Naturism* (St Albans: Five Acres, 2007), p. 5.

110. George Ryley Scott, *The Common Sense of Nudism* (London: T. Werner Laurie, 1934), p. 144. Scott's other books, published during the years he was writing for nudist publications, include *Sex and its Mysteries* (1929), *The New Art of Love: A Guide for the Married and Those About to Marry* (1934), and *A History of Prostitution from Antiquity to the Present Day* (1936).

111. Chesser was a physician and author of many prominent works on women and children's health; she wrote on nudism for *Sun Bathing Review* in the in the 1930s. Chance was a prominent author and campaigner for women's sex education, birth control, and reforms to abortion law. She wrote of her entry into nudism in "How I Passed my Sunbathing Test", *Sun Bathing Review*, Spring 1940, pp. 2–3. Vaughan was a doctor and obstetrician; she contributed to *Sun Bathing Review* in the 1930s on childbirth and clothing for children.

112. Biographical details from Duncan Forbes (ed.), *Edith Tudor-Hart: Under the Shadow of Tyranny* (Edinburgh: National Galleries of Scotland; Wien: Wien Museum, 2013), and Amanda Hopkinson, "Edith Tudor Hart", *Oxford Dictionary of National Biography* (https://www.oxforddnb.com). There is scholarly inconsistency in the hyphen in Edith's surname.

113. See specifically the photograph "Young England" that accompanies the article "Drum Taps of Summer", *Sun Bathing Review* 3:11, Autumn 1935, p. 85.

114. *New Homes for Old* cover by Edith Tudor Hart, illustrated in Robert Radford, "Edith Tudor Hart: Photographs from the Thirties", *Camerawork*, July 1980, p. 2.

115. "Children and the Sun Bathing Movement", *Sun Bathing Review*, Summer 1935, pp. 44–45; "Look at the Children", *Gymnos* 1:4, 1933 pp. 8, 19.

116. "Sexual Education and Sun Bathing Clubs: Report from The World's League of Sexual Reform", *Sun Bathing Review* 1:1, Spring 1933, p. 33.

117. George Ryley Scott, *The Common Sense of Nudism* (London: T. Werner Laurie, 1934), p. 152.

118. *Health and Efficiency* 27:8, August 1947, p. 175.

119. Advertisement for Pinehurst School, *Sun Bathing Review* 3:9, Spring 1935, p. 3; "Gymnosophy and the Child", *Gymnos* 1:8, September 1933, p. 13; "Open Air Life at St Christopher's School, Letchworth", *Sun Bathing Review*, Autumn 1938, pp. 84–85.

120. Dora Russell, "Our Children's Health and Education in Wartime", *Sun Bathing Review*, Spring 1940, pp. 4–5. Russell was a prominent feminist

campaigner for sex education, birth control, and progressive education.

121. J. H. Whittaker-Swinton, "Rocklands School Hastings", *Gymnos* 1:8, September 1933, p. 15.

122. "Letter File", *Sun Bathing Review*, Autumn 1946, p. 20.

123. Beatrix Tudor Hart, "Fortis Green School: Home of Happy Childhood", *Sun Bathing Review* 6:24, 1939, pp. 118–9. Beatrix was also Montessori trained.

124. Edith Tudor Hart, "Vienna: City of Sun Bathing", *Sun Bathing Review*, Spring 1936, pp. 6–8.

125. Hart's photographs were repurposed from a photo-essay produced for an Austrian magazine, "Wildbaden in Der Lobau", *Der Kuckuck*, 21 August 1932, p. 4, illustrated in Duncan Forbes (ed.), *Edith Tudor-Hart: Under the Shadow of Tyranny* (Edinburgh: National Galleries of Scotland; Wien: Wien Museum, 2013), p. 16. Hart also produced photo-essays on children's progressive education for the same magazine.

126. A Clergyman, "Thank God for Nudism!", *Gymnos* 1:10, November 1933, p. 4.

127. "Wake Up England!", *Sun Bathing Review* 1:1, Spring 1933, pp. 3–4.

128. William Welby, *It's Only Natural: The Philosophy of Nudism* (London: Thorsons, 1935), p. 41.

129. J. C. Flugel, "Nature, Nudity and Reason", *Sun Bathing Review* 3:9, Spring 1935, pp. 12–15. See also Welby, *It's Only Natural*.

130. Idrisyn O. Evans, *Sensible Sun-Bathing* (London: T. Werner Laurie, 1935), p. 5.

131. "A Conscientious Objector—to Sun Bathing", *Health and Efficiency* 1:10, May 1932, p. 338, quoted in Peter Fryer, *Mrs Grundy: Studies in English Prudery* (London: Corgi, 1963), p. 227.

132. Idrisyn O. Evans, *Sensible Sun-Bathing* (London: T. Werner Laurie, 1935), p. 6.

133. Julian Strange, "On Meeting the English", *Sun Bathing Review*, Autumn 1936, pp. 118–120.

134. "Rain Bathing", *Sun Bathing Review* 4:15, September 1936, p. 85.

135. Arnold Lane, "Prudery's Veil on the Sun", *Health and Efficiency*, October 1931, p. 81.

136. Julian Strange, "On Meeting the English", *Sun Bathing Review*, Autumn 1936, pp. 118–120.

137. See, for example, "Indoor Nudist Clubs", *Sun Bathing Review* 3:9, Spring 1935, p. 33; "The National Sun and Air Club", *The Naturist*, May 1940, pp. 110–111.

138. Idrisyn O. Evans, *Sensible Sun-Bathing* (London: T. Werner Laurie, 1935), p. 35; Alec Craig, "Indoor Nudism", *Sun Bathing Review*, Autumn 1939, p. 94–95.

139. "Can Indoor Nudism Be Justified?", *Health and Efficiency*, December 1936.

140. Alec Craig, "Indoor Nudism", *Sun Bathing Review*, Autumn 1939, p. 94.

141. Colin Smithson, "The Harm Wrought by Indiscreet Nudists by a Keen Believer in Sane Naturism", *Health and Efficiency*, September 1933, p. 293.

142. Haire quoted in editorial on indoor nudism in *Sun Bathing Review*, Summer 1945, p. 39.

143. Elizabeth King, "The Truth About the Nudists in England", *Health and Efficiency*, January 1933, pp. 183–184.

144. "Looking Back: Alec Craig Reviews Sun Bathing from his Childhood Days", *Sun Bathing Review*, Autumn 1935 pp. 86–89. A *Sun Bathing Review* writer who conducted membership interviews for his nudist club shared insights with Mass Observation in the form of a nudist questionnaire he proposed to carry out for the social research organisation in 1937. In it he queries all aspects of members' attitudes and activities, including statements about class and profession. C. H. B. Cotton, "Nudism Report", 12 July 1938, "Holidays 1937–51, January 1937–December 1951", Mass Observation Archive, University of Sussex Special Collections.

145. Julian Strange, "On Meeting the English", *Sun Bathing Review*, Autumn 1936, p. 119.

146. Idrisyn O. Evans, *Sensible Sun-Bathing* (London: T. Werner Laurie, 1935); Alec Craig, "Are we Too "Select?" *Sun Bathing Review*, Autumn 1947, pp. 51–52; C. E. M. Joad, "Prudery", *Sun Bathing Review*, Autumn 1938, pp. 78–79.

147. A. A. Burall quoted in "Social Reformers: A Lecture on Nudism at Harrogate", *Yorkshire Evening Post*, 9 August 1937, p. 9.

148. Alec Craig, "Nudism is Progressive", *Sun Bathing Review* 1:7, 1933, pp. 86–87. Burall and Craig were both members of the Federation of Progressive Societies and Individuals (FPSI), intended to unite politically left single-issue causes into a united front. Nudism was part of the federation's interests.

149. George C. Foster, "Nudism not a Cult", *Sun Bathing Review* 1:6, 1933, pp. 44–45.

150. "Letter: From a Famous Author" [George. C. Foster], *Health and Efficiency*, April 1934, p. 138.

151. Alec Craig, "Nudism is Progressive", *Sun Bathing Review* 1:7, 1933, p. 87.

152. John Walsh, "Sun-Bathing Societies—A Warning", *John Bull*, 15 August 1931; "Where Nudists Go in the Wintertime", *John Bull*, 28 November 1936, reproduced in *Sun Bathing Review* 4:17, Winter 1937, p. 183.

153. Henry Harris, "Why I am a Nudist", *Daily Mirror*, 30 July 1987, p. 10; "Perverts! Says a Mother; Apollos! Says a Spinster, 34", *Daily Mirror*, 4 August 1937, p. 10.

154. William Welby, "Is Nudism 'Just a Craze'?", *The Naturist* 1:2, January 1938, p. 37.

155. *Sun Bathing Review* was bought by *Health and Efficiency* in 1938. They continued as separate titles under a shared editorship until 1959 when *Sun Bathing Review* fully merged into *Health and Efficiency*.

156. Horace Narbeth [1906–2002], known professionally as Roye, was a prolific photographer of nudes from the 1930s to the late 1950s; he also photographed many British stars of stage and screen, exhibited art photographs at the London Salon of Photography as well as producing his own publications and running a photographic agency. See Roye, *Nude Ego* (London: Hutchinson, 1955).

157. "The Glory that is Perfect Womanhood", *Daily Mirror*, 14 September 1938, p. 14. See Roye, *Nude Ego*, p. 131. Roye identifies the model as Strelsa Brown. Hugh Cudlipp claimed to have published the first nude in a British newspaper as editor of the *Pictorial* in spring of 1938. See Hugh Cudlipp, "Exclusive: The First Nude in Fleet Street", *British Journalism Review* 5:3, 1994, pp. 17–19. There is clearly some kudos for male photographers and editors to be the first to put a naked woman on the printed page Bingham astutely notes that, in fact, "bare breasted black women in exotic imperial locations" had already featured in newspapers. As the subjects were not white and British, they appear not to have counted to editors and photographers. Adrian Bingham, *Family Newspapers? Sex, Private Life and the British Popular Press 1918–1978* (Oxford: Oxford University Press, 2009), p. 208.

158. Roye's photographs appeared in *The World's Best Photographs: Second Series* (London: Odhams Press, n.d. c.1944).

159. "The Naturist's Bookshelf", *The Naturist*, May 1938.

160. Reported in Roye, *Nude Ego* (London: Hutchinson, 1955), p. 130. Roye cherry-picked his reviews. Others dismissed his work. The Royal Photographic Society said *Canadian Beauty* was "ludicrous" with poses and expressions producing "unmitigated ugliness". They concluded, "this volume can serve no useful purpose at all and will add nothing to the prestige of either photography or photographers". See W. J. Pilkington, *The Photographic Journal of the Royal Photographic Society*, February 1953, p. 66.

161. Roye, *Nude Ego*, pp. 134–135.

162. Roye, *Nude Ego*, p. 130.

163. *The Naturist*, March 1938.

164. "Age is No Bar to Nudism", *The Naturist*, June 1940, p. 125.

165. "Roye's Art Interprets Nature", *The Naturist*, July 1938, pp. 240–241.

166. *The Naturist*, January 1940, p. 39.

167. *The Naturist*, July 1940, p. 113.

168. *The Naturist*, July 1940, p. 152.

CHAPTER 2

1. "Newsagents and Bookshops, Report on Bookshops", 1941, Mass Observation 20/3/B; "Bookshops 1941", Mass Observation 20/3/E.

2. "Naturism in the Post-War Days", *The Naturist*, May 1945, p. 83.

3. Books published by The Naturist include Douglas Stewart, *Beauty and Naturism* (1941); Charles Sennet, *Sunshine and Naturism* (1943); Frederick H. Mentone, *The Human Form in Art* (1944); Michael Rutherford, *British Naturism* (1946); Douglas Stewart, *Ideal Manhood* (1948); Roy Watt, *Sussex Maidens* (1949); Frederick H. Mentone, *The Romance of Naturism* (1949); Anne Seton, *Pool of Enchantment* (1950); Anne Seton, *The Garden of Eden* (1952); Paul Jacques, *Nudism in France* (1953); Charles Sennet, *French Maidens* (1954); Mervyn Oakdale, *The Mystery of Naturism* (1956); Charles Sennet, *Nudist Life at Spielplatz: The Story of a Modern Experiment in the Art of Living* (1956).

4. Together Bird, Roye and Everard produced *Eves without Leaves* (London: Pearson, 1941) and *More Eves without Leaves* (London: Camera Studies Club, 1941). Singly, in the war years, Bird produced

Beauty's Self (London: John Long, 1941); Everard produced *Portrait of a Model* (London: Routledge, 1939), *Nymph and Naiad* (London: Routledge, 1940) and *The Judgement of Paris* (London: Routledge, 1940); Roye also produced four books for Routledge, *The English Maid* (1939), *The Scottish Maid* (1940), *The Irish Maid* (1941) and *The Welsh Maid* (1942).

5. "What can Naturists do in Wartime?", *The Naturist*, April 1940, pp. 90–91.
6. Dion Byngham, "Nudism and the War Party", *Gymnos* 1:4, 1933, p. 12; Clifford W. Greatorex, "New Year Resolutions of a Naturist", *The Naturist*, January 1940, pp. 30–31.
7. "What are We Fighting For?", *Sun Bathing Review*, Autumn 1942, p. 55.
8. William Welby, "After the War", *Sun Bathing Review*, Spring 1941, pp. 10–11.
9. Michael Rutherford, *British Naturism* (London: The Naturist, 1946), p. 64.
10. "Sun Societies in War-Time", *Sun Bathing Review*, Autumn 1939, pp. 84–89.
11. "Wartime Nerves: Combating the Strain of Everyday Life", *The Naturist*, December 1943, p. 14.
12. "Sun Societies in War-Time", *Sun Bathing Review*, Autumn 1939, pp. 84–89.
13. Charles Sennet, *Sunshine and Naturism* (London: The Naturist, 1943), p. 62.
14. J. C. Flugel, "The Future of Clothes", *Sun Bathing Review*, Summer 1941, p. 46.
15. *A Confidential Chat about Spielplatz* (St Albans: Spielplatz, 1948), p. 12.
16. William Welby, "After the War", *Sun Bathing Review*, Spring 1941, p. 11.
17. "Nudism in Wartime", *The Naturist*, May 44, pp. 84–85.
18. "What Naturism Has Done for Me", *Health and Efficiency*, October 1947, p. 226.
19. Michael Rutherford, *British Naturism* (London: The Naturist, 1946), p. 17.
20. Stephen Glass, brother of the more famous Zoltan Glass, was a Hungarian photographer who moved to London at the end of the 1930s and photographed regularly for nudist books and periodicals into the 1950s.
21. Michael Rutherford, *British Naturism* (London: The Naturist, 1946), art supplement.
22. Letter to Editor, "Let's Keep the Glamour Girls!", *The Naturist*, December 1951, p. 15.
23. "Generally Speaking", *Sun Bathing Review*, Autumn 1950, p 66.
24. "The English Maid: Foreword", Roye, *The English Maid* (London: Routledge, 1939), n. p.
25. Walter Bird, Roye and John Everard, *Eves without Leaves* (London: Pearson, 1941).
26. *Men Only* was established 1935 as a men's leisure magazine; it became a soft porn magazine in 1964. For wider context, see Jill Greenfield, Sean O'Connell and Chris Reid, "Fashioning Masculinity: Men Only, Consumption and the Development of Marketing in the 1930s", *Twentieth Century British History* 10:4, 1999, pp. 457–476.
27. Reginald Arkell, introduction, *Eves without Leaves* (London, Pearson, 1941), pp. 8–11.
28. "What is a Pin-Up Girl?", *Picture Post*, 23 September 1944, pp. 14–15, 25.
29. "What is a Pin-Up Girl?", *Picture Post*, p. 25.
30. Studies include Maria Elena Buszek, *Pin-Up Grrrls: Feminism, Sexuality, Popular Culture* (Duke University Press, 2006) and Eleni Lipsos, *Anatomy of a Pin-Up: A Genealogy of Sexualised Femininity since the Industrial Age*, unpublished PhD, University of Exeter, 2013.
31. Andre Bazin, "Entomology of The Pin-Up Girl", *What is Cinema*, vol. II (Berkeley: University of Calfornia, 1971); first published in *Ecran Francais*, 17 December 1946.
32. *Sun Bathing Review*, Spring 1938, p. 29.
33. Douglas Stewart, "Unhealthy Stage Nudity", *The Naturist,* May 1940, pp. 104–105.
34. Tony of Woodlands, "From Birth to Manhood as a Naturist", *Health and Efficiency Summer Annual*, 1954, p. 4.
35. Woodsman, "Why are Nudists Hated?", *The Naturist*, December 1948, p. 7.
36. Anne Seton, *The Garden of Eden* (London: The Naturist, 1952), p. 43.
37. Charles Sennet, *Sunshine and Naturism* (London: The Naturist, 1943), p. 59.
38. Ursula Bloom quoted in *A Confidential Chat about Spielplatz* (St Albans, Spielplatz, 1948), pp. 23–31.
39. "Naturism at its Health Benefits", *Health and Efficiency*, October 1955, p. 7.
40. Mervyn Oakdale, *The Mystery of Naturism* (London: The Naturist, 1956), p. 6.
41. Charles Sennet, *Sunshine and Naturism* (London: The Naturist, 1943), p. 56.
42. Woodsman, "Why are Nudists Hated?", *The Naturist*, December 1948, p. 7.
43. Liz Stanley, *Sex Surveyed, 1949–1994: From Mass-Observation's "Little Kinsey" To The National Survey And The Hite Reports* (London: Routledge, 1995), pp. 3–4; Adrian Bingham, "The 'K-Bomb': Social Surveys, the Popular Press, and British Sexual Culture in the 1940s and 1950s", *Journal of British Studies* 50:1, 2012, p. 157.
44. Roy Hayworth, "The Moral Necessity of Naturism", *The Naturist*, March 1938, pp.100–101.
45. Norman Haire, "Foreword", in William Welby, *Naked and Unashamed: Nudism from Six Points of View* (London: Thorsons, 1934), p. 16; "Sex and Nudism", Meeting of the Sex Education Society at Conway Hall, 14 November 1938, *Sun Bathing Review*, Winter 1939, pp. 123–123.
46. For wider context, see Lesley Hall, "Forbidden by God, Despised by Men: Masturbation, Medical Warnings, Moral Panic, and Manhood in Great Britain, 1850–1950", *Journal of the History of Sexuality* 2:3, January 1992, pp. 365–387.
47. Debate staged by "H&E Brains Trust", *Health and Efficiency*, October 1947, p. 232.
48. "The First Moments of Nudism are the Worst", *Health and Efficiency*, July 1933, p. 238.
49. Ernest Stanley, "Conversations at a Sun Club", *Health and Efficiency*, February 1955, pp. 6–7.
50. Seton, *The Garden of Eden* (London: The Naturist, 1952), p. 41.
51. Philosopher, "First Steps", *The Naturist*, December 1945, p. 3.
52. Ken Passingham, "2,000 a Month Go Nudist", *Daily Mirror*, 27 February 1948, p. 2.
53. "Nudism Favoured by Thirty Per Cent", *The Naturist*, October 1946, p. 168.
54. Rex, "Thoughts on British Sunbathing", *The Naturist*, December 1945, pp. 6–7.
55. Anthony Peacock, *Eve* (London: Link House, 1942). Peacock [1898-1981] was a nudist as well as an accomplished photographer.
56. *Sun Bathing Review*, Summer 1941, p. 66.
57. Anthony Peacock, "The Way I Took to Nudes", *PhotoGuide Magazine* 8:5, May 1957, p. 393.
58. Anthony Peacock, "Nudes: English Viewpoint", *Photography*, 1949, p. 21.
59. For those who could not stretch to its cost, it was also available on a five-day loan scheme.
60. John Everard, *Artist's Model* (London: The Bodley Head, 1951), p. 10.
61. Everard, *Artist's Model*, p. 9.
62. Charles Simpson, "Introduction", *Artist's Model* (London: The Bodley Head, 1951), pp. 13–14.
63. Isabel Tang, *Pornography: The Secret History of Civilisation* (London: Macmillan, 1999), p. 100.
64. Charles Simpson, *Artist's Model*, (London: The Bodley Head, 1951), pp. 18, 36.
65. Simpson, *Artist's Model*, p. 46.
66. Donald S. Herbert, review of *Artist's Model*, *The Photographic Journal of the Royal Photographic Society*, April 1952, p. 110.
67. John Everard, *Second Sitting* (London, The Bodley Head, 1955), p. 186.
68. Charles Sennet, review of Kenneth Clark's *The Nude: A Study of Ideal Art*, *The Naturist*, March 1957, p. 55.
69. Kenneth Clark, *The Nude: A Study of Ideal Art* (London: Penguin Books, 1985 [1956]), pp. 1, 3, 4.
70. Clark, *The Nude*, pp. 6, 64.
71. Clark, *The Nude*, pp. 10, 87, 343.
72. Clark, *The Nude*, p. 354.
73. W. M. Whiteman, "2500 Years of Nudity in Life and Art", *Sun Bathing Review*, Spring 1957, pp. 6–7.
74. Woodsman, "Women Won't be Nudists!", *The Naturist*, May 1948, p. 83; "My Wife Won't Join", *Health and Efficiency*, March 1955.
75. Robin Black, "Out of Balance", *Health and Efficiency*, April 1951, p. 7.
76. Illustration accompanying Bamford Stanley, "Radiant Health", *The Naturist*, December 1951, p. 8.
77. "The Ladies—God Bless 'Em!", *The Naturist*, June 1953, p. 109.
78. Little is known about June Hope Kynaston except that she authored *The Mind that Works Miracles: A Book on Christian Psychology* in 1935 and was a member of the Fairy Investigation Society, established in 1927. June Hope Kynaston, "People I'd like to make Naturists", *Health and Efficiency*, September 1947, p. 199.
79. Kynaston, "People I'd like to make Naturists", *Health and Efficiency*, p. 199.
80. Advertisement in *The Naturist*, November 1952.
81. Anne Seton, *The Garden of Eden* (London: The Naturist, 1952), p. 45.
82. Seton, *The Garden of Eden*, pp. 44–46.
83. The shift to mutuality in marriage is discussed in detail in Marcus

Collins, *Modern Love: An Intimate History of Men and Women in Twentieth-Century Britain* (London: Atlantic Books, 2003).

84. Pandora, "Naturism—the Marriage Saver", *Health and Efficiency*, August 1947, p. 174.

85. Elizabeth Brooks, 'Do they Call you "Scraggy"?' *The Naturist*, June 1953, p. 112; S. B. Whitehead, 'Sun-Therapy vs. Obesity', *Sun Bathing Review*, Autumn 1947, pp. 64–65.

86. 'Naturism and Housewives', *Health and Efficiency*, September 1952, p. 15.

87. *A Confidential Chat about Spielplatz* (St Albans: Spielplatz, 1948), pp. 16–19.

88. The Spielplatz Venus contest appears to have been established in around 1946 and ran at least until the end of the 1950s. Latterly an Adonis competition provided a parallel pageant for men.

89. 'H&E Brains Trust', *Health and Efficiency*, September 1947, p. 206.

90. Pam Colbourne, 'Friday: Office Girl—Saturday: Nudist!' *The Naturist*, June 1953, p. 111.

91. 'Generally Speaking', *Sun Bathing Review*, Spring 1949, p. 31.

92. *A Confidential Chat about Spielplatz* (St Albans: Spielplatz, 1948), p. 1.

93. Elizabeth Somers, "Uncommon Proposal", *Health and Efficiency*, December 1951, pp. 26, 30.

94. Mervyn Oakdale, *The Mystery of Naturism* (London: The Naturist, 1956), pp. 49, 50.

95. Most nude models in naturist magazines and art publications were not named; this was also the case with photographic models in magazines and books more broadly. An exception is Dubarry's *Venus Through the Lens* (London: Thorsons, 1942) where 14 of the 20 nude models are listed by forenames evocative of the period—Mavis, Norah, and Doreen—and their occupations are also given, including hairdresser, usherette, and civil servant.

96. "Two Girls Grow Up—at Spielplatz", *The Naturist*, May 1950, pp. 100–111; Charles Sennet, *Nudist Life at Spielplatz: The Story of a Modern Experiment in the Art of Living* (London: The Naturist, 1956), p. 19.

97. Charles Sennet, *Nudist Life at Spielplatz* (London: The Naturist, 1956), pp. 14, 15.

98. Sennet, *Nudist Life at Spielplatz*, p. 46.

99. Pamela Green [1929–2010] has been described by BAFTA as "a cult figure in early British erotic subculture". Yahya El Droubie, who was a friend of Pamela Green later in life and inherited her archive, has a very detailed and well-researched fan site, *Pamela Green: Never Knowingly Overdressed* (https://pamela-green.com).

100. For further biographical information see https://pamela-green.com; Franklyn Wood, *The Naked Truth about Harrison Marks* (Hemel Hempstead: Colonna Press, 1967); Matthew Sweet, "X Appeal: Britain's Oldest Living Sexploitation Star Tells All", *The Independent*, 29 January 2006 (https://www.independent.co.uk/arts-entertainment/films/features/x-appeal-britain-s-oldest-living-sexploitation-star-tells-all-6110509.html).

101. Franklyn Wood, *The Naked Truth about Harrison Marks* (Hemel Hempstead: Colonna Press, 1967), p. 70.

102. Sarah Brown, "In the Flesh" [cutting from Eva Grant family archive; presumed to be *Amateur Photographer*, c.2000; full details missing].

103. Eva Grant, "The Art of Figure Photography" [cutting from Eva Grant family archive; presumed to be from *PhotoART* 5:4, International Edition; full details missing].

104. There are many statements to this effect; for example, "'conquering the nude' has unfortunate connotations to the male ego. When the photographer fails to turn out prints which are both technically and artistically good, it's like a reflection on his virility". Peter Lathendorf, "The Shy Man's Guide to Nude Photography", *Camera Magazine*, February 1967, p. 22.

105. *Figure Quarterly*, January 1964, cover.

106. Russell Gay, "Britain's No.1 Glamour Photographer", *Art and Photography*, May 1957.

107. Ernest Stanley, "Naturism and its Health Benefits", *Health and Efficiency*, October 1955, p. 7.

108. Wallace Arter's "Naturist Notebook", *Health and Efficiency*, October 1955, p. 31. For Arter's early gymnosophy, see Barbara Croom, *Five Acres Country Club: 80 Years of Naturism* (St Albans: Five Acres, 2007).

109. Richard Hoggart, *The Uses of Literacy: Aspects of Working Class Life* (London: Penguin, 2009 [1957]), pp. 189, 207, 300.

110. "Cheesecake", according to the *Oxford English Dictionary*, emerged as slang for female attractiveness and display in the United States in the 1930s. Carol Dyhouse, *Glamour: Women, History, Feminism* (London: Zed Books, 2010), p. 90.

111. Richard Hoggart, *The Uses of Literacy: Aspects of Working Class Life* (London: Penguin, 2009 [1957]), pp. 189, 207, 300.

112. Hoggart, *The Uses of Literacy*, p. 190.

113. For the use of nudists as pornographic models in 1950s Soho, see Helen Wickstead, "Soho Typescripts: Handmade Obscene Books in Post-war London bookshops", *Porn Studies* 7:2, 2000, pp. 187–211.

114. An overview of class consciousness and change in the period is provided by David Kynaston, *Family Britain 1951–57* (London: Bloomsbury, 2009).

115. Hoggart, *The Uses of Literacy: Aspects of Working Class Life* (London: Penguin, 2009 [1957]), p. 163. Further discussions about pin-ups being considered cheap pleasures for working class men are provided in Mark Gabor, *The Pin-Up: A Modest History* (London: Pan, 1972), p. 72, and Adrian Bingham, "Titillation: The Evolution of the Newspaper Pin-Up", *Family Newspapers? Sex, Private Life and the Popular Press, 1918–1978* (Oxford: Oxford University Press, 2009).

116. Woodsman, "Ten Years of Nudism", *The Naturist*, December 1947, pp. 3–4.

117. Ingeborg Boysen, "British Naturism through Foreign Eyes", *The Naturist*, November 1951 pp. 216–217.

118. Michael Wayne, "Why Don't We Tell the Truth?", *The Naturist*, February 1953, p. 43.

119. "How Far Have we 'Progressed'?", *Sun Bathing Review*, Autumn 1953, p. 55.

120. Audrey Whiting, "These Saucy Snaps Went to War", *Sunday Pictorial*, 23 October 1955, p. 15. Claims of Roye's wealth should be taken with a pinch of salt as he went bankrupt in the same year.

121. Roye, *Nude Ego* (London: Hutchinson, 1955), p. 134.

122. Ken Greenwood, "Working with an Experienced Model", *PhotoART* 7:6, n.d. [mid-1950s], p. 2.

123. A John Firth photograph of a Soho bookshop, 1956, shows the publications side by side on the shelf.

124. L. E. Broome, "Portraiture, Figure and Other Work with a Miniature Camera", *The Photographic Journal of the Royal Photographic Society*, August 1953, p. 238.

125. *Photo Studio: Camera Art for the Connoisseur* 1:2, n.d. [mid-1950s], p. 8. Gay, Grant, and Harrison Marks all produced photographs for these kinds of publications.

126. Oswell Blakeston, "The Business of Pin-Ups", *PhotoGuide Magazine*, February 1957, p. 150.

127. "After Hours", *PhotoART* 5.4, n.d. [mid-1950s], p. 41.

128. Roye's figure comes from *Unique Verdict: The Story of an Unsuccessful Prosecution* (London: Art Publications, London, n.d. [c.1959]); Franklyn Wood, *The Naked Truth about Harrison Marks* (Hemel Hempstead: Colonna Press, 1967), p. 154.

129. Dubarry, *Venus Through the Lens* (London: Thorsons, 1942).

130. Underwood Barry, "The Art of Figure Studies", *The Naturist*, June 1941, pp. 126–127.

131. Underwood Barry, "The Ideal Model", *The Naturist*, July 1941, pp. 146–147; Underwood Barry, "Photography Notes", *The Naturist*, September 1941, pp. 188–189.

132. Gordon S. Malthouse, "Photography—and the Principles of Nudism", *Sun Bathing Review*, Spring 1941, pp. 4–5.

133. Strix, "The Passing Scene: Nudist Matters Mostly Controversial", *Sun Bathing Review*, Summer 1951, p. 44.

134. C. S. Frost, "Those Photographic Fiends", *The Naturist*, May 1952. p. 103.

135. S. D. Jouhar, "Figure Photography", *The Photographic Journal of the Royal Photographic Society*, October 1951, p. 293.

136. Anne Seton, *The Garden of Eden* (London: The Naturist, 1952), p. 51.

137. C. S. Frost, "Your First Nude Study: How Not to Set about it", *The Naturist*, July 1952, p. 142.

138. For just two examples: Roye notes that a woman was tricked into disrobing by a man impersonating Walter Bird in *Nude Ego* (London: Hutchinson, 1955), p. 151; John Everard boasted of rewarding his nude models in the Philippines with a box of matches as a fee in Oswell Blakeston, "Dressing Down for It", *PhotoGuide Magazine* 6:1, January 1955, p. 54.

139. "Photographing the Figure: Working Outdoors", *Photo Studio: Camera Art for the Connoisseur* 1:2, n.d. [mid-1950s], p. 5.

140. "The Nude Outdoors", *PhotoART* 4.5, n.d. [mid-1950s], pp. 40, 47.

141. All quotations from Harrison Marks, *How to Take Glamour Studies*, a collection of a series of articles written by George Harrison Marks for *Foto* in the 1950s, republished by https://pamela-green.com.

142. Kenneth Clark, *The Nude: A Study of Ideal Art* (London: Penguin Books, 1985 [1956]), pp. 22–23.

CHAPTER 3

1.   All quotations from Harrison Marks, *How to Take Glamour Studies*, a collection of a series of articles written by Harrison Marks for *Foto* in the 1950s, republished by https://pamela-green.com.

2.   Harrison Marks, *How to Take Glamour Studies*.

3.   A useful study of how the border between legal and sexual categories was performed through the front and back sections of Soho bookshops is provided in Helen Wickstead, "Soho Typescripts: Handmade Obscene Books in Post-war London Bookshops", *Porn Studies* 7:2, 2000, pp. 187–211.

4.   Cocks has noted the impossible nature of defining obscenity and pornography: "the obscene is an empty category, usually legal and cultural, which can include anything and is not necessarily defined by its sexual content. Cultural battles to secure the meaning of pornography and obscenity are therefore inherent in the very formation of the terms". Harry G. Cocks, "Saucy Stories: Pornography, Sexology and the Marketing of Sexual Knowledge in Britain, c. 1918–70", *Social History* 29:4, November 2004, p. 466. For my purposes, I use Stoops' definition of pornography as "any material intended to sexually arouse, regardless of artistic quality, medium, or act depicted", Jamie Stoops, *The Thorny Path: Pornography in Early Twentieth-Century Britain* (Montreal: McGill-Queen's University Press, 2018), pp. 7–8.

5.   Alan Travis, *Bound and Gagged: A Secret History of Obscenity in Britain* (London: Profile Books, 2000), p. 7.

6.   Advert, Economy Educator Services, *The Naturist*, November 1941, p. 228.

7.   Harry G. Cocks, "Saucy Stories: Pornography, Sexology and the Marketing of Sexual Knowledge in Britain, c. 1918–70", *Social History* 29:4, November 2004, p. 481.

8.   Cocks, "Saucy Stories", *Social History*, p. 481; Lesley Hall, *Sex, Gender and Social Change in Britain since 1880* (Basingstoke: Macmillan, 2000), p. 137; Alan Travis, *Bound and Gagged: A Secret History of Obscenity in Britain* (London: Profile Books, 2000), p. 93.

9.   Cocks, "Saucy Stories", *Social History*, p. 467.

10. Police Report, March 1933, *Cases of Indecent Literature, 1932–34*, PRO HO 45/24939, in Cocks, "Saucy Stories", *Social History*, p. 474.

11. Memorandum submitted by the Commissioner of the Police of the Metropolis, Minutes of Evidence Taken Before the Select Committee on the Obscene Publications Bill, Parliamentary Papers 1957–1958 (122), vol. vi, 513, in Harry Cocks, "The Social Picture of Our Own Times: Reading Obscene Magazines in Mid-Twentieth-Century Britain", *Twentieth Century British History* 27:2, June 2016, p. 180.

12. Examples compiled from 1950 police reports located in the National Archive, TNA MEPO 2/9132, in Cocks, "The Social Picture of Our Own Times", *Twentieth Century British History*, pp. 191–192.

13. "Naturally Enough", Lesley Hall, *Sex, Gender and Social Change in Britain since 1880* (Basingstoke: Macmillan, 2000)*The Naturist*, December 1952, p. 12.

14. E. A. Hemingway, "The Guildhall Case", *The Naturist*, December 1952, P. 15; "Naturally Enough", *The Naturist*, p. 12.

15. Example pictured in Sarah Brown, "In the Flesh" [cutting from Eva Grant family archive; presumed to be *Amateur Photographer*, c.2000; full details missing].

16. Roye, *Phyllis in Censorland* (London: Camera Studies Club, 1956). Phyllis Dixey [1914–1964] was known in her own time as the "Queen of Striptease". She began performing during the Second World War, and was a singer, dancer, choreographer, scriptwriter, and director of the Windmill Follies company.

17. Alan Travis, *Bound and Gagged: A Secret History of Obscenity in Britain* (London: Profile Books, 2000), p. 94.

18. Travis, *Bound and Gagged*, pp. 94–95.

19. Roye, *Nude Ego* (London: Hutchinson, 1955), p. 220.

20. "Britain's Number 1 Glamour Girl: An Appreciation of La Dors", *PhotoART* 5.4, n.d. [mid-1950s], p. 49.

21. Advertisement, "Diana Dors in 3D", *Good Photography*, August 1955, p. 429.

22. Notes on sales to American magazines *Playboy*, *Esquire*, *Nugget* and *Cabaret* (Chicago) in 1955–1956, Roye's family archive.

23. Roye, *Nude Ego* (London: Hutchinson, 1955), p. 221.

24. Models included Desirée Cooper, a showgirl from New Zealand whom Roye had been photographing since the 1940s and who appeared in many of his books unnamed, as well as in covers and illustrations for *The Naturist*, in addition to books by Roye under her own name, including *Desirée* and *Desirée Encore*. She appears on the cover of Roye's *Nude Ego*, and he described her as his favourite model in Audrey Whiting, "These Saucy

25. Snaps Went to War", *Sunday Pictorial*, 23 October 1955, p. 15.

26. "New Trial after Jury Unable to Agree", *Bucks Advertiser and Aylesbury News*, 23 May 1958.

27. House of Commons Obscene Publications debate, 16 December 1958, Mr R. A. Butler, the Secretary of State for the Home Department and Lord Privy Seal.

28. House of Commons Obscene Publications debate, Mr Turton, MP for Torrington.

29. House of Commons Obscene Publications debate, Mr Bonham Carter, MP for Thirsk and Malton.

30. Attributed by Roye to Sir Alan Herbert, *Unique Verdict: The Story of an Unsuccessful Prosecution* (London: Art Publications Limited, n.d. [c.1959]), p. 6. In the House of Lords debate on the Obscene Publications Bill, 2 June 1959, the phrase is attributed to Lord Birkett.

31. Roye, *Unique Verdict*, p. 6.

32. Roye, *Unique Verdict*, p. 6.

33. Roye, *Unique Verdict*, p. 14.

34. Roye, *Unique Verdict*, pp. 12–13.

35. "New Trial after Jury Unable to Agree"; "Man of International Repute is Discharged", *Bucks Advertiser and Aylesbury News*, 20 June 1958.

36. Roye, *Unique Verdict*, p. 5.

37. "Ref. L.152, Warwickshire", Roye, *Unique Verdict*, p. 43.

38. "*Unique Editions* prosecution: Worldwide correspondence ensues", *PhotoART* 8:1, n.d. [c.1958], p. 4.

39. "Ref SR.108", Roye, *Unique Verdict*, p. 44.

40. "Ref R.5.77, London", Roye, *Unique Verdict*, pp. 51–52.

41. "Ref L.198, New Zealand", Roye, *Unique Verdict*, p. 46.

42. *A Confidential Chat about Spielplatz* (St Albans: Spielplatz, 1960 edition).

43. L. George, "The Nude in Films", *The Naturist*, July 1959, pp. 120–121.

44. Norman Rich, "Naturist Films: A Reassessment", *The Naturist*, October 1960, pp. 168–169.

45. Gordon Spencer "Generally Speaking", *Sun Bathing Review*, Winter 1959, pp. 16–17.

46. Norman Rich, "Naturist Films: A Reassessment", *The Naturist*, October 1960, pp. 168–169.

47. Matthew Sweet, "X Appeal: Britain's Oldest Living Sexploitation Star Tells All", *The Independent*, 29 January 2006.

48. Pamela Green, *Naked As Nature Intended: The Epic Tale of a Nudist Picture* (Altrincham: Suffolk and Watt, 2013).

49. Full-page ad for *Nudes of the World*, *Health and Efficiency*, January 1962, p. 84.

50. Ernest Stanley, "Those Naturist Films!", *Health and Efficiency*, December 1961, p. 88.

51. Examples can be seen in Pamela Green, *Naked As Nature Intended: The Epic Tale of a Nudist Picture* (Altrincham: Suffolk and Watt, 2013).

52. R. T. Norwich, "Those Nudist Films", *Health and Efficiency*, August 1961, p. 93.

53. "An Open Letter to the British Board of Film Censors", *Health and Efficiency*, November 1961, p. 92.

54. Trevelyan (1964), quoted in Matthew Sweet, "X Appeal: Britain's Oldest Living Sexploitation Star Tells All", *The Independent*, 29 January 2006.

55. Pamela Green, *Naked As Nature Intended: The Epic Tale of a Nudist Picture* (Altrincham: Suffolk and Watt, 2013), p. 18.

56. Trevelyan, quoted in "The BBFC in the 1960s", British Board of Film Classification History (https://www.bbfc.co.uk/education/university-students/bbfc-history/the-1960s).

57. Roland Berrill's same-sex relationship with the photographer Angus McBean is outlined in Adrian Woodhouse, *Angus McBean: Facemaker* (Richmond: Alma Books, 2006), p. 40.

58. Wallace Arter, "Naturist Notebook", *Health and Efficiency*, September 1947, p. 208.

59. "Viewpoint on Men's Clubs", *Sun Bathing Review*, Spring 1949, p. 39.

60. For wider discussion of attitudes in the decade, see David Kynaston, *Modernity Britain 1957–62* (London: Bloomsbury, 2015); quote from Black on p. 253; Lesley Hall, *Sex, Gender and Social Change in Britain since 1880* (Basingstoke: Macmillan, 2000), p. 162.

61. A 1933 survey of "propagandist societies" found clusters of alignment in abstention (vegetarianism, anti-smoking), matters related to sex (including nudism), and politics. Jacques Le Gulf and Pryns Hopkins, "A study of Social and Political Attitudes among Members of Propagandist Societies", *Journal of Social Psychology* 20:2, November 1944. The FPSI aimed to unite single-issue groups on the left, and included many who were nudists, from Joad to Craig. See Cyril E. M. Joad (ed.) *Manifesto: Being the Book of the Federation of Progressive Societies and Individuals* (London: Allen and Unwin, 1934); Lesley A. Hall, "A City That

We Shall Never Find? The Search for a Community of Fellow Progressive Spirits in the UK Between the Wars", *Family and Community History* 18:1, 2015, pp. 24–36.

61.   "Time To Break The Link", *The Naturist*, May 1954, p. 81.
62.   All letters, *The Naturist*, May 1954, p. 91.
63.   Lesley Hall, *Sex, Gender and Social Change in Britain since 1880* (Basingstoke: Macmillan, 2000), p. 164.
64.   Strix, "The Passing Scene", *Sun Bathing Review*, Winter 1958, p. 81.
65.   Robin Black, "Odd Men Out", *Health and Efficiency*, August 1965, pp. 11–13.
66.   Charles Sennet, *Sunshine and Naturism* (London: The Naturist, 1943), p. 3.
67.   Michael Rutherford *British Naturism* (London: The Naturist, 1946), p. 16.
68.   Douglas Stewart, "Modern Naturism is 'Sweeping the Board'", *The Naturist*, December 1952, p. 10.
69.   "Nudism in the New World", *Sun Bathing Review*, Spring 1943, p. 22.
70.   W. Hope-Jones, "Eugenics and Sun Bathing", *Sun Bathing Review* 1:1, Spring 1933, p. 11; Alfred C. Jordan, "Why Civilised Man Needs Doctors", *Sun Bathing Review* 3:9, Spring 1935, pp. 9–10.
71.   "Some Views of Mr. C.E.M. Joad", *Sun Bathing Review* 1:2, Summer 1933, pp. 5–6.
72.   "Children—Savage and Civilised", *Sun Bathing Review*, Summer 1941, pp. 38–39.
73.   Commander J. H. Bowen, "Other People's Clothes", *Sun Bathing Review*, Spring 1945, pp. 8–9, 16.
74.   Commander J. H. Bowen, "Other People's Clothes", *Sun Bathing Review*, Spring 1945, pp. 8–9, 16.
75.   "What Naturism has Done for Me", *Health and Efficiency*, September 1946, p. 209.
76.   Harold Llewes, "Clothes and the African", *Sun Bathing Review*, Winter 1948, pp. 81–2.
77.   Commander J. H. Bowen, "Other People's Clothes", *Sun Bathing Review*, Spring 1945, p. 16.
78.   "Hands Across the Sea", *Sun Bathing Review*, Autumn 1942, p. 49.
79.   "What We Stand For", *Gymnos* 1:1, February 1933, p. 3.
80.   "Wake Up England!" *Sun Bathing Review* 1:1, Spring 1933, p. 4.
81.   Sir Henry Gauvain, "Sun, Air and Sea Bathing in Health and Disease", *Sun Bathing Review* 1:1, Spring 1933, p. 5.
82.   *Sun Bathing Review*, Early Summer Number, 1936, p. 64.
83.   *Cornish Times* female correspondent quoted in Alec Craig, "A Sun-Bathing Survey", *Health and Efficiency* [cutting, n.d. c.1938], pp. 48–49.
84.   "Foreword", *Nudes of All Nations* (London: Routledge, 1936); pp. 7–8.
85.   "Beauties of Three Races: White, Yellow and Black", *The Naturist*, September 1939.
86.   "Dusky Beauties", *The Naturist*, August 1942, pp. 150–151; "Romance of the Near East", *The Naturist*, December 1943, pp. 8–9.
87.   "Dusky Beauties", *The Naturist*.
88.   The illustrations are uncredited in naturist publications, but some can be located in the North African photographic studios of Lehnert and Landrock. The eroticized and exoticized images are in the mould described in Malek Alloula, *The Colonial Harem* (Minneapolis: University of Minnesota Press, 1986).
89.   Jane Everard, "Introduction and Commentary", in John Everard, *Oriental Model* (London: Robert Hale, 1955), pp. 4–5.
90.   Robin Black, "Colour Bar in the Clubs", *Health and Efficiency*, July 1956, pp. 11–12.
91.   For wider context, see David Olusoga, *Black and British: A Forgotten History* (London: Pan, 2016), p. 500.
92.   "Hail Dusky Maidens!", *The Naturist*, January 1958, pp. 24–5.
93.   "Hail Dusky Maidens!", *The Naturist*.
94.   David Olusoga, *Black and British: A Forgotten History* (London: Pan, 2016), pp. 512–513.
95.   Sunny Pepys, "The Naked Truth", *Health and Efficiency*, May 1965, p. 59.
96.   Bainbridge shifted *Health and Efficiency* towards more explicit content during his editorship in the 1960s and 1970s. He was a bodybuilder, a former British representative in the Mr Universe competition, a nude photographer, and the editor of soft porn magazine *Girl Illustrated*. See Murray Wren, "Leslie Bainbridge: A Tribute", *Sunlovers*, March 1999, p. 10; Murray Wren, "The Pubic Pioneer", *H&E*, March 1999, pp. 44–49.
97.   Leslie Bainbridge, "Opinion", *Health and Efficiency* January 1966, p. 7, including quote from *American Sunbather*, June 1965.
98.   *The Naturist* carried on into the 1960s in an American edition that repurposed previously published British articles.
99.   Jan Todd, Joe Roark and Terry Todd, "A Briefly Annotated bibliography of English Language Serial Publications in the Field of Physical Culture", *Iron Game History*, March 1991, pp. 25–40.
100. Guy Burch, *Model Men: Physique Photography and Illustration before 1967* (Mistletoe Towny, 2017); David K. Johnson, *Buying Gay: How Physique Entrepreneurs started a Movement* (New York: University of Columbia, 2021).
101. See, for example, Kate Dorney, "Through the Closet with Ken and Joe: A Close Look at Clothes, Poses and Exposure", *Studies in Theatre and Performance* 37:2, 2017, pp. 269–288; Simon Ofield, "Cruising the Archive", *Journal of Visual Culture* 4:3, 2005, pp. 351–364.
102. Photography competition guidelines, *Health and Efficiency*, December 1951, p. 31.
103. Bill Green, quoted in Nik Cohn, *Today there are no Gentlemen: The Changes in Englishmen's Clothes since the War* (London: Weidenfeld and Nicolson, 1971); Justin Bengry, "Peacock Revolution: Mainstreaming Queer Styles in Post-War Britain, 1945–1967", *Socialist History* 36, 2010, p. 60.
104. Shaun Cole, *'Don We Now Our Gay Apparel': Gay Men's Dress in the Twentieth Century* (Oxford: Berg, 2000).
105. Examples drawn from across naturist magazine advertising in the 1950s and 1960s.
106. Ernest Stanley, "Naturism and the Law", *Health and Efficiency*, November 1962, p. 84.
107. Roy Gill, "I Defend '*Le Minimum*', and Why", *Health and Efficiency*, December 1951, p. 12.
108. These full-page announcements appeared regularly in 1930s *Sun Bathing Review*; these quotations are from Early Summer 1936, p. 37, and Summer 1935, p. 75.
109. The official start date was 1 July 1964. "Unity comes to British Naturism", *British Naturism: The Official Journal of the Central Council for British Naturism* 1, Summer 1964, pp. 1–2.
110. The International Naturist Federation, now known as INF-FEI, was established in 1951 and is still going strong, representing over 40 countries. https://inf-fni.org/about-inf-fni/history-of-inf-fni.
111. Erik Holm, "Naturist Magazines and the Nudist Movement", *British Naturism* 2, Autumn 1964, pp. 8–10.
112. Hugh Shayler, "Problems of Nudist Magazines", *The Naturist*, December 1954, p. 13.
113. Erik Holm, "Naturist Magazines and the Nudist Movement", pp. 8–10.
114. Leslie Bainbridge, "Opinion", *Health and Efficiency*, August 1965, pp. 6–7.
115. "Profile of the Modern British Naturist", *British Naturism* 2, Autumn 1964, p. 20.
116. N. R. T. Finstock, "New Look for Naturism?", *British Naturism* 5, Summer 1965, p. 30.
117. "How You Become a Naturist", *Health and Efficiency Summer Annual*, 1954, p. 22.
118. *Sun Bathing Review*, April/June 1956, p. 7.
119. Peton cartoon, *The Tanners*, *British Naturism* 17, Summer 1968, p. 11.
120. Letter included in Robin Black, "Club versus Beach", *Health and Efficiency*, November 1962, p. 35.
121. "No Nudity Monopoly", *Sport and Sunshine*, Winter 1964, p. 8.
122. Sunny Pepys, "The Naked Truth", *Health and Efficiency*, August 1965, p. 59.
123. "The Naturist Youth of Great Britain", *British Naturism* 16, Spring 1968, pp. 11–14.
124. "Nudism and Youth", *Sun Bathing Review*, Winter 1953, p. 90.
125. "The Future of British Nudism", *Health and Efficiency*, July 1933, p. 237.
126. Strix, "The Passing Scene", *Sun Bathing Review*, Winter 1951, p. 95.
127. "Why not Rock 'n Roll for Nudists? Naturism and the Younger Generation", *The Naturist*, January 1957, pp. 20–21.
128. Sunny Pepys, "The Naked Truth", *Health and Efficiency*, August 1965, p. 59.
129. Sunny Pepys, "The Naked Truth", *Health and Efficiency*.
130. Ken D., "Naturism on the Cheap", *Sport and Sunshine*, Winter 1964, p. 7.
131. "Coy Cranks", *British Naturism* 15, Winter 1967, p.38.
132. Ken D., "Naturism on the Cheap", *Sport and Sunshine*, Winter 1964, p. 7.
133. Sunny Pepys, "The Naked Truth", *Health and Efficiency*, August 1965, p. 58.
134. Ethelred Jean Straker [1913–1984] was known professionally as Jean Straker.
135. The visitor number is from Straker's own publication, *Visual Art* 1, August 1958, p. 10.
136. Occupations of attendees listed in Byron Rogers, "Squire Among the Pin-Ups", *On the Trail of the Last Human Cannonball and Other Small Journeys in Search of Great Men* (London: Aurum Press, 2004), pp. 87–92.
137. Bob Pullen, "Photography and Censorship: The Photographs and Ideals of Jean Straker", *Photography and Culture* 1:2, 2008, pp. 227–238.

138. *Nudes of Jean Straker* (London: Charles Skilton, 1958); cover photograph by Frank Cato. In the 1960s Skilton ran Luxor Press reissuing banned erotica such as *Fanny Hill* and *Venus in Furs*.

139. Advertisements in *The Artist* 74, 1967.

140. Byron Rogers, "Squire Among the Pin-Ups", *On the Trail of the Last Human Cannonball and Other Small Journeys in Search of Great Men* (London: Aurum Press, 2004), p. 90.

141. Full details, including evidence for the prosecution and correspondence by Straker are assembled in The National Archives files Jean Straker: S3 Obscene Publications Act 1959 TNA DPP 2/3377, 1961–1962.

142. Straker's letter to the Director of Public Prosecutions, 6 April 1962.

143. Argument of Claimant, Great Marlborough Street Magistrate's Court, 1 April 1963, p. 7.

144. Argument of Claimant, Great Marlborough Street Magistrate's Court, 1 April 1963, p. 5.

145. Straker's letter to Director of Public Prosecutions, 26 February 1962.

146. Jean Straker (ed.), *Censorship in the Arts: The full text of the Freedom of Vision Teach-in held at Hampstead Old Town Hall, October 2nd 1966 from 3pm till 10pm* (London: Academy of Visual Arts, n.d. [c.1966]).

147. Straker (ed.), *Censorship in the Arts*, p. 57.

148. Straker (ed.), *Censorship in the Arts*, p. 47.

149. Straker (ed.), *Censorship in the Arts*, p. 32.

150. Jean Straker, "Censorship And/Or...", *International Times* 2, 31 October–13 November 1966, p. 13.

151. *British Naturism* 13, Summer 1967, p. 7.

152. *Sun Worship* is backed with the inscription, "She's Not Obscene: The picture that makes the break-through", Jean Straker Collection, National Science and Media Museum, PNRR03/03/02 1998–5060, PA box 785.

153. "Case 3003/66", *OZ* 6, 1967, p.5.

154. *Life*, 30 October 1967, quoted in Bob Peters, "Death of the Sun Clubs", *British Naturism* 15, Winter 1967, pp. 13–15.

155. "Sun Spots", *British Naturism* 14, Autumn 1967, p. 7.

156. Barry Wellfield, "Naturism: A Healthy Movement?", *British Naturism* 14, Autumn 1967, p. 24.

157. "The Struggle within the Naturist Movement", *The Guardian*, 7 November 1969.

158. *British Naturism* 16, Spring 1968, frontispiece.

159. Geoffrey Gorer, *Sex and Marriage in England Today* (London: Nelson and Sons, 1969).

160. Lesley Hall, *Sex, Gender and Social Change in Britain since 1880* (Basingstoke: Macmillan, 2000), p. 173.

161. "The Struggle within the Naturist Movement", *The Guardian*, 7 November 1969.

162. *Sun and Health* advertisement in *Camera Owner* 34, April 1967. Similar advertisements appeared in *International Times*.

163. "Evidence", Director of Public Prosecutions, n.d. [c.1962], Jean Straker: S3 Obscene Publications Act 1959 TNA DPP 2/3377, 1961–1962.

164. Marcus Collins, *Modern Love: An Intimate History of Men and Women in Twentieth-Century Britain* (London: Atlantic, 2003), p. 141.

165. "The World's Top Twenty Films", *Sunday Times*, 27 September 1970, p. 27. *Carry On Camping* was the 17th in the longstanding British comedy film series.

166. House of Commons debate, "Magazines (Seizure)", 8 July 1969.

167. Alex Watford, "Time to Change the Image", *Health and Efficiency*, December 1970, pp. 8–9.

168. The new venture offered a "Holiday 'At Home' with Jean Straker" in "extensive location settings for photography" and "informal optional naturism", *Amateur Photographer*, 23 June 1971, p. 130.

169. Rebecca Loncraine, "Bosom of the Nation: Page Three in the 1970s and 1980s", in Mina Gorji (ed.) *Rude Britannia* (London: Routledge, 2007).

170. Peter Chippindale and Chris Horrie, *Stick it up your Punter: The Rise and Fall of the Sun* (London: William Heinemann, 1990).

171. Alex Watford, "Time to Change the Image", *Health and Efficiency*, December 1970, pp. 8–9.

172. The term "pink wars" has been used to describe the campaigns to show more female flesh in pornographic contexts. See Isabel Tang, *Pornography: The Secret History of Civilisation* (London: Macmillan, 1999), p. 114.

173. Transcript of speech plus reaction in Murray Wren, "The Pubic Pioneer", *H&E*, March 1999, p. 48.

174. Wren wrote under the name Murray James early in his career. Murray James, "Cavalcade", *Health and Efficiency* 918, 21 September 1974, pp. 17–18.

175. At least on some coffee tables; these matters continued to be moderated by class and taste. On changing attitudes to men's magazines, see Kenon Breazeale, "In Spite of Women: 'Esquire' Magazine and the Construction of the Male Consumer", *Signs*, 20:1, Autumn 1994, pp. 1–22.

176. Examples are drawn from across the decade. Finger fucking is in *International H&E Monthly*, 80:1, n.d. [c.1979].

177. Histories of the changes are provided by Wren in "Leslie Bainbridge: A Tribute", *Sunlovers*, March 1999, p. 10; "The Pubic Pioneer", *H&E*, March 1999, pp. 44–49; "How Leslie, Me and H&E Changed the World—A Little", *H&E Naturist*, June 2006, pp. 22–25; "The History of H&E Naturist", *H&E Naturist*, February 2007, pp. 8–11.

178. Wording from a March 1972 promotional leaflet for *Health and Efficiency*; financial detail from Wren, "The History of H&E Naturist", *H&E Naturist*, February 2007, pp. 8–11.

179. Marcus Collins, *Modern Love: An Intimate History of Men and Women in Twentieth-Century Britain* (London: Atlantic, 2003), p. 141.

180. Harry G. Cocks, "Saucy Stories: Pornography, Sexology and the Marketing of Sexual Knowledge in Britain, c. 1918–70", *Social History* 29:4, November 2004, p. 483.

181. *Health and Efficiency* 918, 21 September 1974, cover.

182. Letter from J. A. Watson to *British Naturism*, May 1975, p. 6.

183. David Archer, "Tan Talk", *British Naturism*, Autumn 1970, p. 4.

184. The Women's Liberation Movement protest against Miss World 1970 is recalled by Jo Robinson in the *Sisterhood and After* oral history collection, British Library (https://www.bl.uk/collection-items/jo-robinson-miss-world-contest#)

185. Collins, "Porn Free", *Modern Love: An Intimate History of Men and Women in Twentieth-Century Britain*; Lesley Hall, *Sex, Gender and Social Change in Britain since 1880* (Basingstoke: Macmillan, 2000), p. 173.

186. John Mann, "Come and Join Us, Women's Lib! Let's Fight to End this Degradation", *British Naturism* 31, February 1972, p. 6.

187. "Supermarket Natural Nudes", *Health and Efficiency* 918, 21 September 1974, p. 79.

188. For wider context on sympathetic cultures for paedophilia in Britain in the 1970s, see Mathew Thomson, *Lost Freedom: The Landscape of the Child and the British Post-War Settlement* (Oxford: Oxford University Press, 2013), pp. 168–179.

189. John Berger, *Ways of Seeing* (London: Penguin, 1972), p. 63.

190. See, for example, Laura Mulvey, "Visual Pleasure and Narrative Cinema", *Screen* 16: 3, Autumn 1975, pp. 6–18.

191. Jo Spence [1934–1992] was a feminist photographer and writer who engaged with the image of women in her radical practice; her magazine cuttings are collected in the Jo Spence Memorial Library at Birkbeck; Linder [b. 1954, Linda Mulvey] has been making political collages using magazine images of women since 1976.

192. Frances Borzello, Annette Kuhn, Jill Pack and Cassandra Wedd, "Living Dolls and 'Real Women'", *Camerawork* 12, 1979, pp. 10–11.

193. Lucy Lippard, *From the Center: Feminist Essays on Women's Art* (New York: E. P. Dutton, 1976).

194. Anne McNicholes and Moira Knowles, "Exhibition Review: Self Impressions", *Spare Rib* 59, June 1977, pp. 43–44.

195. McNicholes and Knowles, "Exhibition Review: Self Impressions", *Spare Rib*, p. 44.

CONCLUSION

1. Michael Rutherford, *British Naturism* (London: The Naturist, 1946), p. 67.

2. John Langdon-Davies, *The Future of Nakedness* (London: Noel Douglas, 1929).

3. See, for example, John C. Flugel, *The Psychology of Clothes* (London: The Hogarth Press, 1930).

4. William Welby, *The Naked Truth about Nudism* (London: Thorsons, 1935).

5. "Brighton Bares All", *BBC News*, 9 August 1979 (http://news.bbc.co.uk/onthisday/hi/dates/stories/august/9/newsid_3906000/3906605.stm).

6. Ruth Barcan *Nudity: A Cultural Anatomy* (London: Berg, 2004), p. 170.

7. A further change of title followed, and *H&E Naturist* has endured to this day. Mark Nisbet, "The Naturist Movement is Dead! Long Live Naturism!", *H&E Naturist*, March 2002, p. 1.

8. John Davies, "The Last Nail in the Club Coffin?", *H&E*, February 1999, p. 19.

9. Davies, "The Last Nail in the Club Coffin?", *H&E*.

10. Terry Phillips, "Nudism and the Lost Radical Tradition", *H&E*, January 2000, p. 62.

Appendix

11. John C. Davies, "Human Rights and Human Wrongs: Naturist Lesbians Denied Manchester Sun and Air", *H&E*, December 1999, pp. 7–9.
12. Susan Mayfield, "It's a Guy Thing", *H&E* 97:6, n.d. [c.1997], pp. 2–4.
13. "Homosexuality and Naturism", *Sunlovers* 15, February 2000, p. 23.
14. See, for example, two contrasting letters, "Naturism is not a Sexual Activity… Or is it?", *H&E Naturist*, June 2005, p. 14.
15. *H&E*, July 2007.
16. Jon Williams, "Caught Out by the Camera", *H&E* 97:11, n.d. [1997], pp. 15–17.
17. Petra Vallance, "Give Yourself A Hand", *H&E Quarterly* 69, n.d. [c.1996], pp. 40–41.
18. Nicholas Whittaker, "In Love with *H&E*", *H&E* 95:6, n.d. [c.1995], p. 9.
19. Charlie Simonds, "The Film Service with a Difference", *H&E* 97:11, n.d. [c.1997], p. 72; Simonds, "To all the girls I've filmed before…", *H&E*, June 1999, pp. 76–79; Simonds, *Charlie's Angels: Naturally* (Pewsey: Parafotos, 2006).
20. "Photo Policy", *H&E*, February 2001, p. 71.
21. Helen Ludbrook, "Are we just Body Snobs?", *H&E* 99, n.d. [c.1999].
22. Jane Rowland, "All Right as Long as You're White?", *H&E* 97: 6, n.d. [c.1997], pp. 50–54.
23. Duncan Laurence, "Race and Naturism: Playing the White Man?", *H&E Naturist*, August 2005, pp. 22–23, with additional comment from Sara Backhouse (editor).
24. John Remington Gurney, "Penis Policy", *H&E Naturist*, May 2004, p. 17.
25. Jonathan Margolis, "Dark Side of Fresh Air Utopians", *The Guardian*, 11 June 1999.
26. "Women in Naturism", *All You Need to Know about British Naturism in 2020* (Northampton: British Naturism, 2020), p. 27.
27. *H&E Naturist*, July 2017.
28. Caro Zieringer, *Serious Fun: A Feminist Handbook on How to Use Humour and Joy in Politics, Sisterhood and Everyday Life* (Brighton: Free the Nipple, 2020).
29. "Nearly 4 million Naturists in the UK", *British Naturism*, 9 January 2012 (https://www.bn.org.uk/news/news/nearly-4-million-naturists-in-the-uk-r97/).
30. "Come and Join Us", British Naturism, 2020 (https://www.bn.org.uk/membershipinfo/).
31. John Langdon-Davies, "Introduction", Frances and Mason Merrill, *Among the Nudists* (London: Noel Douglas, 1932), p. x.
32. *All You Need to Know about British Naturism in 2020* (Northampton: British Naturism, 2020), p. 4.

Appendix

Index

Appendix

Index

Image Credits

COVER

John Everard, untitled [from sequence of four photographs of nude woman drinking tea], *Artist's Model* (London: Bodley Head, 1951), plate 125. Courtesy of the John Everard Estate.

ENDPAPERS

Front: Sample page of advertisements, *Health and Efficiency*, January 1946, p. 13. Courtesy of Hawk Editorial Ltd, publisher of *H&E Naturist* magazine.

Back: Sample page of advertisements, *Sun Bathing Review*, Spring 1938, p. 32. Courtesy of Hawk Editorial Ltd, publisher of *H&E Naturist* magazine.

CHAPTER 1

p. 16: Anthony Peacock, "No. 10 Nottingham Sun and Air Society campsite", *Sun Bathing Review*, 1941, p. 33. © A J Peacock Pochin; Courtesy of Hawk Editorial Ltd, publisher of *H&E Naturist* magazine.

p. 21: Uncredited photographer, *Health and Efficiency*, August 1925, cover. Courtesy of Hawk Editorial Ltd, publisher of *H&E Naturist* magazine.

pp. 24–25: Uncredited photographer, "Pioneers of Active Air Bathing in 1930: The Sun Bathing Society", *Sun Bathing Review*, Spring 1938, p. 3. © Keystone-France/Gamma-Rapho via Getty Images.

p. 27: Uncredited photographer, "The Macs of Spielplatz—Three Generations", *A Confidential Chat About Spielplatz* (St. Albans: Spielplatz, 1960 edition), p. 45. Courtesy of the Spielplatz Estate Archive.

p. 28: Uncredited photographer, Hans Surén, *Man and Sunlight* (Slough: Sollux, 1927), frontispiece.

p. 29: Uncredited photographer, Hans Surén, *Man and Sunlight* (Slough: Sollux, 1927), p. 162.

p. 34: Uncredited photographer, C. E. Norwood, *Nudism in England* (London: Noel Douglas, 1933), cover.

p. 38: Uncredited photographer (The Sun-Bathing Society), "A Ball Game" in William Welby, *Naked and Unashamed: Nudism from Six Points of View* (London: Thorsons, 1934), p 17

p. 39: Uncredited photographer, "Sun Worshippers at Sun Lodge", *Sun Bathing Review*, Spring 1933, p. 2. © Keystone/ZUMA Press.

p. 40: Uncredited photographer, *Gymnos*, May 1933, cover.

p. 41: Top: Uncredited photographer, "1880" [original title: "The Boatman Somewhat Rattled"]. Courtesy of Kelvin Ramsey Collection of Lantern Slides and Stereoviews, Special Collections Research Center, William and Mary Libraries. Bottom: Uncredited photographer, "1933". Paired and titled in *Gymnos*, February 1933, p. 9.

pp. 42: Top: Uncredited photographer, "No. 17: A Frieze", *Sun Bathing Review*, Supplement XIV, Winter 1933–1934. Courtesy of William Thuillier; courtesy of Georgia Mosesson. Bottom: Uncredited photographer [identified as Dupré, alias of Yvonne Gregory], "No. 13: Dance Exercises at the Sunbathing Society's Summer School at Haslemere, 1933", *Sun Bathing Review*, Supplement X, Autumn 1933. Courtesy of William Thuillier; Courtesy of Georgia Mosesson.

p. 43: Uncredited photographer [identified as Dupré, alias of Yvonne Gregory], "No. 14: Dance Exercises at the Sunbathing Society's Summer School at Haslemere, 1933", *Sun Bathing Review*, Supplement XI, Autumn 1933. Courtesy of William Thuillier; Courtesy of Georgia Mosesson.

p. 49: Uncredited photographer, "In winter they all work hard and play for warmth: Winter at the Woodland Health Camp", *Sun Bathing Review*, Winter 1942, p. 87. Courtesy of Hawk Editorial Ltd, publisher of *H&E Naturist* magazine.

p. 50: Uncredited photographer, "The New M.D.R.P. Golf Ensemble" [Men's Dress Reform Party clothing advertisement], *Gymnos*, December 1933, back page.

pp. 52–53: All three images: Anthony Peacock, "Camps re-visited: No. 3 Ysha". Top left: "A sloping bank in one corner of the camp provides a perfect sun trap…"; bottom left: "A view inside the pavilion where punch balls, expanders, skipping ropes are provided for their amusement and exercise"; right-hand page: "Agility on the parallel bars is a source of pride…", *Sun Bathing Review*, Autumn 1939, pp. 80–81. © A. J. Peacock Pochin.

p. 55: Uncredited photographer, "Pixillated! The world if young and gay once more…", *Sun Bathing Review*, Autumn 1945, p. 51. Courtesy of Hawk Editorial Ltd, publisher of *H&E Naturist* magazine.

p. 56: Uncredited photographer [identified as Gerhard Riebicke], "A Suren class training in the open", in Hans Surén, *Man and Sunlight* (Slough: Sollux, 1927), p. 118; published as "Concentration", *Gymnos*, April 1933, p. 10. © The Granger Collection Ltd d/b/a GRANGER Historical Picture Archive.

p. 57: Uncredited photographer, "Visitors to the Manor House play croquet at the Seventh Annual General Meeting of the British Sunbathing Association", *Sun Bathing Review*, Winter 1950, p. 77. Courtesy of Hawk Editorial Ltd, publisher of *H&E Naturist* magazine.

p. 58: Uncredited photographer, untitled [boy reading a copy of *Sun Bathing Review*], *Sun Bathing Review*, Summer 1935. p. 56. Courtesy of Hawk Editorial Ltd, publisher of *H&E Naturist* magazine; cover of *Sun Bathing Review* reproduced with permission of the Estate of Robert Gibbings.

p. 62: Uncredited photographer [identified as Bertram Park and Yvonne Gregory], "No. 6: On the Banks of the River Avon", *Sun Bathing Review*, Supplement IV, Spring 1933. Courtesy of William Thuillier; Courtesy of Georgia Mosesson.

p. 63: Uncredited photographer (The Sun-Bathing Society), "…The Water's Fine!", in William Welby, *Naked and Unashamed: Nudism from Six Points of View* (London: Thorsons, 1934), p. 48.

p. 64 Left: Bertram Park, "Perfect Proportions", *Sun Bathing Review*, Summer 1935, p. 54. Courtesy of William Thuillier; courtesy of Georgia Mosesson. Right: Bertram Park and Yvonne Gregory, untitled [nude studio photograph of woman with target and pole], *Curves and Contrasts of the Human Figure* (London: The Bodley Head, 1937), n.p. Courtesy of William Thuillier; courtesy of Georgia Mosesson.

p. 68: John Everard, "Rhythmic Pose", in Walter Bird, Roye and John Everard, *Eves without Leaves* (London: Pearson, 1941), p. 15. Courtesy of the John Everard Estate.

p. 69: Walter Bird, "Grief", in Walter Bird, Roye and John Everard, *Eves without Leaves* (London: Pearson, 1941), p. 14. Courtesy of Walter Bird estate. Thanks to James Culverwell.

p. 70: Uncredited photographer, "The Dancers", *Sun Bathing Review*, Summer 1938, cover. Courtesy of Hawk Editorial Ltd, publisher of *H&E Naturist* magazine.

p. 71: Uncredited photographer, "No. 100", *Sun Bathing Review*, Art Supplement, Summer 1938. Courtesy of Hawk Editorial Ltd, publisher of *H&E Naturist* magazine.

pp. 72–73: Uncredited photographer [identified as Bertram Park], "No. 27: At Yew Tree Camp, 1934", *Sun Bathing Review*, Supplement XXIII, Summer 1934. Courtesy of William Thuillier; courtesy of Georgia Mosesson.

p. 79: Edith Tudor-Hart, "Morning Sun", *Sun Bathing Review*, Autumn Supplement, 1946. © The estate of W. Suschitzky.

p. 80: Uncredited photographer, untitled [two children doing gymnastics], *Sun Bathing Review*, Spring 1944, p. 29. Courtesy of Hawk Editorial Ltd, publisher of *H&E Naturist* magazine.

p. 81 Top: Uncredited photographer [identified as Edith Tudor-Hart], "Children's Football (Haslemere, August, 1933)", *Sun Bathing Review*, Autumn 1933, p. 31. © The estate of W. Suschitzky. Bottom: Uncredited photographer, "Children at Pinehurst School", *Sun Bathing Review*, Summer 1933, p. 13. Courtesy of Hawk Editorial Ltd, publisher of *H&E Naturist* magazine.

p. 82: Uncredited photographer, untitled [children on see-saw], *Illustrated Sun Bathing News*, Summer 1935, p. 13.

p. 83: Edith Tudor-Hart, "The Golden Age", *Sun Bathing Review*, Autumn 1935, p. 91. © The estate of W. Suschitzky.

pp. 86–87: Uncredited photographer, 'A Corner of the Restaurant', *A Confidential Chat About Spielplatz* (St Albans: Spielplatz, 1948 edition), p. 45. Courtesy of the Spielplatz Estate Archive.

p. 89: Uncredited photographer, "Snowballing becomes the Fashionable Game", *Sun Bathing Review*, Winter 1940, p. 105. Courtesy of Hawk Editorial Ltd, publisher of *H&E Naturist* magazine.

p. 90: Uncredited photographer, "This modern Sunbathing Venus of to-day…", *Health and Efficiency*, Christmas 1936, p. 434. Courtesy of Hawk Editorial Ltd, publisher of *H&E Naturist* magazine.

p. 93: Uncredited photographer, "Exhibition of nude photographs was held at Spielplatz recently, and here are some of the visitors inspecting the various studies", *The Naturist*, December 1951, p. 18.

p. 94: Roye [Horace Narbeth], "Sport", *Daily Mirror*, 14 September 1938, p. 14; reproduced in Roye, *Nude Ego* (London: Hutchinson, 1955), facing p. 110. Courtesy of the Colin Narbeth Collection. Thanks to Simon Narbeth and Vanessa Gibson.

p. 97: Roye [Horace Narbeth], untitled [model Desirée Cooper standing with arms raised], *Desirée* (London: Camera Studies Club, 1942 [reprinted mid-1950s]), plate 6. Courtesy of the Colin Narbeth Collection. Thanks to Simon Narbeth and Vanessa Gibson.

CHAPTER 2

p. 98: Anthony Peacock, "The neat huts in and around the family life of Ysha centred are a special feature of the camp…", *Sun Bathing Review*, Autumn 1939, p. 81. © A J Peacock Pochin.

p. 103 Left: Mervyn Oakdale, *The Mystery of Naturism with Photographic Studies of the Nude by Stephen Glass* (London: The Naturist, 1956), cover. Right: Anne Seton, *The Pool of Enchantment: Reflections on the Naturist Movement with Photographic Studies of the Nude by Stephen Glass* (London: The Naturist, 1950), cover.

p. 104: Uncredited photographer, "Knitting for the Troops", *The Naturist*, May 1940, p. 110.

p. 108: "What is a Pin-Up Girl?" *Picture Post*, 23 September 1944, pp. 14–15.

p. 109: Roye [Horace Narbeth], "Contemplation", in *The World's Best Photographs: Second Series* (London: Odhams Press, n.d. [c.1944]), p. 24. Courtesy of the Colin Narbeth Collection. Thanks to Simon Narbeth and Vanessa Gibson.

p. 110: Roye [Horace Narbeth], *Maids: Thirty-two Camera Studies* (Elstree: Elstree Publications, 1947), cover. Courtesy of the Colin Narbeth Collection. Thanks to Simon Narbeth and Vanessa Gibson.

p. 111: Roye [Horace Narbeth], "Beauty on the Beach", *Health and Efficiency*, September 1946, n.p. Courtesy of the Colin Narbeth Collection. Thanks to Simon Narbeth and Vanessa Gibson.

p. 116: Uncredited photographer, *The Naturist*, September 1949, cover.

p. 120: Anthony Peacock, "For Health Unbrought", in Charles Sennet, *Sunshine and Naturism* (London: The Naturist, 1943), p. 41. © A. J. Peacock Pochin.

p. 121: Anthony Peacock, "The Hunter", *Health and Efficiency*, August 1943, n.p. © A. J. Peacock Pochin.

p. 122: John Everard, untitled [sequence of nine photographs of nude woman cooking], *Second Sitting* (London: Bodley Head, 1955), p. 158. Courtesy of the John Everard Estate.

p. 123: John Everard, untitled [man and rock], *Second Sitting* (London: Bodley Head, 1955), p. 168. Courtesy of the John Everard Estate.

p. 129: Ervin Marton, "Last year's hair style!", *The Naturist*, January 1955, p. 27. © Ervin Marton Estate.

pp. 132–133: Uncredited photographer, untitled [Spielplatz Venus Competition entrants and winner, 1959; Iseult Macaskie is fourth from the right]. Courtesy of the Spielplatz Estate Archive.

p. 137: Stephen Glass, "Beauty Unadorned" in Charles Sennet, *Nudist Life at Spielplatz: The Story of a Modern Experiment in the Art of Living* (London: The Naturist, 1956), p. 21. Courtesy of the Stephen Glass Collection at the Pamela Green Archive.

p. 138: Colin R. Clark, "Gymnasts", *Health and Efficiency*, July 1952, n.p. © Colin R. Clark Estate.

p. 139: Colin R. Clark, "East Midland Sunfolk" [East Midland Sunfolk Rally, 19 August 1951], *Health and Efficiency*, November 1951, n.p. © Colin R. Clark Estate.

p. 140: Eva Grant, Untitled [nude on the beach], n.d. [c.1955]. © Eva Grant.

p. 144: Harrison Marks, "In the Warm Sun" [model: Pamela Green], *Health and Efficiency*, October 1955, n.p. © George Harrison Marks Enterprises Limited.

p. 145: Harrison Marks, untitled [Pamela Green as redheaded Parisian model alter ego, Rita Landre], *Kamera* 15 (London: Kamera Publications, n.d. [c.1958]), p. 23. © George Harrison Marks Enterprises Limited.

pp. 148–149: Harrison Marks, untitled [double page spread of contorted nudes montaged onto cloudy skyscape], *Kamera* 15 (London: Kamera Publications, n.d. [c.1958]), pp. 20–21. © George Harrison Marks Enterprises Limited.

p. 151: John Firth, "A peruser contemplates the pornography section at a Soho sex shop in London", June 1956. Courtesy of John Firth/BIPs/Getty Images.

p. 155: Uncredited photographer, "Is the movement actuated solely by the passive pleasure of nudity?", *Sun Bathing Review*, Spring 1941, p. 5. Courtesy of Hawk Editorial Ltd, publisher of *H&E Naturist* magazine.

CHAPTER 3

p. 160: Uncredited photographer, "The first Annual General Meeting of the Federation of British Sun Clubs", *Sun Bathing Review*, Summer 1955, p. 13. Courtesy of Hawk Editorial Ltd, publisher of *H&E Naturist* magazine.

p. 167: Roye [Horace Narbeth], *Phyllis in Censorland* (London: Camera Studies Club, c. 1942 [reprinted 1956]), proof print of cover. Courtesy of the Colin Narbeth Collection. Thanks to Simon Narbeth and Vanessa Gibson.

p. 168 Left: Roye [Horace Narbeth], untitled [retouched photograph of model Desirée Cooper on lilo], *Desirée* (London: Camera Studies Club, 1942 [reprinted mid-1950s]), plate 25. Right: Roye [Horace Narbeth], untitled [unretouched photograph of model Desirée Cooper on lilo], *Unique Editions Number Two* (London: Art Publications, n.d. [1958]). Courtesy of the Colin Narbeth Collection. Thanks to Simon Narbeth and Vanessa Gibson.

p. 170: Uncredited photographer, "WPN 3-D Special: We Proudly Present Roundness-in-space—in print" [Vala on far left; Roye on far right], *World's Press News*, newspaper cutting, n.d. [c.1954], in Roye, *Nude Ego* (London: Hutchinson, 1955), facing p. 191. Courtesy of the Colin Narbeth Collection. Thanks to Simon Narbeth and Vanessa Gibson.

p. 171: Roye [Horace Narbeth], *Diana Dors in 3D* (London: Camera Studies Club, n.d. [c.1954]), cover. Courtesy of the Colin Narbeth Collection. Thanks to Simon Narbeth and Vanessa Gibson.

p. 175: Attributed to Roye [Horace Narbeth], untitled [Roye photographing Diana Dors in his studio], n.d. [c.1954]. Vintage print. Courtesy of the Colin Narbeth Collection. Thanks to Simon Narbeth and Vanessa Gibson.

p. 177: Uncredited photographer, "Film still from the first British nudist film, *Nudist Paradise*. The film crew filming at Spielplatz Nudist Camp. From Left to right: Carl Conway, Anita Love, Katy Cashfield, Dennis Carnell". *Nudist Paradise*, Dir. Charles Saunders, 1958. Courtesy of RGA.

p. 178: Uncredited photographer, "Film still from the first British nudist film, *Nudist Paradise*. Two nudists on a trampoline". *Nudist Paradise*, Dir. Charles Saunders, 1958. Courtesy of RGA.

p. 182–183: Douglas Webb, "Bridget Leonard, Pamela Green, Jackie Salt, and Petrina Forsyth filming *Naked – As Nature Intended*", 1961. Courtesy of Douglas Webb. © Pamela Green Archive.

p. 190: Uncredited photographer [identified as Lehnert and Landrock], "Oriental Model", *The Naturist*, December 1955, p. 10. Courtesy of the Lehnert and Landrock collection.

p. 193: Uncredited photographer, "Zulu Beauties", *Sun Bathing Review*, Spring 1938, p. 28. Courtesy of Hawk Editorial Ltd, publisher of *H&E Naturist* magazine.

pp. 194–195: Bertram Park and Yvonne Gregory, untitled [studio nudes with darker skinned models], *Curves and Contrasts of the Human Figure* (London: The Bodley Head, 1936), n.p. Courtesy of William Thuillier; courtesy of Georgia Mosesson.

p. 197: Tony Crisp, *Health and Strength* [Model: Harry Henry], September 1955, cover. © Tony Crisp.

p. 200: H. J. Atkin, *Vigour* [model: Paul Newington], November 1951, cover.

p. 201: Tony Crisp, untitled [male bodybuilder, studio portrait], n.d. [c.1953]. © Tony Crisp.

p. 202: Krikor Gregor Djololian (Studio Arax), "The Greek Ideal: Robert Duranton, France", *Health and Efficiency*, December 1948, facing p. 233. © 2021 Artists Rights Society (ARS), New York/ADAGP, Paris.

p. 203: Vince [Basil "Bill" Green], untitled [Myrddin Palmer photographed at Gower Peninsula, March 1950]. Courtesy of Stephen Cartwright of the Vince Estate.

p. 208: Uncredited photographer, untitled [female nude model washing a car], *Health and Efficiency*, October 1963, p. 37. Courtesy of Hawk Editorial Ltd, publisher of *H&E Naturist* magazine.

p. 209: Uncredited photographer, "Preparing for the Naturist Season", *Health and Efficiency*, May 1965, n.p. Courtesy of Hawk Editorial Ltd, publisher of *H&E Naturist* magazine.

p. 212: Uncredited photographer, "Scenes at the Pop Concert held in Hyde Park", 18 July 1970. © Mirrorpix/Getty Images.

pp. 214–215: Uncredited photographer, "Drinka-pinta-milka day is the motto at North Kent Sun Club and the milkman makes his regular round", *Health and Efficiency*, Autumn 1963, n.p. Courtesy of Hawk Editorial Ltd, publisher of *H&E Naturist* magazine.

p. 218: David Hurn, "Jean Straker, owner of the Visual Arts Club Soho, c.1960". © David Hurn/Magnum Photos.

p. 219: Jean Straker, "Harvest Festival Queen. Karen gets our first prize. She thrills us to the marrow", *Nudes of Jean Straker* (London: Charles Skilton, 1958), plate LXI. Courtesy of the Jean Straker Photographic Collection.

p. 220–221: Jean Straker, untitled [bespectacled model scrutinises pubic hair], n.d. [c.1958], vintage print. Courtesy of the Jean Straker Photographic Collection.

p. 223: Jean Straker, "Sun Worship". n.d. [c.1958], vintage print. Jean Straker Collection, National Science and Media Museum, PNRR03/03/02 1998–5060, PA Box 785. Courtesy of the Jean Straker Photographic Collection. © Jean Straker/Science Museum Group.

p. 227: Uncredited advertisement, "Be Thankful You Are British: You Can Purchase *Sun and Health*", *Camera Owner* 34, April 1967, p. 39.

p. 234: Beverley Goodway, "...today's Birthday Suit girl" [model: Stefanie Khan], *The Sun*, 17 November 1970, p. 3. Courtesy of Pictorial Press Ltd/ Alamy Stock Photo.

p. 237: Graham Wood, "Devon Nudist Colony", 4 May 1979. © Graham Wood/ ANL/Shutterstock.

pp. 270-271: Uncredited photographer, 'Friezes at Haslemere, 1934, No. 34 and No. 37', Sun Bathing Review, Winter 1933-4, Supplement XXXI, n.p. Courtesy of Hawk Editorial Ltd, publisher of H&E Naturist magazine.

Every effort has been made to trace copyright holders and to obtain their permission for the use of copyright material. The publisher apologizes for any errors or omissions in the above list and would be grateful if notified of any corrections that should be incorporated in future reprints or editions of this book.

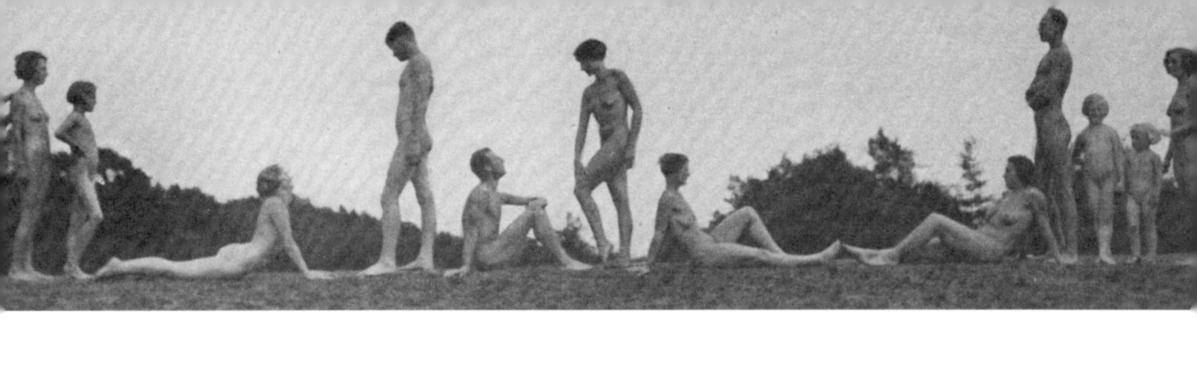

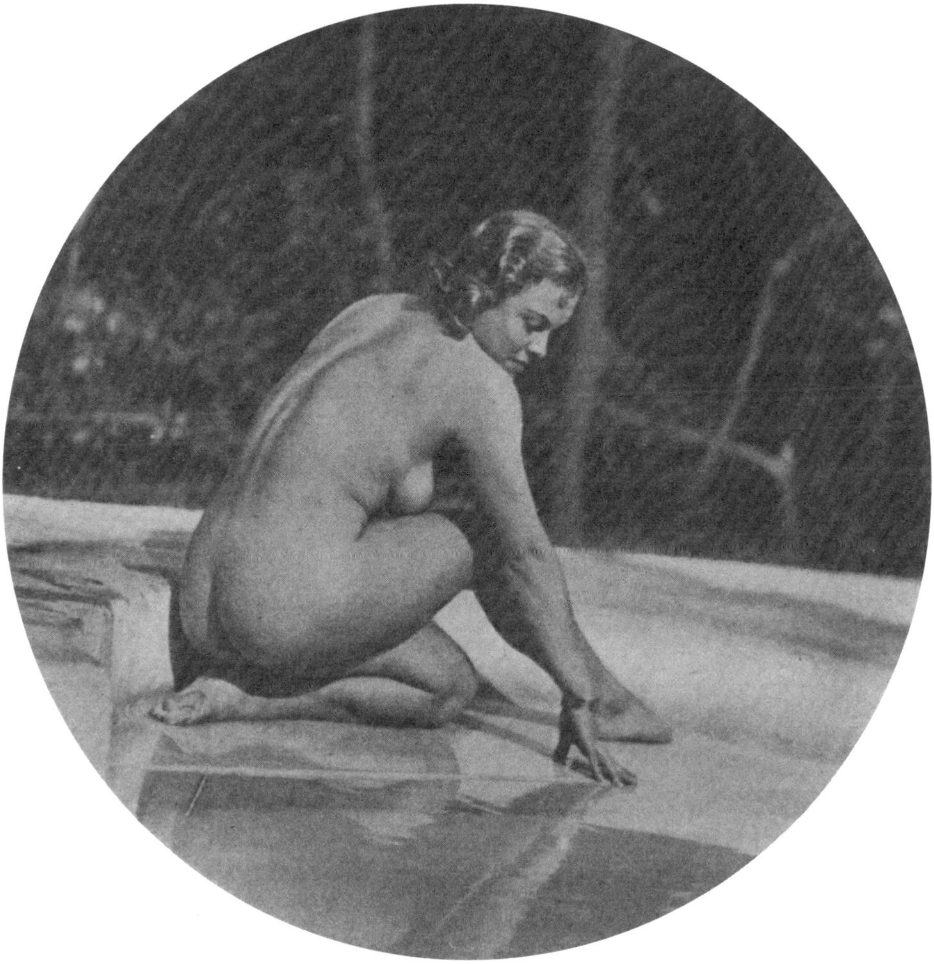

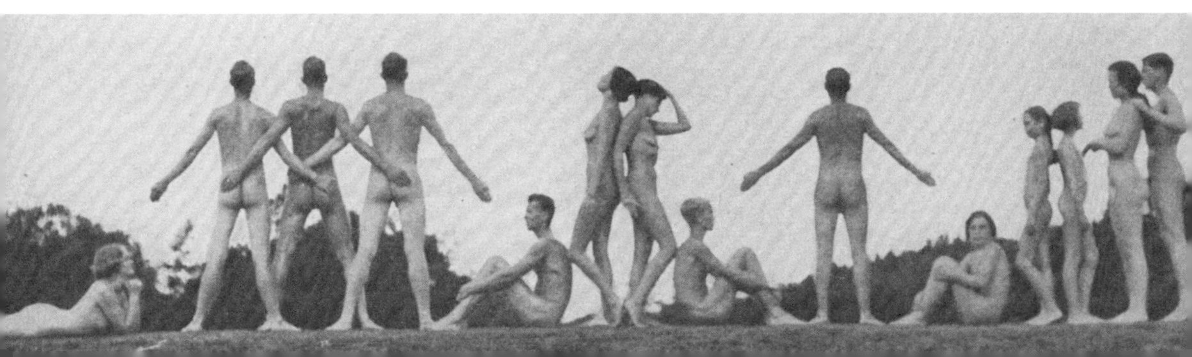